Proceedings of the Workshop on the
Phenomenon known as 'El Niño'

Proceedings of the Workshop on the Phenomenon known as 'El Niño'

Guayaquil, Ecuador
4-12 December 1974
Organized within the
International Decade of Ocean Exploration (IDOE)

by
the Intergovernmental Oceanographic
Commission (IOC)
the Food and Agriculture Organization
of the United Nations (FAO)
the World Meteorological Organization (WMO)
the United Nations Educational, Scientific
and Cultural Organization (Unesco)

Published in 1980 by the United Nations
Educational, Scientific and Cultural Organization
7 Place de Fontenoy, 75700 Paris
Printed by J. Duculot, 5800 Gembloux, Belgium

ISBN 92-3-101509-5

Preface

This publication forms part of the Proceedings of the Workshop on the Phenomenon known as 'El Niño', organized jointly by the Intergovernmental Oceanographic Commission, the United Nations Educational, Scientific and Cultural Organization, the Food and Agricultural Organization, and the World Meteorological Organization, within the framework of the International Decade of Ocean Exploration. The workshop was held at Guayaquil, Ecuador, from 4 to 12 December 1974, under the patronage of the Instituto Oceanográfico de la Armada Nacional del Ecuador.

The present volume contains translations of ten papers contributed in Spanish by marine scientists from the region, and which were presented or distributed at the workshop in their original version. These papers are published here in English in order to make the work of Spanish-speaking scientists

more familiar to their English-speaking colleagues. Two papers presented to the workshop in English by scientists from the region have been published separately and they are therefore not reproduced here.

The FAO publication, *Reunion de Trabajo sobre el Fenómeno Conocido como 'El Niño'* (FAO Informes de Pesca, No. 185) contains the Spanish texts of all twelve papers from the region.

A complementary list of the papers presented or distributed at the workshop which are not included in the present volume is appended to the Introduction; bibliographical references are given for those which have been published.

The opinions expressed in this publication are those of the authors, and do not necessarily coincide with those of the sponsoring organizations.

Contents

Introduction

At the eighth session of its assembly, the Intergovernmental Oceanographic Commission (IOC) adopted resolution VIII-17 in which it instructed the Secretary to organize jointly with the Food and Agricultural Organization of the United Nations (FAO) and the World Meteorological Organization (WMO) a workshop on the phenomenon known as 'El Niño' to: (a) analyse the present state of knowledge concerning the phenomenon; (b) identify the key questions that must be answered to allow understanding and prediction of the phenomenon; (c) devise a co-operative scientific research programme, with priorities, with the direct participation of the coastal countries affected by this phenomenon and with the collaboration and co-ordination of the IOC and other Specialized Agencies of the United Nations; and (d) formulate proposals for a study of the interaction between this phenomenon and the biological resources of the region.

The Steering Committee which was formed to plan this workshop held its first meeting in Callao, Peru, 17–18 January 1974. The members of this committee, under the chairmanship of Dr Warren Wooster, reached the following conclusions: (a) although the resolution stresses the set of anomalous conditions known as 'El Niño', the workshop should also be concerned with variations in the total coupled systems of atmosphere-ocean-biosphere in the eastern South Pacific Ocean; (b) the goal of the investigations to be considered by the workshop should be to predict variations in the ocean environment of the region and the consequences of such variations, and in particular to predict the development of 'El Niño' conditions and their consequences.

Dr Rómulo Jordán (Peru) was invited to serve as Chairman of the workshop.

Twenty-four scientific papers were presented and discussed by sixty scientists from fifteen countries participating in the workshop. The report of the workshop together with the recommendations has been issued in English (*FAO Fish. Rep.*, No. 163, 24 p.) and Spanish (*FAO Inf. Pesca*, No. 163, 26 p.).

In addition to the studies by Spanish-speaking scientists from the region, which have been translated for this publication, the following participants also contributed papers:

Dr David Cushing, Fisheries Laboratory, Lowestoft, Suffolk, United Kingdom: 'Models in Marine Ecology'.

David B. Enfield, INOCAR Guayaquil, Ecuador. 'The Oceanography of the Region North of the Equatorial Front: Physical Aspects'.

Dr Reuben Lasker and Dr Paul E. Smith, National Marine Fisheries Service, Southwest Fisheries Center, La Jolla, California, United States of America: 'Estimation of the Effects of Environmental Variations on the Eggs and Larvae of the Northern Anchovy'.

Dr Jerome Namias, Scripps Institution of Oceanography, La Jolla, California, United States of America: 'Ocean-Atmosphere Interaction of Large Time and Space Scales', *Collective Works of J. Namias, 1934 through 1974*, Vols. 1 and 2, San Diego, University of California, 1975.

Dr Colin Ramage, Department of Meteorology, University of Hawaii, Honolulu, Hawaii, United States of America: Meteorological Aspects of the 1972–73 'El Niño' Phenomenon', *Bull. Amer. Meteorol. Soc.*, Vol. 56, No. 2, 1975, p. 234–42.

A. Hellmut and C. Sievers, Instituto Hidrográfico de la Armada, Valparaiso, Chile, and Nelson Silva

Sandoval, Centro Investigaciones del Mar Valparaiso, Chile: 'Water Masses and Circulation in the Southeast Pacific Ocean' Latitudes 18° S.—33° S. (Operation Marchille VIII)'. Published in English and Spanish by the Comité Oceanográfico Nacional de Chile en Cienci y Tecnología del Mar as Contribución CONA No. 1. Valparaiso, Chile, 1975, 45 p.

Dr Robert Smith, School of Oceanography, Oregon State University, Corvallis, Oregon, United States of America: 'Investigations of Coastal Upwelling Processes'.

Dr Martha Vannucci, Unesco Regional Office for Science and Technology in Asia, New Delhi, India: 'Effects of Environmental Variations on the Distribution of Marine Fauna'.

Dr Klaus Wyrtki, Department of Oceanography, University of Hawaii, Honolulu, Hawaii, United States of America: 'A Review of Recent Research on the Circulation of the Equatorial and Eastern South Pacific Ocean'.

Papers distributed at the workshop:

CPCP Carlós Blandin, Meteorological Service, Quito, Ecuador: 'Caracteristicas del Fenómeno de "El Niño" y la Influencia de la Corriente de Humboldt en las Costas del Ecuador' [Characteristics of the 'El Niño' Phenomenon and Influence of Humboldt's Current on the Ecuadorian Coasts], National Institute of Meteorology and Hydrology, Climatology Section, 1974. (Publication No. 17—1).

Dr Eric D. Forsbergh, Inter-American Tropical Tuna Commission, La Jolla, California, United States of America: 'The Fishery of Skipjack in the Eastern Pacific Ocean'.

Dr Forrest R. Miller, Department of Mathematics, Kansas State University, Manhattan, Kansas, United States of America: 'The "El Niño" of 1972 in the Eastern Tropical Pacific Ocean'. (See also F. R. Miller and R. M. Laws, *Inter-Amer. Trop. Tuna Comm., Bull.,* Vol. 16, No. 5 1975, p. 403—48.

Dr Merritt R. Stevenson and Helen R. Wicks, Scripps Institution of Oceanography, La Jolla, California, United States of America: 'Bibliography of "El Niño" and Associated Publications (in English and Spanish)', *Inter-Amer. Trop. Tuna Comm. Bull.,* Vol. 16, No. 6, 1975, p. 451—501. (This bibliography has now also been made available on microfiche.)

Physical aspects of the 1972–73 'El Niño' phenomenon

Salvador Zuta
David Enfield
Jorge Valdivia
Pablo Lagos
Carlos Blandin[1]

Introduction

The 'El Niño' phenomenon is a spectacular oceano-graphic-meteorological anomaly that develops in the Pacific off Peru. The event causes enormously widespread effects on marine production, fisheries, northern coastal agriculture, and the life of the Peruvian coastal population, all of which finally result in a reduction of the national economy; the economic effects of the 1972–73 even were felt world-wide.

BRIEF HISTORY OF THE PHENOMENON

'El Niño' is a phenomenon that manifested itself off Peru at Christmas. Thus the fishermen of the port of Paita gave it the name of 'Corriente del Niño', in English 'Current of the (Christ) Child' (Carrillo, 1892). This designation was used by many past authors, although today it is a tacit convention to use the term 'phenomenon' instead of 'current', since it involves a transitory irregularity in the ocean-atmosphere system.

Wooster (1960) proposed a definition that tended to generalize the characteristics of 'El Niño' to processes that occur off the coasts of California, South-west Africa, West Australia and Viet Nam.

The first documents referring to 'El Niño' go back to the observations of Captains Colnet in 1795, Lartigue in 1822–23 and Carranza in 1891. According to existing sources, the most notable occurrences were those of 1891 (Schott, 1931), 1925 (Murphy, 1926; Schott, 1931), 1934–41 (Lobell, 1942; Bjerknes, 1961, 1966), 1965 (Guillén and Flores, 1965; Guillén, 1967; Zuta and Guillén, 1970) and 1972–73

(Zuta, 1972, 1973; Zuta *et al.*, 1973; Zuta and Yoza, 1974; Wooster and Guillén, 1974).

PREVIOUS KNOWLEDGE OF 'EL NIÑO'

The present understanding of the principal characteristics is fairly general and cannot clearly explain the generating mechanism of the phenomenon, a fundamental necessity for its prediction.

It is known that 'El Niño' occurs at irregular intervals in time, with variable intensity and peculiarities in the formation process, as for example in 1891 and 1925. Its most apparent physical manifestations off the Peruvian coast are: (a) the abnormal displacement of the tropical surface water layer to $10°–14°$ S. with temperature of $23°–29°$ C and salinities of 34.5–32.4 per mille; and (b) heavy rains typical of the intertropical convergence to about $7°$ S., e.g. rainfalls cited for the port of Zorritos by Peterson in the years 1914 (860 mm), 1925–26 (1,395 mm), 1939 (656 mm), 1953 (632 mm) were approximately three to six times the normal. These abnormalities produce temporary (four- to fourteen-month) modification in the ocean and atmosphere with consequent effects on marine fauna and fishing.

We can summarize current accepted ideas and theories as follows:
The north-east and south-east trade winds, the (north) Equatorial countercurrent, the Peru

---

1. Salvador Zuta and Jorge Valdivia, Instituto del Mar del Perú; David Enfield, Instituto Oceanográfico de la Armada del Ecuador; Pablo Lagos, Instituto Geofísico del Perú; Carlos Blandin, Instituto Nacional de Meteorología e Hidrología del Ecuador.

current, Equatorial front, and the Cromwell
current (Equatorial undercurrent) all play
important roles during the appearance of 'El
Niño'.

In the months preceding 'El Niño', there occurred
an abnormal dropping of the north-east trades,
an intensification of the Equatorial countercurrent and an accumulation of warm water off
the coast of Central America (Bjerknes, 1961;
Namias, 1973; Wyrtki, 1973).

Using the term of Mujica (1972), the 'firing' of
'El Niño' is produced by the abnormal
weakening of the south-east trades, enormously
reducing the upwelling along the Equator and
off Peru.

In some cases, as in 1925 (Bjerknes, 1961, 1966),
there occurred no previous weakening of the
north-east trades, rather a predominance of
north-west winds at Balboa.

A trans-Equatorial circulation, favoured by the
weakening of the south-east trades displaced the
Equatorial front southwards, resulting in the
'El Niño' phenomenon (Bjerknes, 1961).

The 'El Niño' waters proceed from the Equatorial
region, at times advancing from the sector south-
west of the Galapagos Islands; this seems to have
been the case in 1891, and at other times from
the east side of those islands, as seems to have
been the case in 1925.

One can establish or talk of various levels of 'El Niño',
according to intensity, duration and consequences
by taking the area off Peru as a reference.

Materials

All existing information from different sources was
gathered for the purpose of describing the physical
panorama of the 1972–73 occurrence and of increasing
the knowledge of 'El Niño'.

The oceanographic cruises of the Instituto
Oceanográfico de la Armada del Ecuador (INOCAR)
and the Instituto del Mar del Perú (IMARPE) were
fortunately carried out almost simultaneously and
permitted data 'splicing'. In both cases there were
limitations in data on depth and offshore distance at
which readings were taken. The cruises off Ecuador
extended to no further than 86° W. and those off Peru
to a maximum distance of 300 nautical miles from the
coast. These limitations do not necessarily permit the
optimum assessment of the advance of the 'El Niño'
phenomenon, as will be apparent in the following
sections.

ORIGIN AND NATURE OF THE DATA

The oceanographic and meteorological data gathered
and presented here were obtained from oceanographic
cruises, fishery explorations and shore stations.

The oceanographic cruises[1] yielded sea
temperature and salinity from the surface to depths of
500 m, isothermal topographics for 15° to 20° C,
wind, air temperature and surface atmospheric
pressure.

The fisheries explorations of IMARPE, listed
in Table 1, provided sea-surface temperature and
degree of salinity up to about 120 miles offshore
between the latitudes indicated in the right-hand
column of the table.

The shore stations, listed in Table 2, provided
data on sea temperature, air temperature, wind
and precipitation (to the right of the table are
indicated the position and period of each series of
observations).

PROCESSING AND ANALYSIS OF THE DATA

Oceanographic and meteorological data from cruises
were processed by INOCAR (Ecuador) for the area
north of 3°S., and by IMARPE (Peru) for the area
between 4° and 19° S. Data from fixed stations were
processed by SENAMHI and IGP (Peru) and INAMHI
(Ecuador). It is worth noting that salinity data was
processed by INOCAR using a Beckman salinometer
and by IMARPE using an Australian salinometer.
Data from the cruises of the r/v *Mesyatsev* were
processed by silver nitrate titration.

1. The cruises were as follows: INOCAR (Ecuador) 7111
    (23 November–21 December 1971), 7202 (23 February–
    8 March 1972), 7205 (4–9 May 1972), 7209 (14 August–
    2 September 1972), 7211 (20 November–10 December
    1972), 7302 (23 February–10 March 1973), 7305
    (17–30 May 1973); IMARPE (Peru) U7108 (16 August–
    2 September 1971), U7111 (12–27 November 1971),
    U7202 (26 February–10 March 1972), U7204 (26 April–
    24 May 1972), SNP7204 (27 April–16 May 1972),
    U7206/7 (22 June–20 July 1972), M7208/9 (4 August–
    24 September 1972), U7210 (24 October–2 December
    1972), U7212 (4–13 December 1972), U7302 (23
    February–16 March 1973). M7305 (6 May–27 June
    1973). Data from the South Tow expedition (Scripps
    Institution of Oceanography, 3–13 May 1972) and the
    YALOC-71 cruise (Oregon State University, 13 November–
    3 December 1971) were included.

OCEANOGRAPHIC OBSERVATIONS

The basic data used were temperature and salinity. Oxygen measurements, which would have helped in identifying the Cromwell current, were not included since they were not sampled by the INOCAR cruises. It was not possible to perform dynamic (geostrophic) calculations because the appropriate section lacked sufficient depth data to establish a reference level. Instead, we present the 15° and 20° C isothermal topographies; the 20° C topographies are given only for cruises from November to March during which the water off Peru was warm. Only sea surface temperature data were obtained from shore stations, and past measurements permitted the calculation of long-term monthly means (see Figs. 1–5).

The shore temperature and salinity sections of Figures 6, 7 and 8, corresponding to the November/December (1971), February/March (1972) and August/September (1972) cruises respectively, were prepared from cruise stations along or near 82°30′ W., north of 6° S., and about eighty miles offshore further south.

For average seasonal variations of surface temperature and salinity off the coasts of Ecuador and Peru, data from 1° Mardsen subsquares between 82° and 83°W., north of 7° S. and from the subsquares, shown in Table 3, further south were used.

In order to examine the seasonal fluctuations up to 400 m in depth, four areas off Peru were selected (see Table 4) (circular areas of twenty-seven-mile radius), the centres of which are indicated in the right-hand column.

METEOROLOGICAL OBSERVATIONS

The basic data treated are air temperatures, wind and precipitation at selected fixed stations. In addition, we present some of the monthly synoptic atmospheric pressure charts for mid-February 1971-73 (Figs. 9(a),(b),(c)). Distributions of air temperature with altitude and time were prepared by the radiosond stations of Guayaquil and Callao (Figs. 10(a),(b),(c)) and the long-term operation at Callao permitted the calculation of 1961–73 monthly means and monthly deviations for the period 1971–73 (Fig. 11(b)).

For the computation of mean values of winds at fixed stations (Fig. 12), the predominant direction at 13.00 local time (21.00 GMT) was used.

Description of meteorological conditions

In terms of latitude, northern Peru should have a tropical climate. In reality, most of its coast is eminently arid and, north of 7°S., semi-arid. This seems to be the result of several interacting geographic circumstances such as the predominance of oceanic areas in the southern hemisphere; the north-west to south-east trend of the Peru coast; and the high Andean barrier between Atlantic (moist) and Pacific (dry) air masses. The result is a strong and positionally almost invariable anticyclone, strong and persistent south-east trade winds, the north-flowing Peru current made abnormally cold by coastal upwelling and a strong diurnal land–sea circulation. These factors in turn produce powerful atmospheric subsidence, a marked thermal inversion and maximum aridity.

Prohaska (1968a) considered that the subsidence-induced inversions play a decisive role in the coastal climate. According to him (as cited by Mujica, 1972), these inversions at Lima had two types of structures—one in winter from 200 to 1,500 m and one in summer below 700 m. Near the surface, temperature follows a quasi-harmonic cycle ranging from approximately 16° C in August (winter) to 23°C in February (summer). Surface conditions are similar at other coastal stations though with some latitudinal variation.

Surface winds at coastal stations are persistently from the south-east sector throughout the year, south of 14° S. From that point northward to the Equator they are progressively more from the south and south-west, becoming somewhat more variable during the southern summer. Monthly mean wind speeds along the Peruvian coast vary from a summer (S.H.) low of 1.1 m/s to a winter (S.H.) high of 8.8 m/s (Zuta and Guillén, 1970). At a representative coastal station in Ecuador (Salinas) speeds range from 3.6 m/s to 4.6 m/s respectively.

Certain modifications in the atmospheric circulation result in spells of relatively cold or warm weather; in particularly anomalous cases the latter culminate in 'El Niño'. During 'El Niño', wind slackens and may become variable, upwelling is greatly decreased, and the Peru current becomes warmer or is overrun by warm water from the north. Surface air temperatures increase and the inversion is greatly weakened, while subsidence in the air mass probably decreases. The greatly decreased stability then results in torrential rains over much of northern Peru.

The monthly averages during 1971–73 of surface wind at fixed stations in Ecuador and Peru are shown in Figure 12. Data on wind collected during oceanographic cruises are also shown for that period (7111, 7202, 7208, 7212 and 7305). The monthly averages at coastal stations did not generally display well-defined trends of reduced speeds or variable or reversed directions for a single extended period. Some were generally variable in direction (such as Esmeraldas and Pto Pizarro) but with no clear preponderance in a given year. More southern stations (Callao and San Juan) showed only a slight weakening in 1972 but no clear change in direction. Salinas showed a marked decrease in intensity and change from southerly to westerly direction in 1972. Only the wind at Talara showed a clear reduction from February through September 1972, but with no distinct changes in direction.

The cruises (Figs. 13–18) took measurements over shorter periods (one to two weeks) than the fixed stations; their data therefore displays greater extremes of wind conditions.

To give an overall idea of conditions during the quarterly cruises from November 1971 to June 1973, speed ranges and principal direction quadrants can be summarized for the two crucial zones (see Table 5, also Fig. 13).

There were only three periods of significantly abnormal winds. In November–December 1971 (Fig. 14), winds south of 6° S. were weak (2–4 m/s), and were strong to the north. In February–March 1972 (Fig. 15), winds north of 6° S. were very weak and variable in direction. In August–September 1972 (Fig. 16), winds were strong north of 4° S. and from the northern quadrants (data missing south of 4° S.). In the first instance a trans-Equatorial flow would not be favoured due to strong southerly winds in the north; such flow presumably would be possible in the second and third cases. These abnormal wind periods were poorly reflected, if at all, by the monthly averages at coastal stations, suggesting that they occurred over much shorter time scales—possibly days. While the cruises detected extreme conditions, these were at best fortuitous and other interesting wind episodes were probably missed. This suggests that even intermittent, short-lived periods of abnormal wind conditions will allow the development and persistence of 'El Niño' conditions.

There is not enough information to confirm that abnormal wind episodes were as limited as these data seem to suggest. Another view, that abnormal conditions actually predominated over the ocean but were poorly represented by the data at fixed stations is possible.

Lettau and Lettau (1972) theoretically argued that, along the Peruvian coast, land–sea effects produce a thermotidal diurnal oscillation (not strictly a sea-breeze) in the coastal wind. In their model, a marked daytime pressure decrease from sea to land produced a quasi-geostrophic, equatorwards wind that was normally superimposed on the mean wind. Limited observations tend to support their model (Burt *et al.,* 1973). Warmer sea-surface temperatures and reduced upwelling during an 'El Niño' would decrease the intensity of this residual wind but not eliminate it, while offshore its effects would not be felt.

SURFACE PRESSURE DISTRIBUTION

Wooster and Guillén (1974) pointed out the abnormally low atmospheric pressure which occurred along the Peruvian coast during 'El Niño' periods, especially during the 1972 'El Niño'. To see how this might be related to the wind regime off Peru, charts of monthly mean pressure were prepared for February 1971, 1972 and 1973 over the eastern South Pacific (Fig. 9). The lack of data makes pressure analysis over oceanic areas somewhat debatable, though the Easter Island station data helped to position the South Pacific high.

The low pressure referred to by Wooster and Guillén (1974) appears as a pressure trough over the South American Pacific coast. In February 1972, the low pressure was more intense than in either 1971 or 1973. Mostly because the central high pressure east of Easter Island was 3 millibars higher in 1972, the analysis for that month showed a somewhat larger pressure gradient over the Peruvian current. If we accept this analysis, it would suggest that the average south-east trades were not significantly weaker off most of Peru. It would be more plausible, rather, that abnormally weak winds may have occurred in intermittent, short-lived episodes. In view of the mean pressure distribution, the reasons for such behaviour are not clear.

PRECIPITATION AND SURFACE AIR TEMPERATURE

Figure 20 shows the variations of monthly precipitation and surface air temperature from long-term means at coastal stations in Ecuador and Peru.

In 1971 anomalous precipitation occurred in Ecuador, especially in the period February to April. At Machala below-normal amounts were reported for that period, whereas rainfall in Peru was normal for the year. Temperatures were normal or subnormal in both countries in 1971. This would suggest that the rain in Ecuador in 1971 was perhaps associated with the abnormal activity or position of the Intertropical Convergence Zone (ITCZ) but not with large-scale warming of the sea surface.

A marked increase in surface temperature during the second half of 1971 was noted and most stations began to measure abnormally high temperatures at the start of 1972 with particularly large anomalies after May. These lasted until the end of that year and then returned to normal in March—April 1973. After this, most stations measured subnormal temperatures.

During this period of abnormal temperatures (February 1972 to March 1973), there were two periods of unusually heavy rain (in March 1972 and January 1973) at almost all stations as far south as 9° S. Other variations were reported at some stations but no geographical connection was evident for these secondary episodes. The two latitudinally coherent episodes coincided approximately with the two confirmed periods of trans-Equatorial invasions of warm tropical water associated with 'El Niño'.

It seems at first perplexing that during the winter (S.H.) of 1972, when the greatest increases in temperature were reported, there was little increase in precipitation. To understand this, we must first examine the behaviour of vertical temperature structure with time.

TEMPERATURE ALOFT

The vertical distribution of air temperature with time is shown for Callao in Figure 11 (a) and the deviation from the long-term mean in Figure 11 (b). There are two well-defined zones in the 0—3,000 m range—those above and those below 2,000 m. In the upper layer, the isotherms undergo undulatory vertical movements, They are higher (warmer) during the southern winter and lower (cooler) in the summer. In the lower layer, seasonal heating and cooling were much more apparent. During the winters of 1971 and 1972, a temperature maximum formed near 1,600 m (top of the inversion) and a minimum near 600—700 m (inversion base). In 1972 both features

were warmer than in 1971, the inversion base was slightly higher and the inversion layer slightly thinner. During the succeeding summers, the inversion disappeared entirely. A remarkable feature was the non-reappearance of the inversion in the winter of 1973.

The deviation (Fig. 11(b)) indicates abnormally cool air at all levels in 1971 and an early development of the inversion in May of that year. From February 1972 to March 1973, there was strong anomalous warming below the inversion base (800 m), reaching over 3° C in June and July (this was the period of unusually high sea-surface temperature off northern Peru). Beginning in April 1973, the first 100 m above the surface were exceptionally cold while above 1,600 m, temperatures were as much as 3° C above normal.

Positive variations in 1972 were transmitted to the inversion base with relative rapidity in contrast to subsequent cooling in 1973 which was limited to a thin surface layer. This suggests that convection is important below the inversion during 'El Niño'.

The mean monthly profiles of air temperature for February and August at Callao, and February in Guayaquil, are compared to mean profiles in Figure 10. February 1972 and 1973 were nearly normal at Guayaquil. In February 1972, conditions were already significantly abnormal at Callao. By August, the inversion was still marked but only between 1,000 and 1,500 m and the air below was considerably warmer. One year later (August 1973), the inversion had disappeared and the air was almost isothermal up to 1,400 m.

Contrary to what might have been expected, the inversion was not obliterated by convection mechanisms during the 'El Niño' period. This required a much longer time and was undoubtedly a large-scale process involving the entire South Pacific. The great extent of the air mass also explains why normal conditions were not re-established. In fact, since a return to normality requires surface cooling and renewed subsidence (both lower processes), an even longer time should be required for this to happen. Taken a step further, this suggests that the long periods required for the surface-temperature variations to eradicate or regenerate the inversion layer may in some way relate to the longer-term secular changes that occur over several years—that is, the multi-annual cycles of heating and cooling on a large scale, of which 'El Niño' is a manifestation.

The abscence of excessive rain in Peru in the anomalously warm winter (S.H.) of 19.'2 coincided with the presence of the inversion at that time. Heavy rains only occurred during periods of convective warming in the absence of an inversion.

AIR/SEA TEMPERATURE DIFFERENCES

It is well established that a given excess of sea temperature over air temperature in the tropic results in a much greater transfer of heat to the atmosphere (mostly in the form of latent heat) than in temperate latitudes. This is due to the more rapid increase in vapour capacity of air per degree of temperature increase at higher temperatures. Thus, small increases in sea temperature during warm 'El Niño' conditions can be very effective in warming the atmosphere. Figures 20—22 show the distribution of air/sea temp-erature difference $(Ta-Tm)$ in November—December 1971, February—March 1972 and December 1972 respectively. Analysis of these charts indicated that negative values (shaded) were usually associated with advection of air over relatively warm water (usually over 23°–25°C).

In November 1971 the air was generally cooled by the Peruvian current (2°–16°S.) and warming was found only off Ecuador, over the Equatorial front, and near 17°S. By February 1972 this situation was drastically changed when warm 'El Niño' waters and reduced upwelling caused large areas of sea-to-air heat transfer to appear more than 50 miles from the Peruvian coast. This condition persisted throughout the remainder of 1972.

Oceanographic aspects of the 1972–73 'El Niño'

THE PRE-'EL NIÑO' PERIOD

Zuta and Urquizo (1974) considered that the pronounced cooling in March 1971 in the Equatorial Pacific (2° N.–5°S., 110°–150° W.) was symptomatic of the phenomenon to come. At that time the Equatorial Pacific east of 110° W. was significantly warmer than in March of the previous year (Wooster and Guillén, 1974). In works published more recently, authors have felt that abnormally warm conditions may have been established south of 14° S. along the Peruvian coast as early as August 1971.

According to Zuta *et al.* (1973), the 1970–71 period was characterized by sea-surface temperatures off Peru from 2° to 6° C below normal; only in June 1971—south of 14° S.—and in November—over most of the Peruvian coast—did they find markedly higher-than-normal temperatures.

The surface distributions of temperature and salinity in November—December 1971 (Figs. 23(a), (b)) show the Equatorial front (21—24° C.; 33-35 per mille) at a more southern position than was normal for the season; it extended north-westwards from 5° S. near Paita) to about 2° S. west of 82° W. The north—south trend of the front immediately offshore of the Gulf of Guayaquil (3° S.) was due to the runoff of warm, fresh water from the Guayas River. To the north, the warm, low-salinity water had advanced southwards from the Panama Bight. Only two weeks previously, the YALOC-71 cruise detected water of over 26° C and under 28 per mille near 5°N., 80° W. (Enfield, 1974). It is noteworthy that strong S.S.W. winds were encountered over the frontal area in November—December (see Fig. 14). Thus it is possible that the front and the tropical waters were receding northwards at this time, having previously advanced further south.

South of 5° S., the colder coastal waters of the Peruvian current were characterized by temperatures of less than 19° C and salinities less than 35.1 per mille, with widening at the principal upwelling areas off Pimentel (7° S.), Chimbote (9° S.) and San Juan (16° S.). Temperatures at these areas ranged from 0.5° to 1° C below normal and alternated with above-normal values (1°–2° C) in the intervening areas, the latter being the more predominant (Zuta *et al.*, 1972). Subtropical surface water was found offshore as far north as 2°30′ S. (west of 83° W.).

The alongshore hydrographic sections of temperature and salinity with depth (November/December 1971) are shown in Figures 6(a),(b). They are composed of stations along or near 82°39′ W., north of 6° S. and about eighty miles offshore further south. Based on IMARPE seasonal cruises over several years off Peru and 3½ years off Ecuador, the vertical temperature distribution of November—December 1971 was normal. The southern limit of the tropical permanent thermocline was found off Ecuador at depths of from 25 to 50 m. From 2° to 3° S. many of its isotherms surface in the Equatorial front, whereas the rest spread vertically to the south in a transition to the typical structure of the Peruvian current.

Off Ecuador, the 15° C isotherm is found at the base of the tropical thermocline and the 10° C isotherm is found near 400 m. There is a thermostad between 13° and 14° C from 60 m to 200 m. (The weaker gradient is often referred to as '13° water' in the literature.) This is the usual subsurface thermal structure found east of 120° W. and associated with the Equatorial undercurrent west of the Galapagos Islands.

Off Peru the 15° C isotherm was still found near the base of the thermocline at depths from 40 m to 70 m. The thermocline was less intense than off Ecuador, spanning only five isotherms over depth ranges of 20–50 m. The 13°–14° C thermostad could not be indentified south of 10° S.

The salinity distribution off Peru was about normal in November. Off Ecuador there was a very large core of maximum salinity reaching values of over 35.5 per mille and defined by the 35 per mille isohaline (Fig. 23). While it is common to find a high-salinity core east of the Galapagos Islands (Stevenson and Taft, 1971), its size and intensity are not usually so great. The only ultimate source for such saline water is in the subtropical South Pacific; from there it is incorporated into the Equatorial undercurrent and carried eastward.

We can only speculate about the causes of the high salinity which was about 0.3 per mille above normal values. Such increases are typical of the Equatorial undercurrent west of the date-line (Austin and Rinkel, 1957); by the time the water arrives off Ecuador the core salinity is reduced by vertical mixing with the overlying low salinity water of the south Equatorial current. The mixing appears to be a result of equatorial upwelling east of the date line and the vertical shear between the two currents. This suggests that the higher core salinity in November 1971 may have been due to a suspension or weakening of one or both of these processes. Whatever change may have occured on the equatorial Pacific, it could not have been drastic or the temperature structure that is also symptomatic of those processes might have been expected to change as well—it did not. The alternative possibility also exists that evaporation and surface salinity in the subtropical gyre (the sources region) were above normal due to increased south-east trade winds during 1970–71.

THE 'EL NIÑO' PERIOD

The 1972/73 'El Niño' reached full development in January 1972 off Peru and ended in February 1973 having lasted fourteen months and producing an abnormally warm and low salinity period. During this time, the oceanographic conditions showed three well-defined stages which we designate the initial, intermediate and final stages, and whose most outstanding characteristics we now describe. Speaking of these phases, referring only to the Peruvian area, we have as normal southern limit of the surface Equatorial waters (salinities less than 34.8 per mille) the latitudes 4°30′ S. for June; 5°00′ S. for September; 6°30′ for December; and 6°00′ S. for March, according to monthly maps in preparation by Zuta *et al.* (personal communication).

The initial and final phases correspond to the periods of advance and of retreat respectively from or to the normal limit of the waters from the Equatorial zone. The intermediate phase corresponds to the period of absence of such waters south of the normal limit and the dominance of surface subtropical waters over a great part of the Peruvian coast.

Initial phase

The advance of tropical waters to 5° S. in November 1971 (Figs. 23(a),(b)), which could have been the forerunner of the 1972–73 'El Niño', appears not to have continued farther south until February 1972, according to observations made in SNP-1 cruise 7111 (Flores *et al.,* 1972), the monthly maps from November 1971 to February 1972 from *Fishing Information* (1971, 1972) and the temperatures at the port of Paita (Zuta and Urquizo, 1974). On the maps consulted, it is observed that the negative thermal variations with respect to the pattern of many years were accentuated in December 1971 to the east of the Galapagos Islands and disappeared in February 1972.

Evidently the initial phase began off Peru in February 1972 with the advance of a surface tongue of tropical water to the west of 82°30′ W. off Punta Falsa (6° S.) and in a south-easterly direction (Fig. 24(b)).

By 25 February, the northern waters had already reached 9°S. (IMARPE, 1972), and by the middle of March the principal volume had covered all the coastal area north of 10° S. (Huarmey), with a light projection to near to Pucusana (12°30′ S.) within twenty miles of the coast (Fig. 24(b)).

These waters with temperatures of 23°–29° C and salinities of 32.8–34.8 per mille were helped in their advance southward by the southern extension of the Cromwell current and the south Equatorial countercurrent, according to the topographies of the 15° and 20° C isotherms (Figs. 25(b), 26(a)). According to Figure 26(a) (see isoline 120 m), the principal flow of the first of these was north of 2° S. in south-easterly direction.

With the advance of warm and low-salinity waters from the north, two hydric fronts formed at about 7° S. and 9°30′ S. and stand out better in the salinity map of Figure 24. The fronts and the pocket of salinities less then 34.9 per mille off Salaverry could have originated from two pulses which occurred in two intervals in the order of days and weeks, of which the first could have been interrupted by the anticyclonic circulation at the time that the coastal current was still advancing northward on the coastal side, as the 15° and 20° C topographies show (Figs. 25(b), 26(a)).

Another notable aspect of Figures 24(a),(b) is that the coastal upwelling, which prevailed off Punta Falsa and Chicama during the first fortnight of March (observations north of 9° S.) and in February (observations south of 9° S.), was more intense south of 14° S. especially off San Juan and Mollendo (the latter with temperatures as low as 15°C).

The intense thermal and haline gradients of February, south of 15° S., resulted from upwelling and from the considerable mixing, towards the coast, of surface subtropical waters whose maximum temperature approached 27° C and whose maximum salinity was 35 per mille 40 miles off Ilo. The concentrated effect of these waters was related to the intensity of the winds and probably to the unusual approach at this time of the high-pressure centre towards southern Peru (Fig. 15).

In the anchovy operation carried out on 1 and 2 April 1972 (IMARPE, 1972), the Equatorial waters were found to the north of 9° S. (Chimbote). It can be surmised that there was a momentary holdup or reverse of the southward advance, as the data from the operation of Eureka XX of 28/29 of the same month (IMARPE, 1972) showed Equatorial water over the entire coastal area north of 11° S. Further-more it is suggested that some days before it had extended to approximately 14° S. (Pisco). In the area north of Callao (3—17 May) of cruise 7204 (Mejia *et al.,* 1973; Liendo and Guillén, 1973); the tongue of water with a salinity of less than 34.8 per mille to the north of 10° S. (which is shown in Fig. 27(b)) was still a dominant aspects. During Eureka XXI of 17—18 June (IMARPE, 1972), surface Equatorial water was found south of 7° S., thus indicating that in the period of one month it had retreated 180 miles. In Eureka XXII of 18—19 July (IMARPE, 1972), such waters were not seen south of 5° S. yet were found north of Talara (4°30′ S.) during Unanue cruise 7207 (in the area north of Callao) from 8 to 20 July (Guillén and Liendo, 1973). During the

latter a marked broad mixing area (with salinities around 35.0 per mille) was located between Talara and Callao.

From what has been shown here, we can say then that the initial phase began in February and ended in the second half of June with the retreat of the surface Equatorial water to its normal position (4°30′ S. in June). (See also Zuta and Urquizo, 1974; Wooster and Guillén, 1974).

As shown in Figures 28(a),(b), this phase was distinguished by a warm tongue of water of temperature greater than 25° C and salinity less than 34.5 per mille projecting as far as 10° S. In Figure 29 and 30, the initial phase was indicated by the pronounced sinking of the isotherms in the first half of 1972, most marked in the areas of Punta Falsa and Chimbote. Off Punta Falsa, an area with salinity of less than 34.8 per mille above 40 m was noticeable between December 1971 and June 1972.

In the temperature and salinity charts of Figure 7, it can be seen that the depth of water of salinity less than 34.8 per mille rarely extended further than the 50 m from the surface; only at 3°30′ S. did it extend to 70 m in depth. These waters were associated with the very intense thermocline with 9 to 10 isotherms between 20 and 17 m depth (centred approximately at 40 m) north of 10° S., which weakened and came close to the surface further south. This was particularly evident at 14° S. where, as already described, the coastal upwelling was already intense, fed by waters coming from the South Antarctic and contributed to by the dominant south-east winds (Figs. 12 and 15).

In Figure 7, the 13°—15° C isotherms show a notable elevation southwards and between 3° and 6° S., the homothermal layer of 13°—14° C was prominent at depths of 120—300 m with salinities of up to 35 per mille. North of 3° S. and at depths of between 50 and 300 m, a pocket of relatively high salinity exceeding 35 per mille stood out in the layer where the 10°—20°C isotherms formed an appreciable and exceptional gradient. This last aspect represents a great change with respect to the situation of November/December 1971 (Fig. 6), in which the subsurface thermal structure was normal with the exception of the pocket of exceptionally high salinity. It may be supposed that the modification of the thermal structures was due more to advective processes than to convective. This supposition should be further studied, along with the case of high salinity measurements in 1971.

The thermal and saline changes of the initial phase gave rise to thermal increases of 2° to 6° C

above the average which extended over a great part
of the coast in May/June (IMARPE, 1973). However,
in the three months preceding these rises, anomalies
greater than 3° C were measured down to depths of
75 m in areas north of 14° S., associated in the area
north of Callao (12° S.) with salinity falling by the
order of 0.2–0.8 per mille (Zuta and Urquizo, 1974).

Intermediate phase

This phase began towards the end of June 1972,
when the surface Equatorial water was found to have
retreated to the north of Talara (4°30 S.); it
continued until the end of November of the same
year, when such water was found to the north of
6° S. The principal features were observed in the
course of the exploration mentioned in the section
'Origin and Nature of the Data'. General results have
been published in a series of special reports from
IMARPE in the years 1972 and 1973. In this section
only the most outstanding aspects of the change of
oceanographic conditions will be discussed.

It must be recognized that our present
knowledge of 'normal' conditions is still incomplete;
thus the use of the word 'abnormal' or its analogues is
extremely relative. Even for the sea surface, the data
of mean patterns are incomplete and are certainly
not well represented further than fifty miles from the
coast.

In the subsequent evolution of this stage, the
highly saline surface subtropical water (salinity
greater than 35.1 per mille) played a dominant role off
Peru, particularly between August and November
1972. The cruises BAP Unanue 7206 (22–28 June)
and 7207 (8–20 July) showed three important
aspects; that in June subtropical water covered the
area south of Callao (Guillén and Liendo, 1973); that
the area between Talara and Callao was highly
homosaline with salinities of about 35 per mille; and
that Equatorial water was found north of Talara (the
last two cases in the month of July). According to
observations during Eureka XXII of 13–19 July
(IMARPE, 1972), this subtropical water was extending
northwards although with lessening strength by
comparison with that found during June to the south
of 14° S. (Pisco). During Eureka XXIII of 3–6 August
1972 (IMARPE, 1972), the subtropical waters
clearly began to intensify along the Peruvian coast
except in the region between Callao and Atico where
coastal upwelling was weak.

In the cruise 7207–09 of the r/v *Mesyatsev*,
of which the southern part was effected 4–26 August

and the part of north of Callao 6–24 September
(IMARPE, 1973), the surface subtropical water was
found to extend in an unusual manner off the
Peruvian coast south of 5° S. and further north to 2° S.
to the West of 83° W.—including the layer above
100 m (Figs. 31(a),(b); 8(a),(b)). In the north, the
tropical water advanced on two fronts, one on the
coastal side to 4° S. (drawing water from the Gulf of
Guayaquil) with temperatures of 22°–25° C and salinity
of 34.8–33 per mille and the other far off the coast
of Esmeraldas, which advanced in a south-westerly
direction to 2° S. (drawing water from the Gulf
of Panama) whose temperature and salinity were
23–27° C and 34.8–32 per mille. The advance of
the Guayaquil water obeyed the observed pattern
for the month of September (Zuta and Yoza, 1974).
With observations made during Eureka XXIV of 5–8
September 1972 (IMARPE, 1972), it can be deduced
that coastal upwelling appreciably re-established
itself off Pimentel and Salaverry as well as south of
Callao, although with less variability than normal
(Zuta and Santander, 1974), especially to the south
of Callao.

The data of Eureka XXIV of 20–23 October
1972 (IMARPE, 1972) indicated that the upwelling
continued to develop south of Callao and reduced to
the north of it, due to the penetration of subtropical
water which extended noticeably towards the
north—up to 5°30′ S.—of the Peruvian area. The
southern boundary of the Equatorial water was at
5° S., i.e. sixty miles further south than in September.

In the spring (S.H.) explorations were made by
the r/v *Mesyatsev* from 24 October to 3 December
(IMARPE, 1973): between 6° and 12° S. in October
(24–31), 3°30′–17°30′ S. in November (1–30), and
17°30′–10°30′ S. in December (1–3). The most
outstanding aspects were: the dominant presence of
subtropical water south of 6° S., especially between
6°–15° S.; the appearance of Equatorial water as far as
6° S., with a suggestion of an advance of tropical water
to the west of 83° W. (first fortnight of November)
which is shown in Figure 32; and the presence of
gentle winds (speeds < 4 m/s), whose predominant
direction was south-westerly. The situation in the
north, with the isohaline 34.5 per mille at 4°30′ S.
appears to have been the prelude for the second great
advance of tropical water. The Equatorial water
moved sixty miles southwards in November.

The vertical profile of temperature and salinity
of August/September 1972 given in Figure 8(a),(b))
shows marked changes from the situation of February/
March 1972 (Figs. 7(a),(b)) and of November 1971

(Fig. 6), especially at depths of between 50 and 400 m. The pocket of high salinity which was present to the north of 3° S. during February and March was not detected to the north of 4° S. in November; the isothermal layer of 13°–14° C. was much reduced around 7° S.; and the thermal gradient intensified south of 3° S. below 50 m, producing the profile of summer data (S.H.). The warm winter also showed itself in the surface charts of Figures 23(a) and 31(a).

In Figures 29 and 30, the intermediate phase showed rapid decrease in depth of the isotherms between July and November, coming closest to the surface between September and November. This was a time when the positive thermal changes decreased, having attained increases of 3°–6° C between March and October 1972 (IMARPE, 1972); such a phase is represented in Figure 28 by the relatively cold waters (temperatures less than 23° C with salinity greater than 35 per mille) projecting northwards to 2° S. principally between July and October.

The principal characteristics of the intermediate phase were an abnormal zone of predominantly surface tropical water off Peru—principally between August and November—with reduced upwelling, and appreciable slackening of winds in November. There were very high positive thermal anomalies (3°–6° C) until August, and reduction of the same between September and November.

Final phase

The final phase was a broad repetition of the initial phase with certain peculiar features. Under normal conditions, the February/March period of Equatorial current disappears east of 100° W., the intertropical convergence (ITC) is very close to the Equator and the anticyclonic eddy (with a centre at about 5° N., 88° W.) develops to its maximum, with one of its branches displacing in a south-westerly direction, transporting Gulf of Panama waters at velocities which exceed 1 knot in Fenruary (Wyrtki, 1965a, b). In the normal December panorama, the Equatorial countercurrent moves eastwards to 85° W., at speeds of about 0.5 knot; the ITC is found more to the north of the Equator and the cyclonic eddy off the Colombian coast reaches its maximum, with a branch which displaces to the south-west at speeds of around 0.4 knot; this can cross the Equator carrying water from the Gulf of Panama. Under abnormal conditions, as in 1972, a greater transport southwards of tropical water was produced among the summer (S.H.) with more permanent effects than usual.

It has already been established that, during the first fortnight of November 1972, the northern water had advanced to 6° S. to the west of 83° W. and that in that month the winds had weakened significantly (dominant speeds less than 3 m/s off Peru, (IMARPE, 1973), with predominantly south-westerly direction along the Peruvian coast (see also Fig. 17 —to the south off Callao). In the first fortnight of the following month, during the cruise Unanue 7212 of 4–12 December (Zuta and Urquizo, 1974), the water coming from the Equatorial zone had advanced southwards to Huarmey (10° S.) in the form of a coastal tongue with temperatures of 23°–25° C and salinities of 34–34.8 per mille (Figs. 33(a),(b)).

Taking the 34.5 per mille isohalines as a reference, we can say that this water moved 450 (nautical) miles in the first fortnight of December. Then, although apparently the situation was similar to the one observed in November, the water did not continue its advance until the following month, yielding a mean speed of displacement of approximately 23 miles/day (Zuta and Urquizo, 1974).

There is some evidence suggested by Figure 33(b) that the warm tongue of water advanced along the coast from at least as far as Esmeraldas (Ecuador), at a time when the dominant south-east winds were appreciably stronger than they had been in the preceding month (November).

Surface Equatorial water (S. < 34.8 per mille) was measured in a hydrographic survey made off Callao (12° S.) at the end of December, on board the IMARPE-1. That suggested that the December advance reached at least the area off Callao, with a progress of approximately 120 miles in the second fortnight of that month (8 miles/day).

At the end of January 1973 on the cruise of the Eureka XXVI of 20–23 January (IMARPE, 1973), the surface Equatorial water was located already at some distance from the coast, west of 81° W. and north of 8° S. It had been displaced and replaced by a strong invasion of surface subtropical waters (with salinity of up to 35.4 per mille close to the coast) which covered almost all the rest of the coast to the south.

In the Unanue cruise 7302 of 23 September– 16 March (Liendo and Carbajal, 1974), the surface Equatorial water was found to have already retreated to north of Talara (4° 30′ S.). Further south, the surface subtropical water covered almost all the coastal area (excluding the part between Punta Doña María and Ilo) with salinities ranging from 35–35.1 per mille (see Figs. 34(a),(b)).

The sequence followed implies that the final phase of 'El Niño', which began in December, must have reached its end at least by the last days of February. Data from the fixed stations (Figs. 1–5) also support this, showing the fall in temperature in February—especially to the north of Callao.

The final phase is marked in Figures 28(a) and (b) by the warm tongue of water of very low salinity projecting south to approximately 10°30′ S. between December 1972 and June 1973. It is evident that the final phase was shorter and less intense than the initial phase, a fact which also can be seen in Figure 29(a) and (b) in the area off Punta Falsa.

Although data is limited for the Peruvian area, the evidence presented by Zuta and Urquizo (1974) showed that the 'El Niño' effect extended through the first 30 to 70 m with temperatures 25–22° C and salinities 34–34.8 per mille. Also, immediately below the subtropical water it formed a subsurface tongue which extended to depths of 200–250 m with salinities greater than 35.1 per mille. For the area north of 3° S., data was presented by Enfield (1974) in which the layer 0–100 m (temperatures 21–27° C, salinity 35–33.8 per mille) and a layer from 100 to 400 m (temperature 10°–20° C and salinity 35–35.4 per mille) are apparent (the pocket of high salinity with a maximum at about 150 m). This profile is notably different from that of February/March 1972 (a reduced sheet of lower salinity and a less pronounced gradient below 100 m; and the salinity pocket which did not exceed 35.2 per mille salinity) and from that of November/December 1971 (homothermal layer, 12°–15° C, between 50 and 300 m and regional salinities varying from 35.5 to 25.1 per mille between 50 and 400 m). It is sufficient to emphasize that the 15° C isotherm appeared at about 50 m in November/December 1971, between 80 and 150 m in February/March 1972 and between 200 and 250 m in November/December 1972. The pockets of high salinity of November 1971 and November/December 1972 represent high values if the value established by Wyrtki (1965a) is considered.

The topographies of the 15° and 20° C isotherms also showed variations, The 15° C topography showed much greater depths in December (Fig. 35(a)) than throughout the rest of the period considered in this article (1971–73). It indicated a flow from the west at about 3° S. which would come to be the southern extension of the Cromwell current (CCSE) and, at 6° S., another flow from the west (see the 150 m isoline) probably corresponding to the south Equatorial counter current (SECC).

The 20° C topography of December 1972 (Zuta and Urquizo, 1974) showed much greater depths than in Figure 25(b) of February/March. That same December chart showed more clearly the flow of the CCSE near 82° W., which in the 15° C chart appeared around 82°30′ W. The common feature was that both in February/March and in December the centre of the tongue (minimum salinities) corresponded closely with the principal flow of the CCSE.

The thermal anomalies began in this final phase in contrast to the normal pattern (Zuta and Urquizo, 1972), reaching increased values of 2°–6° C off much of the Peruvian coast (IMARPE, 1973). On the other hand both in the areas of Sechura (CM308–51) and Salaverry (CM307–89) for December, increases of 5°–7.5° C down to 100 m of depth and negative salinity anomalies of 0.1–0.7 per mille down to 50 m were noted. But the temperature and salinity variations from November to December 1971 were 5° C and 1 per mille respectively for area 307–89 and 6° C and 0.6 per mille for the area 307–51, significantly higher than normal. (The normal thermal variations for both areas are less than 1° C). The warming which occurred in the final phase was thus of much shorter duration than that of the initial phase since it continued to no longer than March 1973.

THE POST-'EL NIÑO' PERIOD

Bjerknes (1966) introduced the terms pre-'El Niño' years and post-El Niño' years in connection with the phenomenon of 1957/58, and described their general aspects—principally the meteorological. In the summer in the southern Pacific, the trades weakened yearly from 1955 to 1957 and intensified in the period 1959–62).

The post-'El Niño' period is considered to have begun in the sea when the surface tropical waters had recovered their normal position after their final advance southwards, and continued until the time by which the sea conditions had returned to normal or near-normal. From this point of view, this section refers to the initial part of the period, particularly over 1973, and attempts to describe its principal effects in the coastal area off Ecuador and Peru.

The transition from the 'El Niño' period (final phase) to the post-'El Niño' period (initial phase) occurred rapidly, somewhat similar to the transition from the pre-'El Niño' period to the 'El Niño' period (initial phase). One of the notable forerunners of the post-'El Niño' period was the widespread, steep thermal decline in February on the Peruvian coast, and even off Ecuador during March/April 1973. The mean sea-surface temperatures, which in the preceding December/January had been 2°–5° C higher than normal, in April was 2°–4° C below normal south of 4° S. (IMARPE, 1973). Temperatures markedly lower than normal were maintained until April 1974, frequently some 2°–5° C below temperatures consistent with the season. These were values very similar to the anomalies of summer and spring of the years 1970–71 (Zuta, 1973). In May 1974 variations above normal up to 1.5° C appeared over much of the coast; in the following months further drops from the normal (in the order of 0.7° C) predominated with some intensification over September.

The conditions encountered between the end of February and the middle of March during the cruise 7302 of INOCAR and of IMARPE (Liendo and Carbajal, in press) belong to the post-'El Niño' stage, Figures 34(a),(b) show their important differences. The surface subtropical water was the dominant feature principally south of 4°30′ S. with greater penetration to the coast between 12° and 15° C and south of 17° S. North of 4°30′ S., the surface Equatorial water extended but was generally limited to the coastal band east of 82° W.

The unusual projection of the surface subtropical water towards the coast and the north continued to be a notable feature in the cruises 7305 of INOCAR (May) and IMARPE (May/June) in which a strong re-establishment of coastal upwelling was observed off Peru (Figs. 36(a),(b)), with predominating south-east and south-west winds most intense between 9° and 11° S. in the Peruvian area and north of 2° S. on the coastal side of the Equatorial area (Fig. 18).

The surface subtropical water manifested itself very distinctly during the Eureka XXVII voyage of 23–26 September 1973 (IMARPE, 1973). But in Eureka XXVIII of 12–13 November 1973 (IMARPE, 1973), their intensity diminished appreciably, with a slight persistence between Chimbote and Callao and San Juan and Atico.

The November situation underwent few changes until February 1974 (IMARPE, 1974). In March of that year there appears to have been a brief invasion by surface Equatorial water to about 9° S. (IMARPE, 1974), but from May to September the Peruvian coastal waters appeared relatively saline with occasional abnormal rises of temperature no greater then 2° C, as was shown by the Eureka Operation of 28–30 May (IMARPE, 1974), of June (IMARPE, 1974), 3–5 August (IMARPE, 1974) and 5–7 September.

The predominance of surface subtropical water to the south of 5° S. is evident in Figure 28(b) (shaded part) for the three periods dealt with in this article, and in Figure 28(a), the cold temperatures (those shaded with values less than 17° C) of the post-'El Niño' period were very similar to those of the pre-'El Niño' period.

The process which took place off Peru between July 1971 and July 1973 is represented in Figures 29 and 30. The rapid cooling which took place in 1973 especially in the areas off Punta Falsa and Chimbote (Figs. 29(a),(c)) is indicated. The Punta Falsa area is that which most clearly distinguishes the three periods. The Punta Doña Maria area, Figure 31(a),(b) identifies the initial phase of 'El Niño' (with a delay of one or two months) and the Ilo area, Figure 31(c),(d) distinguishes the intermediate phase of the 'El Niño' period.

Thus we can say that the principal features of the post-'El Niño' period were lower-than-normal temperatures (with deviations of from 2° to 5° C below normal in the autumn and springs of 1973 and the summer of 1974), a somewhat abnormal presence of surface subtropical waters principally until before November 1973. In addition there was a notable re-establishment of coastal upwelling off Peru, especially after May 1973.

SYNTHESIS

In this section of the article the principal evidence is extracted from marine observations, with respect to the abnormal effects over the years 1971–73, and the final interpretation is translated into a scheme of the possible circulation during the 1972–73 'El Niño'. The synthesis refers exclusively to areas off the coasts of Ecuador and Peru.

Sequence of hydrographic events

The events began with abnormal cooling of the sea in the years 1970–71, with temperatures as low as 6° C below normal and a somewhat abnormal invasion by surface subtropical waters off the Peruvian coasts and to the north. To this must be added the area of abnormally high salinity (from 35 to 35.5 per mille) at 3° S. (Fig. 16), the layer of the southern extension of the Cromwell Current (50–300 m), at a time when the south-east and south-west winds were already strong to the north of 6° S. (Fig. 14) and the notable Equatorial upwelling according to the maps in *Fishing Information* (1971).

The warming of the sea, especially off Peru, occurred between February 1972 and February 1973. In this lapse of time, the surface tropical water became apparent to the south of 6° S. (Punta Falsa) on two occasions: between February and June 1972 (initial phase) and between December 1972 and February 1973 (final phase). In the first case the advance was to approximately 14° S. (Pisco) and in the second case to 12° S. (Callao) with mean speeds of displacement of up to 23 nautical miles/day in the intermediate phase. The rise in mean temperatures continued markedly in May, and very high values (3°–5° C higher than normal) were registered in the period from June to August, affecting principally the 0–100 m layer. There was an appreciable reduction in September and November, only to be followed by very high values again after in the final phase (3°–6° C). The coastal area to the south of 14° S. was less affected by the anomalous warming, and the upwelling did not disappear from it.

The February/March advance was associated with heavy rainfall and slight winds or calm zones (Fig. 15) at the axis of the warm tongue—and very low salinity (Fig. 24)—which appears to have carried a great quantity of water from the Gulf of Panama to the east of 85° W. These waters produced salinity changes of 0.1–0.8 per mille in the 0–50 m layer.

The December advance was not accompanied by such rainfall and the winds (Fig. 17) were well re-established after an appreciable weakening in the preceding month. In this case, the northern tongue (Fig. 33) appears to have been displaced to the south from the area off Esmeraldas (Ecuador) with the principal initial quantity coming from the Gulf of Panama (and possibly a small contribution from the Gulf of Guayaquil).

In these two advances, the northern tongue occupied the first 50 m depth and in only a few cases reached depths of 70 m. But the thermal structure down to 400 m also showed great changes. Salient among these changes was the disappearance of the thermostatic layer associated with the southern extension of the Cromwell current (Montgomery and Stroup, 1962), principally in the intermediate and final phase (Fig. 8).

The sea temperature in the beginning of the post-'El Niño' period suffered sharp falls in April 1972 approaching values frequently as much as 3°–5°C lower than normal (particularly in autumn and spring 1973 and summer of 1974). Figures 1(a),(b);

28(a),(b); 29(a),(b); and 30(a),(b) effectively illustrate the major events of 1971 and 1973.

Circulation scheme

The analysed data gave indications that over the 'El Niño' period there had been two advances towards the south carrying principally waters from the Gulf of Panama east of 85° W.: that of February/March away from the coast, and that of December closer to it (Figs. 24 and 33).

The vertical sections of temperature and salinity (Fig. 8) as well as the topographies of the 15° and 20° C isotherms (Figs. 25(b), 26(a), and 35(a)) showed that the southern extension of the Cromwell current (Cochrane and Zuta, 1968, unpublished) and the south Equatorial counter current (Reid, 1959), favoured the southward surface flow, by the first advance eastward to the north of 2° S. and by the second to 6° S. (taking 86° W. as reference). The aforementioned topographies, as well as the distribution of the masses of water, insinuate that the principal turn of the Peruvian current took place south of 8° S. at the time of maximum advance of the 'El Niño' waters.

On the other hand there is evidence that the northern waters, with salinity of less than 34.5 per mille, came close to 14° S.; that to the south of this latitude upwelling prevailed; and that far away from the coast in the south and to the west of the Equatorial waters in the central part of Peru, the surface subtropical waters had extended (for the scheme, it is sufficient to limit them with the 35 per mille isohaline).

Putting all these factors together resulted in the diagram in Figure 37 whose scheme could be further enlarged by more data from the west and north. In this theoretical analysis, it is established that the southern extension of the Cromwell current (CCSE) and the south Equatorial countercurrent (SECC) at about 6° S., combine into a single flow named the Peruvian surface current (Peru–Chile surface current). A large part of the waters of 'El Niño' joined the Peruvian current; however there are indications that at the culmination of the initial and final phases, part of the warm surface Equatorial waters turned north in a coastal flow which could merge as part of the Peruvian coastal current. Unfortunately the limitation of the data, both in depth and in area covered, did not permit the formation of a more complete scheme of the last 'El Niño'.

Comparison between
the previous phenomena

Until now no systematic investigations have been
made of the 'El Niño' phenomenon. As a consequence
the available data—especially the hydrographic—
are not sufficient for a valid comparison with other
previous events. Continuation of programmes such as
EASTROPAC (Love, 1971, 1972, 1973, 1974), but for
much longer periods, could fill many gaps in the
knowledge of the eastern Pacific where 'El Niño' is
formed.

Relation with respect to origin

There are indications in the analysis presented here
that the tropical waters which invaded the Peruvian
coast in 1972—73 came mainly from the Gulf of
Panama with a small contribution from the Gulf of
Guayaquil. This establishes a similarity with the
occurrences of 1925 (Schott, 1931) and to those we
can add the events of 1939—41 and 1957—58, according
to the data presented by Bjerknes (1961, 1966).

According to the maps of Stevenson *et al.*
(1970), the great advance in 1965 southwards almost
to 12° S. must have been produced in March/April
with a coastal flow from off Punta Ventura
(Colombia); that is, similar to the advance of December
1972. In November/December 1965, there was a
similar flow which reached only to 7° S.

With respect to the occurrence of 1891 (Schott,
1931), we have already stated that the waters
advanced to the southern and western sides of the
Galapagos Islands and not to the east as in the case of
other occurrences cited in previous paragraphs.

With reference to phenomena of lesser magnitude,
such as that of 1953, Posner (1957) established
that the 1953 'El Niño' carried Equatorial countercurrent waters as well as some from the Central
American region. Examining abnormally high salinities
of 36 per mille off Peru, he added that the western
areas of Central America contributed to 'El Niño'.
The salinities up to 35.6 per mille observed near the
Peruvian coast in 1972 appeared to be related to the
coastward flow of surface subtropical waters, favoured
by the anticyclone of the South Pacific centred
around 23° S. in 1971—73 (Fig. 9).

Relation to characteristics

The most well documented information indicates that
the phenomenon of 1891 was truly extraordinary,

those of 1925, 1939—41, 1957—58, and 1972—73 were
of great magnitude, that of 1965 was of medium size
and those of 1951—53 and 1969 were small. Bjerknes
(1961) and Wooster and Guillén (1974) used the term
'principal Niño' for the three first groups and
'secondary Niño' for the last group. On the other
hand, Zuta *et al.* (1973) established for such groups
the categories 'giant Niño', 'large Niño', 'medium
Niño', and 'small Niño' with durations of
approximately seventeen, fourteen, ten and four
months respectively. Wooster and Guillén (1974)
established similarities between the occurrences of
1972—73 and 1965 such as the invasion of tropical
waters in the first quarters of the year and the advance
of such waters to 12° S.

Zuta (1973) and Zuta and Urquizo (1974),
on the basis of thermal anomalies, established
similarities between the 1972—73 phenomenon and
those of 1957—58 and 1925—26.

The surface temperature at fixed stations shown
in Figures 2—4 revealed various aspects of the 1957—58,
1965 and 1972—73 phenomena. In 1965, a single
warming peak appeared in March. In 1957—58 and in
1972—73, apparently two pronounced warming peaks
appeared: one in February/March of the first year and
the other in January/February of the second, the first
greater than the second at the Talara stations (Fig. 2)
and Don Martin (Fig. 3) with the reverse at San Juan
(Fig. 4) and Pta Coles (Fig. 5) (The second peak
being much more pronounced than the first, which
appeared in May/June with a one- or two-month
delay). In Figure 1 of Sta Cruz (Galapagos), only
a single warming maximum occurred in May 1965
and in 1972—73 there were two maxima, very similar
in size, one in April 1972 and the other in January
1973.

In 1972, the advance of the tropical waters was
associated with an appreciable slackening of the trade
winds in the area of extension of the warm tongue
even though, according to the coastal stations, no
great changes in the wind pattern were detected. It
can be said of this then, that it obeyed the
prerequisites established by Bjerknes (1961).

Examining atmospheric pressures at coastal
stations off Peru, Wooster and Guillén (1974) found
that during the 'principal' and 'secondary' Niños
negative pressure anomalies occurred and, for the
period observed at Callao (1949—73), the largest
anomaly (2.6 m) was during August 1972. The high
pressures of the 1962—64, 1967—68 and 1970—71
periods were associated with drops in sea
temperature.

Relation with respect to periodicities

The surface temperature data show trains of variations with irregular periods. It can be said that, in a prolonged sequence, normal periods are followed by moderately cold and hot, extremely cold (2° C or more below mean) and hot (3° C or more above the mean).

The cold period of 1933–38 preceded the 1939–41 'Niño'; those of 1950, 1954–55 the 1957–58 'Niño'; that of 1961–64 the 1965 'Niño'; and those of 1967–68 and 1970–71 the 1972–73 'Niño'. Between these occurrences of abnormal warmings there are intervals to five to eight years of cold and normal years.

Conclusions

The conclusions given, based on limited data and non-systematic observations cannot be definite and could be improved or amplified with more information:
The 1972–73 'El Niño' can be catalogued as a
    phenomenon of great magnitude, comparable
    with those which occurred in 1957–58 and
    1925–26.
There is evidence that the 1972–73 'El Niño'
    waters advanced from the Gulf of Panama to the
east of 85° W. both in February/March and in
    December, in very coastal form in the latter case.
The invasion to the south of 6° S. of warm and very
    low salinity waters took place between February
    and June 1972 and between December 1972 and
    February 1973; approaching 14° S. (Pisco) in the
    first case and 12° S. (Callao) in the second. To the
    south of 14° S. the conditions remained much
    closer to normal and the coastal upwelling prevailed.
The February/March 1972 advance was associated
    with light winds or zones of calm and heavy rainfall
    at sea. The December 1972 advance took place
    when the winds were re-established after weakening
    in November. In both cases the mean winds at
    coastal stations did not show great variations.
In the 1970–71 pre-'El Niño' period, the sea was
    abnormally cold and the atmospheric pressures
    were high off Peru. During the 1972–73 'El Niño'
    there was considerable warming and low pressures.
    In the post-'El Niño' year, 1973, the sea was
    abnormally cold. The surface subtropical water
    made abnormal invasions both off the Peruvian
    coast and towards the north in 1971, between
    July and September 1972 and in 1973 (October/
    November).
The extension of the Cromwell current received a
    large contribution from the southward flow of
    tropical water during the 1972 advance.

Table 1

Expedition	Number of vessels	Date	Latitudes
Peladilla	11	24—25 February 1972	7—14° S.
Anchoveta	11	2 April 1972	7—17° S.
Eureka XX	23	28—29 April 1972	7—18°30′ S.
Eureka XXI	18	17—18 June 1972	7—18°30′ S.
Eureka XXII	16	18—19 July 1972	5—18°30′ S.
Eureka XXIII	25	3— 6 August 1972	6—18°30′ S.
Eureka XXIV	36	5— 8 August 1972	6—19° S.
Eureka XXV	35	20—22 October 1972	5—18°30′ S.
Eureka XXVI	42	20—23 January 1973	5—18° S.
Eureka XXVII	60	23—26 September 1973	6—18°30′ S.
Eureka XXVIII	51	12—13 November 1973	5—18°30′ S.

Table 2

Station	Latitude	Longitude	Temperature Sea	Temperature Air	Precipitation	Wind	Pressure
Ecuador							
Pto Baquerizo (Guayaquil)	0°54′	89°37′ W.		X		X	
I. Sta Cruz	2°12′ S.	79°53 W.	X				
Salinas	2°59′ N.	80°59′ W.				X	
Esmeraldas	0°59′ N.	79°39′ W.		X	X	X	
Ancón	2°20′ S.	80°51′ W.		X	X		
Machala	3°16′ S.	79°57′ W.		X	X	X	
Peru							
Pto Piz	3°30′S.	80°23′ W.		X	X	X	
Talara	4°30′ S.	81°17′ W.	X	X	X	X	
Chimbote	9°05′ S.	78°31′ W.		X	X	X	
I. Don Martín	11°00′ S.	77°45 W.	X	X			
Callao (Corp)	12°00′ S.	77°07′ W.		X		X	X
San Juan	15°20′ S.	75°10′ W.	X	X		X	
Pta Coles	17°30 S.	71°20′ W.	X	X		X	
Pimental	8°50′ S.	79°57 W.		X	X		

Table 3

Marsden	Interval	Marsden	Interval
308—71	7— 8° S.	343—46	14—15° S.
308—80	8— 9° S.	343—55	15—16° S.
307—99	9—10° S.	343—64	16—17° S.
343—08	10—11° S.	343—73	17—18° S.
343—18	11—12° S.	343—82	18—19° S.
343—27	12—13° S.	343—91	19—20° S.
343—37	13—14° S.		

Table 4

Areas	Latitude	Longitude
Pta Falsa	6°10′ S.	81°20′ W.
Chimbote	9°40′ S.	79°20′ W.
Pta Doña Maria	14°50′ S.	76°20′ W.
Ilo	17°40′ S.	71°40′ W.

Table 5

Cruise	1°N.—6° S. speed (I: m/s) [1]	Direction [2]	6° S.—12° S. speed (II: m/s) [1]	Direction [2]
7111	4—8	S.W., S.E.	2—4	S.W., S.E.
7202	0—3	S.E., S.W., N.E.	2—6	S.E.
7205	2—6	S.E., S.W.		
7208	4—8	N.E., N.W.	—	—
7201	2—8	S.E., S.W.	4—9	S.E.
7302			3—7	S.E.
7305	2—8	S.W.	3—9	S.E., S.W.

1. Mean — standard deviation to mean + standard deviation, rounded
2. In order of decreasing frequency.

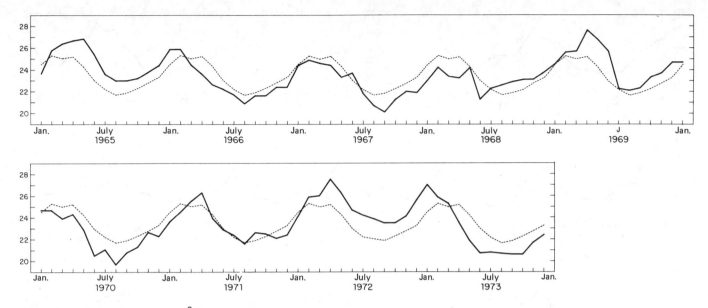

Fig. 1. Surface sea temperature (°C) on the Isle of Santa Cruz
(Galapagos). Broken lines corresponds to long-term average,
1965–73.

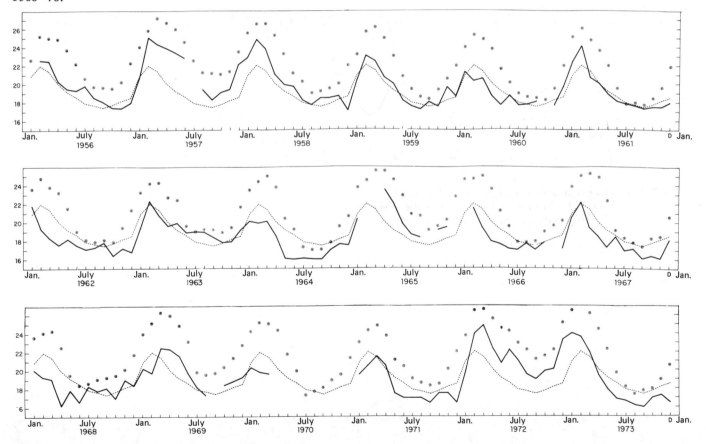

Fig. 2. Surface sea temperature at Talara (4°34′ S., 81°15′ W.).
The broken line corresponds to the long-term mean, 1956–73.
The encircled points represent air temperature (°C).

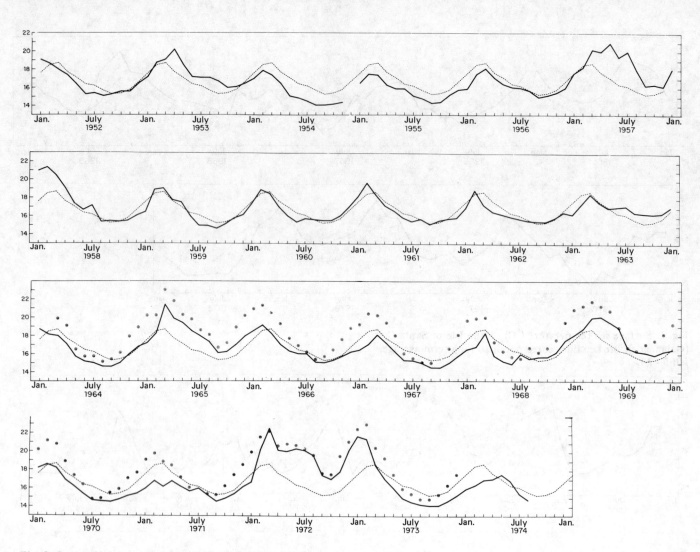

Fig. 3. Sea surface temperature on the Isle of Don Martin
(11°02′ S., 77°41′ W.). The broken line represents the long-term
mean, 1952—74. The encircled points represents air temperature (°C).

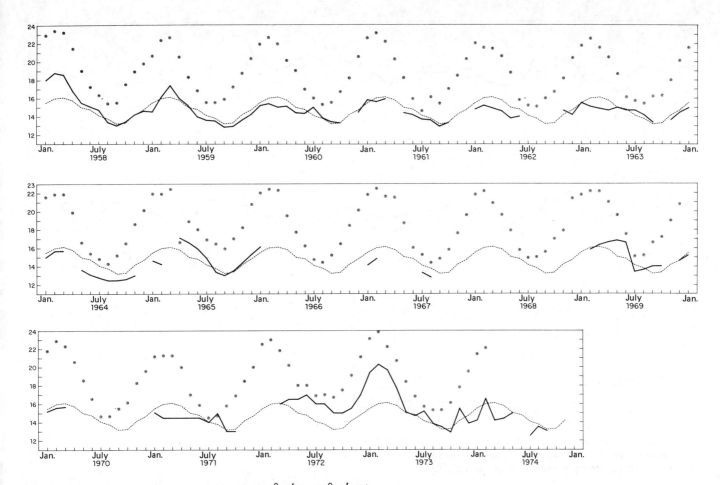

Fig. 4. Sea surface temperature at San Juan (15°20′ S., 75°10′ W.).
The broken line corresponds to the long-term mean, 1958—74,
The encircled points represent air temperature (°C).

Salvador Zuta, David Enfield, Jorge Valdivia, Pablos Lagos,
Carlos Blandin   30

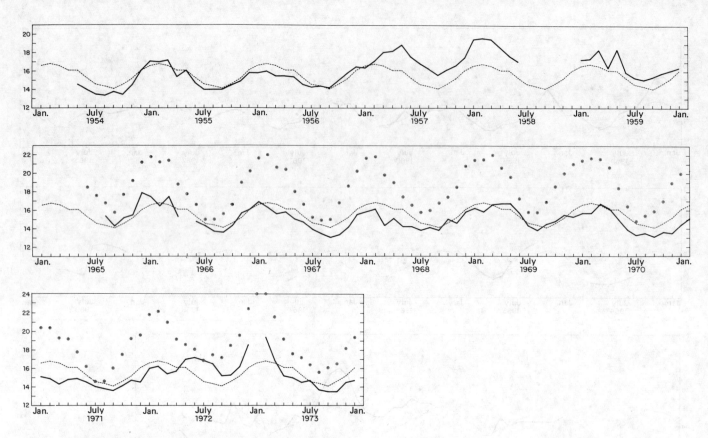

Fig. 5. Sea surface temperature at Pta Coles (17°50′ S., 71°20′ W.).
The broken line corresponds to the long-term mean, 1954—73.
The encircled points represent air temperature. (°C).

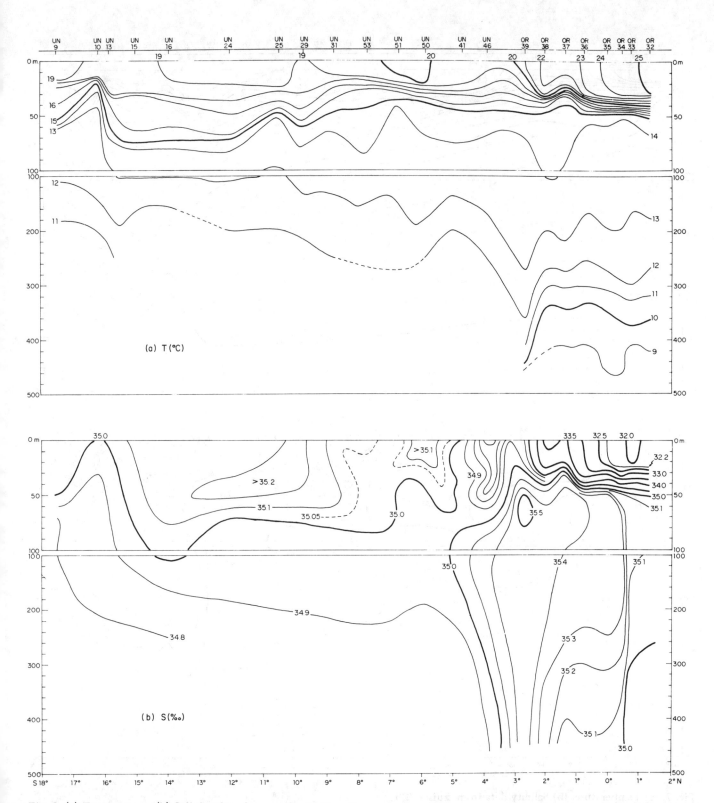

Fig. 6. (a) Temperature. (b) Salinity data from cruise 7111
(November 1971) from the boats *Unanue* (UN) and *Orión*
(OR).

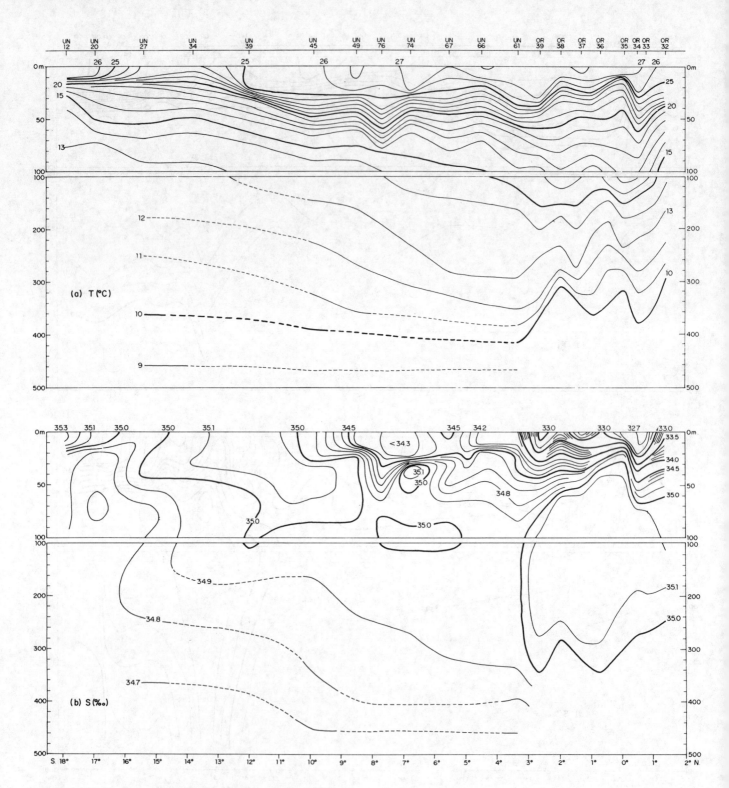

Fig. 7. (a) Temperature. (b) Salinity data from cruises 7202
and 7203 (February–March 1972) from the boats *Unanue*
(UN) and Orión (OR).

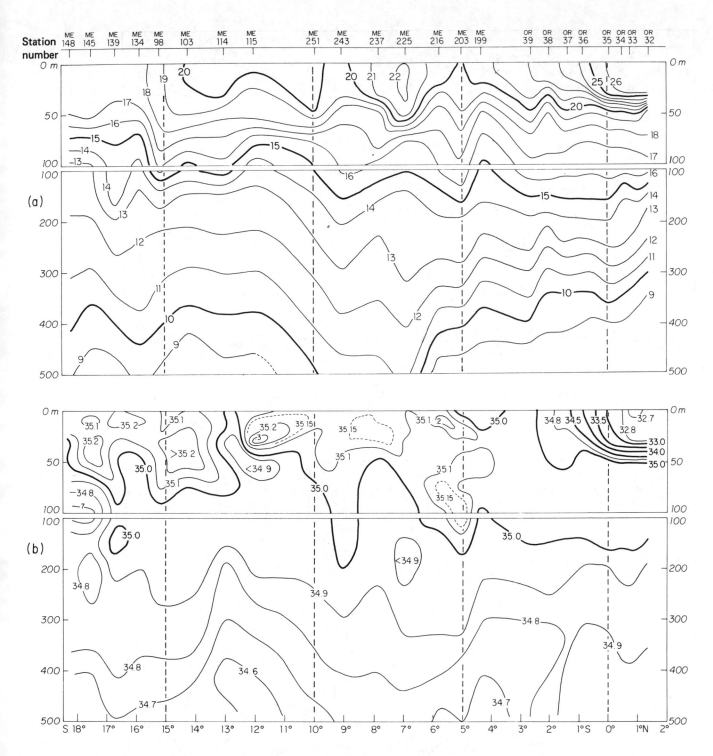

Fig. 8. (a) Temperature. (b) Salinity data for August and
September 1972 from the boats *Mesyatsev* (ME) and Orión
(OR).

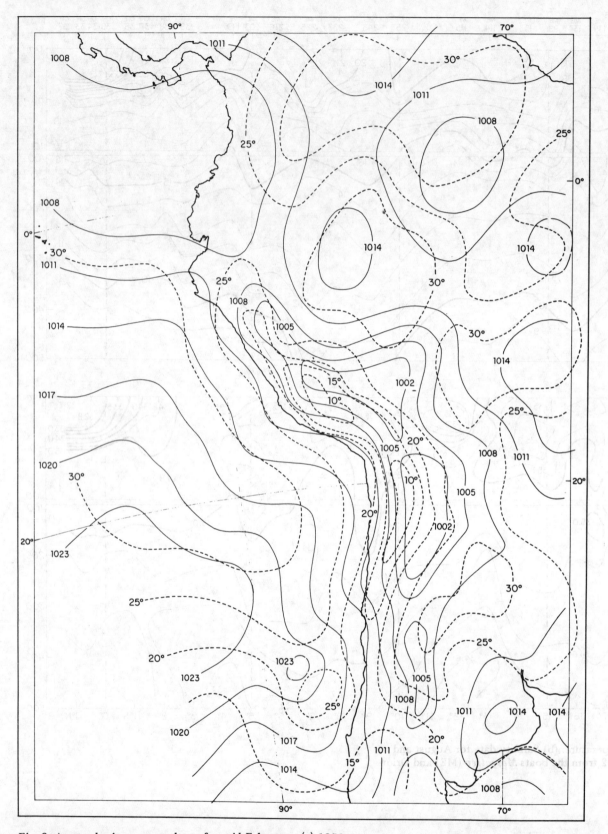

Fig. 9. Atmospheric pressure charts for mid-February: (a) 1971.

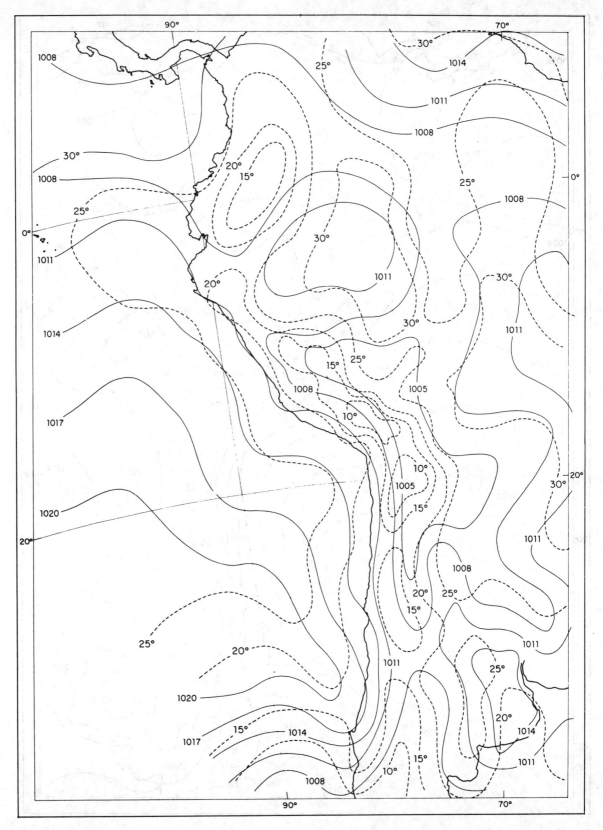

Fig. 9(b) 1972.

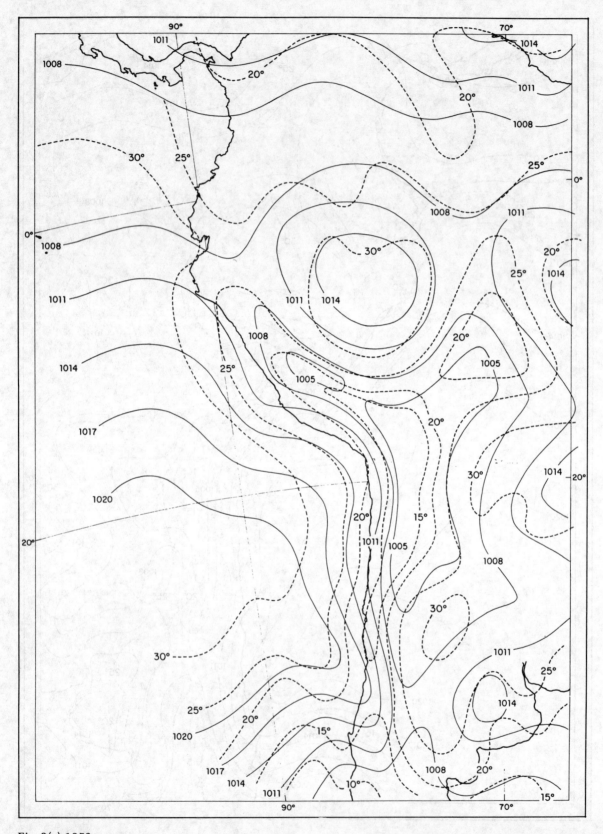

Fig. 9(c) 1973.

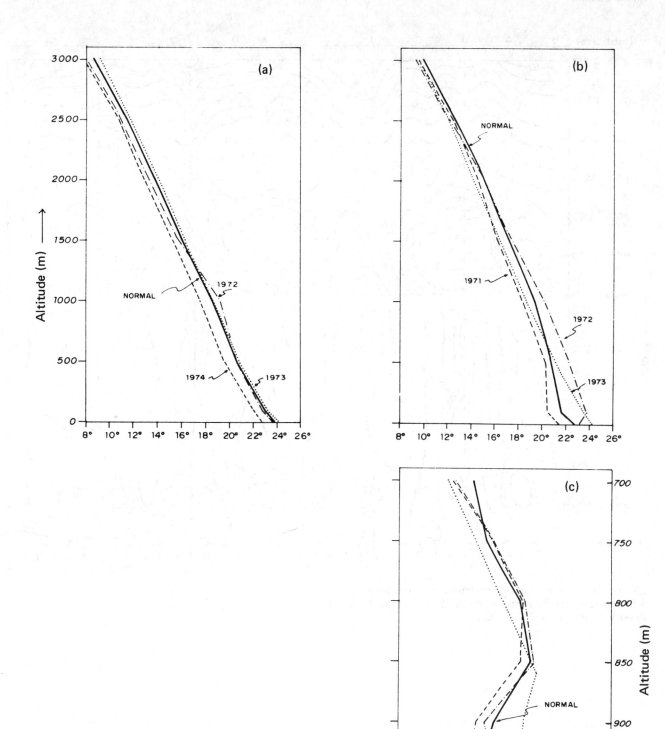

Fig. 10. Vertical air temperature distribution
for: (a) Guayaquil; (b) and (c) Callao in February
and August during the years 1971—74 (° C).

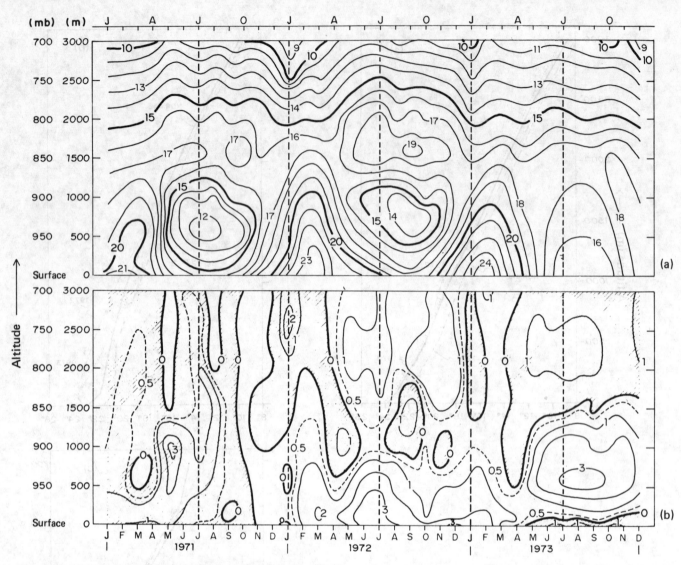

Fig. 11. Station variation of air temperature between 0 and
3,000 metres: (a) the nine-year mean 1957–73; (b) the monthly
deviations during 1971–73 (°C).

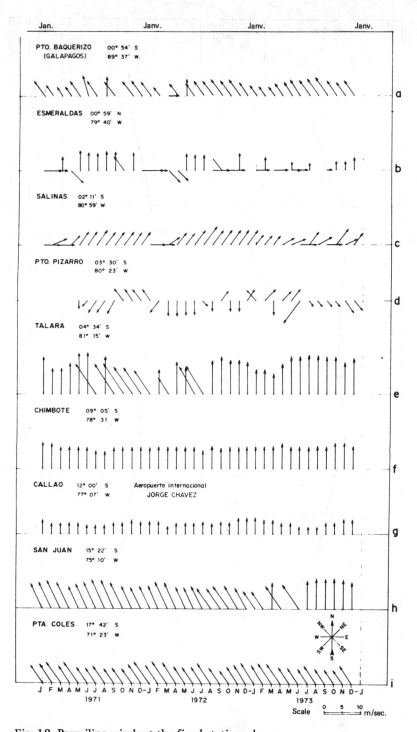

Fig. 12. Prevailing winds at the fixed stations shown.

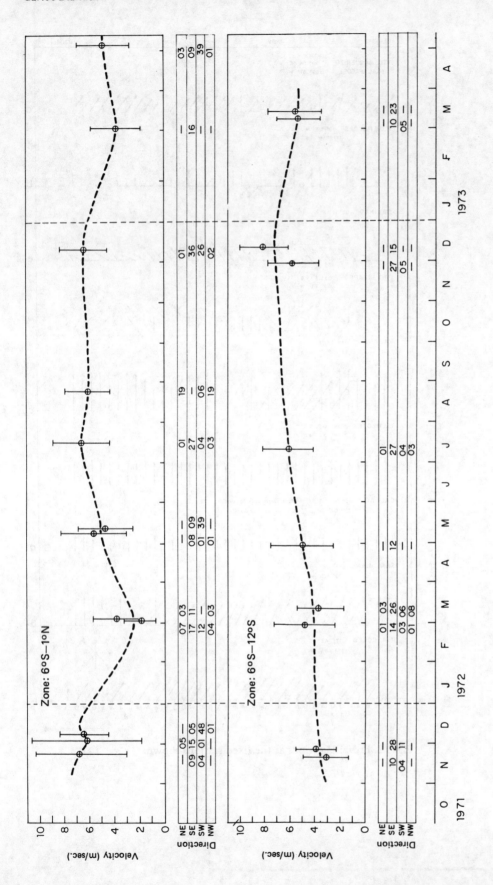

Fig. 13. The winds during cruises 1971—73. In the left margin
is indicated the frequency of the wind directions.

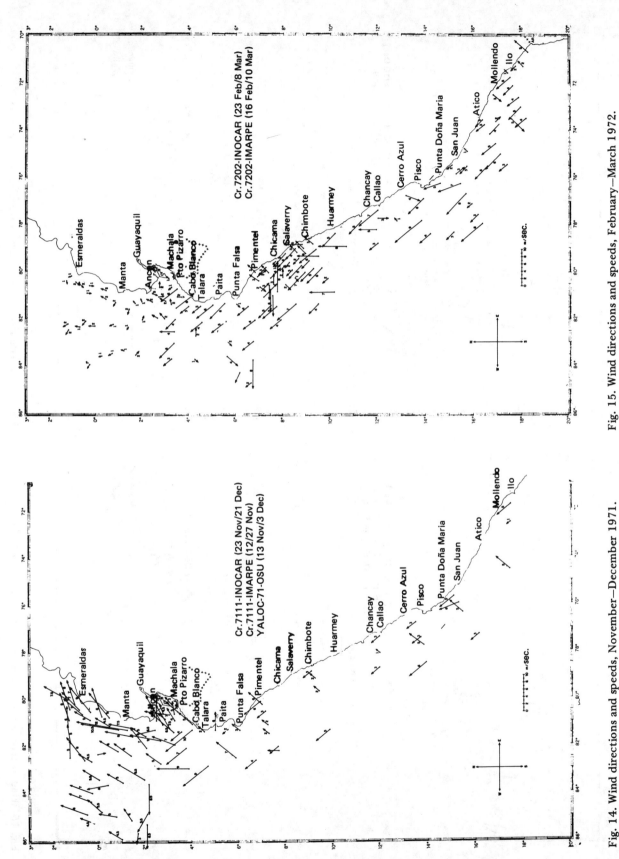

Fig. 15. Wind directions and speeds, February–March 1972.

Fig. 14. Wind directions and speeds, November–December 1971.

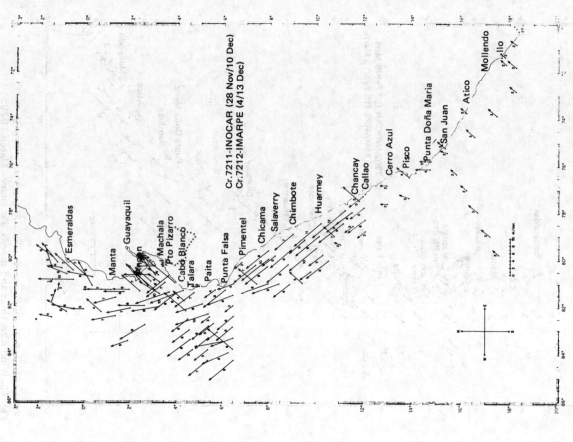

Fig. 17. Wind directions and speeds, November—December 1972.

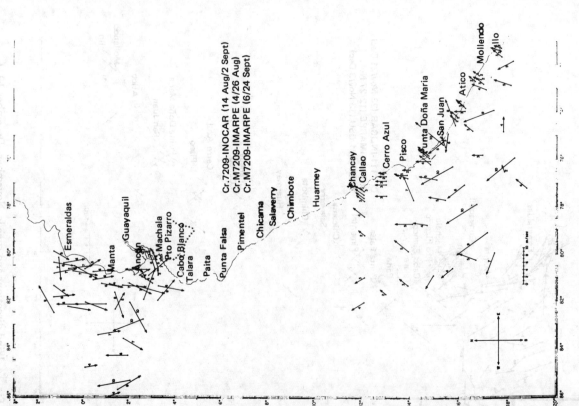

Fig. 16. Wind directions and speeds, August—September 1972.

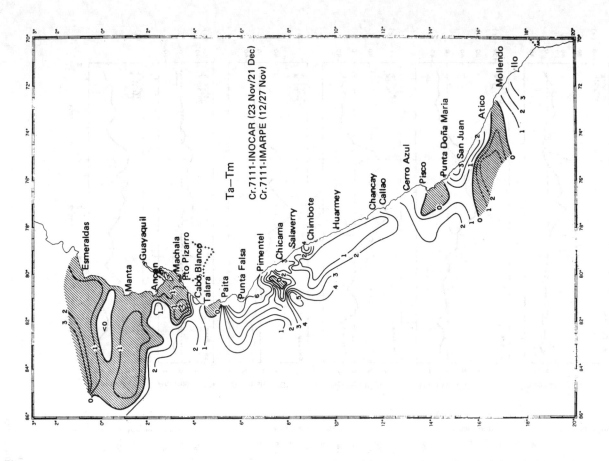

Fig. 19. Air/sea temperature difference, November–December 1971.

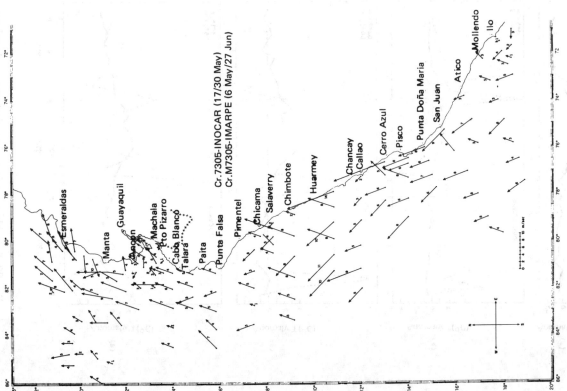

Fig. 18. Wind directions and speeds, May–June 1973.

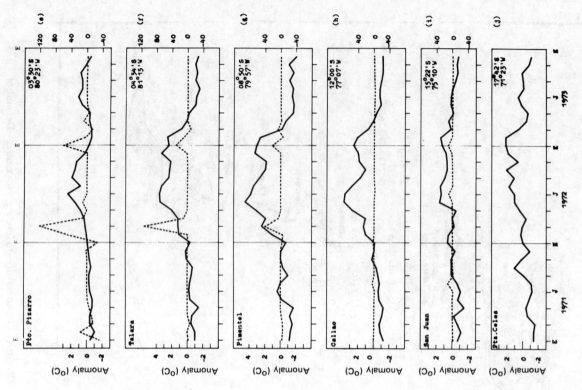

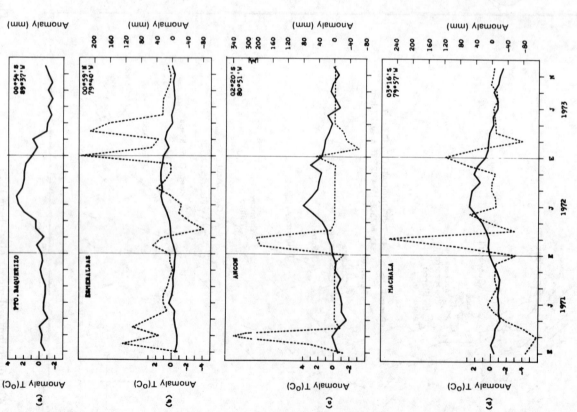

Fig. 20. Monthly variation of precipitation and surface air temperature from long-term means at coastal stations as indicated over the period 1971–73. (Broken lines represent precipitation; unbroken lines correspond to temperatures.)

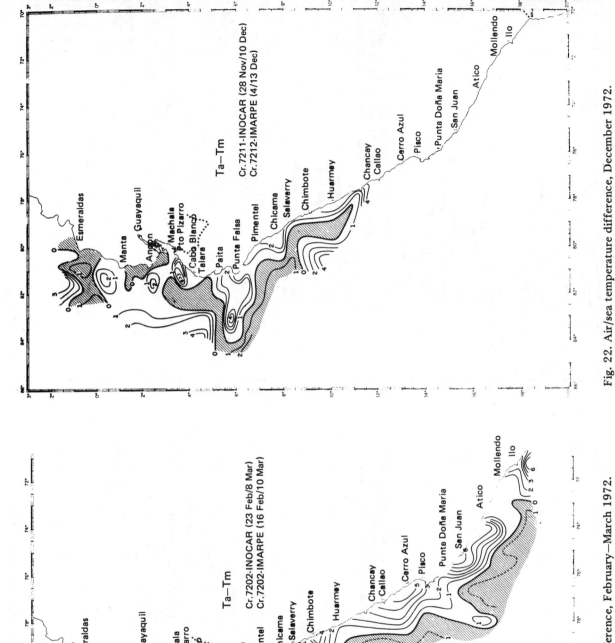

Fig. 22. Air/sea temperature difference, December 1972.

Fig. 21. Air/sea temperature difference, February–March 1972.

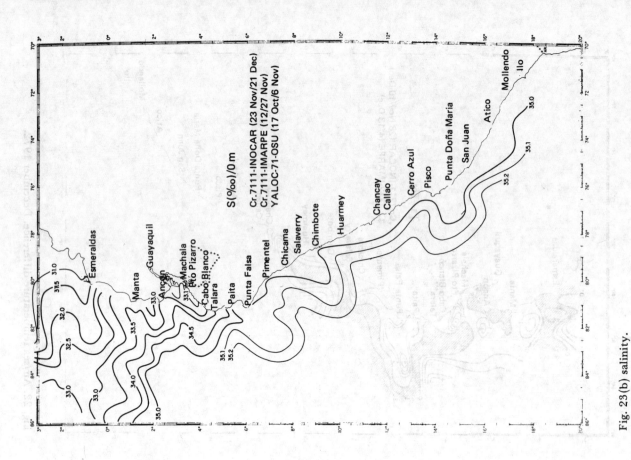

Fig. 23(b) salinity.

Fig. 23. Surface distributions, November–December 1971:
(a) temperature.

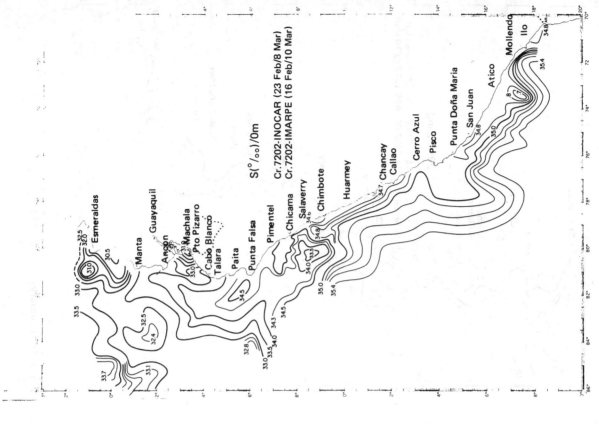

Fig. 24. Surface distributions, February–March 1972:
(a) temperature.
Fig. 24(b) salinity.

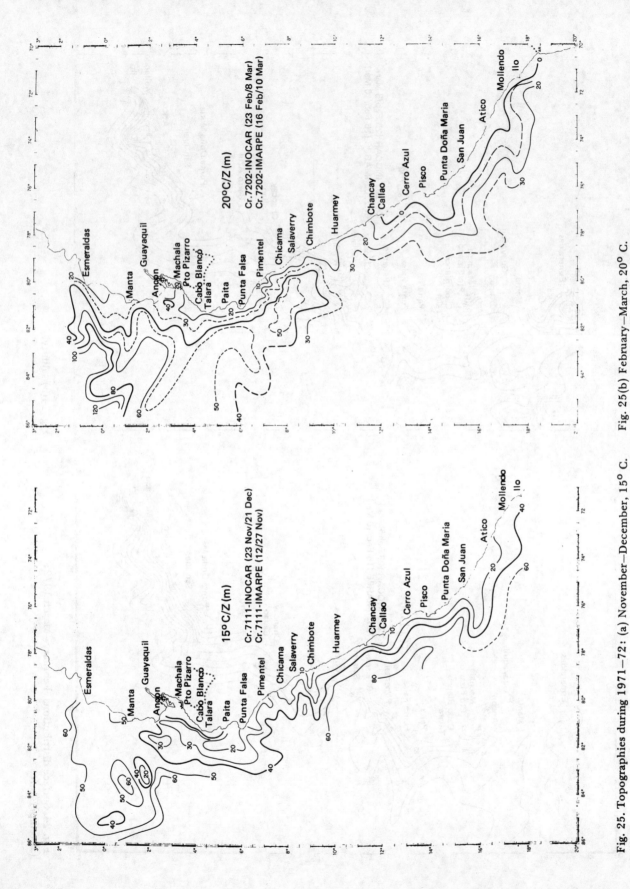

Fig. 25. Topographies during 1971—72: (a) November—December, 15° C.   Fig. 25(b) February—March, 20° C.

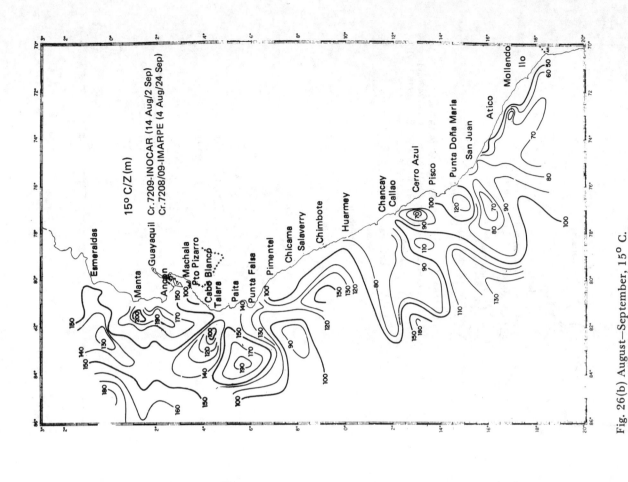

Fig. 26(b) August–September, 15° C.

Fig. 26. Topographies during 1972: (a) February–March, 15° C.

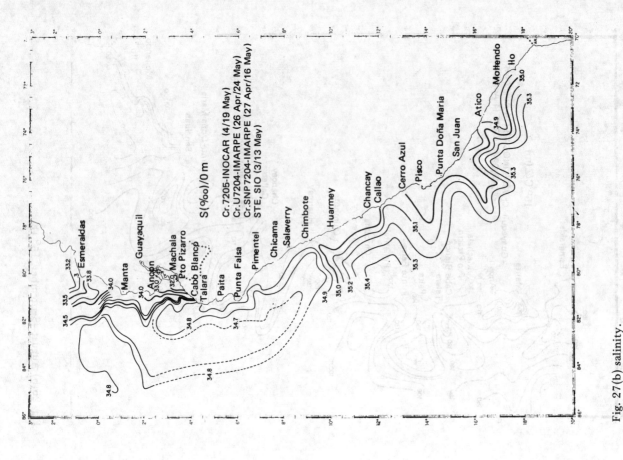

Fig. 27(b) salinity.

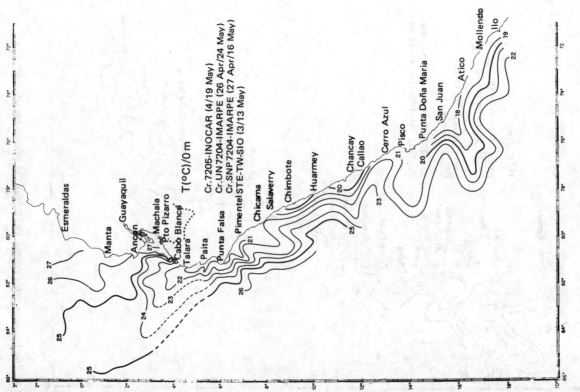

Fig. 27. Surface distributions, April—May 1972: (a) temperature.

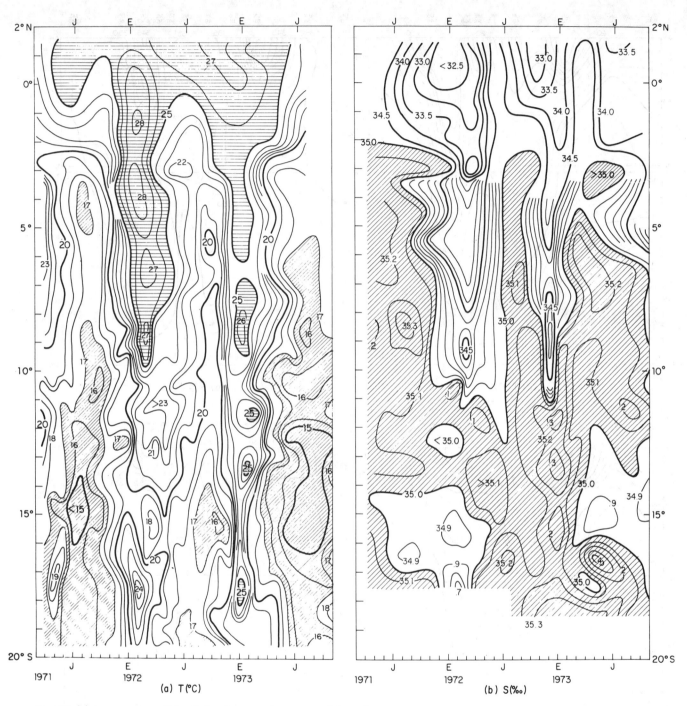

Fig. 28 (a) temperature; (b) salinity data on the coasts of Ecuador and Peru during 1971–73. Dates represent average for selected stations. (E = January; J = July.)

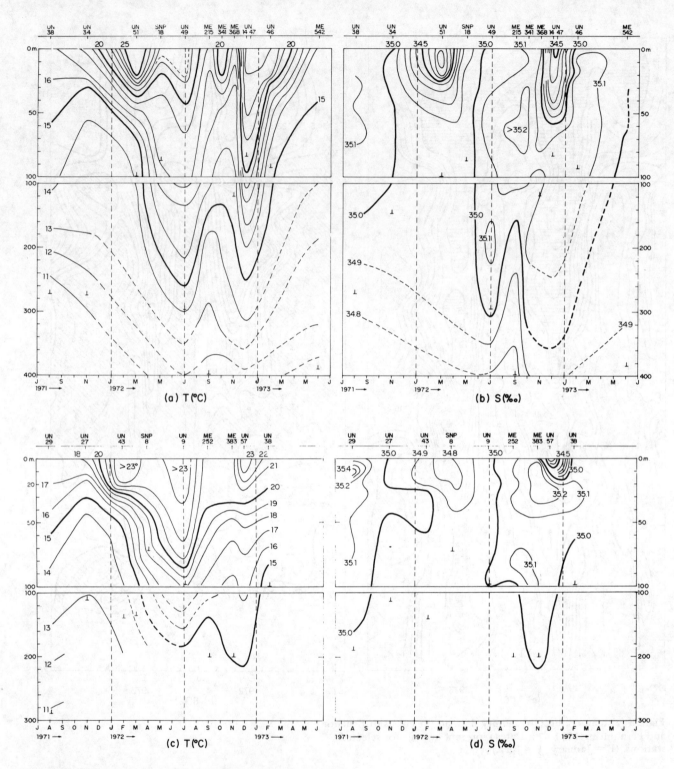

Fig. 29. The Pta Falsa area: (a) temperature; (b) salinity. The
Chimbote area: (c) temperature; (d) salinity. The sign ⊥
represents maxima observed. Dates of cruises of the ships
Unanue (UN), *SNP–1* (SNP) and *Mesyatsev* (ME).

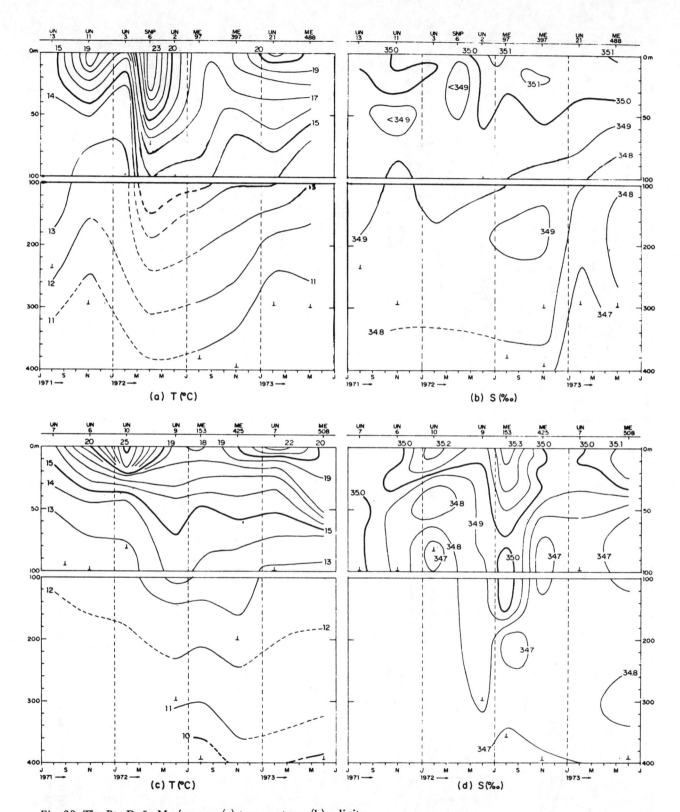

Fig. 30. The Pta Doña María area: (a) temperature; (b) salinity
The Ilo area: (c) temperature; (c) salinity. The sign represents
maxima observed. Dates of cruises of the ships *Unanue* (UN),
SNP–1 (SNP) and *Mesyatsev* (ME).

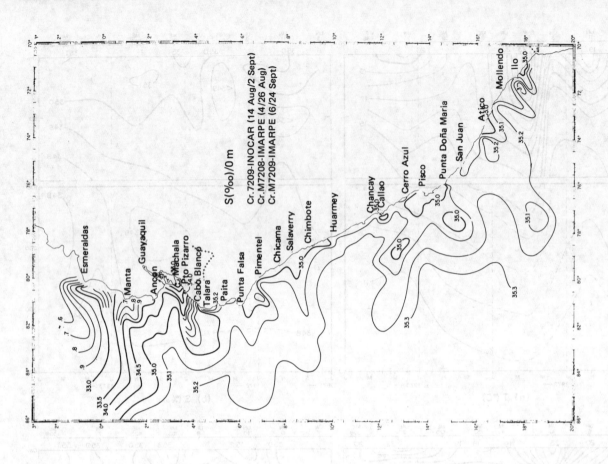

Fig. 31(b) salinity.

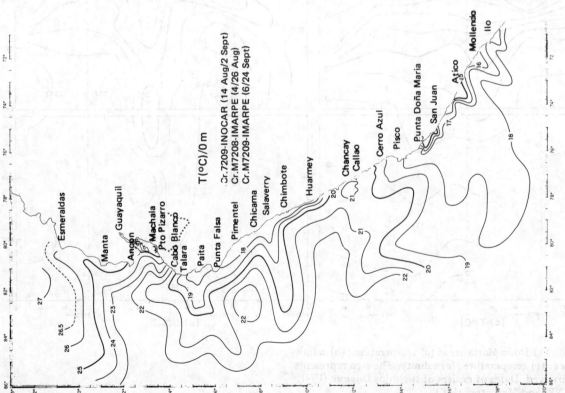

Fig. 31. Surface distributions, August–September 1972:
(a) temperature.

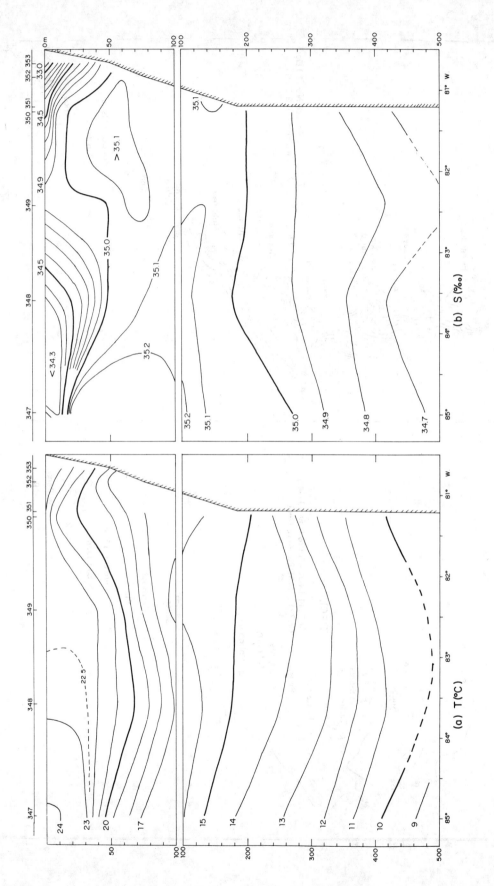

Fig. 32. Data at Pto Pizarro, 3–5 November 1972: (a) temperature; (b) salinity. (*Mesyatsev*, cruise 7210).

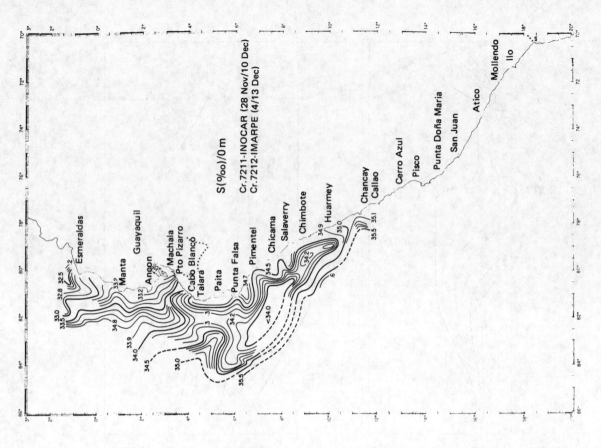

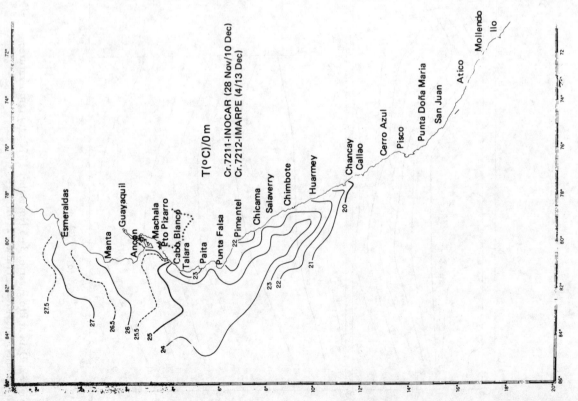

Fig. 33. Surface distributions, December 1972: (a) temperature.

Fig. 33(b) salinity.

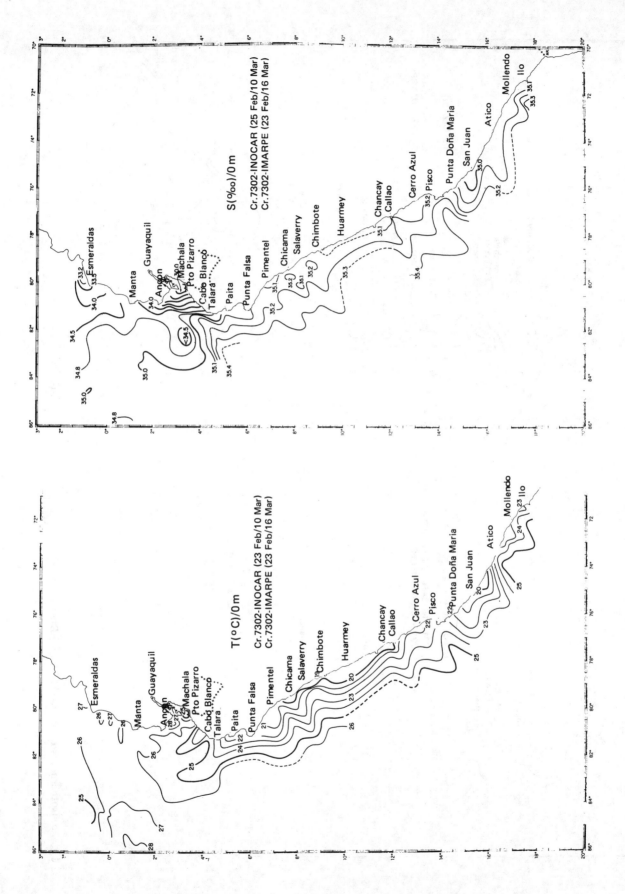

Fig. 34. Surface distributions, February–March 1973:
(a) temperature.

Fig. 34(b) salinity.

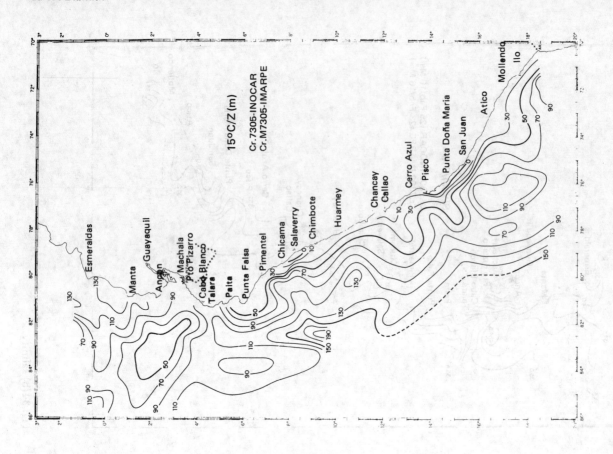

Fig. 35(b) May—June 1973.

Fig. 35. Isotherm distributions, 15° C: (a) December 1972.

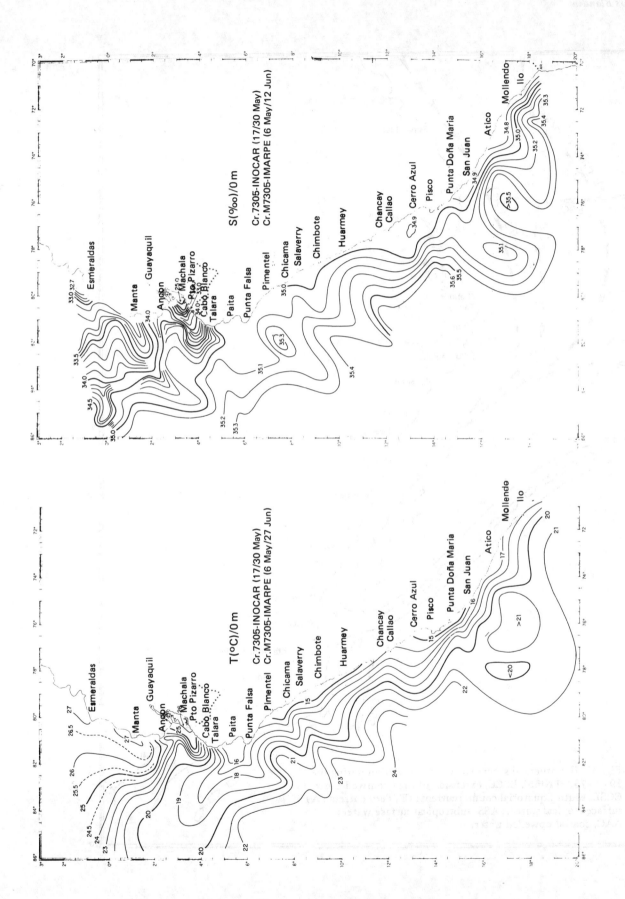

Fig. 36. Surface distributions, May–June 1973; (a) temperature.

Fig. 36(b) salinity.

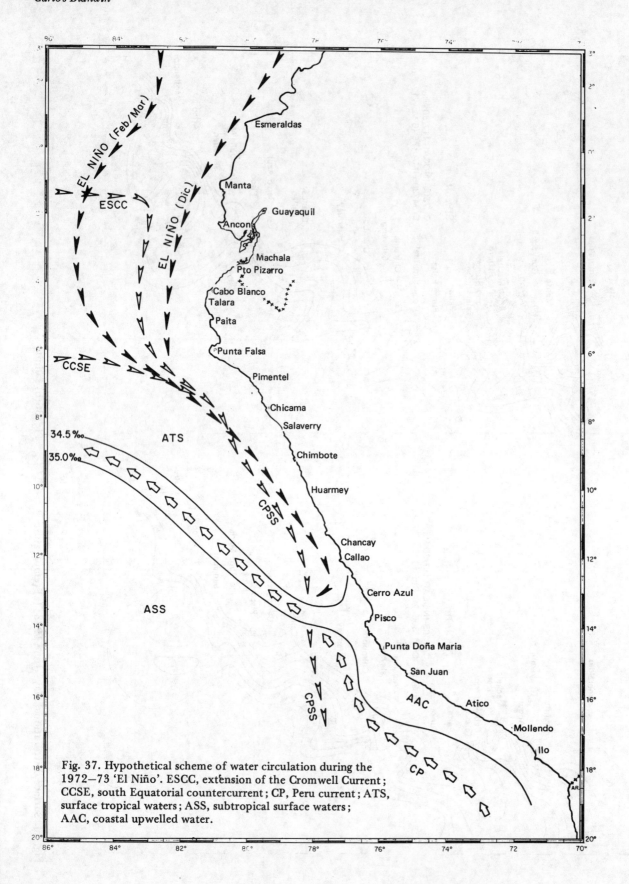

Fig. 37. Hypothetical scheme of water circulation during the
1972–73 'El Niño'. ESCC, extension of the Cromwell Current;
CCSE, south Equatorial countercurrent; CP, Peru current; ATS,
surface tropical waters; ASS, subtropical surface waters;
AAC, coastal upwelled water.

References

Bjerknes, J. 1961. 'El Niño' Study on Analysis of Ocean Surface Temperatures 1935–37. *Inter-Amer. Trop Tuna Comm. Bull.*, Vol. 5, No. 3, p. 217–307.

——. 1966 Survey of 'El Niño' 1957–58 in its relation to Tropical Pacific Meteorology. *Inter-Amer. Trop. Tuna Comm. Bull.*, Vol. 12, No. 2.

Burt, W. V., Enfield, D. B., Smith, R. L.; Crew, H. 1973. The Surface Wind over an Upwelling Area near Pisco, Peru. *Boundary-Layer Meteorology*, Vol. 3, p. 385-91.

Carillo, Camilo N. 1892. Disertación Sobre las Corrientes Oceánicas y Estudios de la Corriente Peruana ó de Humboldt. *Bol. Soc. Georgr. de Lima*, Vol. 11, p. 72–100. (P/0–02–00315).

Cochrane, J. D.; Zuta, S. 1968. Equatorial Currents East of the Galapagos Islands in February–March 1967. (Mimeo.).

Enfield, D. B. 1974. The Region North of the Equatorial Front: Physical Aspects. Paper presented at 'El Niño' Workshop, Guayaquil, Ecuador.

Fishing Information. 1971. Monthly Sea Surface Temperature Charts of the Pacific Ocean, Nos. 1–12. National Marine Fishery Services, United States of America.

Flores, L. A., Cany, P.; Hartley, H. 1972. *Informe Preliminar del Crucero SNP-1, 7111.* (Serie Inf. Esp. No. IM-106, IMARPE).

Guillén, O. 1967. Anomalies in the Waters off the Peruvian Coast During March and April 1965. *Stud. Trop. Oceanography* (Miami), Vol. 5, p. 452-65.

Guillén, O.; Flores, L. A. 1965. Exploración de la Región Maritima Máncora–Callao–Arica, Cruce 6504. *Inf. Instituto del Mar del Perú–Callao*, No. 4, May.

Guillén, O.; Liendo, V. 1973. *Informe Preliminar de los Cruceros Unanue 7206 y 7207* (Serie Inf. Esp. N IM-150, IMARPE.)

Instituto del Mar del Perú (IMARPE). 1972. Serie Inf. Esp. No. IM-98, IM-100, IM-105, IM-110, IM-111, IM-112, IM-113, IM-115, IM-117.

——. 1973. Serie Inf. Esp. No. IM-122, IM-128, IM-129, IM-130, IM-141, IM-145, IM-146.

——. 1974. IM-156, IM-157, IM-158, IM-159, IM-164.

Lettau, H.; Lettau, K. 1972. *Exploring the World's Driest Climate;* University of Wisconsin.

Liendo, V.; y Carbajal, G. 1974. *Informe Preliminar del Crucero Unanue 7302.*

Liendo, V.; Guillén, O. 1973. *Informe Preliminar de los Cruceros SNU-1, 7204 y Unanue 7204,* (Serie Inf. Esp. No. IM-144, IMARPE).

Lobell, J. M. 1942. Some Observations on the Peruvian Coastal Current. *Trans. Amer. Geophys. Union,* Vol. 2, p. 332–6.

Love, C. M. (ed.). 1970. *Eastropic Atlas,* Vol. 4.

——. 1971. *Eastropic Atlas.* Vols 2, 3.

——. 1972. *Eastropic Atlas.* Vols. 1, 5 and 6.

——. 1973. *Eastropic Atlas.* Vol. 7.

——. 1974. *Eastropic Atlas,* Vol. 8.

Mejia, J., Flores, L. A., Castillo, J.; Hartley, H. 1973. *Informe del Crucero SNP–1, 7205.* (Serie Inf. Esp. No. IM–149, IMARPE.)

Mugíca, R. 1972. Oceanografía del Mar Peruano. *Historia Marítima del Perú.* Vol. 1, p. 219–474.

Murphy, R. C. 1926. Oceania and Climatic Phenomena Along the West Coast of South America During 1925. *Georgr. Rev.*, Vol. 16, p. 26–54.

Montgomery, R. B.; Stroup, E. D. 1962. Equatorial Waters and Currents at 150° W., July–August 1952. *Johns Hopkins Oceanography Studies,* Vol. 1,

Namias, J. 1973. Response of the Equatorial Counter-current to the Subtropical Atmosphere. *Science,* Vol. 181, p. 1244–5.

Posner, G. S. 1957. The Peru Current. *Bull. Bingham, Oceanography.* (Coll.), Vol. 16, No. 2, p. 106–55.

Prohaska, F. 1968a. Climatic Consequences of the Inversion Layer at the Peruvian Coast. *19th Annual Meetings, Ass. Amm. Geography,* p. 1–5.

——. 1968b. The Inversion Layer at the Peruvian Coast. *7th National Fall Meeting, Am. Geoph.*

Reid, J. L., Jr. 1959. Evidence of a South Equatorial Countercurrent in the Pacific Ocean. *Nature,* Vol. 184, p. 209–10. (P/0–02–00041).

Schott, G. 1931. *Ann. Hidrogr. u. Mar. Meteorol.,* Vol. 59, p. 161–253.

Stevenson, M. R.; Guillen, O.; Santoro, J. 1970. *Marine Atlas of the Pacific Coastal Waters of South America.* University of California Press. 23 p. + charts.

Stevenson, M.; Taft, B. 1971. New Evidence of the Equatorial Undercurrent East of the Galapagos Islands. *Jour. Mar. Res.,* Vol. 29, No. 2, p. 103–15. (P/0–02–00023).

Wooster, W. S. 1960. 'El Niño'. *California Coop. Ocean. Fish. Invest., Rept.* 7, p. 43–5.

Wooster, W. S.; O. Guillén, 1974. Characteristics of El Niño in 1972. *Jour. Mar. Res.,* Vol. 32, No. 33, p. 387–404. (P/0–02–00176).

Wyrtki, K. 1965a. Surface Currents of the Eastern Tropical Pacific Ocean. *Inter-Amer. Trop. Tuna Comm. Bull.,* Vol. 9, No. 5, p. 270–304. (P/0–02–00129).

—— 1965b. *Summary of the Physical Oceanography of the Eastern Equatorial Pacific Ocean.* San Diego, University of California IMR Ref. 65–10.69 p. (P/0–02–00134).

Zuta, S. 1973. El Fenómeno 'El Niño' 1972–73. *Revista de la Asociación de Oficiales Generales, ADOGEN,* Vol. XX, No. 35, p. 29–44.

Zuta, S.; O. Guillén, 1970. On the Oceanography of the Peru Coastal Waters. *Inst. Mar. Peru. Bol.*, No. 5 (P/O—02—00131, 00132).

Zuta, S.; Santander, H. 1974. *El Ambiente Marino y su Relación con los Recursos Biológicos* (in press).

Zuta, S.; Urquizo, W. 1972. Temperatura Promedio de la Superficie del Mar Frente a la Costa Peruana, Periodo 1928—1969. *Inst. Mar. Peru,* Vol. 2, No. 8, p. 462—519 (MET—02—00004).

—. 1974. *Informe de los Cruceros 7211 y 7212 del BAP Unanue. Condiciones Oceanográficas Anormales Frente al Perú en la Primavera de 1972.* (Serie Inf. Esp. No. IM—160, IMARPE).

Zuta, S.; Urquizo, W.; Liendo, V. 1973. *Informe del Crucero Unanua 7202. Condiciones Oceanográficas Anormales Frente al Perú en el Verano de 1972* (Serie Inf. Esp. No. IM-142, IMARPE).

Zuta, S.; Yoza, L. 1974. *El Niño un Fenómeno de Interacción del Sistema Océano-Atmósfera.*

Biological aspects of the 1972–73 'El Niño' phenomenon. 1: Distribution of the fauna

Aurora C. de Vildoso [1]

Introduction

The 'El Niño' phenomenon is a typical example of the influence that changes of habitat can have on the distribution of different species. In effect, by causing a warming of the waters within the limits of the coastal current, the distribution of stenothermal species is modified and a further, indirect effect is exerted on other species related to the stenothermal group through food-chain interrelationships.

Reliable background information on this matter started at the turn of this century, and relates to 'El Niño' phenomena recorded in 1911–12, 1917, 1925, 1932, 1939–42, 1953, 1957–58 and 1965. The works of Lavalle (1917), Murphy (1926), Vogt (1940), Hutchinson (1950) and Jordan and Fuentes (1966) all mention mortalities and/or migrations of the guano birds caused by the displacement of fish which, like the anchovy *Engraulis ringens* J., serve as their food.

The references on the hydrobiological upsets of the 'El Niño' bearing on other zoological groups are fewer. The works of Del Solar (1942), Fiedler *et al.* (1948) and Schweigger (1953) recorded that during the 'El Niño' phenomenon of 1939–42, as well as of that of 1953, with the invasion of warm waters approximately to the level of Pisco (14° S.), latitudinal displacements of tropical fauna occurred towards the central coast of Peru. Oceanic species approached the coast and, furthermore, the elements of the true Peruvian current fauna were absent from their normal habitat.

Observers of 'El Niño' of 1972–73 had the advantage, from the scientific point of view, of more systematic information than had been available in previous years. The Instituto del Mar, due to its obligation to monitor constantly the changes in achovy population level, carried out ten bio-oceanographic surveys ('Eureka' operations) over those two years along the entire length of the Peruvian coast and three other surveys in various regions of the coast. Although the investigation was oriented towards the anchovy, alterations of the marine environment in general were also recorded.

The present work presents a summary of some of the results with respect to biological aspects of the 1972–73 'El Niño' phenomenon, results which have been partially published in various official documents of the Instituto del Mar.

Distribution of pelagic fish during the 1972–73 'El Niño'

RECORD OF RARE FISH TYPES OFF THE CENTRAL AND SOUTHERN COAST OF PERU

Within the normal distribution of the pelagic resources of Peru, it is possible to distinguish between a coastal fauna and another open-sea fauna in the surface-water habitat. The former consists of: (a) coastal fish typical of the coastal current as well as those of southern origin whose latitudinal distribution

1. Instituto del Mar del Perú, Esq. Gamarra y Gral. Valla, Chucuito, Callao (Perú).

extends along the entire southern and central coast to approximately 6° S.; and (b) the tropical neritic fishes which inhabit waters from 6° S. to the north of the littoral. The open-sea fauna consists of species of wide distribution and which approach both the north as well as south coasts.

During the 1972 summer, warm waters (around 30° C) whose salinity was less than 33 per mille and of Equatorial origin approached the coasts. They covered the northern and central area from Cabo Blanco to Pisco and showed a change of up to 5° C above the forty-year mean. Between Pisco and Arica (14°–18° S.), the temperature remained about average. Until June the positive thermal deviations (0.5–5° C) extended as far as Arica, although always with greater values from Pimentel to Pisco. Although the low salinity Equatorial waters had disappeared by July, the thermal anomalies were maintained by a strong invasion by superficial subtropical water, maintaining positive deviations between 3° and 5° C, principally between Punta Doña Maria and the north. By the end of 1972, a great new advance of Equatorial water appeared; the warm conditions continued until 1973, the conditions returning to normal about March of that year. (IMARPE 1972, Serie Inf. Exp. Nos. 104, 110, 111, 112, 115, 117, 122; Zuta and Urquizo, 1974).

Associated with the above-mentioned invasion of warm water after the beginning of the 1972 summer there was clear evidence that the distribution patterns of many fish had altered; this alteration continued until approximately the middle of 1973. Fish types characteristic of the lower latitudes extended and distributed themselves southwards, thus indicating the tropicalization of the environment; this invasion was largely by coastal pelagic species, which are typical of the northern littoral and extended as far as Pisco (14° S.). This was the limit up to which the thermal anomalies were most marked. At the same time, oceanic pelagic fishes were recorded near the central coast. A survey carried out in September 1973 showed that the distribution of the species was once more back to normal.

Table 1 (on page 68) shows a list of fish species for which an enlargement of normal distribution was recorded. A greater part of these results were obtained in the Eureka operations by experimental undirected fishing—although, as mentioned earlier, it was oriented to the anchovy. Other species were brought to the IMARPE laboratory by fishermen of that zone who were surprised by their presence. The identifications were made by Chirichigno (1973 *a, b*).

The greatest number of the recordings regarded as anomalous were obtained in the central coast up to 14° S., agreeing well with thermal reports. It will be observed that the scombrid, *Auxis rochei* (frigate mackerel), was one of the invading species which characteristically showed itself with high frequency throughout the 'El Niño' period. This species, with the skipjack (*Katsuwonus pelamis*), the yellow-fin tuna (*Thunnus albacares*) and the dolphin (*Coryphaena hippurus*) remained associated with the 20° C isotherm, which is within the change of their optimum environmental temperatures. The records in Table 1 thus confirmed that the yellow-fin tuna, the skipjack, the Spanish mackerel (*Scomberomorus maculatus*), the dolphin and the manta (*Manta birostris hamiltoni*) were species which could be regarded as biological indicators of the presence of warm water.

However, contrary to expectations, over the entire littoral (Table 2), the commercial catches of the yellow-fin tuna and the skipjack were considerably less in 1972 than in preceding years; this distinguished the event from the years 1953 and 1957–58, when the fishing for yellow-fin tuna was slight off Mexico and Central America, whereas it increased off Peru and the northern coast of Chile. Only small catches of skipjack and Spanish mackerel were landed at Callao, and those at Pisco were considerably reduced (Table 2).

Table 1 also shows that the effects of 'El Niño' are reflected not only in the distribution of pelagic fishes since the hake (which is considered demersal or meso-pelagic) was also affected. While enlarging its distribution, this species maintained the normal pattern of size distribution, with the larger individuals to the north, and the smaller ones towards higher latitudes. The presence of *Chanos chanos* also constituted the first record of the family Chanidae in Peruvian waters (Chirichigno, 1973).

CHANGES IN LEVELS OF ABUNDANCE

The proportion of the species Sardina (*S. sagax*), jural (*Trachurus murphyi*), cabalia (*Scomber japonicus peruanus*) and machete (*Brevootria maculata chilcae*) in experimental and commercial fishing, as well as the quantity of these species caught in 1972 and 1973, suggested by comparison with previous years that the population levels might have increased. (Although within the limitations of the statistical information there is no sufficient basis to confirm this increase in population, the catch statistics presented in Table 3 and Figure 1 strongly suggest this.)

In the case of the sardine, in addition to the increased catch taken commercially in 1973, its proportion in the anchovy nets was remarkable. Until 1971 the greater part of the sardine catch taken for human consumption was caught to the north of Chimbote. The sardine caught by the anchovy fleet in 1972 could, as in previous years, be considered insignificant. By contrast, in March and April 1973, the proportion of sardine in the commercial anchovy fishery reached 14 per cent, totalling some 160,000 tons in those two months. The large quantity during March was distributed principally between Supe and Callao, plus a little in the south. After April the distribution widened, extending over the entire southern Peruvian littoral.

The rapidity and magnitude of this increase in sardine catches suggested that it was due more to an unusually high annual class than to distribution of the stocks over non-habitual areas. This deduction was supported by the fact that in 1972, an extension of the sardine spawning areas was noted; these, which normally extend to Callao, reached as far as Ilo (Santander and Castillo, 1974). Until 1971, the number of sardine larvae recorded was very small. After 1972 it was considerably increased.

The sardines found in these incidental catches were smaller than those taken in the sardine catches for human consumption. The latter normally comprises modal groups of approximately 25 to 33 cm long. The specimens in the incidental fishing of March–April 1973 had a dominant mode of 17.5 cm (with a range of 16.5 and 18.5 cm between Chancay and Punta Doña María and between 12 and 13 cm from San Juan to the south). In regard to the ages of the sardine (*S. sagax*) there is a lack of data with which to interpret these indicated modes; however, it is probable that the predominant mode came from the heavy spawning of February 1972. The success of this class or classes could be related to the prolonged bio-oceanographic alteration and in some way to the reduction of the anchovy population, since the two species have a similar diet. During the s surveys carried out in November 1973, the sardine was still frequently observed to the south of its usual distribution (IMARPE, 1973, Inf. Esp. 146), even when the size of the catch was considerably less than that recorded in March and April of that year. It should be noted also that the proportion of sardine in the commercial catches in 1974 was once again insignificant

Of the jack, mackerel and the machete and other species for which there are indications of population increase during the 1972–73 'El Niño', commercial landings were considerably higher than in preceding years (Table 3) and their proportions in the experimental fishing came after the sardine in order of importance; the mackerel was found principally in the northern and central regions and the jack in the southern region. In Chimbote, one of the areas of greatest machete landings, the catch and catch per unit of effort data showed an increase in 1972 and 1973 compared with previous years.

Alternate fluctuations between populations of anchovy, sardine, jack and mackerel, noted before in other regions of the world, were generally interpreted as effects of ecological factors on species with different requirements.

It will be seen in Table 3 and Figure 1 that the catches of the bonito (*Sarda chilensis*) fell. It was assumed that the population had declined. As this species feeds chiefly on anchovy, it is highly probable that exploitation and the unfavourable effect of 'El Niño' of 1972–73 on the anchovy had deleterious effects on the bonito. In addition, attempts were made to examine whether the changes in the environment produced by the 'El Niño' modified the bonito reproductive cycle—as had been known to occur for the anchovy—the data available in the Food Fishes Department made it possible to demonstrate this clearly for both bonito and the machete.

This effect is represented in Figures 2 and 3, which show the percentage distribution of two accumulated sexual stages, V and VI (mature and spawning), comparing one year taken to be normal (1969 or 1970) with those of 1972 and 1973. The bonito had a reproductive period in the year 1969 covering spring and summer—which is characteristic of this species—and had a rest period during autumn and winter; in 1972 and to a lesser extent in 1973, reproductive activity was still marked in autumn. The principal reproductive wave of the machete occurs in autumn and a minor wave occurs in spring; in 1972, it was observed that the sexual activity was much more continuous, though by 1973 a trend towards normality was evident.

Distribution of invertebrates

Characteristic of tropical waters and observed very frequently during the entire period of oceanographic abnormality, the pelagic crab (*Euphylax dovii*) was massively displaced to the south of the coast and was captured during fishing for anchovy, saury, sardine and jack mackerel. Moreover, this crab was present in significant numbers off the Peruvian coast during the second half of 1971, even though at that time the surface water temperature off the coast was less than average. According to Wooster and Guillen (1974), the warming of the central coast off Peru could have begun in August 1971, and, if this is so, this crab might be a highly sensitive indicator of such changes.

Normally, phytoplankton is more abundant in the northern and central regions of Peru between 6° and 16° S. and the zooplankton more abundant to the south. During 'El Niño', however, a paucity of phytoplankton in the northern and central regions was observed, contrasting with a predominance of zooplankton.

Organisms characteristic of tropical and oceanic waters, especially copepods, dinoflagellates and diatoms (which are rarely encountered in these waters) appeared; among the latter was *Skeletomema costatum f. tropicum*.

Among the dinoflagellates detected were: *Ceratrium paradoxides*; *C. gravidum*; *C. trichoceros*; *C. azoricum*; *C. hexacanthum f. contortum*; *C. lunula*; *C. furca var. eugrammum*; *C. declinatum*; *C. breve*; *C. teres*; *C. carriense*; *C. massilensii*; *C. aristinum*; *C. candelabrum f. curvatulum*; *C. gibberum*; *Pyrocystis robusta*; *Peridinum elegans*; and genus species of *Ornithocerus*.

Among the copepods detected were: *Eucalanus attenuatus*; *Temora discaudata*; *T. stylifera*; *Pleuromamma abdominalis*; *P. gracilis*; *Centropages furcatus*; and *Lucicutia flavicornis*. Identifications made by de Mendiola and collaborators in the Plankton Department).

The guano birds

The effect most discussed in the literature with respect to the 'El Niño' phenomenon has been that concerning the reduction in the population levels of the guano birds. These consist of three species: the cormorant (*Phalacrocorax bougainvillii*), the gannet (*Sula variegata*) and the pelican (*Pelecanus occidentalis thagus*). Their populations indirectly reflect the fall in available food, predominantly anchovy.

It is known that periodic fluctuations occur on the Peruvian coast adversely affecting the guano birds. The adults desert the nesting areas, great numbers die at sea, others appear great distances away in Chile and even Ecuador and, although part of these nomadic populations return to the islands, most perish outside their normal area of distribution. These disasters have often been attributed to thrusts of warm water towards the coast, south of its normal distribution.

A chronological series of these population fluctuations is presented in Table 4. From the high level of 28 million individuals in 1955/56, the population fell to 6 million as a consequence of the 1957/58 'El Niño'. It recovered to reach a relatively stable level of 18 million by 1962/64. After the 1965 'El Niño', it fell to 5 million, stabilizing for a period of seven years as was shown in the censuses from 1965/66 to 1971/72; its failure to reach previous levels was probably connected with high commercial exploitation of the anchovy.

As a consequence of the 1972/73 'El Niño', the population again fell drastically to about 2 million. It was noted after February 1972 that the guano birds had abandoned the islands in the north and, as a result, there was high mortality of the chicks and a huge loss of eggs. The birds settled principally in the central zone under conditions which were more satisfactory until the middle of April when they moved further south leaving the islands and headlands practically deserted (with the exception of those in the extreme south off the north of Chile where further mortalities probably occurred). Undoubtedly these migrations were related to the distribution and availability of the anchovy schools.

The reproductive cycles of the cormorant did not take place in the months of September and April as was normal, but the onset of reproductive activity started in July, which signifies that the 1973/74 reproductive cycle was advanced. In the middle of October on the island of Mazorca, it was observed that 48 per cent of the nests had eggs and 52 per cent had chicks whose age varied from one to ten weeks; at the same time, hatching was beginning in gannet and pelican colonies. The last 1973/74 census (mean of November and March) showed an increase to 2.5 million which was attributable chiefly to chicks (which are not usually a major factor of guano bird populations).

During 1972, other marine bird species characteristic of the tropical zones, such as the camanay (*Sula nebouxi*) and the Galapagos seagull (*Creagnus furcatus*) were observed on the central coast. The camanay had last been recorded in Peru during the 1939 'El Niño' (Vogt, 1940).

Summary

Evidence of changes during 1973/74 in the fauna off the Peruvian coast is presented, with invasions of the area by species whose distributions normally lie further north and with the displacement of endemic species. These changes were attributable to the change in temperature and salinity of the water masses altering the fish population on which these birds depend and which constitutes an aspect of the 'El Niño' phenomenon. The species referred to in this article are biological indicators, sigalling environmental change by change in distribution and population levels. Evidence is mostly discussed with respect to the guano birds, the sardine, the frigate mackerel and the pelagic crab.

Table 1. List of fishes of anomalous distribution recorded during the 1972–73 'El Niño'

Species	Peruvian name	Name of species or group in English	Family	Regular geographic distribution	Enlargement of distribution
Auxis rochei	Melva on barrilete negro	Frigate mackerel	Scombridae	From Huntington Bay, California to Lobos de Afuera (Peru). Also found in Western and Central Pacific, the Atlantic and the Mediterranean Sea.	Southern and central coast of Peru to Mollendo
Katsuwonus pelamis	Barilete	Skipjack	Scombridae	From Huasco (Chile) to Vancouver Island (Canada) and the Galapagos Islands. It does not occur in the area of the coastal current of Peru	Central and southern coast of Peru (to 12° S.) 16°35′ S.[1]
Thunnus albacares	Atún de aleta	Yellow-fin tuna	Scombridae	From Pta Conception (California) to San Antonio (Chile). It does not occur in the area of the coastal current of Peru.	Central coast of Peru to 11°45′ S.[1]
Scomberomorus maculatus	Sierra	Spanish mackerel	Scombridae	From Southern California to the Bay of Sechura (Peru)	Central coast (to 14° S.)[1]
Merluccius gayiperuanus	Merluza	Hake	Merlucciidae	From 00°30′ S. (Ecuador) to 09° S. (Peru)	Southern and central coast of Peru.
Coryphaena hippurus	Dorado	Dolphin	Coryphaenidae	San Diego (California) to northern Chile. From tropical waters	Central coast (to 14° S.)
Trachinotus paitensis	Pampano	Paloma	Carangidae	From northern Chile to the Bay of California (Mexico)	Supe to Pisco (14° S.)[1]
Seriola mazatlana	Fortuno	Yellow tail	Carangidae	From Mazatlán (Mexico) to Chimbote (Peru) and From Ialtal (Chile), Juan Fernández Islands, San Ambrosio, San Feliz and the Galapagos Islands	Callao (Peru) 12° S.[1]
Naucrates ductor	Piloto	Pilotfish	Carangidae	From the Bay of California to northern Peru	Callao (Peru) 12° S.[1]
Caranx hippes caoninus	Cocinero	Crevalle jack	Carangidae	From the Bay of California to northern Peru	Callao (Peru) 12° S.[1]
Caranx crysus caballus	Cocinero	Green jack	Carangidae	From San Pedro, California to Lobos de Tierra Islands (Peru) and the Galapagos Islands	Callao (Peru) 12° S.
Oligoplites refulgens	Chaqueta de cuero	Leather jacket	Carangidae	Mexico to Cabo Blanco (Peru)	Callao (Peru) 12° S.
Anchoa naso	Anchoveta blanca	Anchovy	Engraulidae	The Bay of San Juanico, Bay of California (Mexico) to Cabo Blanco (Peru)	Central coast of Peru to Cerro Azul[1]
Etrumeus teres	Sardina redonda	Round herring	Clupeidae	Gulf of California to Lobos de Afuera Islands (Peru) and the Galapagos Islands	Callao (Peru) 12° S.
Opisthonema libertate	Machete de hebra	Thread herring	Clupeidae	San Pedro (California) to Bay of Sechura (Peru) and the Galapagos Islands	Callao (Peru) 12° S.
Opisthonema bullori	Machete del norte	Slender thread herring	Clupeidae	Mazatlán (Mexico) to Pta Sal and Pta Pisco (Peru)	Pimentel (Peru)

					Central and Southern coast to Mollendo (17° S.)
Sardinops sagax sagax	Sardina	Pilchard	Clupeidae	Bay of Sechura (Peru) to Callao and the Galapagos Islands	Around the coast
Exocoetus volitans	Pez volador	Tropical two-wing flying fish	Exocoetidae	Mexico to the centre of Chile and the Galapagos, Hawaii, Marshall and other islands in oceanic waters	
Fodiator acutus rostratus	Pez volador	Flying fish	Exocoetidae	Mexico Cabo Blanco (Peru). Galapagos Islands and Hawaii	Callao (Peru) 12° S.
Sphyrna Zygaena	Pez martillo	Common hammer head	Sphyrnidae	Central California, Gulf of California, Panama Galapagos Islands and Ecuador to Chile. Mainly in tropical waters	Central coast (to 14° S.)
Manta birostris hamiltoni	Manta	Blanket fish	Mobulidae	Gulf of California (Mexico) to Morro Sama (Peru) and the Galapagos Islands. Mainly in oceanic waters	Central coast (to 14° S.)
Diodon hystrix	Pez erizo	Porcupine fish	Diodontidae	Bay of California (Mexico) to Pto Pizarro, Pascua and Galapagos Islands	Callao (Peru) 12° S.[1]
Sphoeroides lobatus	Tomborín	Puffer fish	Tetraodontidae	Gulf of California (Mexico) to Pto Pizarro (Peru) and the Galapagos Islands.	Callao (Peru) 12° S.
Alutera sp.	Pez lija	Unicorn file fish	Monocanthidae	North coast of Peru, Pto Pizarro to Talar.	Callao (Peru) 12° S.
Albula vulpes	Zorro	Ocean white fish	Albulidae	Bay of Monterrey (California) to Chimbote (Peru)	Callao (Peru) 12° S.
Prionotus ruscarius	Falso volador	Sea robin	Triglidae	Gulf of California (Mexico) to Chimbote (Peru)	Callao (Peru) 12° S.[1]
Caulolatilus cabezón	Peje blanco	Ocean white fish	Branchiostegidae	Manta (Ecuador) to Chimbote (Peru)	Callao (Peru) 12° S.
Brachydepterus leuciscus	Roncador	Grunt	Pomadasydidae	Bay of California (Mexico) to Lobos de Tierra (Peru)	Callao (Peru) 12° S.
Kyphosus	Gallinazo	Sea chub	Kyphosidae	Gulf of California (Mexico) to Chimbote	Callao (Peru) 12° S.
Hemirhampus saltator	Medio pico	Longfin–half beak	Hemirhamphidae	Mexico to Lobos Islands (Peru)	Callao (Peru) 12° S.
Pseudopriacanthus serrula	Semáforo	Popeye catalufa	Priacanthidae	Cabo San Lucas, Bay of California (Mexico) to Huacho	Callao (Peru) 12° S.
Nematistius pectoralis	Pepe pluma	Roosterfish	Nematistiidae	Gulf of California (Mexico) to Chimbote on Galapagos Islands	Callao (Peru) 12° S.
Synodus sechurae	Iguana marina	Lizard fish	Synodontidae	Gulf of California (Mexico) to Bay of Sechura (Peru)	Callao (Peru) 12° S.
Synodus sciuliceps	Pez lagarto	Lizard fish	Synodontidae	Gulf of California (Mexico) to Paita (Peru) on Galapagos Islands	Callao (Peru) 12° S.
Pseudopenaeus grandisquamis	San Pedro rojo	Red goat fish	Mullidae	Gulf of California (Mexico) to Chimbote on Galapagos Islands	Callao (Peru) 12° S.
Chanos chanos	Liza blanca and sabalote (Mexico)	Milk fish	Chanidae	Tropical and subtropical waters of the Pacific and Indian Oceans from longitudes 40° E. to 100° W. and latitudes 30°–40° N. to 30°–40° S.	La Punta, Callao (12° S.)
Dormitator maculatus	Camote	Fat sleeper	Electridae	California to Tumbes (Peru)	Laguna Medio Mundo (10° S.).

1. Generally associated with the presence of warm water.

Table 2. Annual landing in tons of three species for the entire littoral and at three ports, 1966—72

	Species											
	Yellow-fin tuna				Skipjack				Spanish mackerel			
Year	Total littoral	Chimbote	Callao	Pisco	Total littoral	Chimbote	Callao	Pisco	Total littoral	Chimbote	Callao	Pisco
1966	5,461.0	5,441.3	0.3	—	6,387.8	6,374.0	0.4	—	1,318.8	2.4	—	—
1967	3,359.5	—	—	—	13,377.9	—	—	—	442.1	4.9	0.2	—
1968	3,447.3	3,091.6	—	—	6,528.4	5,575.3	—	—	710.1	—	—	—
1969	4,021.5	2,482.4	—	—	11,842.7	7,682.6	—	—	508.6	—	—	—
1970	6,704.5	1,675.0	—	—	6,719.0	2,472.3	—	—	546.5	—	—	—
1971	6,275.1	1,128.7	—	—	5,575.5	1,041.5	—	—	1,669.7	—	—	—
1972	2,008.0	2,008.0	0.0	0.0	2,425.0	76.0	112.0	0.1	799.7	0.0	7.6	0.3

Table 3. Annual landings of different fish species, 1963—73 (in tons)

Year	Species				
	Bonito	Sardine	Machete	Jurel	Caballa
1963	88,179	2,201	7,863	1,954	7,911
1964	63,315	10,159	4,585	1,718	2,084
1965	68,488	7,419	7,376	2,561	3,887
1966	74,154	1,902	13,420	4,271	7,559
1967	63,574	2,138	18,416	3,071	13,432
1968	54,274	1,847	11,880	2,790	7,187
1969	59,332	1,121	13,018	4,176	7,161
1970	57,371	449	19,719	4,711	8,791
1971	73,043	6,051	22,754	9,189	10,113
1972	64,160	6,337	38,611	18,618	8,707
1973	33,612	132,252	44,624	42,705	60,383

Table 4. Census of guano birds (cormorant, pelican and gannet)

Reproductive cycle	Number (in millions)	Reproductive cycle	Number (in millions)
1955	28.0	1965	4.4
1956	22.0	1966	4.6[1]
1957	6.6	1967	4.3[1]
1958	6.1	1968	5.2[1]
1959	11.1	1969	4.7[1]
1960	12.6	1970	4.5[1]
1961	17.0	1971	6.5[1]
1962	18.1	1972	1.8[1]
1963	14.7	1973	2.5[1]
1964	16.5		

1. Average figures from two or more censures from 1955 onwards.

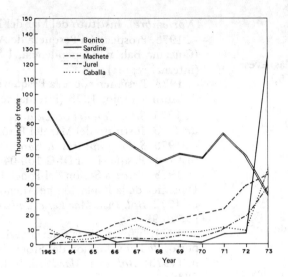

Fig. 1. Annual catch of five fish species, 1963–73.

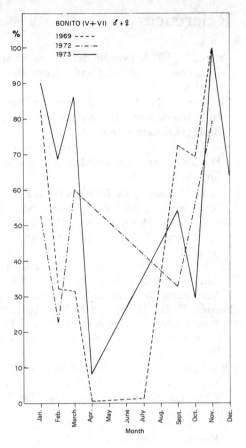

Fig. 2. Sexual maturity distribution
of the bonito.

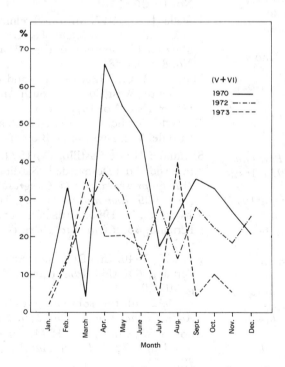

Fig. 3. Distribution of the state of sexual maturity
of the machete.

References

Ballen, F., 1924. Estudio del Colera Aviario en las Aves Guaneras. *Cía. Adm. Guano, Nem. Dir.,* No. 15, p. 93-4.

Chirichigno, N., 1973a. Registro de Peces no Comunes en la Isla de San Lorenzo. Instituto del Mar. Div. de Biología (internal report).

——. 1973b. Registro del *Chanos chanos* en Aguas Peruanas. Instituto del Mar. Div. de Biología (internal report).

——. 1974. Clave para Identificar los Peces Marinos del Perú. *Inf. Inst. Mar. Perú, Callao,* No. 44, 388 p.

Del Solar, E., 1942. Ensayo sobre la Ecología de la Anchoveta. *Bol. Cía. Adm. Guano,* Vol. 18, No. 1, p. 1-23.

Fiedler, R., Jarvis, N., Lobell, M., 1943. La Pesca y las Industrias Pesqueras del Perú. Informe de la Misión Americana. *Bol. Cía. Adm. Guano,* 367 p.

Forbes, H. O., 1914. Puntos Principales del Informe Presentado al Supremo Gobierno el Estudio de las Aves Guaneras. *Mem. Dir. Cía. Adm. Guano,* No. 5, p. 57-80.

Hutchinson, G., 1950. Survey of Contemporary Knowledge of Biochemistry. 3. The Biogeochemistry of Vertebrate Excretion. *Bull. Am. Mus. Nat. Hist.,* No. 96, 521 p.

IMARPE, 1972. *La Anchoveta en Relación con el Fenómeno "El Niño" 1972.* Instituto del Mar del Perú. (IMP-104.)

——. 1973. *Informe sobre la Primera Semana de Pesca de Anchoveta Realizada del 5 al 9 de Marzo de 1973.* Instituto del Mar Perú. (IMP-124.)

——. 1972. *'Operación Eureka XXI, 17-18 Junio de 1972).* Instituto del Mar del Perú. (IMP-110.)

——. 1972. *'Operación Eureka XXII', 18-19 Julio de 1972.* Instituto del Mar del Perú. (IMP-111.)

——. 1972. *'Operación Eureka XXIII', 3-6 Agosto de 1972.* Instituto del Mar del Perú. (IMP-112.)

——. 1972. *'Operación Eureka XXIV', 5-8 Septiembre de 1972.* Instituto del Mar del Perú. (IMP-115.)

——. 1972. *'Operación Eureka XXV', 20-23 Octubre de 1972.* Instituto del Mar del Perú. (IMP-117.)

——. 1973. *Operación Eureka XXVI (20-23 Enero de 1973).* Instituto del Mar del Perú. (IMP-122.)

——. 1973. *Operación Eureka XXVII, 23-26 Septiembre de 1973.* Instituto del Mar del Perú. (IMP-141.)

——. 1973. *'Operación Eureka XXVIII', 12-13 Noviembre y la Pesca de Comprobación (14-17 Noviembre).* Instituto del Mar del Perú. (IMP-146.)

——. 1973. Prospección Pesquera de Anchoveta (Chicama Bahía Independencia, 1-3 Agosto de 1973) (internal report).

——. 1973. Resúmen sobre la Pesquería de Anchoveta de de Abril a Junio, 1973 (internal report).

——. 1973. *Situación del Stock de Anchoveta a Principios de 1973.* Instituto del Mar del Perú. (IMP-125.)

——. 1973. *Sobre Capturas de Sardina.* Oficio al Sr Ministro de Pesquaría: FDI-G-100-044 (August 1973).

——. 1973. Tercera Sesión del Panel de Expertos sobre la Dinámica de la Población de Anchoveta Peruana. Julio de 1972. *Bol. Inst. Mar Perú, Callao,* Vol. 2, No. 9, p. 525-99.

——. 1974. Informe de la Cuarta Sesión del Panel de Expertos de la Evaluación del Stock de Anchoveta Peruana (1973). *Bol. Inst. Mar Perú,* Vol. 2, No. 10, p. 603-723.

Jordán, R., Fuentes, H., 1966. Las Poblaciones de Aves Guaneras y su Situación Actual. *Inf. Inst. Mar. Perú,* No. 10, 30 p.

Lavalle, J. A., 1917. Informe Preliminar sobre la Causa de la Mortalidad Anormal de las Aves Ocurrida en el Mes de Marzo del Presente Año. *Cía. Adm. Guano, Mem. Dir.,* No. 8, p. 61-88.

Murphy, R. C., 1926. Oceanic and Climatic Phenomena Along the West Coast of South America during 1925. *Geogr. Rev.,* No. 16, p. 26-54.

Rojas de Mendiola, B., 1972-73. Reports (various). Instituto del Mar, Division de Biología.

Santander H.; de Castillo, O., 1974. Variaciones en la Intensidad del Desove de la Sardina en la Costa Peruana. *Trabajo presentado al IV Congreso Nacional de Biología (24-29 Noviembre de 1974),* Trujillo, Perú.

Schweigger, E., 1953. Situación Veraniega en el Litoral Peruano. *Bol. Cient. Cía. Adm. Guano,* Vol. 1, No. 1, p. 9-18.

Vogt, W., 1940. Una Depresión Ecología en la Costa Peruana. *Bol. Cía. Adm. Guano,* Vol. 16, No. 10, p. 307-29.

——. 1942. Informe sobre las Aves Guaneras. *Bol. Cía. Adm. Guano,* Vol. 18, No. 3, p. 1-132.

Wooster, W., Guillén, O., 1974. Características de 'El Niño' en 1972. *Bol. Inst. Mar Perú,* Vol. 3, No. 2, p. 44-72.

Zuta, S.; Urquizo, W., 1974. *Informe de los Cruceros 7211 y 7212 del B.A.P. 'Unanue'. Condiciones Oceanográficas Anormales frente al Perú en la Primavera de 1972.* Instituto del Mar del Perú. (IMP-160).

Biological aspects of the 1972–73 'El Niño' phenomenon. 2: The anchovy population

Julio Valdivia [1]

Introduction

An understanding of the population characteristics of the anchovy, *Engraulis ringens,* is particularly important because of the enormous size of this resource. It is unique among the single species resources which populate the seas of the earth. The fishery that operates on these stocks is to be considered foremost among the many that exist not only with regards to the quantities taken, but also because the fishmeal derived therefrom provides the world with a significant proportion of total animal foodstuffs, apart from the economic benefits which accrue to the exploiting country.

It is well known that this species lives in a zone adjacent to the coast of Peru and Chile where special oceanographic phenomena occur, such as the large upwellings which make these regions highly productive and favourable for the development of high concentrations of fish. From time to time, when changes in these phenomena occur, the species responds through complex biological and behavioural processes which are not yet understood. These processes, combined with the tremendous fishing pressure, bring about abrupt and sudden changes which lead to a substantial reduction of population levels.

In this article an attempt is made to describe, in general terms, the events which occurred immediately before, during and after the time that the habitat of this species was changed by the phenomenon known as 'El Niño' 1972–73.

The documentation for this summary is given in the Bibliography at the end of the article.

State of the anchovy stock before the 1972–73 'El Niño'

REPRODUCTION

Studies based on the quantity of eggs deposited in the sea per unit area, microscopic analysis of gonads and fat content show that, in general, spawning took place over a period of seven months with two peaks of maximum intensity.

During the period before the 1972–73 'El Niño', spawning was more or less constant with between-year fluctuations (Fig. 1, Table 1). It is believed that fluctuations in spawning are not directly related to changes in numbers of the generations to which they give rise, but that generation size depends on the small variations in the rate of survival of the aionomorph eggs, larvae and post-larvae stage. This rate of survival is certainly determined by environmental conditions during the time that those stages are present in the sea.

DISTRIBUTION OF THE STOCKS

On the basis of acoustic fishery prospecting ('Eureka') over various years, it has been determined that, in general, the pattern of distribution of anchovy results in large concentrations in areas close to the coast during summer, while in winter the fish disperse into

1. Instituto del Mar del Perú, Esq. Gamarra y Gral. Valle, Chucuito, Callao (Peru).

much smaller schools distributed over large areas. These facts correspond fairly well to the oceanographic characteristics of summer and winter in normal years. However, these general considerations do not provide a full explanation of the behaviour of these species. It must be determined by, among other factors, the complex biological processes of reproduction, feeding, and competition with other species.

Unfortunately, the location of the fishing areas in which the commercial fleet operates could not be determined in the years before the 1972—73 'El Niño'. Nevertheless, on the basis of limited sampling, information was obtained concerning the entire Peruvian coast and was listed by distance from the coast for the month of March from 1970 to 1973 (Table 2). From this it is calculated that in the year before the 'El Niño' phenomenon the catches were taken within thirty miles of the coast. There are reasons to believe that in previous years, the location of the accessible and vulnerable schools was similar to that described for 1970 and 1971.

CATCH AND EFFORT

A catch of about 10 million tons was taken annually between 1967 and 1971. However, the fishing effort has increased sharply (Table 3), with consequent risks of overfishing.

It became necessary to regulate the effort in an indirect manner through closed seasons and catch quotas. These quotas were taken rapidly owing to strong competition between the fleets of different companies. Each year the days of work at sea were reduced and concentrated in periods when new recruits were joining the fishable stocks, thus increasing the fishing pressure on fish in their first year of life and perhaps even those which were sexually immature. Since 1967, 5 million tons of young fish have been taken, increasing to 6—7 million tons in later years and each time making the population balance more dramatically unstable.

COMPOSITION OF THE CATCH

Taking composition by size, age and length as a source of information, it was estimated that during 1970 the fishable population consisted of six cohorts: two of them came from the spawning cycle of 1966, and were particularly important because of their great abundance; two cohorts which originated in the

spawnings of 1968; and two weak cohorts, almost at the end of their life, which came from 1967. This catch composition is similar to that of years before 1970.

RECRUITMENT

In a species with short life, such as the anchovy, recruitment strength is of vital importance for the maintenance of population equilibrium. Quantitative data with respect to this force is available only as indices of number per unit of effort (Table 4). It is clear that variations of this index over the period in question did not reach twice the average index of previous years—contrary to other pelagic species such as the herring in which the abundance of successive generations varies in the order of fifteen to twenty times. The stability of the anchovy was the main factor in the maintenance of the stock as the levels indicated up to 1971.

ESTIMATE OF BIOMASS

For the period 1966—70 the population was comparatively stable, that is to say, the mortality caused by fishing and natural causes was countered by recruitment and growth. This balance in terms of fishable biomass, calculated by means of the virtual population model, gave a monthly mean of about 16 million tons (with fluctuations between 11 and 22 million for the stocks to the north of 15° S.). This figure is increased by 10 to 15 per cent if, instead, the stocks distributed between 6° and 18° S. are considered (Fig. 3, Table 6).

The events during the 1972-73 'El Nino' phenomenon

REPRODUCTION

Both production of eggs and the frequency of spawning stage shown by macroscopic classification during the spawning cycle of 1971, showed that the spawnings of winter/spring were low by comparison with previous years (Fig. 3, Table 4). In addition, the fat content was unusually high, reaching values of between 12 and 15 per cent—values which are almost twice as high as the mean. These facts were not considered to be alarming since they had been low in the preceding years of 1969 and 1970 (Fig. 3). however, strong annual classes, such as those recruited in 1970, had come from those years (Table 1).

In summary, spawning was very low, and the best indication of disturbance of the reproduction process was that of the fat content, a phenomenon which should be taken into future account when predicting oceanographic anomalies. In addition it is clear that the poor spawning was not due to a low stock of spawners, since between September 1971 and June 1972, 10 million tons of spawners greater than 12 cm in length and one year old were caught.

During autumn, winter and spring of 1973, there was constant reproductive activity throughout, thus differing from the pattern observed in previous years. Apparently, the most intense spawning took place in November, it is only from the spawning point of view that there was any basis for expecting a good year class.

DISTRIBUTION

According to the quantity of catch taken per day in the second half of 1971, it can be established that these were unusually large concentrations close to the coast, greatly increasing the density in normally low areas. This fact, one could speculate, could have had an effect on the spawning pattern. When the fishing season reopened in March 1972, these great densities remained close to the coast but the area of distribution had shrunk latitudinally, significant catches taking place only to the south of 10° S. In that month, a record catch per day was taken, with quantities exceeding 170,000 tons. This abnormal distribution can also be appreciated from Table 5, where 91 per cent of the catches were taken within ten miles of the coast.

During April 1972 it became clear that rapid displacement of the schools to the south was taking place; the fishing areas were located to the south of 12° S.—and later at 14° S., and the catches began to fall abruptly until the operations became uneconomical and fishing had to cease (Table 2). Moreover, the catch statistics of the Chilean fleet showed a strong decline in this period, proving that the schools migrating to the south did not reach Chilean waters.

In 1973 there was evidence of a redistribution of the schools which had migrated south in 1972.

This restocking of the coast must have been, in part, a consequence of changes in behaviour; that is to say, the aggregations which in 1972 were inacessible and invulnerable in the northern and central regions, made themselves abundant close to the coast—as was shown by the March—April catches of 1973.

CATCH AND EFFORT

The catch per unit of effort during the phenomenon did not measure the relative abundance of the total stock but rather the level of densities of the aggregation, since the area normally occupied by the species has markedly diminished both latitudinally and longitudinally. In Table 6, it can be seen that the catch per unit of effort for the months of September 1971 and June 1972 remained more or less constant even while the stocks were falling rapidly. It was only after April that the decline was noted—when in fact the fishery could no longer be maintained.

With ten months of closed season during 1973, the catches of 2.3 million tons in March and April and with fishing effort reduced to almost a quarter of that operating before the crisis, the catch per unit of effort again reflected the level of concentration, rather than the relative abundance of the population, a situation similar to that in 1972.

CATCH COMPOSITION

The cohorts which supported the fishery during the crisis were identified. Only four were apparent: two from the 1970 spawning cycle and two from the 1969 spawning cycle. The latter were exceptionally abundant. However, those that should have composed an important part of the catch (that is to say those spawned in 1971) were practically absent, a fact which determined the abrupt fall of population levels due to the low recruitment.

RECRUITMENT

Neither size composition of catches of December 1971—March/April 1972, nor the fishery acoustic surveys from research vessels and fishing vessels in February 1972, showed the presence of recruits drawn from the 1971 spawnings thus showing that recruitment had failed. This produced population stability, even though replenishment by recruitment is the most important factor when a stock is submitted to heavy fishing pressure. The evidence also indicated that the survival of eggs, larvae and juveniles had been very poor and may have been effected by anomalies in the water masses even before the more marked temperature and salinity changes had taken place. Qualitatively it was established that the recruitment index reached only 0.56; this represents a level six to seven times lower than the mean of the preceding eleven years (Table 1).

The 1973 index of recruitment (Table 4) was greater than that of 1972, but was still below that of the eleven-year mean. Even so, this showed that a small recovery of the population had occured.

BIOMASS ESTIMATES

Based on the relation of recruitment and total production from a class, it was possible to estimate that the remnants of the 1969 and 1970 spawning classes consisted of 1.5 million tons, plus a small contribution from the 1971 spawning class. At the beginning of 1973 the stocks were at levels around 4 million tons, a figure which is subject to behaviour patterns and may be an underestimate. Moreover, it must be emphasized that it was impossible to find evidence—in spite of continuous and intense operations at sea—that the oceanographic disturbance had caused mass mortality of the anchovy or that its principal influence lay in greatly altering the distribution, making the fish more accessible and vulnerable to the fleet on the one hand, and in some manner changing its reproduction habits on the other; the latter speculation is not yet fully understood.

Towards the end of 1973, the calculations of biomass from data of various sources indicated a value between 5 and 6 million tons. A moderate increase from recruitment, the low exploitation rates during autumn and the changes of behaviour would seem to have been the major causes of the increase.

The events after 'El Niño' 1972–73

FISHERY

The fishery reopened from March to June 1974, reaching a catch of 2.3 million tons with a fishing effort similar to that of 1973. The fishery began again in October with an effort similar to that of the first half of the year, reaching in that month a catch of about 800,000 tons.

COMPOSITION OF CATCH

The outstanding fact in the 1974 catches is that between 40 and 50 per cent were composed of large fish of between 15 and 18 cm in length. This stock was thus of fish of 2 to 3 years old. Comparing the size composition of 1973 and 1974, it was found that these fish were not accessible to the fishery of 1973, partly because they were the cohorts of 1971 spawning and thus almost at the end of their life (Fig. 2). This is clear evidence that population estimates represented only fishable stocks in the sense of recruits and adults, and that behaviour was a factor of considerable influence which must be studied in relation to changes in oceanographic characteristics.

RECRUITMENT

The index of recruitment reached during March and April 1974, a value of four, is similar to that of 1965; this represents something less than half of the eleven-year mean. It must be indicated that no evidence appeared of a relationship between the magnitude of spawning and the class of which it was the origin. In fact, the spawning during 1973 was continuous and reached high values in November, but the 1974 recruits did not immediately present themselves in great numbers, which again indicates that the recovery process is a slow one.

BIOMASS ESTIMATES

After catching more than 2 million tons in the first half of 1974, the biomass at the end of September was estimated at 6 million tons; however, although detailed calculations have not been considered, the population was numerically reduced and the fish between 16 and 18 cm (cohorts from the 1971 spawning), although weighing on the average about 55 g, constituted almost half the biomass. This low numerical strength of the population was due to weak recruitment in 1973 and 1974.

Conclusions

The evidence presented in this brief summary leads to three conclusions:

A substantial decline occured in the anchovy population level.

Changes in the anchovy habitat began to appear before the obvious changes in temperature and salinity appeared off the Peruvian coast; thus changes in the normal distribution of the species took place in the second half of 1971 and complex mechanisms inhibited 'reproduction' with respect to the intensity of spawning and the survival of eggs and larvae.

The behaviour of the species changed as a consequence of oceanographic disturbances, modifying the patterns of accessibility and vulnerability of the schools.

Table 1. Percentage of mature mates (stage V) over 13 cm for two different areas

Year	Chimbote	Callao
1966	44.9	69.0
1967	74.4	68.3
1968	74.4	62.1
1969	78.9	62.1
1970	72.2	49.6
1971	28.6	12.8
1972	77.2	54.0

Table 4. Index of recruitment by catch per unit effort for years 1966—73

Year	Recruitment index	Year	Recruitment index
1966	439	1970	553
1967	383	1971	539
1968	338	1972	56
1969	377	1973	160

Average 1961—71, 361.

Table 2. Percentage distribution of catch by distance from the coast for March 1970—73

Distance from the coast (miles)	March			
	1970	1971	1972	1973
0—10	42	47	91	88
10—20	33	33	7	11
20—30	16	13	1	1
30—40	5	5	1	—
40—50	4	1	—	—
50—60	—	1	—	—
Total	100	100	100	100

Table 5 Estimates of biomass (average monthly for each year) based on cohort analysis

Year	Average stock (in millions of tons)	Year	Average stock (in millions of tons)
1965/66	18.3	1968/69	13.9
1966/67	16.9	1969/70	14.7
1967/68	19.7		

Average 1963—70, 16.3.

Table 3. Catch, effort and catch per unit of effort by year for the whole of Peru, 1966—71.

Year	Catch (in thousands of tons)	Effort	Catch per unit of effort
1966	8,523.0	22,740.2	0.375
1967	9,824.6	23,418.1	0.420
1968	10,262.7	25,417.8	0.404
1969	8,960.5	28,557.6	0.314
1970	12,277.0	32,938.2	0.374
1971	10,281.8	19,484.0	0.528

Table 6. Catch, effort and catch per unit of effort for each month, over the whole of Peru, during 'El Niño' 1971—73

Year	Month	Catch (in thousands of tons)	Effort	Catch per unit of effort
1971	September	1,205.2	2,875.9	0.419
	October	1,357.8	2,787.9	0.487
	November	1,155.2	1,856.3	0.622
	December	1,342.1	2,197.4	0.611
1972	January[1]	17.3	26.4	0.656
	February[1]	159.5	271.7	0.587
	March	1,841.9	3,341.0	0.551
	April	1,567.4	4,644.6	0.337
	May[1]	531.1	3,681.8	0.144
	June[1]	153.6	1,780.2	0.086

1. Only in the south.

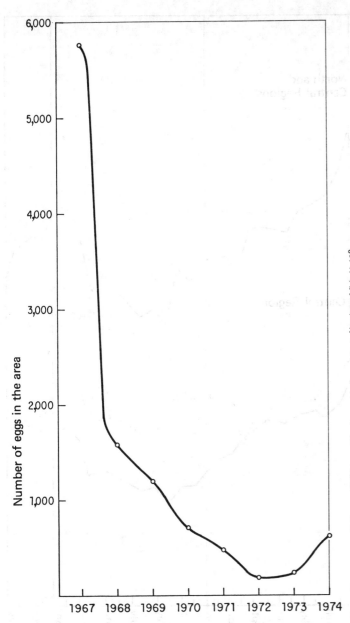

Fig. 1. Average number of anchovy eggs by station between
6°—14° S. during August/September 1967—74.

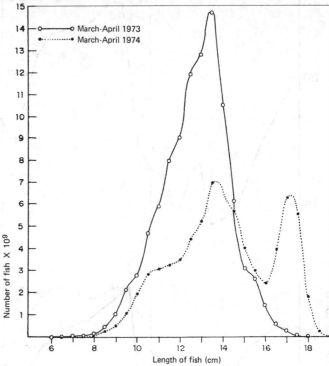

Fig. 2. Size distribution comparison of absolute numbers of
fish caught during March—April 1973 with the same of March—
April 1974.

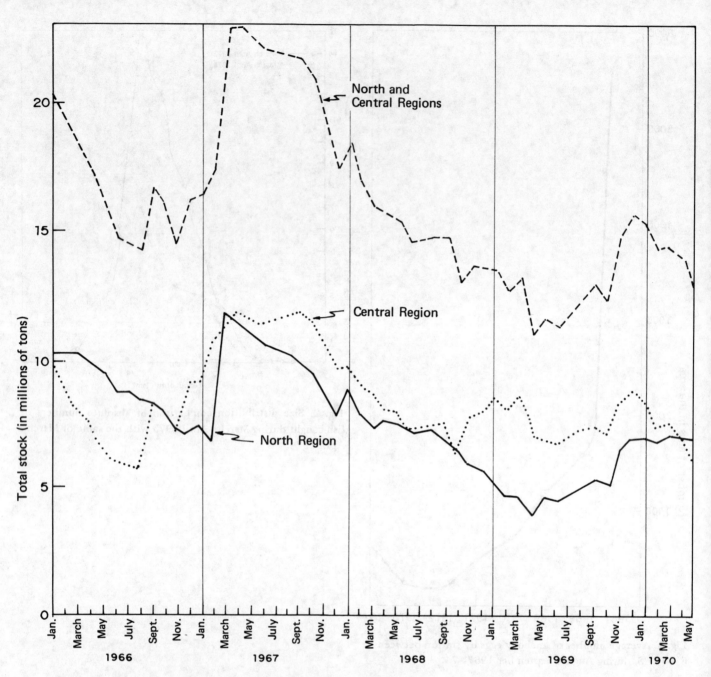

Fig. 3. Monthly fluctuations of the size of the anchovy population
for the north, central, and north plus central regions, based on
cohorts analysis from 1966 to 1970.

Bibliography

Boerema, L. K. Informe sobre los Efectos de la Pesca en el Recurso Peruano de la Anchoveta. *Bol. IMARPE,* Vol. 1, No. 4, 1965.

Burd, A.; Valdivia, J. E. *El Análisis de Población Vittual con Datos de la Anchoveta Peruana.* n.d.

Guillén, O.; Liendo, V. *Informe Preliminar de los Cruceros Unánue 7206 y 7207,* 1973. (Inf. Especial No. IM–150).

Gulland, J. A. Informe sobre la Dinámica de la Población de Anchoveta Peruana. *Bol. IMARPE,* Vol. 1, No. 1, 1968.

Instituto del Mar. Informe del Cuadro de Expertos sobre Dinámica de la Población de Anchoveta Peruana. *Bol.* Vol. 2, No. 2, 1970.

——. Informe sobre la Segunda Reunión del Panel de Expertos en Dinámica de Poblaciones de la Anchoveta Peruana. *Bol.,* Vol. 2, No. 7, 1972.

——, *Regulación de la Pesquería de Anchoveta para el Año Calendario 1972.* 1972. (Inf. Especial No. IM-97.)

——. *Exploración de Peladilla y Distribución de Cardúmenes de Anchoveta.* 1972. (Inf. Especial No. IM–98).

——. *Operación Anchoveta.* 1972. (Inf. Especial No. IM-100.)

——. *La Anchoveta en Relación con el Fenómeno de 'El Niño' 1972.* 1972. (Inf. Especial No. IM-104.)

——. *Operación Eureka XXI.* 1972. (Inf. Especial No. IM-105.)

——. *Operación Eureka XXI.* 1972. (Inf. Especial No. IM-110.)

——. *Operación Eureka XXII.* 1972. (Inf. Especial No. IM-111.)

——. *Operación Eureka XXIII.* 1972. (Inf. Especial No. IM-112.)

——. *Operación Eureka XXIV.* 1972. (Inf. Especial No. IM-115.)

——, *Notas sobre el Estado Actual del Stock de Anchoveta a Base del Informe del Panel de Expertos Realizado en Julio 1972 y de los Ultimos Estudios pecciones Bio-oceanográficas Efectuadas por el y Prospecciones Bio-oceanográficas Efectuadas por el Instituto del Mar.* 1972. (Inf. Especial No. IM-116).

——. *Operación Eureka XXV.* 1972. (Inf. Especial No. IM-117.)

——. *La Pesca en el Sur y la Situación del Stock de Anchoveta.* 1972 (Inf. Especial IM-119.)

——. *Resultados de la Pesca Exploratoria Realizada del 4 al 7 de Diciembre de 1972.* 1972 (Inf. Especial No. IM-121.)

——. Tercera Sesión del Panel de Expertos sobre la Dinámica de la Población de la Anchoveta Peruana. Julio 1972. *Bol.* Vol. 2, No. 9, 1973.

——. *Operación Eureka XXVI.* 1973. (Inf. Especial No. IM-122.)

——. *Situatión del Stock de Anchoveta a Principios de 1973.* 1973. (Inf. Especial No. IM-125.)

——. *Operación Eureka XXVII.* 1973. (Inf. Especial No. IM-141.)

——. *Diagnóstico del Estado del Stock de Anchoveta en Noviembre 1973.* 1973. (Inf. Especial No. IM-146.)

——. *Informe del Cateo No. 4.* 1974. (Inf. Especial No. IM-156.)

——. *Operación Eureka XXIX.* 1974. (Inf. Especial No. IM-158.)

——. *Informe Sobre el Estado del Recurso Anchovetero a Fines de Setiembre y los Perspectivas para la Pesquería en la Temporada de Octubre-Diciembre 1974.* 1974. (Inf. Especial No. IM–165).

——. Informe de la Cuarta Sesión del Panel de Expertos de la Evaluación del Stock de Anchoveta Peruana. *Bol.,* Vol. 2, No. 10, 1974.

Wooster, W.; Guillén, O. Características de 'El Niño' en 1972. *Bol. IMARPE,* Vol. 3, No. 2, 1974.

Zuta, S. *et al. Informe Preliminar del Crucero Unanue 7111.* 1972. (Inf. Especial No. IM-99.)

——. *Informe del Crucero Unanue 7202 Condiciones Oceanográficas Anormales frente al Perú en el verano de 1972.* 1973. (Inf. Especial No. IM-142.)

Zuta, S.; Urquizo, W. *Informe de los cruceros 7211 y 7212 del BAP Unanue Condiciones Oceanográficas Anormales Frente a Perú en Primovera 1972.* 1974. (Inf. Especial No. IM-160.)

Water masses in the northern Chilean zone and their variations in a cold period (1967) and warm periods (1969, 1971–73)

Fernando Robles
Elías Alarcón
Alvaro Ulloa[1]

Introduction

The descriptions of waters off the Chilean coast mainly refer to the northern region (Gunther, 1936; Wyrtki, 1964, 1965 and 1967; Wooster and Gilmartin, 1961; Robles, 1966 and 1968; Wooster, 1970; Brandhorst, 1971; Sandoval, 1971; Inostroza, 1972). Seasonal oceanographic conditions in the region as related to distribution and abundance of pelagic fisheries of economic interest—mainly anchovy and sardine—have been described by Brandhorst and Rojas (1967, 1968) and Brandhorst and Cañón (1967); a summary of these relationships has recently been presented by Cañón.

Systematic collection of oceanographic information was commended when the Chilean Fisheries Development Institute (IFOP) was established in 1963. Seasonal cruises, although not sequential, are nevertheless sufficient to permit the water masses off the Chilean coast to be described in terms of oceanographic variables relevant to an examination of the environment of the fish species of economic importance. The Oceanographic Section of IFOP, as well as the biological and fisheries sections, have performed around 140 different types of cruises, concentrating mainly on the waters adjacent to the northern and central-south zones of the country; the preliminary results of these investigations have been published elsewhere.

The main pelagic fisheries are situated adjacent to the northern zone of the country. The major commercially important species is the anchovy (*Engraulis ringens*), with annual catches of approximately a million tons from 1966 to 1971. Other species of commercial importance are: the sardine (*Clupea bentinki* and *Sardinops sagax*); the machuelo (*Brevoortia maculata*); the bonito (*Sarda chilensis*), and the jurel (*Trachurus murphyi*). The jurel has proved to be extraordinarilly abundant during the last few years with annual catches of over 150,000 tons. Finally, the potential importance in terms of fisheries of the agujilla (*Scomberesox equirrostrum*), has recently been examined (Guzmán and Ulloa, in press).

The regional climate is controlled by the high pressure cell of the eastern South Pacific interacting with the cold coastal waters and the continental depressions; this results in an arid climate with minimal rainfall, but with large day/night thermal variations and slightly developed coastal seasonal patterns. The prevailing winds over most of the year come from the south and south-west; easterly winds blow only during the night, when the continental land mass cools.

The oceanographic regime of the coastal waters is determined, in general terms, by the combined action of: the Humboldt current transporting waters from the subantarctic region towards the north; the upwelling phenomena, supported by the south and south-west winds; and the intrusion of high temperature and salinity subtropical waters from the north and towards the coast. Beneath the surface, the most characteristic feature is the subsurface Equatorial water mass (of relatively high salinity and low oxygen content) that flows southerly as part of the Perú–Chile undercurrent; this water mass extends over the shelf and part of the slope and is apparently

1. Fernando Robles, Department of Oceanography, University College, Swansea, South Wales (United Kingdom), Elías Alarcón and Alvaro Ulloa, Universidad del Norte, CIS, Coquimbo (Chile).

responsible for the absence of demersal fisheries in the zone.

The investigation described in this article is based on analyses of oceanographic information collected by IFOP and other institutions, with the intention of describing in more detail the water masses and their circulation in the northern Chilean zone, taking into account variations during cold and warm periods. Upwelling and variations in the relative abundance of four commercially important pelagic species are considered in the same perspective.

Data and methods

This investigation is based mainly on the analysis of oceanographic information collected over twenty-four cruises; twenty-two were carried out by IFOP and the remaining two by other institutions (see Table 1 and Fig 1).

The general area covered by the investigation is that contained latitudinally by Arica (18°30' S.) to Valparaíso (33°00' S.) on the Chilean coast and between the coastline and 80°00' W. However, the main research was concentrated into an area between Arica (18°30' S.) and Caldera (27°10' S.) and between the coastline and 73°00' W.; this restriction was related to the amount of data involved in the analyses. The general and specific areas of investigation are shown in the composite of Figure 1, in relation to the annual and seasonal availability of data.

In order to construct the average seasonal temperature/salinity (T/S) curves for the area Arica–Caldera to 73° W. (Figs. 2(a),(b),(c) and (d), temperature and salinity data corresponding to thirty-five cruises carried out between 1960 and 1973 were considered; thirty of these cruises were carried out by IFOP and the five remaining cruises by other national and foreign institutions (see Table 5). Reference has also been made to charts of the *Atlas Oceanográfico de Chile* (Inostroza, 1972) in order to describe average seasonal characteristics (Figs. 3, 4, 5 and 6); the figures include the horizontal variation in temperature and salinity at various depths, and the oxygen concentration at 200 m.

The twenty-four cruises analysed for the present study relate to periods between May 1967 and January 1974, in accordance with the detailed information presented in Table 1; these have been further grouped into twelve seasonal periods (Fig. 1). Data obtained during the IFOP cruises was processed through 'a one-step oceanographic data-reduction programme of modular design (IFOP–51) for the IBM 360/50' (Cummings, 1969), by the Oceanographic Section of IFOP.

The analysis and comparison of the oceanographic parameters and water masses of the area is based on the production of horizontal seasonal distributions of temperature, salinity and oxygen at different water depths. At selected locations on the coast, vertical distributions of T °C, S per mille, O_2 (ml/l) and sigma-t were also drawn; this information was complemented by comparison with average T/S curves computed for the seasonal periods considered.

The following information was derived in order to analyse the circulation patterns: the horizontal topographies of sigma-t; the dynamic topographies at different surfaces; and profiles of relative geostrophic velocities.

To describe the features of the coastal upwelling, the variation in depth and distance from the coast of sigma-t values representative of the subantarctic and Equatorial subsurface water masses (as obtained from the T/S curves) were averaged seasonally. Horizontal distribution charts (of S per mille, O_2, and percentage of saturation of O_2, traced at 20 m) were analysed in order to determine the extension of the upwelling phenomena and the location of the upwelling focus for each of the seasons.

Data relating to fish catch and catch per unit of effort were provided by the Data Processing Section of IFOP; this was utilized to compute tables of annual catch by ports and to examine quarterly and annual averages of catch per unit of effort for various fishing areas; these were compared with the quarterly averages of surface water temperature and salinity for each of the areas, and with the annual deviations of surface temperature (based on a nine-year average), respectively.

Description and results

WATER MASSES

This investigation, as previously discussed, was restricted to the area 18°30' to 27°10' S., and between the coastline and 73°00' W.; consequently, it was an attempt to describe oceanographic conditions on a mesoscale. However, over certain periods and according to the availability of data, a larger oceanic area was covered, in order to relate features to more general oceanographic characteristics; therefore, the boundaries of the zone are extended in some cases to approximately 80° W. and 33° S.

The zone covered by the study represents, from the oceanographic and meteorological point of view, a transition between the subtropical and subantarctic regimes. The characteristics of the water masses in the area under investigation reveal their origins in the subtropical and subantarctic areas.

The description of the water masses between the surface and 1,000 m was based mainly on graphical representation of lateral variation in T/S; graphical representation of densities (sigma-t) was also utilized. The preceding analyses were supplemented with averaged T/S diagrams and vertical profiles of

The water masses in the zone

Between the surface and 1,000 m, several different water masses can be distinguished.

Subtropical surface water

This water mass has been defined by, among others, Wyrtki (1965); it is characterised by high S per mille values—which can vary from 35.0 per mille to more than 36.0 per mille in the zone influenced by the south-east anticyclone. Accordingly for the purposes of this study, all surface waters with values of this order of magnitude will be considered subtropical surface water. The value of 35.0 per mille can also be compared with the lower limit (35.1 per mille) given for this water mass off the Peruvian coast by Zuta and Guillén (1970).

In the zone, this water is present as a thin layer extending to depths of no more than 30 m, which penetrates (or is formed) from the north towards the coast between spring and autumn; it is not noticeable during winters of cold periods. The appearance of the water mass coincides, in general terms, with that of the 19° C isotherm and (more specifically) with that of the 25 sigma-t. This sigma-t value is equivalent to the 300 cl/ton thermostatic anomaly (δt) given by Zuta and Guillén for this water mass.

Subantarctic water

This water mass originates in the northern part of the Polar Front and is characterized by the low $T°$ C and S per mille. Wyrtki (1967) proposed that the northern portion of this water should be regarded as the 'South Pacific temperate waters'; characteristic temperatures are between 8° and 15° C, and salinities less than 34.5 per mille. The nomenclature adopted by Wyrtki has similarly been used by Zuta and Guillén in their reference to '*Aguas templadas de la subantártica*'.

In the zone covered by this investigation—as well as in the southern coastal area of Peru—this water mass is located between the lower limit of the seasonal thermocline and at depths of about 80 m; in regions further from the coast (i.e. 80° W.), it can extend to a depth of more than 150 m. It is characterized by temperatures of between 13 and 15° C and salinities or less than 34.8 per mille. A sigma-t value of 25.9 is characteristic of this water mass and is associated with a salinity minimum which at the coast fluctuates between approximately 34.45 per mille and 34.75 per mille. This water supplies, with few exceptions, the coastal upwelling at the north and centre of Chile; it becomes a distinct surface feature from approximately 27° S. southwards, especially during winters of cold periods. The formation of this salinity minimum seems to be closely related to the seasonal variation of the surface thermal structure (Wyrtki, 1967).

Equatorial subsurface water

This water mass is formed in the subsurface oriental Equatorial Pacific region, where the anticyclonic circulation does not penetrate or has only a minor influence. The formation of this water mass appears, in one way or another, to be dependent upon the equatorial undercurrent ('Cromwell current'), the south Equatorial countercurrent and the subsurface subtropical salinity maximum. The southern extension of the water mass coincides with the development of a layer of minimum oxygen content; this is caused by the combined effect of weak circulation, long residence time and coincidence with surface layers of high productivity. However, the extent of the water mass is not strictly coincident with the minimum oxygen layer, as this oxygen layer often extends down to the upper limit of the Antarctic Intermediate Water, situated under the Equatorial subsurface water (Wyrtki, 1967).

Zuta and Guillén proposed a differentiation in this water mass along the Peruvian coast. Waters associated with relatively high salinities (34.9—35.1 per mille) and oxygen, which would be related to the Cromwell current and subsurface circulation off northern Peru, were distinguished as *aguas ecuatoriales subsuperficiales* (AESS) (Equatorial subsurface waters); those with lower salinities (34.9(8)—34.6 per mille), coinciding with the oxygen minimum and extending to the south, were distinguished as *aguas ecuatoriales profundas* (AEP) (deep Equatorial waters); the AESS would correspond to a δt of 200 cl/t, and the AEP to 180 cl/t.

In the northern Chilean zone, the core sigma-*t* value for this water mass is 26.4, which is equivalent to a δt value of 160 cl/*t* as presented by Wooster and Gilmartin (1961) and Brandhorst (1971) for the waters of the 'Peru–Chile undercurrent' or 'Gunther current', respectively. Although the proposed sigma-*t* value (26.4) and its other characteristics are more closely related to those waters defined as AEP by Zuta and Guillén, a common denomination of 'Equatorial subsurface' will nevertheless be used in this situation for this type of water. At the northern Chilean zone, this water mass is approximately located between depths of 100 m and 400 m, and of temperatures between 8° and 14° C; this is correspondingly associated with a salinity maximum that fluctuates between 34.76 per mille in autumn/winter, and 34.91 per mille in summer. The corresponding oxygen minimum is generally lower than 0.5 ml/l, with values of below 0.25 ml/l in coastal areas.

In its southerly extension—and due to the influence of the Humboldt current (also sometimes referred to as the Chilean current along the Chilean coasts, and the Peru coastal current along the Peruvian coasts)—the upper layers of the Equatorial subsurface water are influenced in such a way that two salinity maxima and corresponding O_2 minima are developed: one is distinctly coastal, associated with the undercurrent; and the other is oceanic and weaker, perhaps related to the 'Peru countercurrent' described at 80° W. by Wyrtki. The southern coastal extension of the undercurrent has been specifically suggested, in addition to the authors previously cited, by Robles (1968) and Alarcón and Pineda (1969) to reach 41° S. or more. The oceanic extension has not been studied in such detail but probably penetrates to a latitude 33° S. or more.

Intermediate antarctic water
This water mass has its origin at the Polar front and is located at the northern part of Chile, at depths greater than 500 m. It is characterized by a temperature less than 7° C, associated with a salinity minimum of about 34.5 per mille and an oxygen maximum in excess of 2 ml/l. Its core density value can be identified by a sigma-*t* value of 27.2 located between 600 m and 800 m. This density coincides, in general terms, with the δt values of 90–100 cl/ton presented by Wyrtki for the zone south of the 15° S. and the δt 80 cl/ton presented by Zuta and Guillén for the coast of Perú.

Seasonal variations

Figures 2(a), (b),(c) and (d) illustrate seasonal *T/S* curves based upon the average of temperature and salinity data listed in Table 5 for the zone 18°30′ to 27°10′ S., 73°00′ W. The number of observations considered and their distribution throughout the area were more or less similar for all the seasons; during summer, the number of cruises and data were fewer. On each of the curves is shown the approximate position and average depth of the sigma-*t* core values characteristic of each of the water masses between the surface and 1,000 m. The seasonal description of these water masses are also complemented (see Figs. 3, 4 and 5) by horizontal distributions of $T°$ C and *S* per mille (as adapted from Inostroza, 1972) for depths (at 0.5 and 100 m.) near the average depths of the sigma-*t* core values for three (subtropical, subantarctic and Equatorial subsurface) of the four water masses described previously. In addition to the above, and in order to describe the oxygen minimum layer (Fig. 6), seasonal charts of O_2 corresponding to 200 m depth were adopted.

Subtropical surface water
During average winter conditions (Fig. 3(a)), this water mass is virtually absent from the zone; it is only present in the northern portion of the area (35 per mille isohaline in Fig. 3(a)). The temperature and salinity distribution illustrates the penetration of subantarctic waters from the south. North of 29° S., this phenomenon is separated from the coast and might be an expression of the Humboldt current which is to be found off the coast in such latitudes.

In spring, this water mass is sufficiently developed to be detected by its core sigma-*t* (25 in Fig. 2(b)), and additionally by the surface distribution of temperature and salinity (Fig. 3(b)). The penetration and formation of the water mass is mainly observed in the northern coastal area; from there it extends as a thin layer (average depths of only 15 m for sigma-*t* 25) to the south, forming (as will subsequently be described) a coastal surface countercurrent. This countercurrent contributes to the separation of the Humboldt current and delimits the zone of upwelling between itself and the coast. The upwelling also coincides with coastal and surface drift to the north, which is the result of dominant winds from the south and south-west. This coastal drift, formed mainly of subantarctic waters in a manner similar to the Humboldt current, will be referred to as the Chilean coastal current.

During summer, the subtropical surface water appears to reach its maximum distribution; it is concentrated in the northern coastal portion, although it is also possible to observe an isolated focus further to the south (Fig. 3(c)). The average depth of its density core remains at about 15 m (Fig. 2(c)).

In autumn, seasonal cooling and the relative weakness of the circulation diminishes the presence of this water mass (Fig. 3(d)). This is particularly noticeable in the coastal zone south of 27° S. However, the subtropical surface water is particularly noticeable as a lens which remains in the Arica–Mejillones (Antofagasta) area and it is eventually related to the coastal countercurrent referred to previously. The increasing isolation and cooling of the high-salinity water lens can also be observed in the vertical development of the subtropical layer for this season (average depth of 20 m for sigma-*t* 25, Fig. 2(d)). This phenomenon (discussed below) appears to determine particular conditions governing the general distribution and circulation of water masses and the type of upwelling which occurs in the northern Chilean zone.

Subantarctic water
In winter, the subantarctic salinity minimum, as defined by a core sigma-*t* value of 25.9, reaches its maximum average depth (approximately 50 m, Fig. 2(a)); this must be mainly related to a convection process. Due to the influence of circulation and upwelling, colder temperatures are located in the coastal area (Fig. 4(a)). However, the salinity distribution clearly demonstrates that these subantarctic waters of minimum salinity leave the coast from about 30° S. as a manifestation of the Humboldt current. Equatorial subsurface water is distinct on each side of this current (especially in the coastal area). At 50 m, waters which are probably subtropical in origin (salinities over 35.0 per mille, Fig. 4(a)) are still observed off Arica.

In spring, as a probable consequence of the more intense circulation of subantarctic origin, the salinity minimum is observed to be shallower (sigma-*t* 25.9 at only 30 m, Fig. 2(b)). Also more evident are mixing and upwelling in the coastal zone as well as an increase in the warming in the oceanic zone (Fig. 4(b)). The penetration (and formation) of subtropical waters from the north and subantarctic water from the south are now more extensive; salinities of less than 34.2 per mille are observed off Valparaíso. Separation of the Equatorial subsurface waters is

similar to that in winter. The distinct high-salinity lens is again present in the northern coastal zone and is developed on the eastern side of the subantarctic circulation. This zonal lens is persistent and, as discussed previousuly, appears to have peculiar characteristics in its formation and influence (for example, in the development in the zone of the Equatorial subsurface layer and its possible relationship with a reinforcement of the Peru–Chile undercurrent to the south). The lens also seems to play an important role in the development of the coastal surface countercurrent which contributes to the separation of the Humboldt current further to the south. The high salinity of this lens seems to indicate that important *in situ* processes take place in the Arica–Mejillones coastal zone which determine (or reinforce) the characteristics of waters extending to the south both at the surface and at deeper levels.

During summer, the mean depth of the 25.9 sigma-*t* value is at about 30 m (Fig. 2(c)); this corresponds to a minimum average salinity which has increased to more than 34.75 per mille, and is probably due to advection of waters of high salinity and to the influence of warmer waters situated to the west (see Fig. 4(c)). For the same reasons, low-temperature waters are restricted to a zone very close to the coast. The distribution of salinity at 50 m (Fig. 4(c)) clearly illustrates the southerly penetration of saltier and warmer waters and the relative retreat of the subantarctic waters. This intrusion corresponds to subtropical waters in the northern exterior region, and to equatorial subsurface waters in the coastal zone. The western portion of the subantarctic circulation (Humboldt current) is, in this way, dominant towards the coast and to the south. Waters of Equatorial subsurface characteristics are now dominant in the Arica–Mejillones coastal area.

During autumn, the sigma-*t* value of 25.9 is evident at an average depth of 40 m; this is related to the seasonal cooling, convective mixing, and the relative weakness of the circulation towards the north. The subantarctic salinity minimum has returned to its mean values (34.7 per mille, Fig. 2(d)). At 50 m the temperature and salinity decrease, in general terms, over the whole zone; lowest values are at the southern coastal portion, which suggests the beginning of reinforcement of the subantarctic circulation in that area (Fig. 4(d)). The distinct configuration of the Arica–Mejillones lens can again be appreciated in the same zone as previously observed; this is probably a residual effect of the *in situ* process developed during summer.

Equatorial subsurface waters

In winter, this water mass develops a large vertical display with its core sigma-*t* value (26.4) at approximately 140 m (see Fig. 2(a)); this seems to be the combined effect of the presence of water belonging to the undercurrent at that depth and the autumn turnover. Temperatures at 100 m are, as usual, lower in the coastal zone and correspond to the Equatorial subsurface values ($< 13°$ C., Fig. 5(a)). Temperatures between 13° and 15° C appear to correspond to the lowest layers of subantarctic water of the Humboldt current. The distribution of salinity shows an extensive central zone with low values equivalent to those of the subantarctic waters and probably associated with the divergence from the coast of the Humboldt current. These low salinities may correspond to the lower layers of surface circulation towards the north and divide, as previously discussed, the southerly Equatorial subsurface penetration into two branches—one coastal and well developed, and the other oceanic and not so well developed.

In spring, and in apparent association with the general activation of horizontal and vertical circulation, the Equatorial subsurface water layer starts rising (and also decreasing in width), reaching its sigma-*t* core value at average depths of about 130 m (Fig. 2(b)). Low temperatures in the coastal zone correspondingly become more noticeable; at the same time, seasonal warming starts at the northern exterior zone (Fig. 5(b)). Other characteristics can be better appreciated by reference to the salinity distribution at 100 m (Fig. 5(b)), where both the subantarctic central penetration to the north ($S < 34.5$ per mille) and the separation of the Equatorial waters (prevously referred to) can be distinguished. In the northern exterior zone the high salinities referred to correspond to high temperatures; this could indicate a subtropical surface origin for these waters.

During summer, the conditions which prevail in spring seem to reach their maximum. The core density of Equatorial subsurface water is now situated at a depth of only 90 m (Fig. 2(c)). Although less information was available for tracing this average *T/S* curve, the preceding conclusions seem to agree with the temperature and salinity distributions at 100 m (Fig. 5(c)). The closeness of the 13°–14° C isotherms demonstrate that the central circulation has been well developed; the salinity distribution shows the same pattern. The location of the 34.5 per mille isohaline is somewhat remarkable and can be observed near 20° S.; correspondingly, the high salinity Equatorial subsurface waters are on both sides of this minimum,

and are considerably extended to the south. (In the *T/S* curve of Fig. 2(c), the subsurface salinity maximum reaches salinities greater than 34.9 per mille.) The coastal extension, although narrowing to the south, can be observed down to 33° S., or further. The oceanic penetration of Equatorial subsurface waters reaches 30° S. or even further south. It is conceivable that this oceanic penetration, as previously mentioned could be related to the Peru countercurrent described by Wyrtki (1967). The distribution of temperatures on either side of the 13°–14° C isotherm also appears to correspond to previous considerations (Fig. 5(c)).

During autumn, the relative weakness of circulation, in addition to the seasonal convective process, again makes the core of the Equatorial subsurface water sink to 130 m (see Fig. 2(d)); the shape of the sector of the *T/S* curve at the Equatorial subsurface maximum clearly illustrates this situation, with a reduction in the difference between the subantarctic minimum and the Equatorial subsurface maximum This situation suggests that convection reaches considerable depths during this season. This is also noticeable since waters at 100 m depth are very homothermic over the whole zone with the exception of the exterior warmer area (Fig. 5(d)). The same pattern can be observed in the salinity distribution because both the salinity minimum and the two branches of Equatorial subsurface waters are, in general, less consistent, especially in the oceanic sector.

The oxygen minimum layer

This layer coincides with the horizontal display of the Equatorial subsurface water in the zone. However, it has larger vertical development, reaching the upper limits of the antarctic intermediate water; its axis is located at a depth of approximately 200 m in contrast with 100 m for Equatorial waters. In order to analyse the seasonal pattern of this variable distribution, diagrams related to 200 m depth, adapted from Inostroza (1972), are shown (Fig. 6).

In winter, this layer seems to have only minor horizontal development (Fig. 6(a)); this is probably due to the influence of convective processes.

In spring, the layer starts developing to the south and west (Fig. 6(b)), in response to a process probably associated with the dynamics of lower layers of the Equatorial subsurface water. Oxygen contents of less than 0.25 ml/l appear in the northern region during this season.

In summer (Fig. 6(c)), the horizontal display of this layer remains very narrow at the coast but appears to reach its maximum manifestation towards the south, in accordance with corresponding conditions observed for the Equatorial subsurface water during the same season.

In autumn (Fig. 6(d)), the formation of conditions which eventually prevail in winter commences; the coastal layer seems to be elongated. Oxygen contents lower than 0.25 ml/l disappear from the northern coastal zone, probably in response to the generalization of the convection process. Convection is also indicated by the lateral expansion in the 0.5–1 ml/l isolines.

Antarctic intermediate water

This water mass does not present any noticeable seasonal variations in the zone; throughout all the seasons it remains at depths greather than 500 m and with a core sigma-*t* value of 27.2 remaining at about 700 m. The salinity minimum associated with this density is also very stable and remains very close to 34.5 per mille throughout the year (see Figs. 2(a), (b),(c) and (d).

The water masses during cold and warm periods

Figures 7, 8 and 9 show the average *T/S* curves for the winters, springs and summers as presented in Figure 1 for the Arica–Caldera, 73° W. zone. The curves are based upon the oceanographic data in each zone from each of these periods. The position of core sigma-*t* values corresponding to the subtropical, subantarctic and Equatorial subsurface waters and their mean depths—calculated from the computation listings (see Table 3)—are shown in these figures. Also repeated are the average seasonal *T/S* curves as shown in Figure 2. Only surface data was available for autumn 1972, and summer and winter 1973, and it was not possible to include an average *T/S* curve for those seasons; accordingly, there is no average *T/S* curve for any summer period as part of the present investigation.

Comparison between average *T/S* curves for cold (1967) and warm periods (autumn 1969, and late 1971 to late 1973) are complemented by: surface salinity and temperature charts for the identification of the surface layer; distributions of the salinity minimum for the demarcation of subantarctic waters; and distributions of the subsurface salinity maximum and oxygen minimum for the delineation of Equatorial subsurface waters. Charts showing the salinity distribution at 10 m were preferred to those of the surface (0 m) because of their improved

representation of the interaction between subtropical and subantarctic waters at the surface layer.

Winter conditions

During the cold winter of 1967, subtropical waters ($S > 35.0$ per mille) were noticeable only in the northern exterior zone (Fig. 10(a)). At the same time, the important central penetration of subantarctic water (Humboldt current) could be observed within longitudes 72° to 74° W.; in this area the 34.5 per mille isohaline extended up as far as 23° S. This northerly penetration was adjacent to the Arica–Mejillones lens; in the northern coastal region, this lens extends to the south and forms what has been referred to as the Chilean coastal countercurrent. This countercurrent segments the northerly flowing subantarctic flux; between the countercurrent and the coast and originating from 28° S., there exists a coastal drift oriented towards the north. Surface temperatures (Fig. 10(b)) reproduce similar general characteristics to those illustrated by salinity, and in particular to the formation of the Arica–Mejillones lens and the central subantarctic penetration to the north (located at 73° W.). Low coastal temperature centres, probably related to upwelling, are also indicated; the most relevant ($< 14°$C) is that located near the Mejillones Peninsula. The average depth for the 25.9 sigma-*t* value corresponding to the subantarctic water core is located at about 40 m; the corresponding salinity of this minimum is slightly lower than the average (Fig. 7).

The surface situation was remarkably different during the warm winter of 1972. The subtropical waters were present along almost the whole of the coastal zone and were indicated by salinities greater than 35.0 per mille (Fig. 11(a)). This intrusion (or formation) of subtropical waters seemed to deflect the central circulation of low-salinity waters towards the west. Nevertheless, these low salinities were considerably higher than during the winter of 1967 (Fig. 10(a)). Temperatures (Fig. 11(b)) were correspondingly higher (on average about 1° C higher) and the Arica–Mejillones lens was better outlined and developed. The (conjectural) upwelling centres had almost disappeared and temperatures greater than 15° C that were observed at 20° S. in winter 1967 were seen only down to 27° S.

The salinity minimum distributions (Figs. 10(c) and 11(c)) coincided with the preceding interpretations. During the winter of 1967, the subantarctic penetration towards the north (centred at about 73° W.). and the position of the highly saline Arica–

Mejillones lens were clearly demonstrated (Fig. 10(c)); the coastal countercurrent was also detectable as an extension to this lens. On the oceanic side of the subantarctic flux at 73° W., a high-salinity tongue which penetrated from 77° W. towards the south-east could then be clearly observed; this created a westerly limit to the central flux.

In winter 1972 (Fig. 11(c)), the distribution of the salinity minimum showed that both the highly developed Arica—Mejillones lens and the central subantarctic waters ($S < 34.5$) were displaced towards the west. Along the coastal zone, the subantarctic minimum was practically absent and the 25.9 sigma-t value had reached an average depth of 60 m in comparison to the 40 m depth of the cold year of 1967 (Fig. 7).

During winter 1973 (Figs. 12(a) and (b)), surface salinities and temperatures seemed to have recovered, but had not yet reached conditions similar to those observed during the winter of 1967. High salinities and temperatures were located at a latitude some 2° further north than in 1972; temperatures in the southern region (15° isotherm) reacted similarly. The centres of upwelling were remarkably consistent in their locations in comparison with winter 1967 and seemed to have recovered their stability and to be supplied with waters of subantarctic origin.

The distribution of the subsurface salinity maximum for the winter of 1967 (Fig. 10(d)) showed the two aforementioned Equatorial subsurface penetrations towards the south on both sides of what can be considered the lowest limit of the Humboldt current (at 73° W.). The oceanic penetration was weaker and appeared to be limited to the extreme south-west zone, by what might have been the lower layers of the oceanic Chile—Peru current system. The coastal penetration, corresponding to the undercurrent, was more defined and was located between 73° W. and the continent—its relationship to the Arica—Mejillones lens was particularly marked. During winter 1967, the sigma-t 26.4 average depth was approximately 120 m, associated with salinities lower than the average (Fig. 7).

In the winter of 1972, the Equatorial subsurface coastal penetration was clearly distinguishable, especially in the coastal zone ($S > 34.9$ per mille, see Fig. 11(d)); this seems to indicate that the penetration was, in some way, reinforced by conditions prevailing during summer and winter of 1972. The corresponding sigma-t value of 26.4 was at an average depth of 170 m (Fig. 7) and the shape of the corresponding T/S curve indicated a clear relationship between the surface processes and the development of this subsurface 'Equatorial' water mass. These processes probably originated north of 18°30′ S. but quite possibly were reinforced, to a large extent, in the Arica—Mejillones lens.

In the winter of 1967, the oxygen minimum distribution (Fig. 10(e)) coincided with the considerations given above for the subsurface salinity maximum; however, as referred to previously, it covered wider ranges and average depths (see Table 4). The southerly penetrations generally corresponded to O_2 values lower than 0.25 ml/l; the coastal penetration was again more noticeable and better developed. The relationship, at the coastal zone, between this low O_2 concentration and the Arica—Mejillones lens also seemed to be clear. In the winter of 1972 (Fig. 11(e)), the minimum O_2 distribution was consistent with the previous data and, in general, exhibited a well developed horizontal minimum.

Comparing the ranges and average values (given in Table 4) for the winters of 1967 and 1972, it can be seen that this O_2 minimum layer was developed more vertically during the winter of 1972 in comparison with 1967, in relation to average depths and mean O_2 contents. Similar comparison can be applied to the subantarctic salinity minimum and the Equatorial subsurface salinity maximum, as demonstrated by the means and ranges for the corresponding sigma-t values in Table 3.

Spring conditions

During the spring of 1967, the waters were, on average, colder and less saline at all levels (Fig. 8); the subtropical surface water had an average depth of only 10 m and was only observed in the zone corresponding to the Arica—Mejillones lens (Figs. 13(a) and 13(b)). The salinity and temperature surface distributions showed, at about 72° W., a well-developed flux towards the north (Humboldt current), slightly separated from the coast by the southerly extension of the coastal countercurrent. The coastal flux towards the north (the Chilean coastal current) also appeared to be well developed. The persistence of the upwelling centres was again noticeable in the temperature distribution (Fig. 13(b)); the centres generally coincided with temperatures of less than 15° C. The upwelling focus situated just north of 21° S. seemed to be supplied preferentially by Equatorial subsurface water ($S > 38.0$ per mille); the southern centres were supplied preferentially with subantarctic waters ($S < 37.0$ per mille). The salinity minimum (Fig. 13(c)) was consistent with the pattern described above both with regard to the flux towards the north and to the separation that this flux produced in the saltier waters. During the spring the 34.5 per mille isohaline reaches as far north as 21° S. The information presented in Figure 13(c) further indicates a low-salinity area situated off Mejillones, related to a quasi-permanent subantarctic type of upwelling centre, in contrast to the higher coastal salinities observed further to the north, the latter being related to an Equatorial subsurface type of upwelling. Nevertheless, the subantarctic minimum is still predominant over the whole zone with lower than average salinities occurring at mean depths of only 30 m (Fig. 8); this must be connected to the general activity observed for the northerly circulation. The southerly penetration of the coastal subsurface salinity maximum is clearly demonstrated in Fig. 13(d). The O_2 minimum (Fig. 13(e)) coincides with the salinity maximum in the zone corresponding to the Arica—Mejillones lens: however, the 0.25 ml/l isolines become increasingly narrower towards the south extension, probably due to mixing processes caused by the Mejillones Peninsula.

In the spring of 1971, the surface distribution of salinity and temperature (Figs. 14(a) and 14(b)) illustrated the warming and intrusion (or formation) of subtropical surface waters from the north. Temperatures were clearly higher than in spring 1967, with the 19° C reaching 24° S. Salinities in excess of 35.0 per mille were only observed in the coastal region, although this may have been caused by a lack of data collected towards the boundary of the zone. The tongue of water which extended from the Arica—Mejillones lens was not well defined in the salinity distribution (Fig. 14(a)) but the fact that the 17° C isotherm reaches 27° S. (or further) suggested that the tongue was well developed (Fig. 14(b)). Subantarctic salinities ($S < 34.5$ per mille) that were observed in 1967 at around 23° S. retreated to 26° S. (Fig. 14(a)). The salinity minimum (Fig. 14(c)) suggested an interesting interaction between the warm conditions at the surface and the cold characteristics which persisted in the subsurface layer. Off the Mejillones Peninsula, salinities less than 34.2 per mille were recorded; however, the 34.5 isohaline had retreated one degree latitude further south than in the spring of 1967. The pattern shown by this and the other isohalines also indicated that higher salinity waters tended to spread towards, the south on both sides of the subantarctic flux. This interesting contrast between warmer conditions which formed in the surface waters and the exceptionally low salinities in

the subantarctic layers was also illustrated by low salinities in the offshore zone (Fig. 14(c)) and in the shape of the corresponding T/S curve (Fig. 8). This T/S curve, in spite of having been constructed from data mainly derived from coastal and oceanographic stations to the south, was so different by comparison with the average curve that it seemed to suggest that 1971 was an exceptionnally cold year. (Zuta and Guillén (1970) and Wooster and Guillén (1974) discussed how warm periods, such as that in 1972—73, were preceded by exceptionally cold periods.) Similar conclusions can be obtained by considering the subsurface salinity maximum and the corresponding O_2 minimum distributions (see Figs. 14(d) and (e)). Salinities were lower in 1971 than in 1967, and corresponding O_2 contents were higher in the southerly region dominated by subantarctic waters; this would correspond to a relatively minor intrusion of Equatorial subsurface water towards the south during 1971—a situation which appears to be related to cold periods.

During spring 1972, the warmer pattern was generalized; high salinities and temperatures existed over the whole area, affecting even the coastal area between Arica and Mejillones (see Figs. 15(a) and 15(b)). The low-temperature upwelling centres were reduced to their minimum manifestation. The Arica—Mejillones lens was very well developed at this time and was undoubtedly related to conditions to the north. The countercurrent which is an extension of the lens was clearly defined and extended far to the south (salinities of less than 34.5 per mille were no longer in the surface layer). The salinity minimum distribution (Fig. 15(c) may be interpreted in a similar way and the whole zone could be seen to have been invaded by high-salinity waters; the characteristic salinity minimum of the Mejillones Peninsula disappeared and the 34.5 per mille isohaline had noticeably retreated to the south. The distributions of the salinity maximum and O_2 minimum (see Figs. 15(d) and 15(e)) were in accordance with the general interpretation; waters of high salinity (> 34.5 per mille) and of low O_2 content (< 0.25 ml/l) penetrated, as an extraordinarily narrow entity, towards the south. The abnormal situation which existed during the spring of 1972 can also be detected in the corresponding T/S curve of Figure 8, in which temperatures and salinities throughout the upper layer were above average. The shape of this curve, in addition to that of winter 1972 (Fig. 7), was indicative of a close relationship between the different water masses of the upper layers during the periods of stability:

this may have been generated by the warm conditions and their relationship to the weak circulation to the north. This situation was confirmed by a mean depth of 170 m for a sigma-*t* value of 26.4 during the spring of 1972 (Fig. 8).

Only coastal and surface information, i.e. data only down to a depth of 100 m, is available for spring 1973; however, the shape of the corresponding *T/S* curve (Fig. 8) suggested that conditions were close to the average. The surface distributions (Figs. 16(a) and (b)) exhibited patterns which tended to be close to the average; coastal circulation was reactivated in the north but it was not as developed as during the spring of 1967. Similar general conclusions are reached by observing the distributions of the salinity minima, the subsurface salinity maxima and the O_2 minima (Figs. 16(c), (d) and (e)); these interpretations are, however, seriously hindered by the lack of information from more than a limited depth.

According to data not included in the present work, cold conditions prevailed along the Chilean coast during 1974; thus, it can be assumed that conditions observed during the spring of 1973 were representative of the transition from a warm (1972–73) to a cold (1974) period.

Summer conditions
Data collection for this season was limited to surface temperatures in the southern coastal area of the zone during the summer for 1973 (Fig. 17); this distribution data cannot, therefore, be compared with any other summer within the present investigation. However, the general pattern show in Figure 17 demonstrates that one of the climaxes of the warm period of 1971–73 was reached during this season, with very warm waters adjacent to the Chilean coast far to the south. This conclusion is confirmed by the position of the 19° C isotherm; during the spring of 1972 this was observed at a latitude of 24° S. whereas in the summer it was located at 27° S. or still further south.

Autumn conditions
Conditions during the autumn season are generally characterized, as discussed previously, by a relative weakness in the circulation pattern; this, in association with cooling, favours vertical mixing. Mixing might reach considerable depths and extend as far down as the lowest layers of the Equatorial subsurface waters. In comparison to other seasons, the average depths of the sigma-*t* core values seem to support this interpretation with respect to all the water

masses. The mixing situation is further confirmed by the shape of *T/S* curves (Fig. 9); inflexions in the upper mayers, which characterize water masses in the curves corresponding to the other seasons, disappear and all the layers are seen to be homogeneous with respect to salinity. The homogeneity causes the variations between the various autumn seasons to be less marked. It should be pointed out that the salinity during this period ranges between 34.7 per mille and 34.8 per mille; this is exactly the range of overlapping between Equatorial subsurface and subantarctic waters in the zone.

During the autumn of 1967, subtropical waters were present over the exterior oceanic zone and the area corresponding to the Arica—Mejillones lens (Figs. 18(a) and (b)); these displays were separated by the northern extension (centred at 72°–73° W.) of the subantarctic waters. At a longitude of 80° W. (Fig. 18(a)), high-salinity waters extended towards the south and were probably related to the Peru countercurrent; this, as will be discussed later, is a seasonal extension restricted to the surface and is not observed during winter. The maximum development of the extension occurred during summer (Robles, 1968). The relationship between the 35.0 per mille and the 19° C isolines, as an index of the southern limit of the subtropical surface water, is particularly noticeable during the autumn season. As in other seasons of the year, the northerly extension (between 72° and 73° W.) of the subantarctic waters is adjacent to a southerly penetration known as the Chilean coastal countercurrent; this is clearly related to the Arica—Mejillones lens and is particularly well defined during the autumn season. Between this countercurrent and the coast, and extending from the south to the Mejillones Peninsula, is—based on the salinity distributions depicted in Figure 18(a)—a northerly coastal drift which is referred to as the Chilean coastal current. With the possible exception of the Mejillones Peninsula area, coastal upwelling centres are not in evidence; this situation is in accordance with the stable conditions which are prevalent during this season. The distribution of the salinity minima (Fig. 18(c)) emphasizes the characteristics described previously and, in particular, the oceanic countercurrent at 80° W., the subantarctic extension at 72°–73° W., the southerly countercurrent extending from the Arica—Mejillones lens and the coastal drift towards the north. During this season, subantarctic waters seem to extend to latitudes lower than 20° S., because they extend parallel to the coast, they leave a narrow strip of high-salinity water at the Arica—Mejillones coastal zone. The average depth of the 25.9 sigma-*t* value was at 30 m for the autumn of 1967 (see Fig. 9); however, this value and the general shape of the curve were influenced by the coastal origin of the data. In particular, the lowest sector of the curve was distorted; salinities were higher than the average values in accordance with the high salinities observed in the northern coastal area. For the same reason, the average depth of the 26.4 sigma-*t* value was nearer to the surface.

The subsurface salinity maxima and oxygen minima (Figs. 18(d) and (e)) demonstrate, as during other seasons, the penetration of water of high salinity and low oxygen content on both sides of the subantarctic flux towards the north (centred about 73° W.). The coastal instrusion (the undercurrent) is very narrow with salinities greater than 34.9 per mille and even 35.0 per mille at the northern extreme: the intrusion generally corresponds with O_2 contents of greater than 0.25 ml/l. Although similar O_2 contents can be associated with the oceanic intrusion, lower salinities than those associated with the coastal penetration are observed as having occurred during other periods of the year. The oceanic penetration, as in winter, seems to come from the north-west at a longitude of 77° W. (the relationship between this countercurrent and that described by Wyrtki as the Peru countercurrent at 80° W. should again be noted here). At this longitude, it seems that this countercurrent only goes directly to the south in the surface and in the subsurface layers, turns towards the coast due to a major influence. The influence at that depth and longitude is the general oceanic subantarctic circulation towards the north (the 'Chile–Peru' oceanic current'). The situation would be in agreement with the low salinity and high O_2 contents observed to the west and south-west of the area covered by Figure 18(d) and (e). Further evidence of the two subsurface intrusions is provided by latitudinal cross-sectional profiles (see Fig. 19, based on data of the Scorpio expedition shown in Table 1): lenses of salinity maxima, and their corresponding O_2 minima, occur at 20 and 220 miles from the coast.

During the autumn of 1969 (see Figs. 20(a) and (b), warmer surface conditions extended over the whole zone. The northerly subantarctic circulation was distinctly displaced towards the west by a well-developed Arica–Mejillones lens. Subtropical waters (S > 35.0 per mille) extended to a latitude of 24° S. over the central portion and to 20° S. in the coastal area. Only coastal data was available for the southern part of the area but the isohalines and isotherms

suggested that the coastal countercurrent was well developed and that the coastal surface drift to the north was diminished. Upwelling centres were not evident. The salinity maxima (Fig. 20(c)) were indicative of conditions similar to those of the spring of 1971, i.e. an abnormally warm surface situation in opposition to a well-developed subsurface, subantarctic flux, although never reaching the extremes described for the latter period. The subantarctic flux was well developed on both sides of the coastal countercurrent, which was also distinct. Waters with salinities less than 34.5 per mille extended up to 20° S. in the offshore zone and to Mejillones, or further, adjacent to the coast. A strip of high-salinity coastal water was detected between Arica and Mejillones (Fig. 20(c)). The salinity maximum and O_2 minimum (Figs. 20(d) and (e)) indicated a well-defined equatorial subsurface penetration. The penetration was better illustrated by the O_2 minimum; however in contrast to autumn 1967, salinity values of 34.9 per mille were almost totally absent. The corresponding *T/S* curve (Fig. 9) appeared to indicate that, in general, conditions were warmer than the seasonal average.

During the autumn of 1972 (Figs 21(a) and (b)), only coastal surface salinity and temperature data is available. The salinities indicated extremely warm conditions over the whole of the coastal area, with subtropical waters covering practically the whole zone down to 26° S. The temperature data confirmed this; the 19° C isotherm was evident at 23° S., and from there northwards, the whole of the coastal region was extremely warm (> 19° C). It appears that the warm surface conditions for autumn 1972 were more extreme than for autumn 1969; this being in accordance with the general situation described for the other seasons of the 1972–73 period.

Data available for autumn 1973 are also restricted to coastal and surface waters, and in particular to the northern part of the zone. Surface salinities and temperatures (see Figs. 22(a) and (b)), showed a partial recovery, with subtropical waters moving offshore. To the south of the region, the subantarctic flux (S < 34.5 per mille) had been partially restored, as had the coastal upwelling centres. Similar conclusions can be drawn by reference to distribution of salinity minima (Fig. 22(c)). The subsurface salinity maximum and O_2 minimum distribution charts (Figs. 22(d) and (e)) suggest that the recovery was faster at depths influenced by the equatorial subsurface waters, since salinities of greater than 34.8 per mille were present only within a narrow northerly strip which generally coincided with low O_2 contents. This situations seems to have differed from conditions observed for the atutumns of 1967 and 1969 but all these considerations are based solely on coastal and surface data. Conditions near the average for this season (see Fig. 9) are indicated by the *T/S* curve and the mean depths for the sigma-*t* cores.

CONSIDERATIONS ABOUT THE CIRCULATION IN THE ZONE

The large-scale, general water circulation, defining the interaction between horizontal fluxes from both the south and the north, has not been described for the region bounded by 18° 30′−33° 00′ S. and the coastline and 80° W. Some of the general features of the zone have been presented (Wyrtki, 1967; Wooster 1970; Sandoval, 1971; Zuta, 1972) although these have always been related to more extensive descriptions which concentrate on the exterior (offshore) and northern areas. Aspects of the coastal circulation adjacent to central and northern Chile have been mentioned by (among others) Gunther (1936), Wooster and Gilmartin (1961), Brandhorst (1963, 1971), Brandhorst and Inostroza (1969), Robles (1968) and Inostroza (1973).

In this section, an attempt is made to give additional consideration to a description of water-circulation patterns. The analyses, relating to some of the periods covered by the present investigation, were made by examining the following: charts of sigma-*t* cores topographies; dynamic topographies; and selected relative geostrophic velocity profiles. The sigma-*t* topographies were traced from data which was interpolated from computer listings. The dynamic topographies were traced at the nearest standard surface to the mean depths of the subantarctic and equatorial subsurface sigma-*t* core values (averaged in this case from all data available for the given season). The reference level chosen was 500 db because it corresponded, on the one hand, to the depth to which samplings were made during most of the cruises and, on the other because it seemed to be an appropriate level of 'no-motion' located between the Equatorial subsurface and the intermediate antarctic water (as can be deduced from the relevant *T/S* curves). At the coast, and where the 500 m depth was not reached, dynamic highs were extrapolated from neighbouring deeper stations. The same criteria was followed in tracing the relative geostrophic velocity profiles.

The series of charts relating to the winter of 1967 confirm the circulation pattern already described.

Fluxes from the west to the coast could be distinguished in both the topography of sigma-*t* 25.9 and in the corresponding dynamic topography (see Figs. 23(a) and (b)) as follows:

From the far south-west, the flux of the Chile—Peru oceanic current towards the north. During this particular season, this current would reach depths of 200 m or more with relative geostrophic velocities slightly greater than 0.1 knot (see profile of Fig. 24(a)). The origin of this current is primarily subantarctic. In Figure 23(b), and 'eddy' can be observed in the zone of influence of this current (centred at about 28° S. 79° W.). This 'eddy system' also appeared in similar charts traced for autumn 1967 (these have not been included to avoid unnecessary repetition).

Proceeding further toward the coast, a flux toward the south could be observed. To the west, it was partially surface; towards the coast it was subsurface. The velocity of the flux was again slightly greater than 0.1 knot but the flux apparently reached greater depths than the current mentioned above (Fig. 24(a)). Figures 23(a) and (b) show that this current (Peru oceanic countercurrent) enters the zone at 77° W.; it then proceeded in a south-easterly direction and contributed to the exterior subsurface salinity maximum and corresponding to the O_2 minimum observed in Figure 19. This indicated that it was predominantly of Equatorial subsurface origin. As referred to previously, it would be of interest to examine the relationship between this countercurrent and that described as the Peru countercurrent by Wyrtki for the 80° W. longitude off Peru.

A main subantarctic flux to the north, corresponding to the Humboldt current was evident for the whole area *but* centred at 73° W. During this season— according to Figure 24(a)—it seemed to be present at considerable (> 400 m) depths; its higher velocities (> 0.3 knot) appeared to remain on the coastal side. This current probably extends to the Peruvian coast as the 'Peru coastal current', in accordance with Zuta and Guillén (1970).

The countercurrent which appeared nearer to the coast corresponds to that known as the Chilean coastal countercurrent. This flux towards the south, referred to by Brandhorst (1971), seems to have marked seasonal variations. This author has described the current reaching, during summer, as far south as Talcahuano (37° S.). The dynamic topography (Fig. 23(b)) indicated that, during cold winters, the current would extend to approximately

31° S. The relationship between the countercurrent and the Arica—Mejillones lens also appears in Figure 23(b). In warm periods, this countercurrent could be the southern part of the warm coastal tongue as shown in the surface temperature charts published by Bjerknes (1961) and Wyrtki (1964). The depth of this countercurrent, which divides the subantarctic coastal flux towards the north, seems to be considerable; its velocity would be higher than 0.3 knot during the summer (Fig. 24(a)). The possible relationship between this surface countercurrent and the 'undercurrent' can be postulated from its subsurface display as a similar interaction to that observed for the oceanic countercurrent. In fact, both countercurrents (oceanic and coastal) are indicated at the surface by their subtropical characteristics and in subsurface layers by their Equatorial subsurface characteristics. These interactions become more evident during warm periods.

Immediately adjacent to the coast and originating at about 28° S., the so-called Chilean coastal current can be observed; in this particular winter season, this current seemed to extend northwards to the latitude of the Mejillones Peninsula or further (Fig. 23(b)). The current was not well defined in the profile of Figure 24(a), due to the peculiarities of the Arica—Mejillones lens. However, it probably attained or surpassed velocities of 0.5 knot. Figures 25(a) and (b), corresponding to the topography of the 26.4 sigma-*t* value and the dynamic topography at 150 m respectively, define conditions which agree with the previous description. It should be noted that the circulation of the Chile—Peru oceanic current (the south-westerly portion of the charts) does influence the subsurface orientation of the Peru oceanic countercurrent at these levels. Also the charts illustrate separation at the coast as the Humboldt current divides the Equatorial subsurface flux to the south and eventually reinforces the Peru—Chile undercurrent produced by the Arica—Mejillones lens.

In addition to the above information, a velocity profile relating to autumn 1967 is shown (Fig. 24(b)); this relates to a position 28°15′ S. and is based upon the data of the Scorpio profile shown in Figure 19. It can be deduced from this section that, during autumn, the Chile—Peru oceanic current circulation was displaced towards the west because it does not appears in the profile. At the western extremity of the zone, a narrow surface flux moving south could be detected; this was possibly associated with the Peru oceanic countercurrent. This flux, as described previously, would be found at higher latitudes during autumn and appears to be separated from its subsurface manifestation. The subsurface flux would attain lower velocities than in winter and in the profile reproduced (Fig. 24(b)), it is observed to be displaced toward the east approximately 300 miles from the coast. The Humboldt current, with characteristics and location similar to those during the winter of 1967, can also be observed, although its velocities were slightly lower than in winter (> 0.2 knot). Closer to the coast and reduced in both depth and velocity (Fig. 24(b)), the Chilean coastal countercurrent can be seen. Finally—immediately adjacent to the coast—a northerly surface flux (corresponding to the Chilean coastal current) underlain by the Peru--Chile undercurrent, can be observed; the latter with velocities in excess of 0.3 knot. The eventual relationship between the coastal countercurrent and the undercurrent can again be appreciated.

Winter 1972, which was generally warm (Figs. 26(a) and (b)), showed a general weakness in the circulation towards the north. The general direction of movement of the fluxes was towards the south and the Chilean coastal current was practically absent. This situation was confirmed by the depths of the 25.9 sigma-*t* value adjacent to the coast (Fig. 26(a)), which was sometimes deeper than those in the central zone of the area. The velocity profile (Fig. 27) progressing from west to east shows a weak (> 0.1 knot) and shallow flux, corresponding to the Humboldt current and the whole of the remaining coastal zone with a dominant flux towards the south extending to depths of about 400 m and subsurface velocities occasionally greater than 0.8 knot. This pattern indicated that the coastal countercurrent and the undercurrent formed, in exceptionally warm conditions, a combined flux towards the south. The topographies corresponding to a sigma-*t* value of 26.4 (Figs. 28(a) and (b)) clearly coincided with the previous interpretation, of particular interest was the great depth (> 300 m) reached by the Equatorial subsurface sigma-*t* core value in some if the coastal regions.

Examining the topography for the 25.0 sigma-*t* value in spring 1972 (Fig. 29), it was possible to observe the subtropical water penetration towards the south. The topographies corresponding to the sigma-*t* value of 25.9 (Figs. 30(a) and (b)) seemed to indicate a partial, though weak, recovery of the subantarctic flux towards the north (both the Chilean coastal current and the Humboldt current) during this season.

However, the coastal countercurrent remained a well-developed feature between both subantarctic fluxes. The velocity profile (Fig. 31) again, as in winter 1972, illustrated the weakness of the Humboldt current and the combined fluxes towards the south of the coastal countercurrent and the undercurrent. Nearer the coast was the Chilean coastal current, with velocities in excess of 1.0 knot. The topographies corresponding to a sigma-*t* value of 26.4 (Figs. 32(a) and (b) confirmed the above interpretation; the depth reached (Fig. 32(a), by this Equatorial subsurface water indicator at the coast was again remarkable reaching greater depths than observed for winter 1972. This coastal sinking of Equatorial subsurface water seemed to be a consequence of the stable conditions prevailing during warm years.

In order to establish comparisons with other warm periods, charts representing the autumn of 1969 are included. During autumn 1969, the 25.0 sigma-*t* topography (Fig. 33) enables the extension and depth of subtropical water layer penetration to be observed. Conditions are less relevant than those observed during spring 1972 (Fig. 29); however, topographies corresponding to the 25.9 sigma-*t* value (Figs. 35(a) and (b)) demonstrated similarities to the aforementioned period, mainly with respect to the relative weakness of the coastal circulation towards the north (the Chilean coastal current). The Humboldt current, centred about a longitude of 73° W., was relatively important and the coastal countercurrent towards the south also seemed to be well developed—though in this case confined to the north and to the coast. The velocity profile data presented in Figure 34 are in general agreement with these considerations; the Humboldt current was better developed in autumn 1969 than in spring 1972 with correspondingly greater velocities (> 0.3 knot) and the Chilean coastal countercurrent apparently was not combined with the Peru—Chile undercurrent. However, the situation could be distorted by the location of the profile (Antofagasta) where local conditions, i.e. the upwelling, might create peculiarities in the circulation. In the topographies corresponding to sigma-*t* values of 26.4 (Figs. 36(a) and (b)), the depth reached at a coastal strip north of Mejillones by the Equatorial subsurface water density can again be appreciated (Fig. 36(a)); the southward extension of these waters in a narrow coastal zone should also be noted as an expression of the Peru—Chile undercurrent (Fig. 36(b)).

UPWELLING

As has already been stated; the zone is under the influence of the meteorological regime determined by the south-eastern Pacific anticyclone. Accordingly, the dominant winds are from both the south-west (Figs. 37(a) and (b)), and from the south (Fig. 37(c)). For the period covered by this investigation (1967—73), the average measured annual wind forces were 8 knots for Arica, 5 knots for Iquique and 10 knots for Antofagasta. Due to the persistence and dominance of the south-westerly and southerly winds, the sea-surface drift (Ekman drift) was directed towards the north and north-west.

The relationship between air temperature and atmospheric pressure is shown in Figures 38(a), (b) and (c), for Arica, Iquique and Antofagasta respectively. Temperature and pressure are inversely related and cyclic, in terms of positive (shaded areas in Fig. 38) and negative anomalies from the average values for 1967—73. Two cold periods (1967—68 and 1970—71), with negative thermal deviations, corresponded to positive pressure trends; warm periods (1969 and 1972) had inversely related patterns. The correlations were more noticeable for Arica and Iquique (Figs. 38(a) and (b)). In order to determine common characteristics and seasonal or zonal differences in the water that upwells along the coast of the area, the variations in depth of the subantarctic and Equatorial subsurface sigma-*t* cores have been analysed (for twenty-eight density--sigma-*t*--vertical profiles, corresponding to eleven cruises carried out during the period covered by this work). The horizontal extension of the upwelling centres was determined by analysing twenty-seven seasonal horizontal charts of salinity, O_2 and unsaturated O_2 (per cent sat.) at 20 m. The seasons covered by the analysis were: winter, 1967 and 1972; spring 1967, 1971, 1972 and 1973; and autumn 1967, 1969 and 1973.

From vertical sections of the sigma-*t* values the following general characteristics for upwelling in the zone were deduced:

The subantarctic density core (25.9) upwelled from a mean depth of 64 m and from an average distance of 45 miles from the coast;

The equatorial subsurface density core (26.4) upwelled from a mean depth of 163 m up to an average depth of 85 m at distances that fluctuated between 34 and 42 miles from the coast.

The maximum inclination for the core value isopycnal (25.9) corresponding to the subantarctic water, was observed at a latitude of 28°10′ S. during autumn 1967; here the density core of this water upwelled from 100 m to the surface over a distance of 26 miles (Fig. 39(a));

The maximum inclination for the core value isopycnal (26.4) corresponding to the Equatorial subsurface water, was observed at Mejillones during late winter 1971; here the density core of this water upwelled from 190 up to 40 m over a distance of 35 miles (Fig. 39(b)).

Examination of seasonal charts for the above-mentioned properties at 20 m, indicated the following characteristics:

The area under investigation normally presents a strip of unsaturated oxygen waters in the surface layers near the shore. During the periods considered, this strip varied in width from 3 to 100 miles (Figs. 39(c) and (d) for autumn 1967 and spring 1971, respectively).

The insaturated strip corresponded, in general terms, to relatively low salinity coastal areas (subantarctic upwelling) which were narrower than the unsaturated strip (Fig. 40).

The upwelling focus could eventually be identified by centres of low insaturated values (< 40 per cent), low oxygen contents (< 2.0 ml/l) and relatively low surface temperatures (< 15° C).

Seasonal variations

During the winter of 1967, the upwelling seemed to be mainly supported by subantarctic waters and/or mixing of this water with Equatorial subsurface water. These conditions are clearly illustrated by Figure 41(a) (salinity at 20 m), for the area between 18° 30′ and 21° 00′ S.; here, it is possible to observe a thin strip of water near the coast, with salinities lower than those of the coastal waters. This type of upwelling was dominant in the Arica—Mejillones area. Coastal upwelling centres could be detected at 18° 30′ S., 19° 30′—20° 30′ S. and probably existed in other coastal areas located between 23° and 29° S. (see Fig. 41(b)).

The vertical distribution of sigma-t along 23° S. (Mejillones, Fig. 39(b)) showed that at the end of winter 1971, strong upwelling in the sigma-t cores of both the subantarctic and Equatorial subsurface waters; the former upwelled from 55 m to the surface and the latter, as referred to previously, rose from a depth of 190 m.

During the winter of 1972, the subtropical waters intruded into the whole of the coastal areas as far as or futher than, Antofagasta, making the subsurface water masses more stable (Fig. 42(a)). In the vertical distribution of sigma-t, corresponding to a latitude of 20° 10′ S. through Iquique (Fig. 42(b)), the subantarctic sigma-t core was observed to be stable at a depth of 80 m and the Equatorial subsurface core sank towards the coast. The same situation existed at the cross-section corresponding to 23° 40′ S. (Antofagasta, Fig. 42(c)). The upwelling focus was small and can be observed at 18° 30′ S. (Arica), and (possibly) at 23° 40′ S. (Fig. 42(a)).

In spring 1967, the upwelling was strong but restricted to a narrow strip due to the beginning of subtropical seasonal penetration. It would appear that the low salinity tongue of coastal water ($S <$ 34.8 per mille, Fig. 43(a)), was reinforced by upwelling of subantarctic origin; however, at Arica (18° 30′ S.) this water did not apparently reach the surface (Fig. 43(b)), but established a strong pycnocline. Upwelling centres could be detected at Arica, at 105 miles to the west of this port, between 19° 20′ S. and 21° 00′ S. and at 23° 40′ S. (Fig. 43(c)).

In spring 1971, subtropical water retreated from the coast and left a strip of upwelling; this corresponded to O_2 values of less than 2 ml/l located between 22° 30′ and 28° 10′ S. A remarkable centre of upwelling occurred at the Mejillones Peninsula 23° 10′ S. (Fig. 43(d)).

During spring 1972, the subtropical water was a little further from the coast than during the winter of the same years and consequently the upwelling zone was wider (fig. 44(a)). Figures 44(b), (c) and (d) show interesting variations in the sigma-t cores corresponding to subtropical, subantarctic and Equatorial subsurface waters at three profiles located at Arica, Mejillones and Caldera respectively. In the first profile (Fig. 44(b)), it was mainly mixed subtropical—subantarctic water which was upwelling. In the second (Fig. 44(c)), upwelling was related to mixed subtropical—subantarctic water at the exterior zone, and mixed subantarctic and equatorial subsurface water in the coastal zone; in the third (Fig. 44(d)), subantarctic water at the exterior zone and mixed subantarctic—Equatorial subsurface at the coast upwelled. Upwelling centres could be detected at 19° 50′ S., 20° 50′ S., 22° 40′ and 27° 50′ S. (Fig. 44(a)).

Conditions during spring 1973 were similar to those observed during spring 1967, with subtropical water intruding towards the coast and a tongue of water of relatively low salinities ($S <$ 34.7 per mille) moving from south to north (Fig. 45(a)). The sigma-t profiles for this season indicated subantarctic and Equatorial subsurface upwelling at Arica and

Mejillones (Figs. 45(b) and (c)). The former upwelled from 50 m to the surface and the latter from a depth of 80 m. The intense upwelling centres were probably located between 18°30′ and 20°20′ S. and between 21°40′ and 23°00′ S. (Fig. 45(d)).

In autumn 1967, subtropical water had retreated from the coast (Fig. 40) with coastal upwelling centres at 18°30′ S., between 19°10′ and 19°40′ S. and at 23°40′ S. (Fig. 39(c)). The profile presented (Fig. 39(a)) for a latitude of 28°10′ S. shows the subantarctic sigma-*t* core rising from 100 m depths to the surface.

In autumn 1969, subtropical water penetrated as far as 21° S. (Fig. 46(a)) and stabilized the subsurface conditions over the whole area except for a lens of low-salinity water at a latitude of 22° S. The strong stratification, which resulted from this situation, can be seen in the sigma-*t* profile at Iquique for this period (Fig. 46(b)).

Similar conditions to those observed during autumn 1967 seem to have been re-established during autumn 1973: subtropical waters retreated from the coast (Fig. 46(c)), which is a situation favouring the formation of several upwelling centres (expressed as a wide coastal strip of unsaturated O_2 values—see Figure 47(a). Upwelling foci were detected to the north and south of Arica at 21°20′ S. and at 23°00′ S. Sigma-*t* profiles traced for Mejillones and Caldera showed the subantarctic core rising to the surface from 75 and 50 m respectively (Figs. 47(b) and (c)).

Considerations of the upwelling during cold and warm periods

In cold winters (e.g. 1967 and 1971) the subantarctic water core ascended to the surface from an average depth of 48 m and from a position of about 40 miles offshore. The equatorial subsurface water core sank at a latitude of 20°10′ S. (Iquique) and ascended at 23°10′ S. (Mejillones).

During the warm winter of 1972, the subantarctic core was observed to be stratified at a depth of about 80 m and the Equatorial subsurface sank all along the coastline. These conditions were observed in association with the penetration or formation towards the coast of subtropical surface water.

Coastal upwelling centres, common to both warm and cold winters have been observed at 18°30′ S. (Arica), between 19°30′ and 20°30′ S. and at 23°40′ S. (Antofagasta). The O_2 values at these centres during the warm winter were higher than during similar cold periods.

During cold springs (1967 and 1973), the subantarctic core was rising from an average depth of 49 m and from a mean distance of 45 miles offshore. The Equatorial subsurface core ascended from a depth of 95 m to 36 m from a mean distance of 39 miles off the coast.

In the warm spring period of 1972, the subantarctic core upwelled from 58 m to 28 m from a mean distance of 27 miles offshore at 18°30′ S., 19°50′ S., 22°10′ S., and 23°40′ S.; also, from 83 m depth up to the surface at 23°00′ S., 25°10′ S. and 27°10′ S. The Equatorial subsurface core is observed to have stratified or sunk over the whole area, except at latitudes 18°30′ and 27°10′ S., where some weak uprisings could be seen.

The common upwelling foci for both warm and cold springs were located at 18°50′ S., 23°00′ S., 25°00′ S. and 28°00′ S.

In cold autumns (1967 and 1973), the subantarctic core rose from an average depth of 71 m up to 9 m and from a mean distance of 35 miles from the coast. The Equatorial subsurface core rose from 150 m to 100 m depth and from a mean distance of 32 miles offshore.

During the warm autumn of 1969, the subantarctic core upwelled from 50 m to the surface and from a distance of 20 miles offshore of Arica (18°30′ S.). However, to the south of this area and at 20°10′ S. and 23°40′ S., this core was observed to be stratified at a depth of 53 m. The Equatorial subsurface core was stratified at 18°30′ S. (Arica) and had sunk at latitudes corresponding to Iquique and Antofagasta.

The coastal upwelling foci, common to both warm and cold autumns were located at 18°30′ S., 19°30′ S., 22°00′ S. and 23°40′ S.

THE PELAGIC FISHERIES AS RELATED TO COLD AND WARM PERIODS

The surface layers of the coastal zone (which support the anchovy, sardine, jack and bonito fisheries) are usually formed by the upper portions of the subantarctic waters. The feature that best indicates the deepest limit of these waters is the layer of minimum O_2, which can reach the surface through the upwelling processes; this has important biological implications.

The anchovy, one of the best studied pelagic species, seems to be well adapted to an upwelling type of environment—its vertical distribution generally does not extend to a depth of more than 50 m. During warm conditions the species is normally observed either concentrated at some points along the coastline (when it is particuarly vulnerable to fishing) or dispersed throughout the whole of the coastal waters. The horizontal distribution of the species does not seem to exceed 50 miles from the coast and is probably limited by the warmer conditions further offshore. The sardine and jack seem to behave in a similar way; however, the bonito seems to prefer warmer waters. The catches of these four species, divided into fishing areas (see Table 2), can be generally associated with cold and warm periods. The anchovy data (representing 1966—73) showed a constant decrease in annual catch, interrupted only by 1971 which was a cold year. In 1971, nearly a million tons of anchovy were caught in the three fishing areas. Figures for the sardine and jack catches conversely show a constant rise though also with maxima during 1971. By contrast, the bonito catches were at their maximum during the exceptionally warm year of 1972 and decreased considerably the following year.

In the following paragraphs, an attempt is made to describe in more detail the possible relationship between variations in the relative abundance of these resources and the observed surface oceanographic conditions. Three graphs have been prepared for this purpose, which present the anchovy catch per unit of effort (c.p.u.e.) as an index of the relative abundance of this species for each quarter of the year. The quarterly average of surface $T°$ and S per mille are plotted against this index, for the Arica (Fig. 48(a)), Iquique (Fig. 48(b)) and Antofagasta (Fig. 48(c)) fishing areas. The temperature and salinity have been averaged from data collected between the coastline and a longitude of $71°$ W. A fourth diagram (Fig. 49) relates, for the same three areas, the monthly average of the annual c.p.u.e. of anchovy (1964—73), Spanish sardine, jack and bonito (1969—73) to the annual, thermal sea-surface deviations (as compared with a nine-year average—1965—73).

Arica and Iquique

The areas are described together because they both showed similar tendencies in variation of surface temperature and salinity, and the relative abundance of anchovy (c.p.u.e.). Figures 48(a) and (b) show a general seasonal pattern in the c.p.u.e. and in the surface oceanographic conditions; high values are centred about spring/summer and low values during autumn/winter. Superimposed upon this general seasonal pattern is the influence of the warm and cold periods. This influence, as expected, has a lag effect in relation to the c.p.u.e.

Thus, the dominant warm period during 1965 could influence the c.p.u.e. corresponding to both that year and the following summer (note the reduced maximum centred about the first quarter of 1966), in such a way that they are, on the average, lower than during the other years. A further warm period centred about the first quarter of 1967 could overlap on the conditions observed for 1965—66, and create an abnormal seasonal pattern with low c.p.u.e. during that summer (1967). This is more clearly shown in Figure 48(a) for the Arica fishing area.

Exeptionally cold conditions during the last half of 1967 may have aided the recovery of the anchovy, as shown in the c.p.u.e. for the whole of 1968 and the first quarter of 1969. This tendency would be countered by the appearance of a new warm period over virtually the whole of 1969 so that it seems to have repeated during 1970, (with both a higher intensity and extremes) the conditions observed during summer 1967.

The dominant cold period from the end of 1970 and into most of 1971 corresponds to the very high c.p.u.e. in 1971. In contrast to the seasonal pattern prevalent in the other years, the maximum c.p.u.e. in 1971 occurred during the autumn/winter quarters and was not centred about summer.

The extraordinarily warm period that followed, and whose first effects were detected at the end of 1971, seemed to affect the relative abundance of anchovy during 1972 and 1973 in such a way that only at the end of 1973 and early 1974 was recovery observed. This, as described, coincided with the new cold period late in 1973 (and was apparently well developed during 1974 though data is not included in this article).

Antofagasta

This zone is more influenced by subantarctic waters, as shown by the lower average temperatures and salinities; this is due to the dominant subantarctic upwelling regime which is particularly marked in the zone throughout the year.

The general seasonal and periodic patterns exhibited by Arica and Iquique are reproduced here (Fig. 48(c)). However, and probably as a consequence of the dominant subantartic regime, fluctuations in c.p.u.e. were more extreme with respect to warm and cold periods and sometimes behaved differently from those in the other two areas. This can be deduced by observing the c.p.u.e. for the warm period of 1969–70; after a partial recovery during the first quarter of 1970, high c.p.u.e. values were not observed until the following cold period centred about 1971. However, the remarkably warm period which followed (1972–73), would have greatly affected the relative abundance of anchovy in this area where, as in the other areas, a recovery was not detected until the end of 1973 and the first quarter of 1974.

Figure 49 emphasizes the possible relationships between cold and warm years and the annual monthly average c.p.u.e. of anchovy for each of the three fishing areas; included in the figure are similar comparisons for the c.p.u.e. of Spanish sardine, jack and bonito. Bonito appears to have behaved differently from the other three species, i.e. its relative abundance increased during warm periods. This is in accordance with the preference that bonito show for warmer and more oceanic environments. If the c.p.u.e. curves are examined and correlated—particularly those from the Iquique and Antofagasta fishing areas—interesting interrelationships between the relative abundance of these species appear to exist, particularly as expressed in differences in c.p.u.e. between anchovy, jack and Spanish sardine.

These considerations seem to indicate a relationship between cold and warm periods and the relative abundance of fish (as expressed as c.p.u.e.). In order to establish better correlations and eventually to be able to create model systems, improved and increased oceanographic information and biological and biological—fishery parameters will be required. Anadditional (and substantial) problem to solve is how variations in the fishing effort affect these environmental changes; it is also necessary to examine the probable cumulative effects of all the oceanographic, biological and fisheries variables on long-term changes in the yield of these resources. From the pointof view of fishery—oceanography, a further aspect of particular interest is to examine how the different rates of change from a warm to a cold period can contribute in increasing the relative abundance of coastal pelagic resources during the subsequent fishing season. Examples of this effect seem to be evident in comparing observations made of conditions in 1967 and 1968 and particularly in 1969–70 and 1971.

Conclusions

The methodology developed for data analysis and the discussions presented in the preceding articles

confirm that water masses between the surface and 1,000 m and originating in subtropical and subantarctic zones can be described by their characteristics and in terms of their influence on the zone covered by the present investigation. The method followed, based mainly on the determination of the sigma-*t* core values which characterize these water masses, makes it possible to compare the properties and positions of the water masses in the zone with those previously described for similar depths in more extensive offshore areas of the south-eastern Pacific.

Variations observed in the subtropical, subantarctic and Equatorial subsurface waters indicate that these water masses exhibit marked seasonal fluctuations. Interaction between these waters, particularly in the coastal zone, seems also to be very important. In relation to this interaction, it is possible that, predominantly during the autumns, the surface conditions reinforce subsurface water characteristics to depths of 400 m or more. This mixing process and eventual formation of water masses seems to be more prominent during dominantly warm periods at the surface, closely related to the large-scale meteorological and oceanographic conditions that cause them.

The horizontal circulation, as a dynamic expression of these processes, in its surface and subsurface characteristics, has also been described in a way more detailed than in the past. The most important features observed in the surface circulation are the confirmation of the separation of the subantarctic flux towards the north (Humboldt current) at about 30° S. and the eventual development of a seasonal coastal countercurrent towards the south of subtropical characteristics (Chilean coastal countercurrent) between the position of the subantarctic flux and the coastline. Although exhibiting a marked zonal notation, these two fluxes, in their origin and development, must be dependent on larger-scale processes which, in turn, are reinforced during cold and warm periods. Thus, during cold periods the subantarctic flux of the Humboldt current towards the north must contribute to reinforce the circulation at the Peruvian coast known as the 'Peru coastal current'. Conversely, during warm periods, the prevailing conditions in the north and west of the zone (apparently reinforced locally in the so-called 'Arica-Mejillones lens') should manifest themselves in the coastal subtropical penetration towards the south—defined as the Chilean coastal countercurrent. In the subsurface layers, the most important feature described is the actual separation of the Equatorial subsurface flux towards the south into two branches on either side of the Humboldt current; these demonstrate considerable latitudinal extension, particularly on the coastal side (Peru—Chile undercurrent).

The upwelling processes, supported by the dominant south and south-west winds also show interesting seasonal and zonal fluctuations in relation to cold and warm periods and the interaction of different water masses. It can thus be deduced that coastal upwelling is stronger is the zone from late winter to the early summer of cold periods. Upwelling is generally weak during warm periods and seasons. However, this general pattern can have important local exceptions.

In the northern part of the area (Arica—Iquique) and related to the development of the Arica—Mejillones lens, the upwelling seems to be preferentially supplied by Equatorial subsurface waters; south of Mejillones, the upwelling seems to be preferentially subantarctic. The location of the upwelling centres is also persistent, particularly those observed off the Mejillones Peninsula.

Finally, the investigation seems to have demonstrated the close relationship between the seasonal and periodical environmental changes and the variation in the relative abundance of coastal pelagic resources of the northern Chilean zone.

The general review of the main conclusions derived from the present study emphasizes only some of the many interesting problems that require the attention of oceanographers, biologists and fishery specialists interested in the zone. The peculiarities observed in the area (for example, its sensitivity—particularly in its coastal region—to the large-scale processes that produce the warm and cold conditions) are so attractive as to justify integrated research effort in the area. The size of the zone permits such an investigation to be performed with comparatively limited resources and support. In addition to investigating the characteristics of the area, it is also possible to speculate about the small-scale similarities shown by the oceanographic, biological and fishery conditions in this zone to the large-scale processes along the Peruvian coast. For example, the following similarities should be considered: at the northern limit of both areas there appears to be a dominantly subtropical regime with upwelling primarily supported by Equatorial subsurface waters; there are also mainly subantarctic regimes in the south of both zones (the large upwelling centre of San Juan—located off southern Peru — and the quasi-permanent upwelling focus of Mejillones—south of northern Chile); and the largest pelagic catches of both regions are made in their northern parts (north of about 14° S. in Peru, and approximately between Arica and Iquique in Chile).

All the preceding information indicates a number of interesting problems which require examination:

Possible correlation between Equatorial subsurface upwellings and the relative abundance of coastal pelagic resources which seem to be associated with them.

The role that a subantarctic reinforcement from the south has in increasing the upwellings and the general circulation.

The processes resulting in the stable presence (or formation) of water of Equatorial subsurface characteristics during warm periods and its subsequent upwelling during the next cold period.

The actual correlation existing among all these oceanographic factors with critical stages in the life cycle of the coastal pelagic species (e.g. spawning, larval drift, food, recruitment etc.) in turn, related to the fluctuations in the relative abundance of these resources.

Solutions to all these problems will require an increasingly integrated and multidisciplinary study of all these factors and will require international co-operation among countries already directly involved. The establishment of regional monitoring systems, with ample exchange of oceanographic—meteorological information of high quality, would also contribute significantly to this end and assist in the more specific study of selected areas.

Acknowledgements

The authors wish to thank the following for their help in processing the information covered in the present study (all from the Oceanographic Section of IFOP): J. R. Cañón for computation listings; J. Pineda for vertical profiles of temperature, salinity, oxygen and sigma-t; R. Golusda, L. Contreras, J. Echeverría, B. Mariangel and B. Lorca for tabulation and graph plotting.

In addition, this study would not have been possible without the support and collaboration of many people from the Chilean Fisheries Development Institute (IFOP). A large number of people took part in the collection and processing of the data used; many of these people are not now at IFOP (for reasons not related to them or the oceanographic sciences), but their dedication and efforts are to be acknowledged.

Also instrumental in completing this article were the facilities provided by the head of the Resources Department of IFOP, Mr Oscar Guzmán.

The authors' gratitude is also expressed to: Ethel Nario and Maria Antonieta de la Jara for preparing the graphics; Patricia Valenzuela, Eliana Veas and Marión Reid for typing the manuscript; and Sergio Meneses for the final presentation.

The Soviet scientists and crews of the vessels *Nogliki* and *Ecliptica* are to be recognized and thanked for their co-operation during eight of the twenty-four cruises (as one of the many valuable attributes of the former Chile—U.S.S.R. Agreement on Fisheries Development).

Heartfelt thanks are extended to Carlota de Robles and Dr M. B. Collins (Department of Oceanography, University College Swansea) for their collaboration in, respectively, organizing the manuscript and revising the English version of this article.

Finally, the authors wish to thank Ms J. Greengo for typing the English version of the manuscript.

Table 1. Data, periods and zones covered by twenty-four oceanographic cruises (see also Fig. 1)

Cruises	Zone	Period (month/year)	Ocean station	$T^\circ C$ to depths of (m)	S to depths of (m)	O_2 ml/l to depths of (m)
IFOP 34 (2) 67 CD	Arica—Caldera,74° W.	May, June 1967	48	500	500	500
Scorpio	28°15' S., 81° W.	June 1967	11	1,000	1,000	1,000
IFOP 35 (2) 67 CD	Iquique—San Felix, 80° W.	June 1967	35	500	500	500
IFOP 37 (3) 67 CD	Arica—Caldera, 72° W.	August 1967	18	500	500	500
Marchile VI	Arica—Valparaíso, 80° W.	September 1967	104	1,000	1,000	1,000
IFOP 41 (4) 67 CD	Arica-28°30' S, 74° W.	November, December 1967	58	500	500	500
IFOP 66 (2) 69 CD	Arica—Valparaíso, 74° W.	May, June 1969	56	800	800	800
IFOP 95 (3) 71 NG	19°30' S.—30°00' S., 75° W.	September 1971	17	300	300	300
IFOP 97 (4) 71 NG	24°13' S.—25°00' S., 75° W.	October, November 1971	—	0	0	—
IFOP 98 (4) 71 NG	22°00' S.—30°00' S., 73° W.	November, December 1971	18	300	300	300
IFOP 100 (4) 71 NG	Iquique 30°00' S., 73° W.	December 1971	9	300	300	300
IFOP 105 (2) 72 NG	Antofagasta—Caldera, 72° W.	May 1972	—	0	0	—
IFOP 106 (2–3) 72 CP	Arica 28°00' S., 74° W.	June, July 1972	53	1,000	1,000	1,000
IFOP 107 (3) 72 NG	Arica—Caldera, 74° W.	July, August 1972	—	0	0	—
IFOP 109 (3) 72 NO	Arica—Mejillones, 71° W.	September 1972	11	250	250	250
IFOP 113 (4) 72 NG	22°00' S.—25° 30' S., 72° W.	November 1972	—	0	0	—
IFOP 114 (4) 72 CP A & B	Arica—Caldera, 73° W.	November, December 1972	114	1,000	1,000	1,000
IFOP 116 (1) 73 CP	Antofagasta 28°00' S., 72° W.	February, March 1973	—	0	—	—
IFOP 118 (2) 73 CP	Arica—Antofagasta, 72° W.	March, April 1973	67	200	200	200
IFOP 121 (2) 73 EC	25°30' S.—30°00' S., 74° W.	March, April 1973	13	200	200	200
IFOP 129 (3) 73 CP	Antofagasta—Caldera, 72° W.	July 1973	—	0	0	—
IFOP 130 (3) 73 CP	Arica—Mejillones, 73° W.	July, August 1973	43	0	0	—
IFOP 133 (4) 73 NO	Arica—Mejillones, 72° W.	July 1973	20	100	100	100
IFOP 134 (1) 74 NO	Arica—Mejillones, 72° W.	January 1974	—	0	0	—

Table 2. Catches of four species of fish, divided into fishing areas (in tons)

Fishing areas	Species	Year							
		1966	1967	1968	1969	1970	1971	1972	1973
Arica (18°20'-19°30' S.)	Anchovy	385,947	173,552	462,046	266,763	173,538	483,118	149,729	77,923
	Sardine				949	4,228	10,050	5,151	3,080
	Jack				212	26,536	20,052	16,588	2,225
	Bonito				395	61	691	1,246	30
Iquique (19°30'-31°30' S.)	Anchovy	494,475	341,058	380,643	227,503	307,531	287,504	121,429	60,768
	Sardine				148	4,431	13,538	381	29,946
	Jack				729	137,297	150,985	36,844	54,382
	Bonito				339	365	464	643	342
Antofagasta (21°30'-24°02' S.)	Anchovy	147,126	176,016	113,621	145,752	140,602	138,279	29,151	7,438
	Sardine				1,860	5,227	2,235	5,299	17,771
	Jack				2,615	11,378	13,463	9,204	15,155
	Bonito				101	293	7	25	31

Table 3. Sigma-*t* 25.9 and 26.4 averages for the Arica-Caldera, 73° W. zone during the seasons considered.

Seasons	Year	Sigma-*t* 25.9			Sigma-*t* 26.4		
		Mean depth (m)	Range (m)	Data	Mean depth (m)	Range (m)	Data
Autumn	1967	34	0–73	44	119	63–215	35
Winter	1967	40	7–108	40	115	42–217	43
Spring	1967	31	2–129	47	107	20–147	47
Autumn	1969	60	27–139	33	159	102–214	29
Spring	1971	37	1–67	25	110	54–204	27
Winter	1972	63	42–103	47	168	90–267	36
Spring	1972	41	9–112	85	167	75–327	52
Autumn	1973	30	3–70	44	113	20–170	27
Spring	1973[1]	28	3–78	19	63	21–92	12

1. Data only down to a depth of 100 m.

Table 4. Averages for the O_2 minimum layer, for the Arica–Caldera, 73° W. zone, during the seasons under consideration.

Seasons		Average O_2 (ml/l)	Average (m)	Range (m)	Data
Autumn	1967	0.56	149	10–400	46
Winter	1967	0.41	175	30–380	50
Spring	1967	0.34	149	20–500	40
Autumn	1969	0.36	141	20–302	45
Spring	1971	0.30	229	47–298	44
Winter	1972	0.36	192	50–457	51
Spring	1972	0.33	131	25–438	76
Autumn	1973	0.36	141	20–302	45
Spring	1973[1]	0.74	70	20–100	19

1. Data only down to a depth of 100 m.

Table 5. $T°$ C and S per mille data used to derive the average seasonal T/S curves in Figures 2(a),(b),(c) and (d) for the research area 18°30'-27°10' S., 70°00' W.

Cruise	Year	T/S data	Cruise	Year	T/S data
Winter			*Summer*		
Marchile II	1962	742	IFOP 8	1965	447
IFOP 13	1965	410	IFOP 18	1966	105
IFOP 25	1966	124	IFOP 57	1969	126
Marchile VI	1967	462	IFOP 59	1969	166
IFOP 37	1967	143	Total		844
IFOP 106	1972	148			
IFOP 109	1972	25	*Autumn*		
IFOP 129	1973	89	CHIPER	1960	62
IFOP 130	1973	292	IFOP 11	1965	464
Total		2,435	IFOP 24	1966	71
Spring			IFOP 34	1967	411
STEP 1	1960	104	IFOP 35	1967	48
IFOP 15	1965	654	IFOP 44	1968	28
IFOP 28	1966	63	IFOP 66	1969	265
IFOP 41	1967	415	IFOP 81	1970	156
Ak. Kurchatov	1968	260	IFOP 106	1972	26
IFOP 50	1968	113	IFOP 118	1973	215
IFOP 74	1969	166	IFOP 121	1973	51
IFOP 95	1971	105	Total		1,797
IFOP 98	1971	94			
IFOP 100	1971	49			
IFOP 114	1972	647			
IFOP 133	1973	95			
Total		2,765			

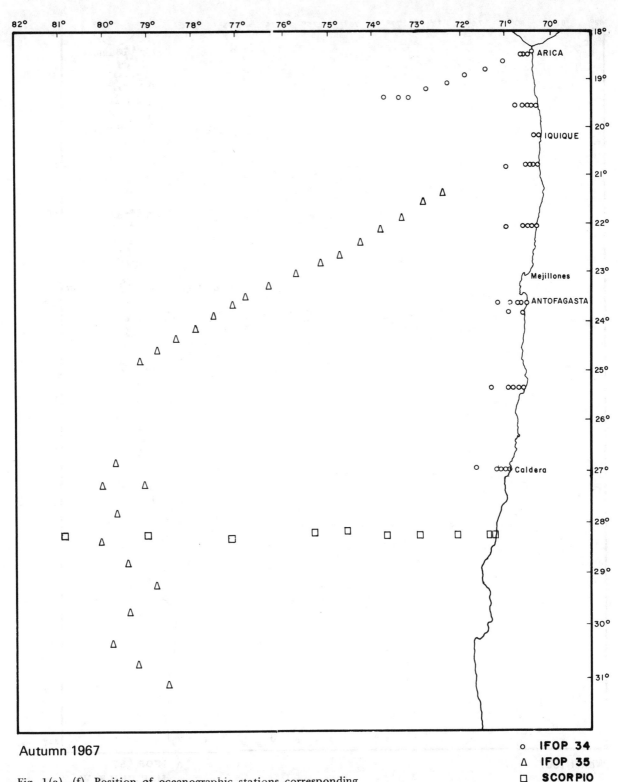

Autumn 1967

	o	IFOP 34
	△	IFOP 35
	□	SCORPIO

o ,△ □ Oceanographic stations

Fig. 1(a)–(f). Position of oceanographic stations corresponding to the twenty-four cruises covered, grouped in twelve seasonal periods (see Table 1).

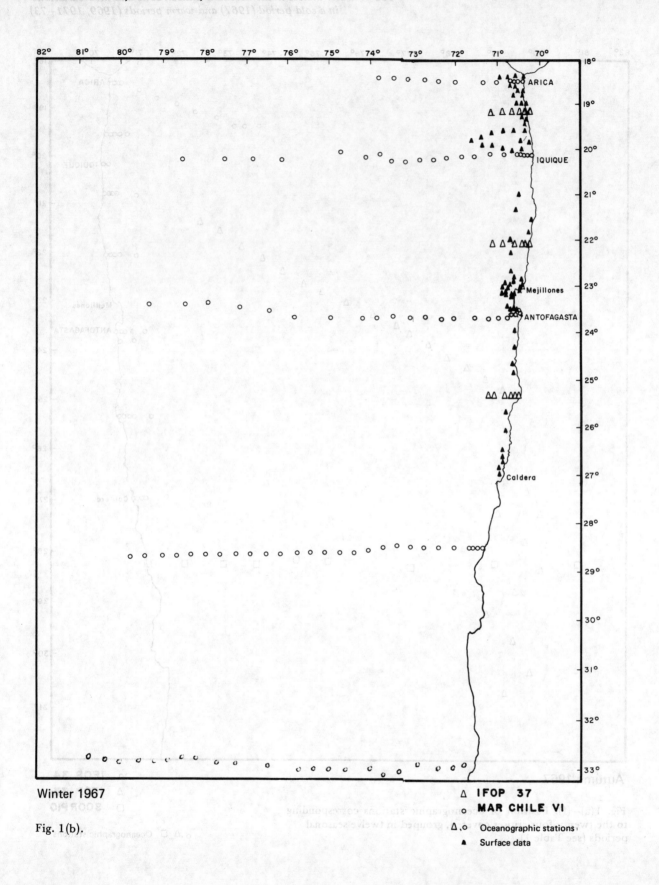

Winter 1967

Fig. 1(b).

△ **IFOP 37**
○ **MAR CHILE VI**

△,○ Oceanographic stations
▲ Surface data

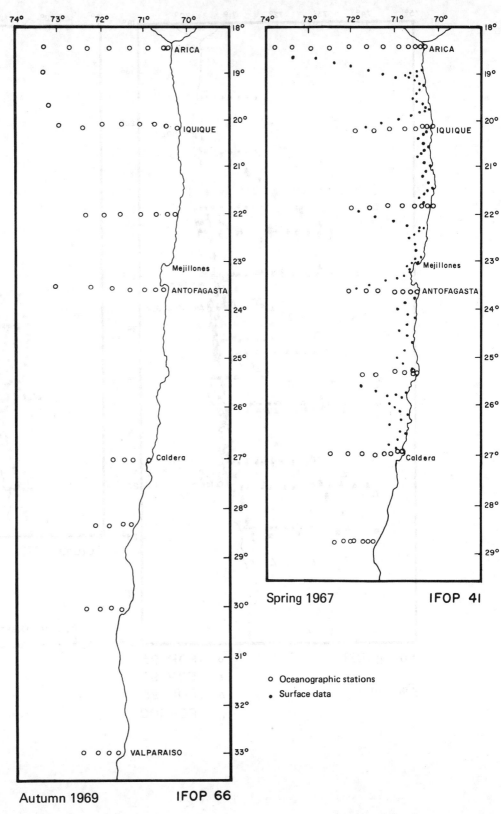

Fig. 1(c).

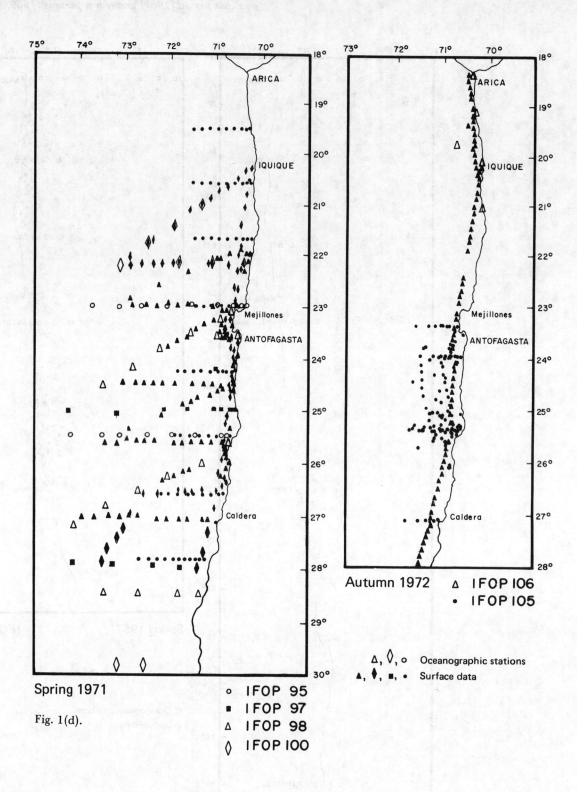

Spring 1971

Fig. 1(d).

	IFOP 95
o	IFOP 95
■	IFOP 97
△	IFOP 98
◊	IFOP 100

Autumn 1972

| △ | IFOP 106 |
| • | IFOP 105 |

△, ◊, o Oceanographic stations
▲, ◆, ■, • Surface data

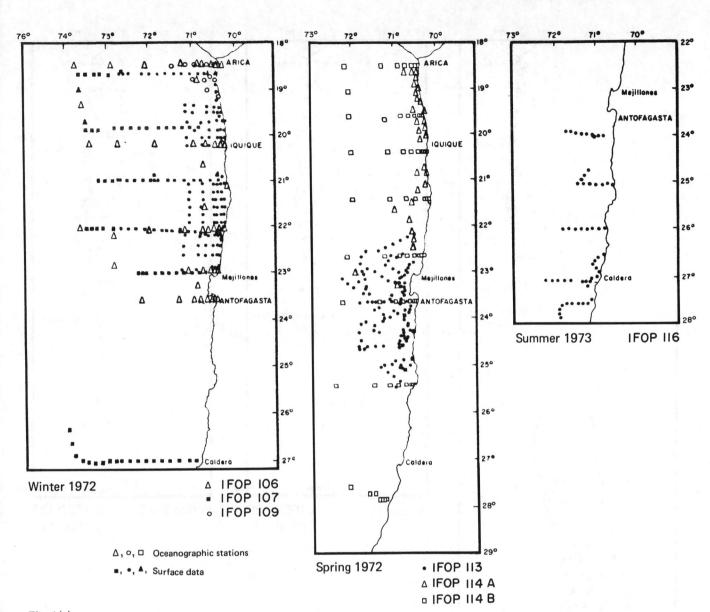

Winter 1972   △ IFOP 106
                               ■ IFOP 107
                               ○ IFOP 109

△, ○, □ Oceanographic stations

■, ●, ▲, Surface data

Spring 1972   ● IFOP 113
                     △ IFOP 114 A
                     □ IFOP 114 B

Summer 1973   IFOP 116

Fig. 1(e).

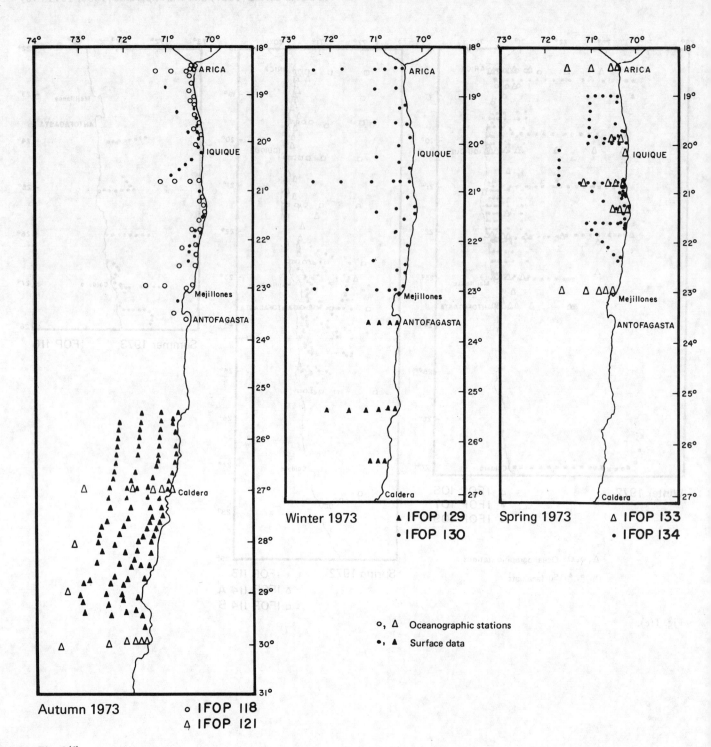

Autumn 1973   o **IFOP 118**
                     Δ **IFOP 121**

Winter 1973   ▲ **IFOP 129**
                     • **IFOP 130**

Spring 1973   Δ **IFOP 133**
                     • **IFOP 134**

o, Δ Oceanographic stations
•, ▲ Surface data

Fig. 1(f).

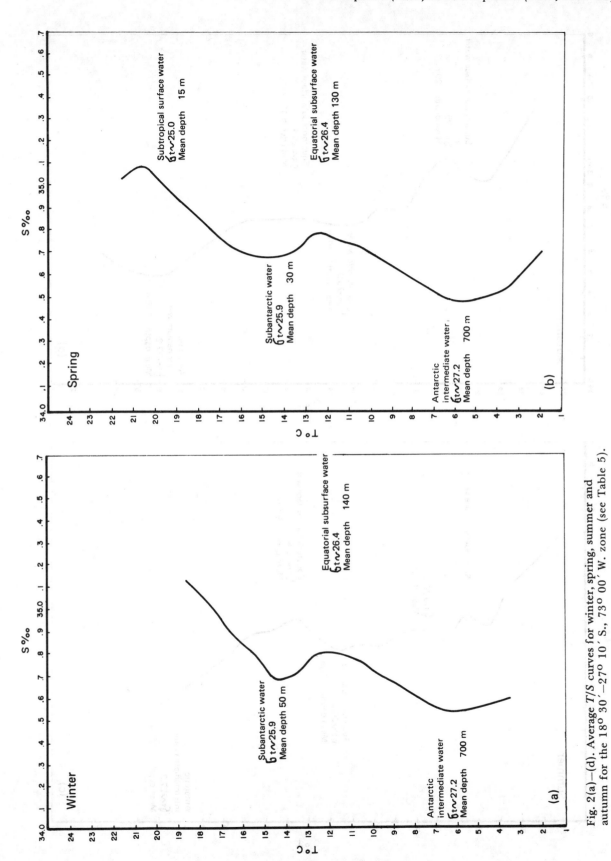

Fig. 2(a)–(d). Average *T/S* curves for winter, spring, summer and autumn for the 18° 30′–27° 10′ S., 73° 00′ W. zone (see Table 5).

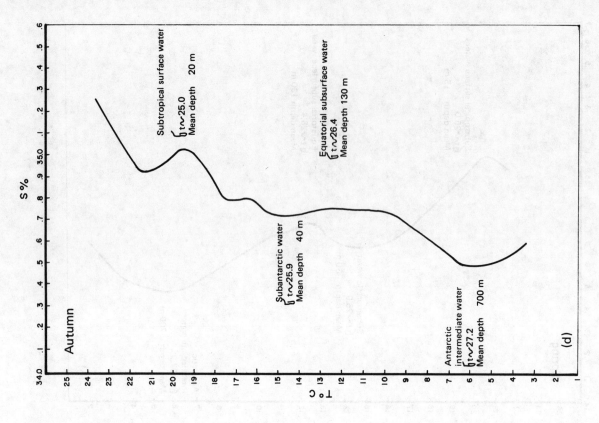

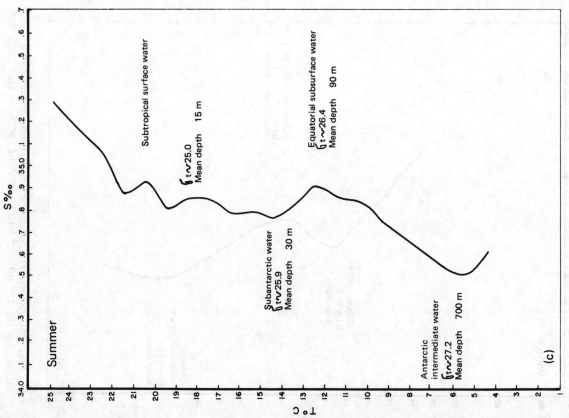

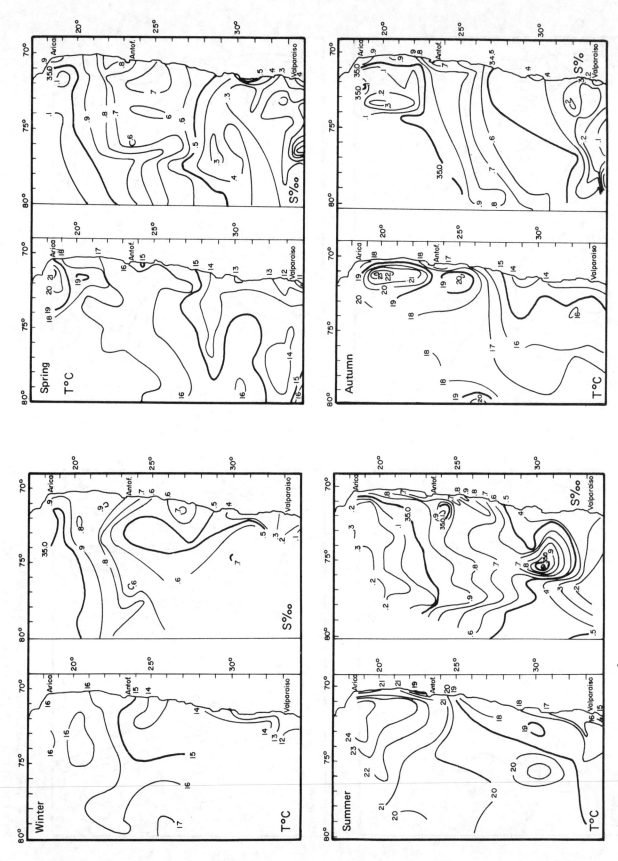

Fig. 3. Average distribution of T° C and S per mille at zero m for winter, spring, summer and autumn (Inostroza, 1972).

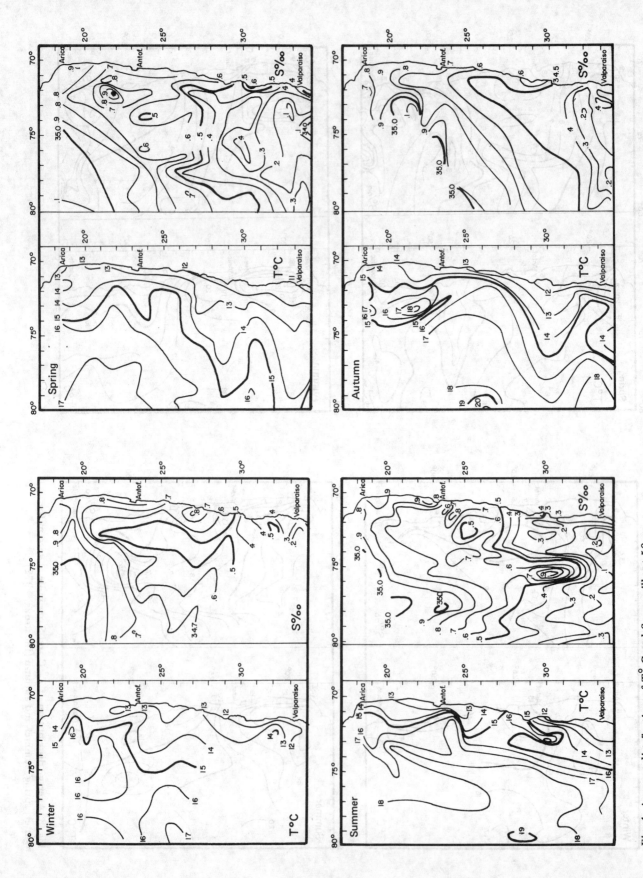

Fig. 4. Average distribution of $T°$ C and S per mille at 50 m for winter, spring, summer and autumn (Inostraza, 1972).

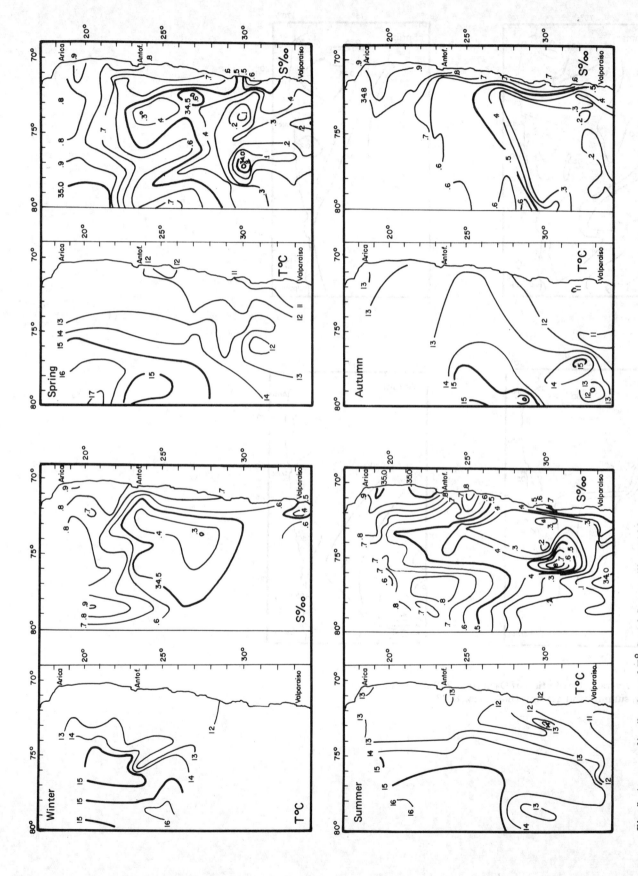

Fig. 5. Average distribution of T° C and S per mille at 100 m for winter, spring, summer and autumn (Inostraza, 1972).

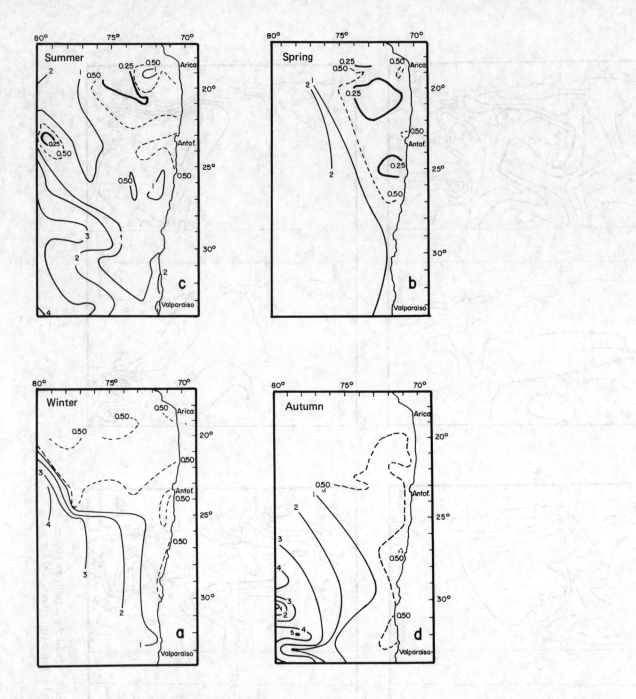

Fig. 6. Average distribution of O_2 ml/l at 200 m for winter, spring, summer and autumn (Inostraza, 1972).

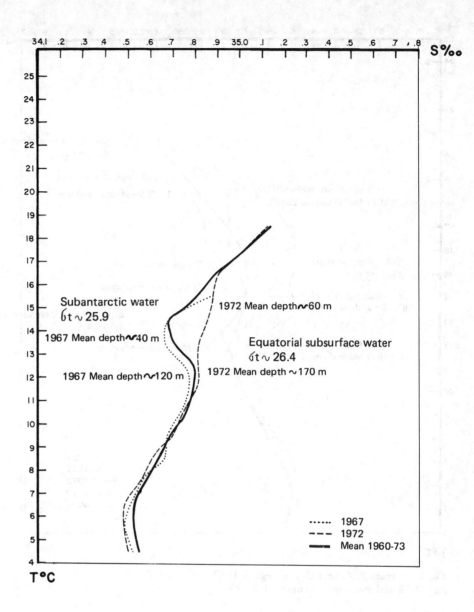

Fig. 7. Average *T/S* curves for winters of 1967 and 1972 and
mean winter curve 1960—73.

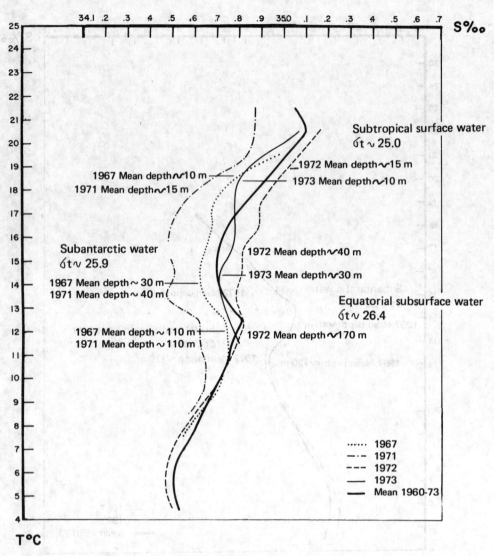

Fig. 8. Average *T/S* curves for springs of 1967, 1971, 1972
and 1973 and mean spring curve 1960—73.

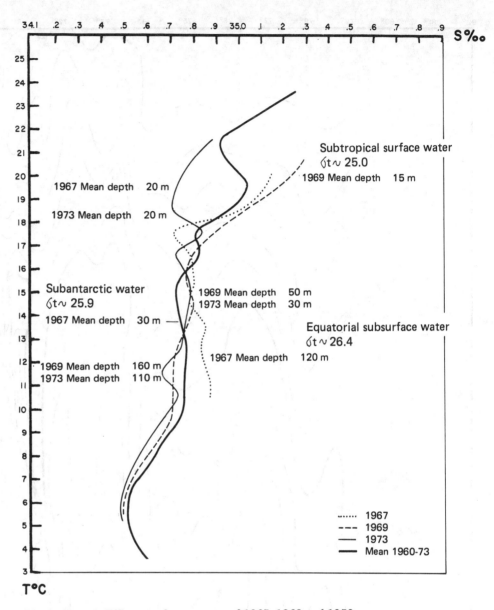

Fig. 9. Average *T/S* curves for autumns of 1967, 1969 and 1973 and mean autumn curve 1960—73.

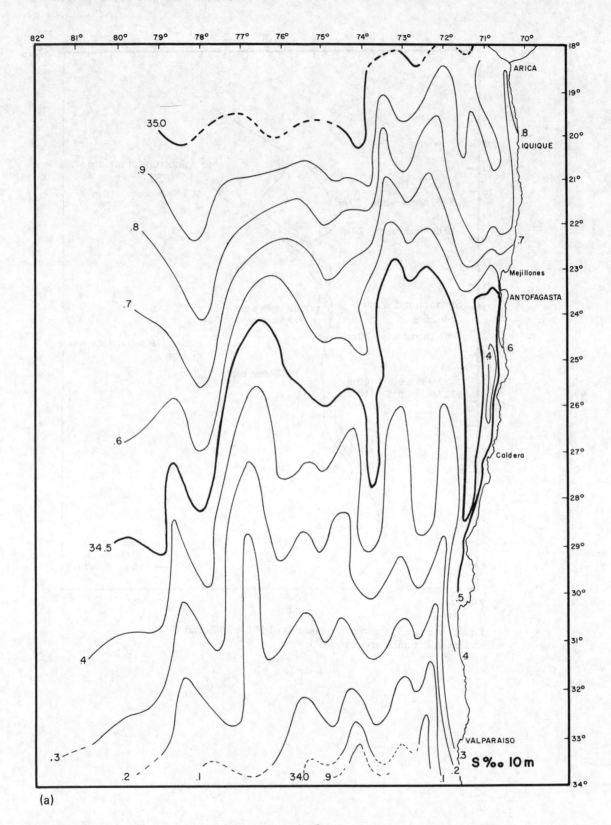

(a)

Fig. 10. Winter 1967: (a) *S* per mille, at 10 m; (b) *T*° C
at zero m; (c) *S* per mille minimum; (d) *S* per mille
maximum; and (e) *O*$_2$ ml/l minimum.

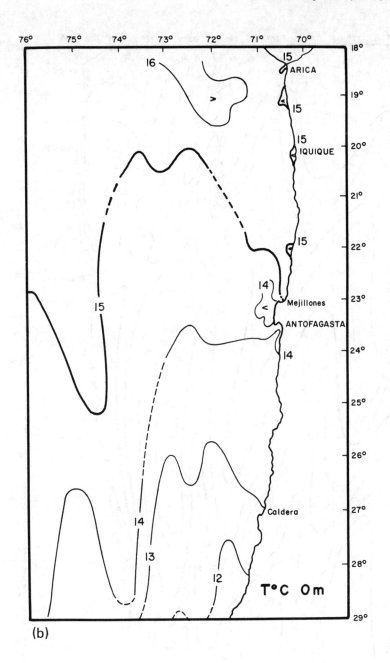

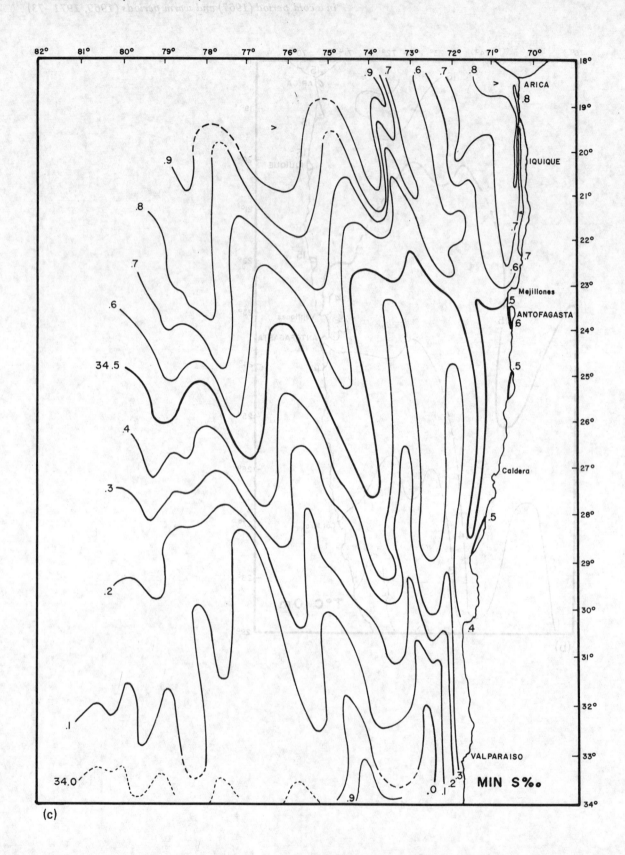

(c)

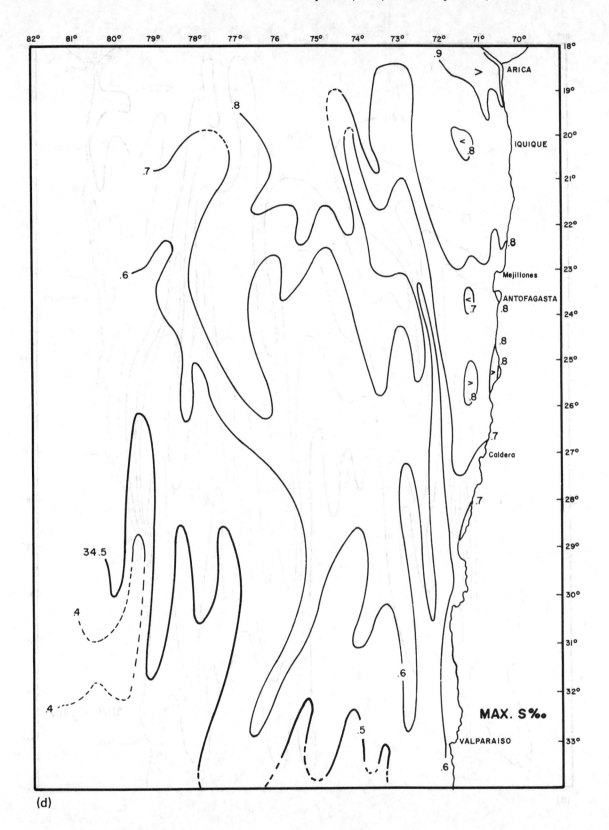

(d)

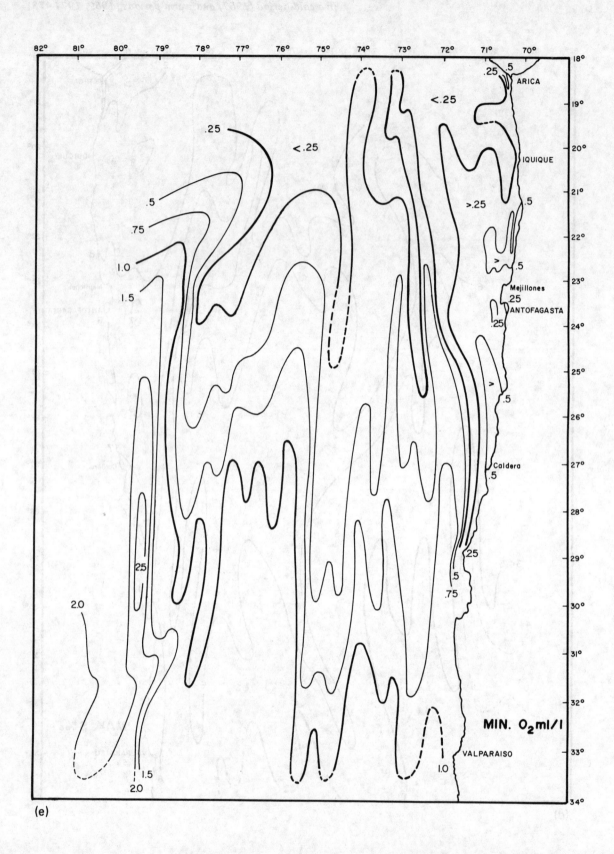

(e)

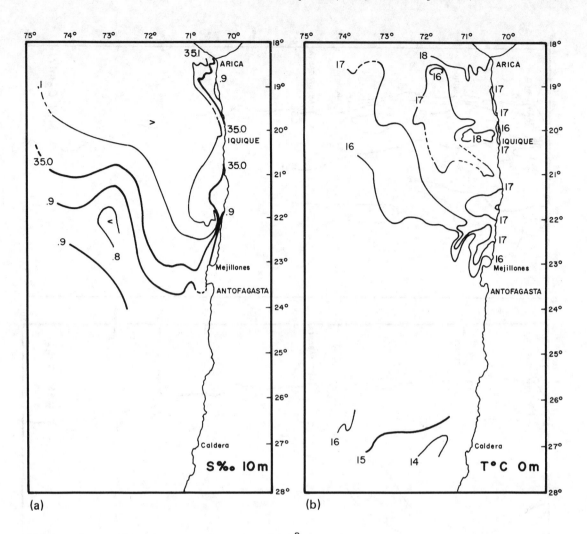

Fig. 11. Winter 1972: (a) *S* per mille at 10 m; (b) *T*° C at
zero m; (c) *S* per mille minimum; (d) *S* per mille maximum;
and (e) O$_2$ ml/l minimum.

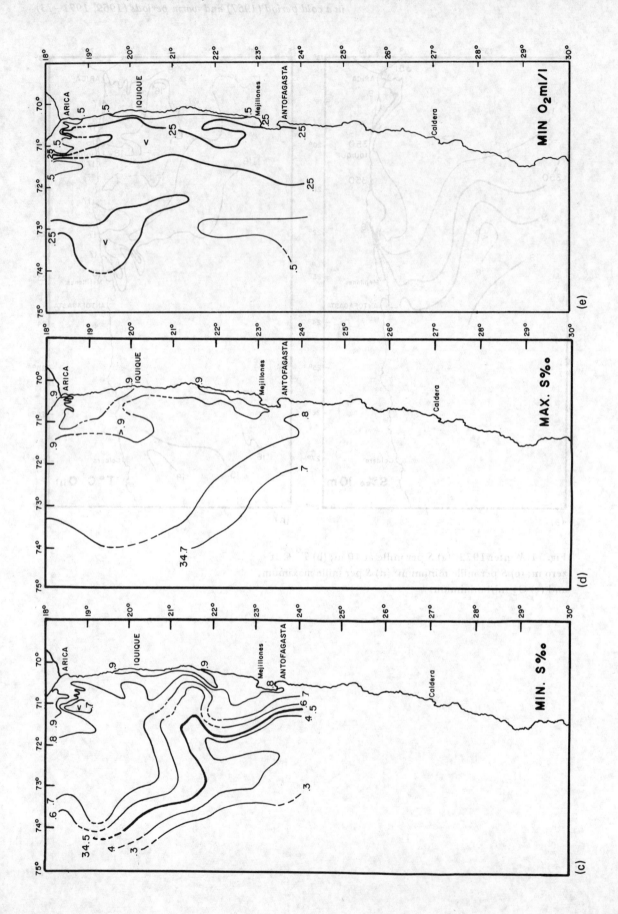

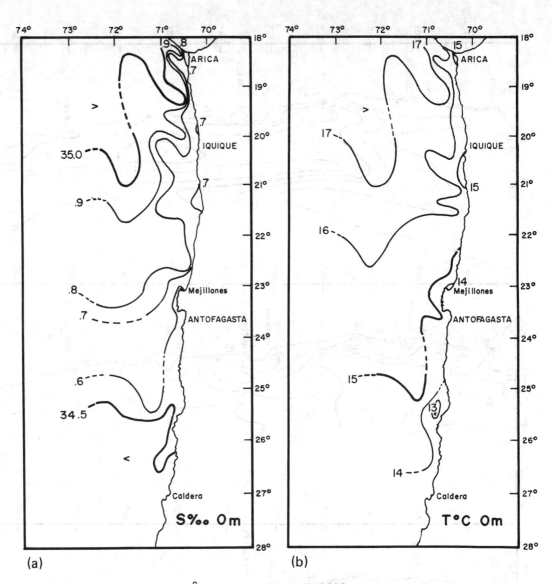

(a)

(b)

Fig. 12(a),(b). *S* per mille and *T*° C at zero m for winter 1973.

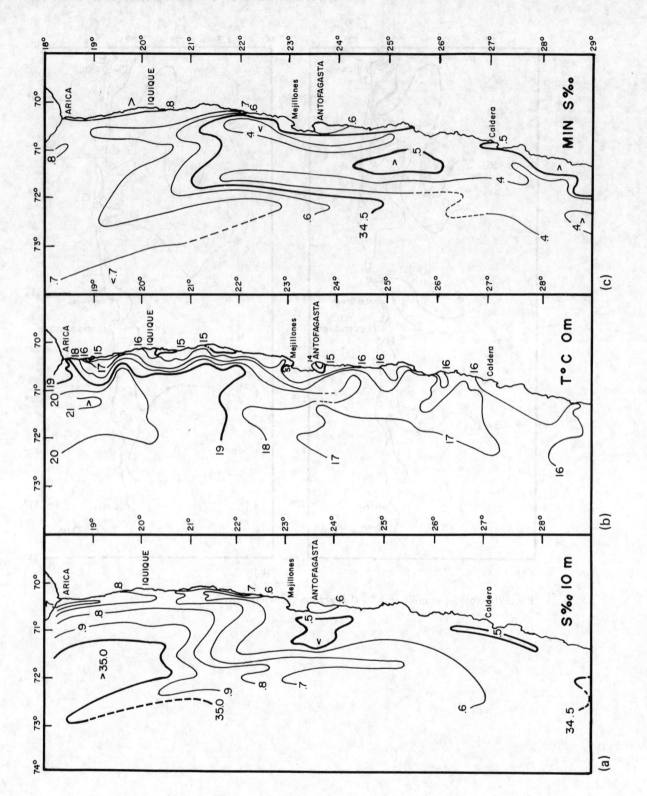

Fig. 13. Spring 1972: (a) *S* per mille at 10 m; (b) *T*° C at zero m; (c) *S* per mille minimum; (d) *S* per mille maximum; and (e) O$_2$ ml/l minimum.

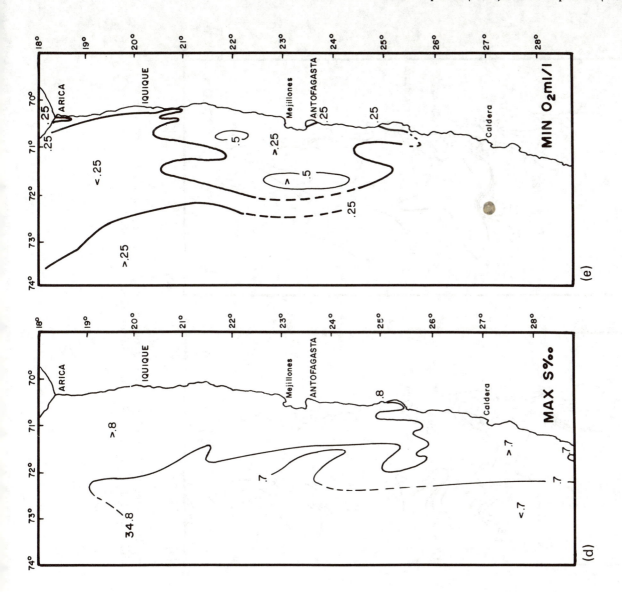

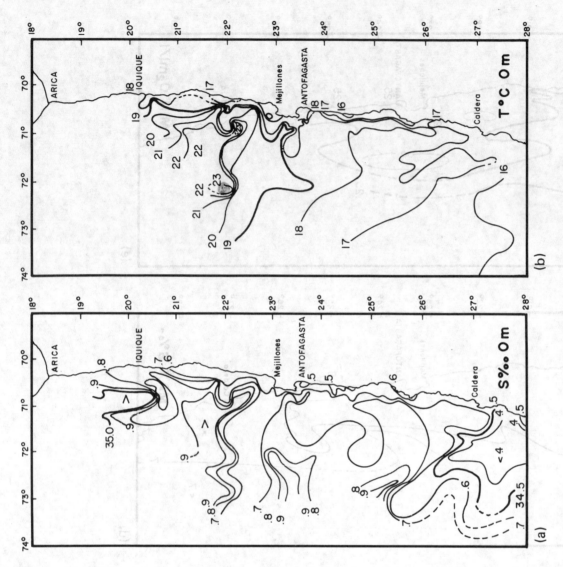

Fig. 14. Spring 1971 : (a) *S* per mille at zero m ; (b) *T°* C at zero m ; (c) *S* per mille minimum; (d) *S* per mille maximum ; and (e) O$_2$ ml/l minimum.

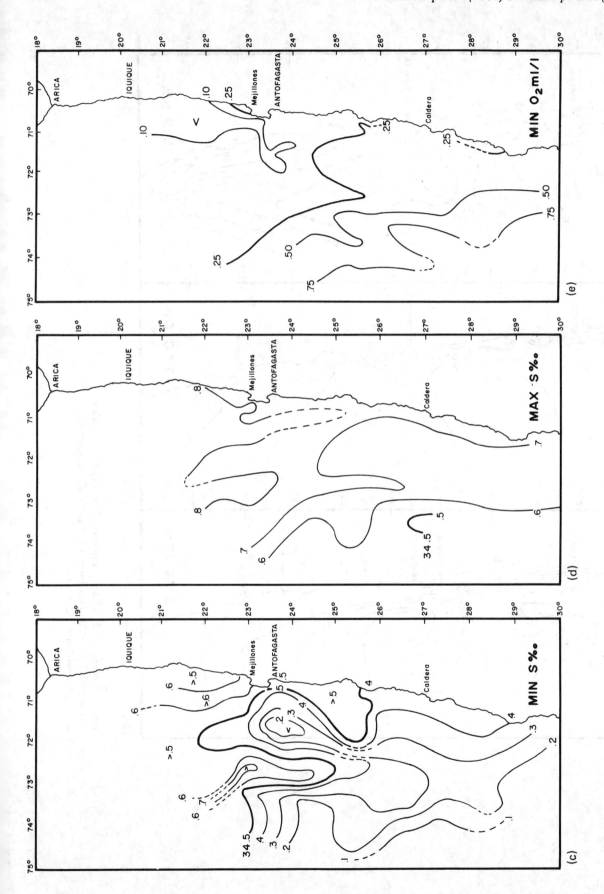

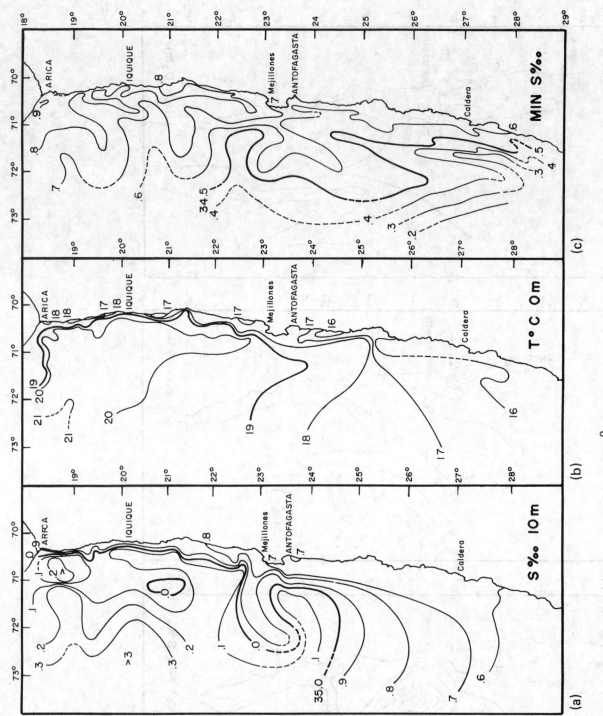

Fig. 15. Spring 1972; (a) *S* per mille at 10 m; (b) *T*° C at mille, zero m; (c) *S* per mille minimum; (d) *S* per mille maximum; and (e) O$_2$ ml/l minimum.

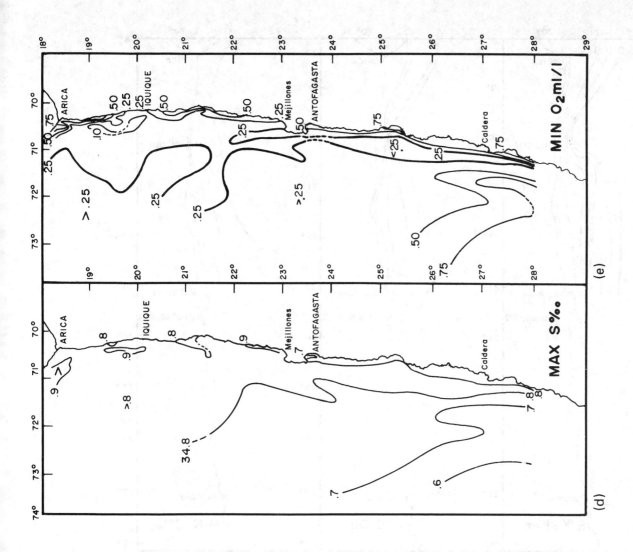

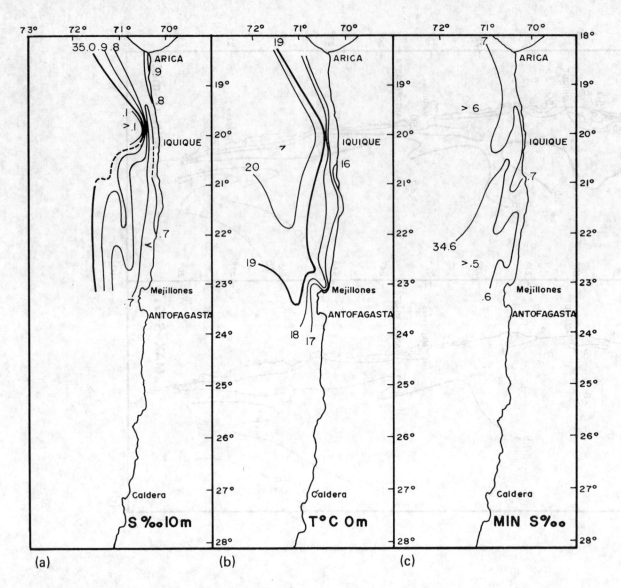

Fig. 16. Spring 1973: (a) S per mille at 10 m; (b) T° C at
zero m; (c) S per mille minimum; (d) S per mille maximum;
and (e) O$_2$ ml/l minimum.

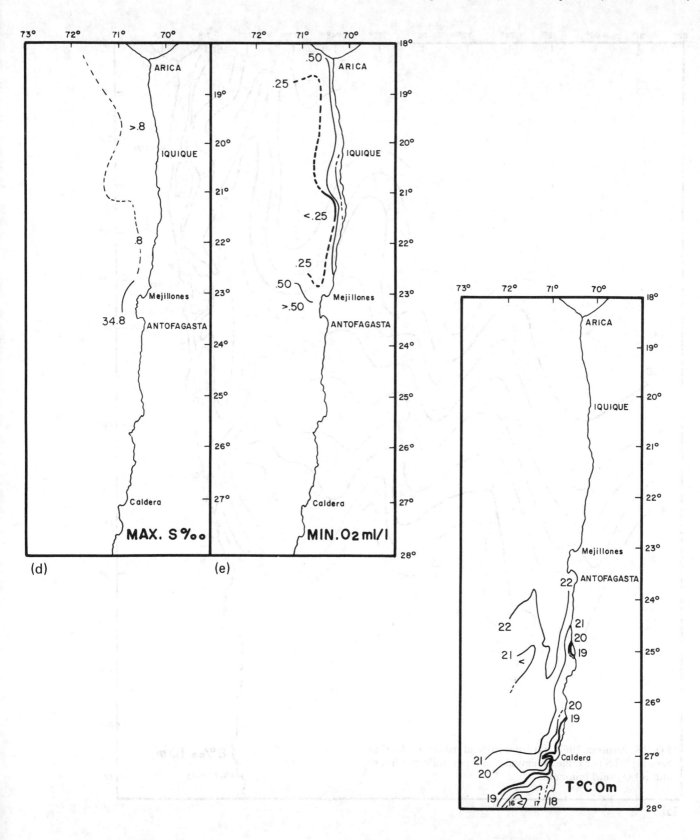

(d)   (e)

Fig. 17. T° C at zero m for summer 1973.

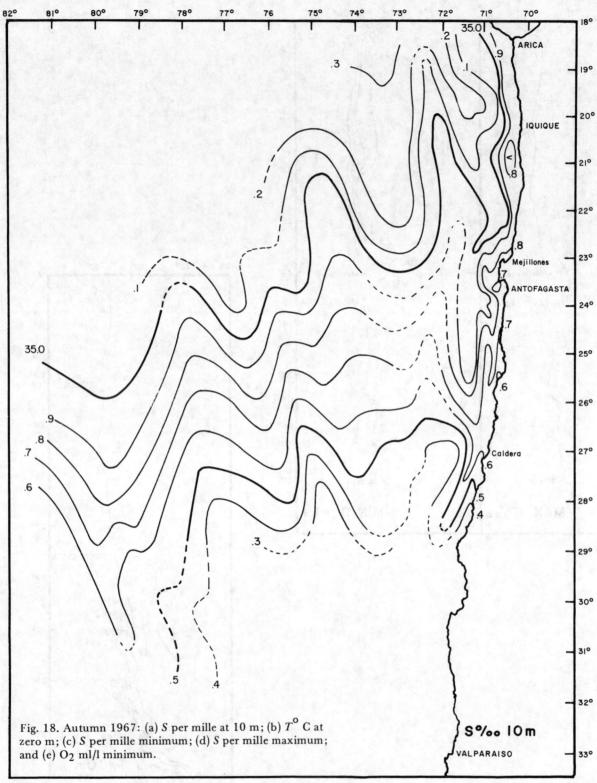

Fig. 18. Autumn 1967: (a) *S* per mille at 10 m; (b) *T*° C at zero m; (c) *S* per mille minimum; (d) *S* per mille maximum; and (e) O_2 ml/l minimum.

(a)

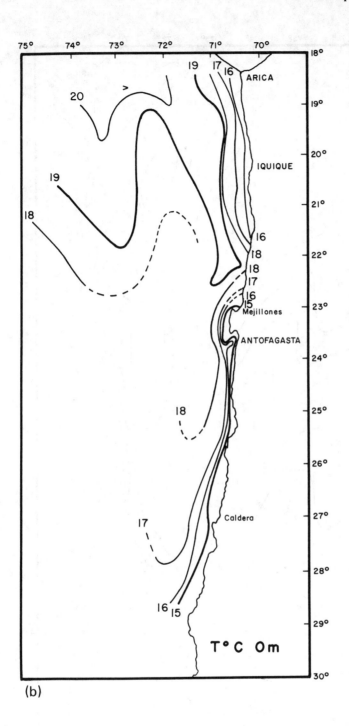

(b)

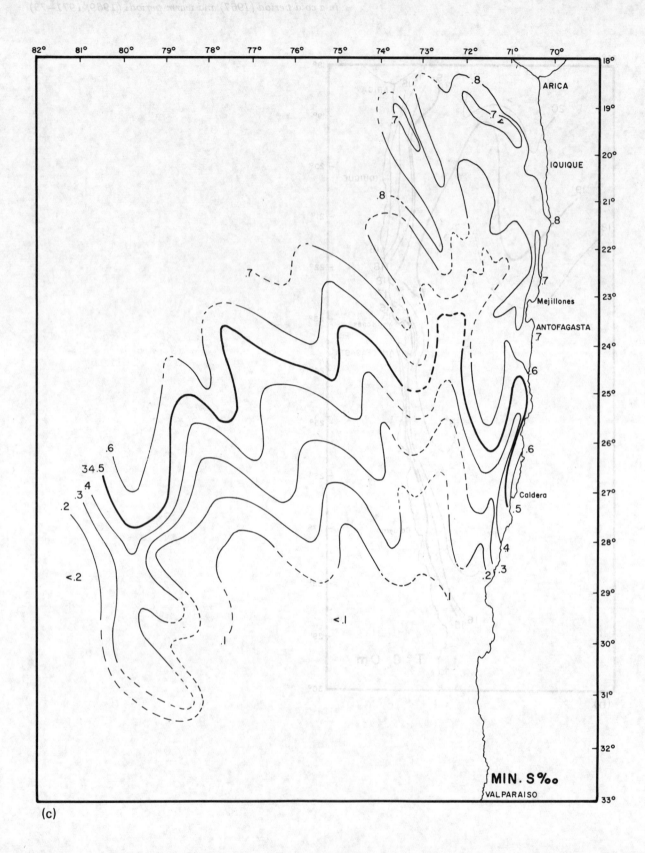

(c)

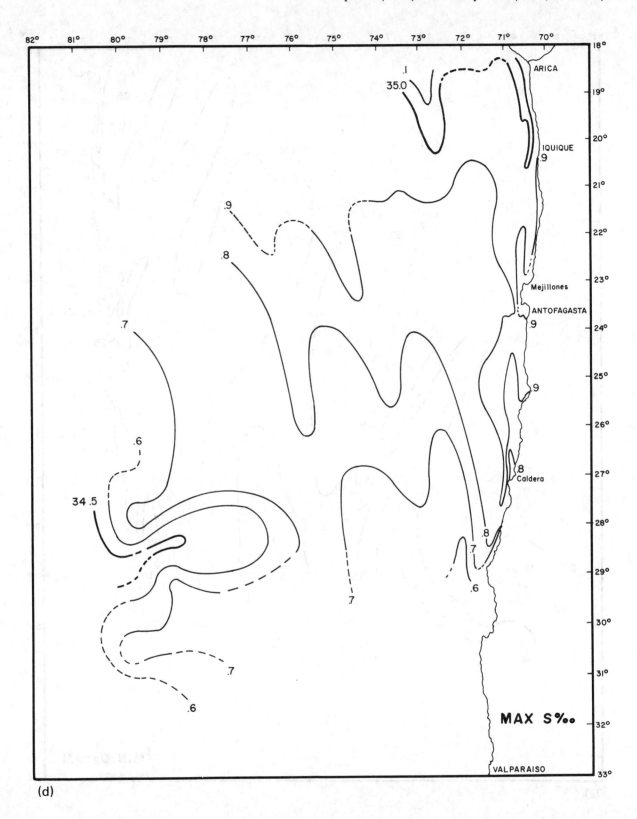

(d)

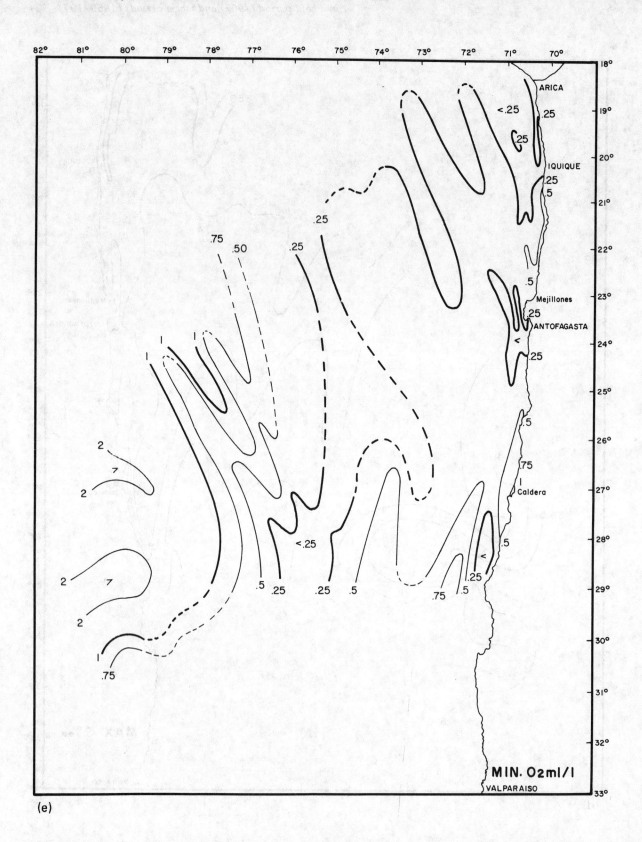

(e)

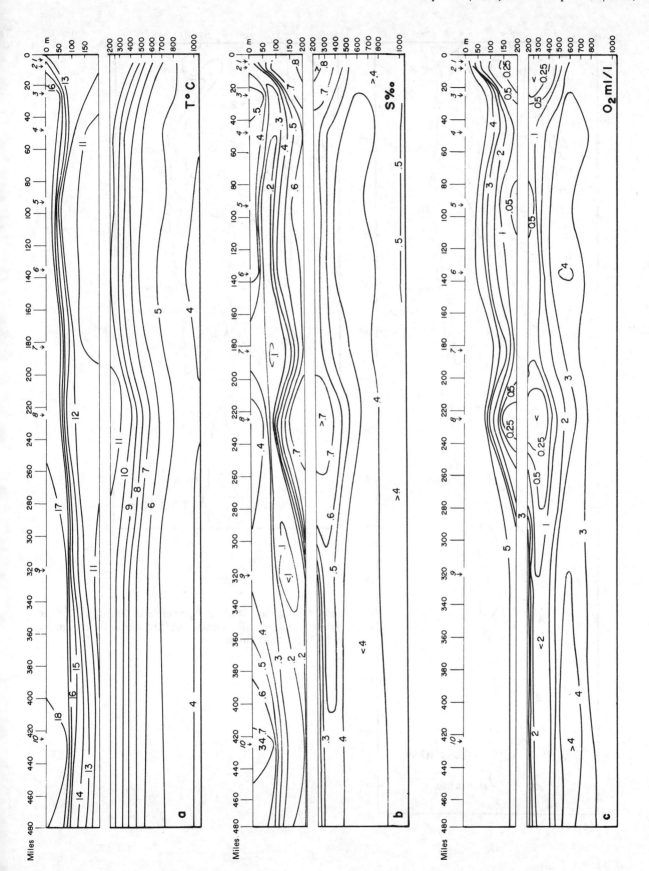

Fig. 19. Autumn 1962 at latitude 28°15′ S.; (a) $T°$ C.; (b) S per mille; and (c) O_2 ml/l profiles.

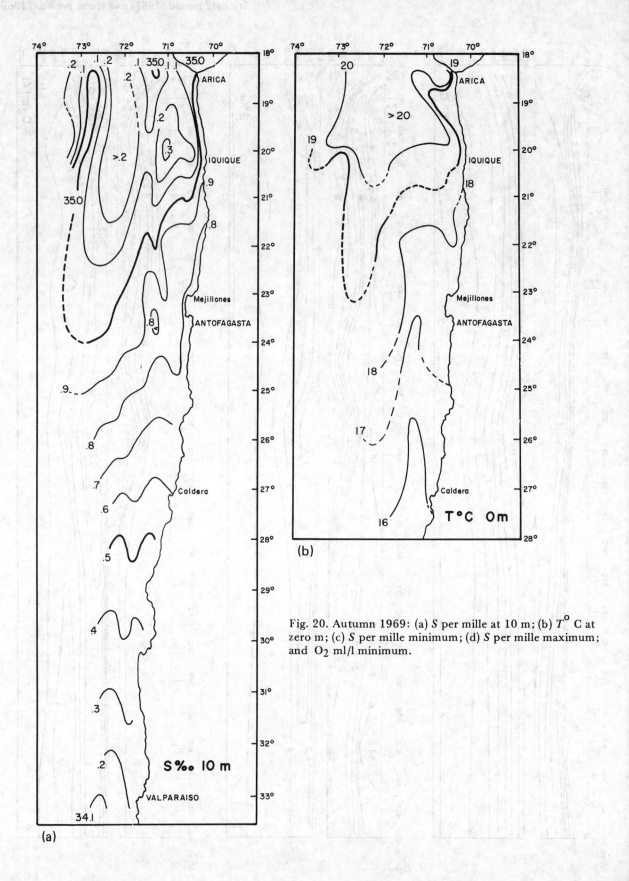

Fig. 20. Autumn 1969: (a) *S* per mille at 10 m; (b) *T*° C at zero m; (c) *S* per mille minimum; (d) *S* per mille maximum; and O₂ ml/l minimum.

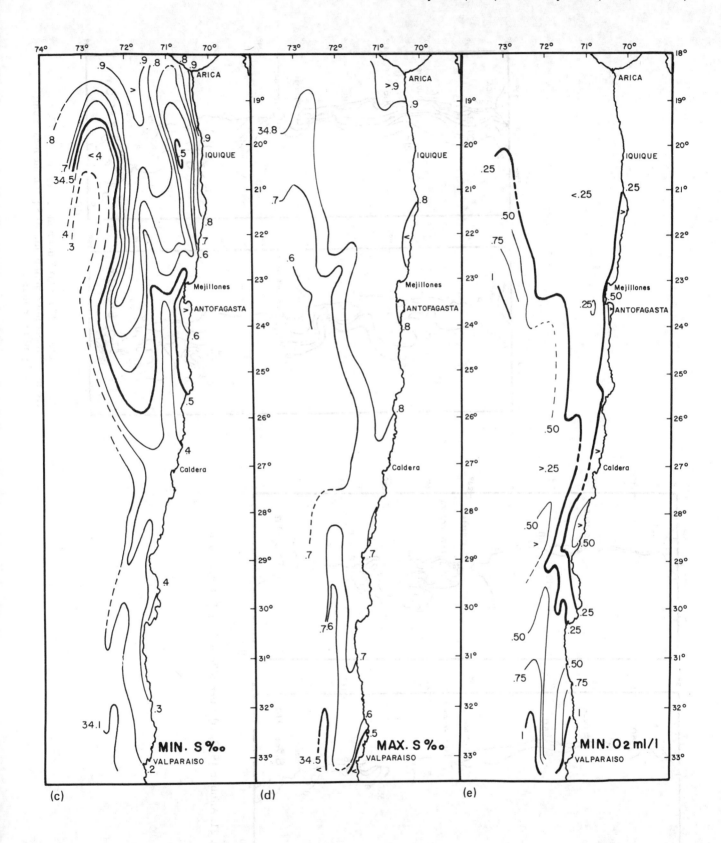

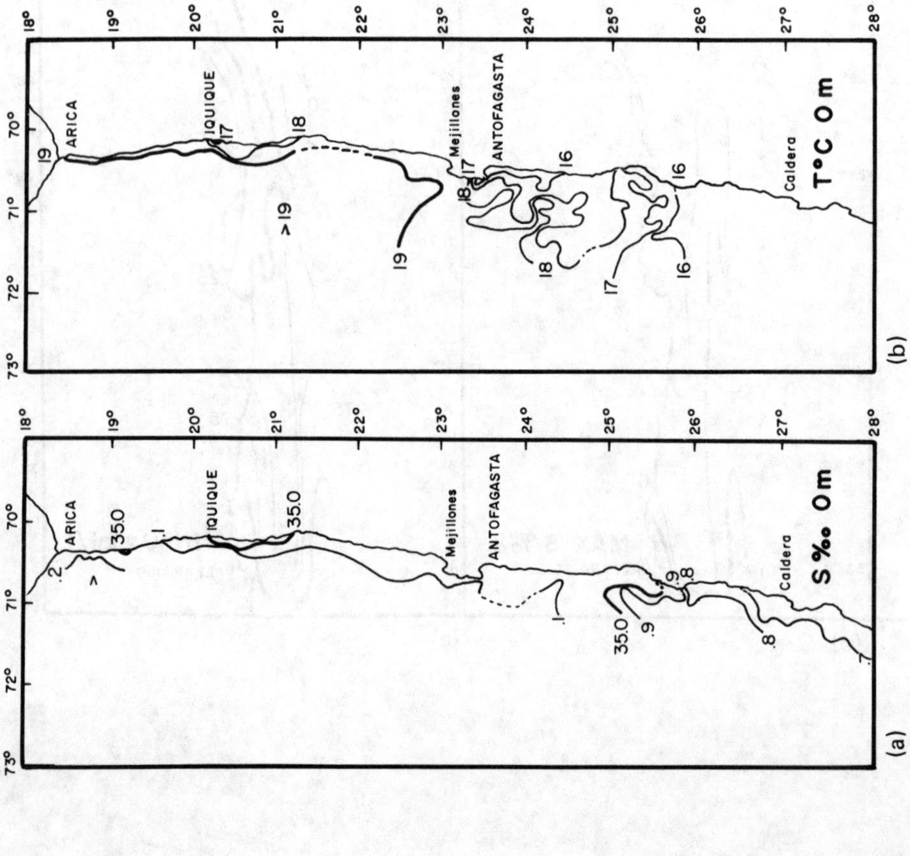

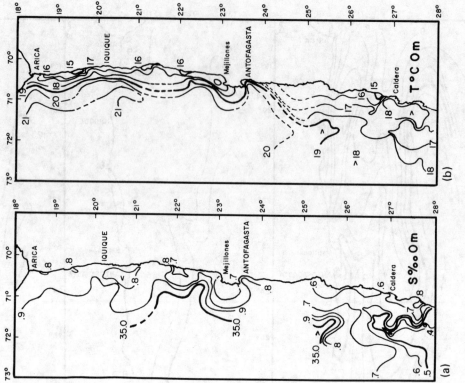

Fig. 22. Autumn 1973: (a) *S* per mille at zero m; (b) *T*[o] C at zero m; (c) *S* per mille minimum; (d) *S* per mille maximum; and (e) O$_2$ ml/l minimum.

Fig. 21. Autumn 1972: (a) *S* per mille and (b) *T*[o] C at zero m.

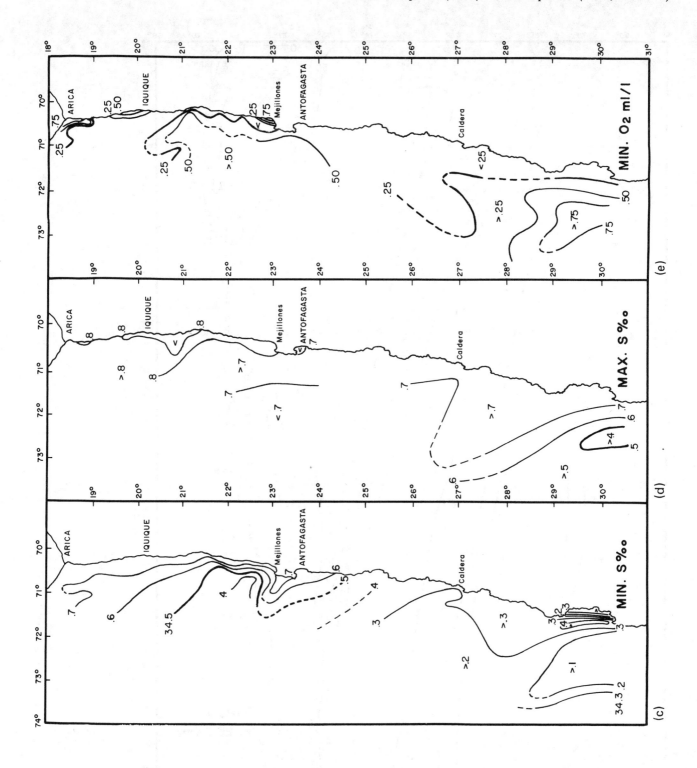

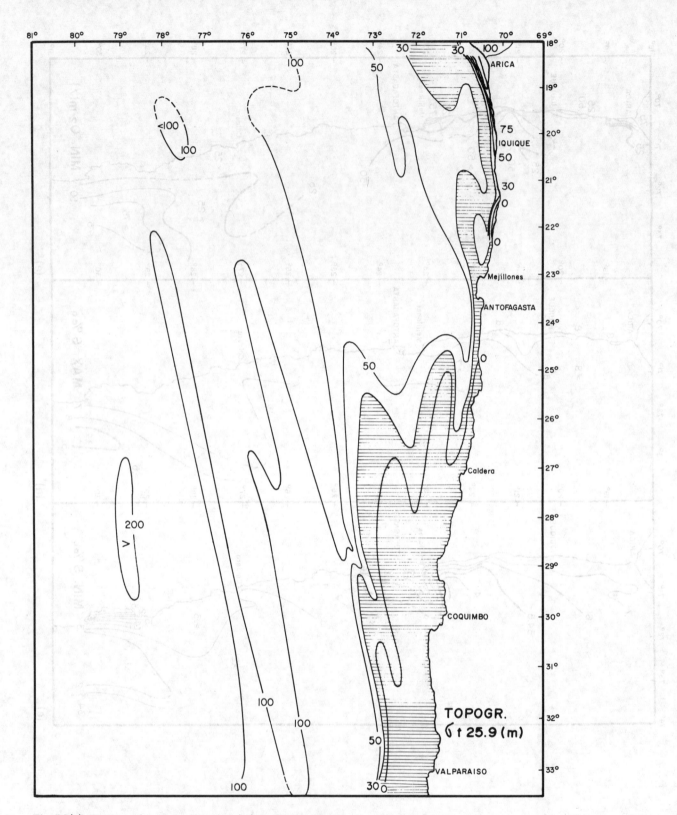

Fig. 23(a). Topography of sigma-*t* 25.9 (m) for winter 1967.

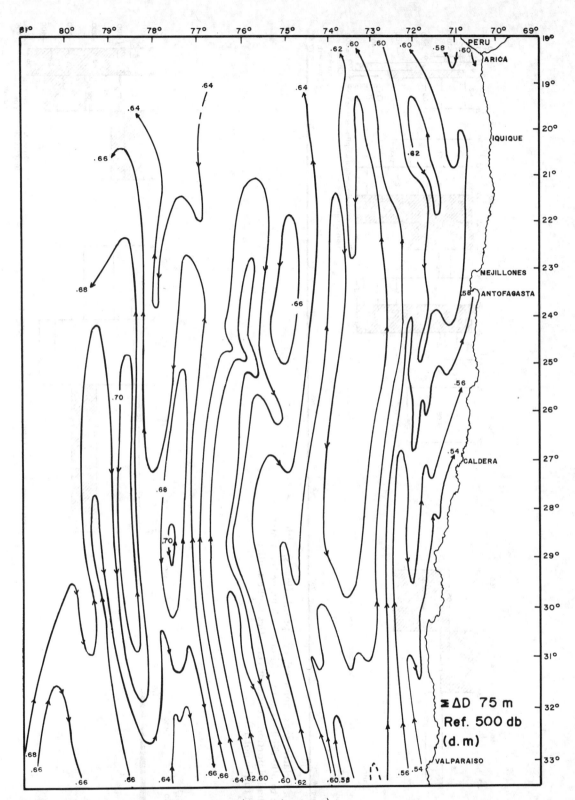

Fig. 23(b). Dynamic topography at 75 m (dynamic metres)
with reference to 500 decibars for winter 1967.

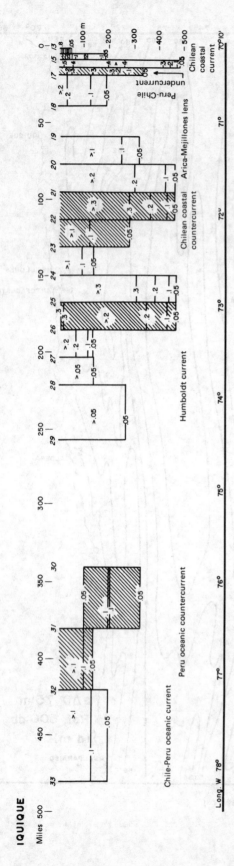

Fig. 24(a). Relative geostrophic velocity profile (knots) with reference to 500 decibars at the latitude of Iquique for winter 1967. (Shaded portions represent velocities to the south; unshaded to the north.)

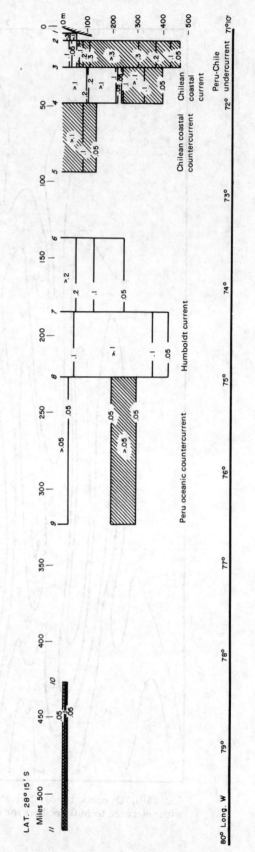

Fig. 24(b). Relative geostrophic velocity profile (knots) with reference to 500 decibars at 28° 15' S. latitude for autumn 1967. (Shaded portions represent velocities to the south; unshaded to the north.)

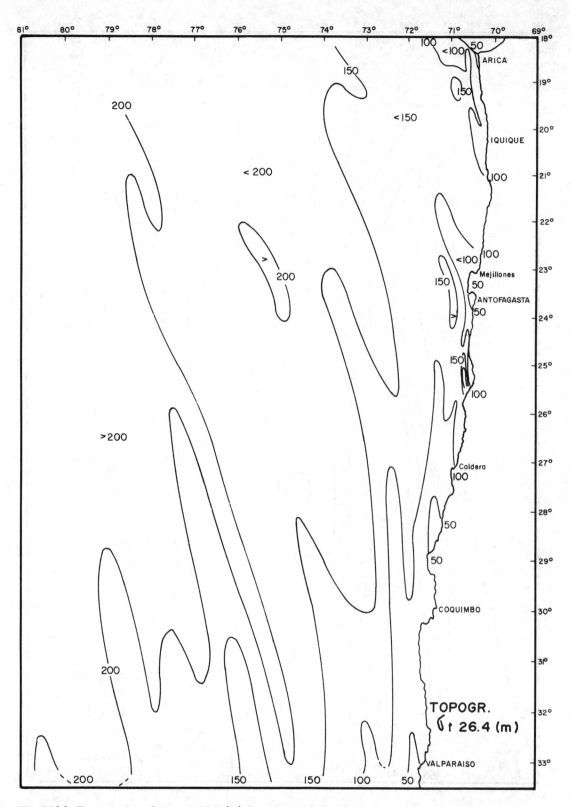

Fig. 25(a). Topography of sigma-*t* 26.4 (m) for winter 1967.

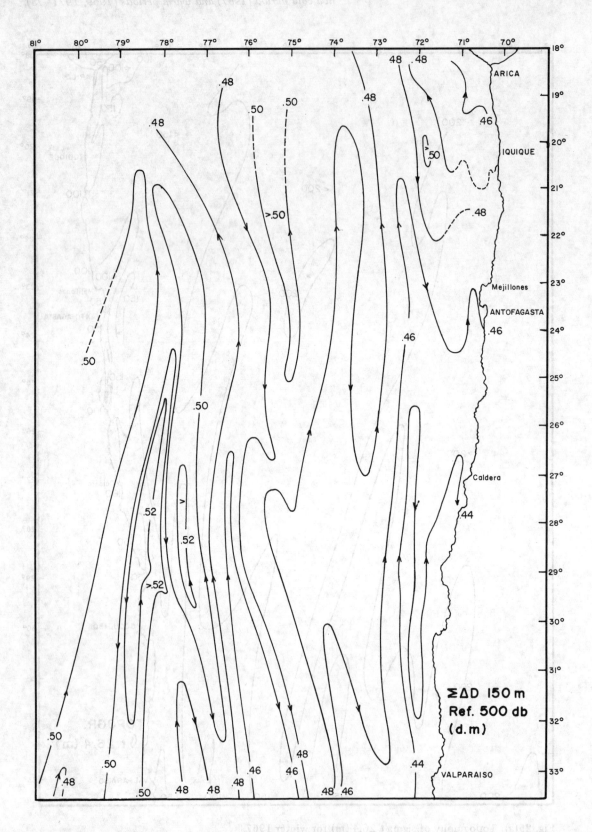

Fig. 25(b). Dynamic topography at 150 m (dynamic metres)
with reference to 500 decibars for winter 1967.

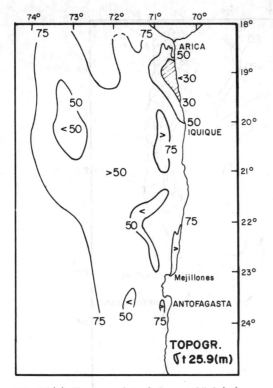

Fig. 26(a). Topography of sigma-*t* 25.9 (m) for winter 1972. (Shaded area represents topographies less than 30 m).

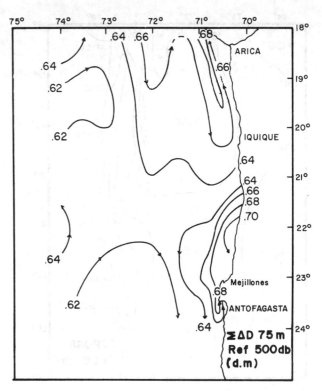

Fig. 26(b). Dynamic topography at 75 m (dynamic metres) with reference to 500 decibars for winter 1972.

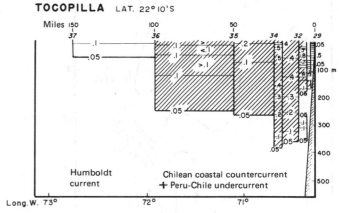

Fig. 27. Relative geostrophic velocity profile (knots) with reference to 500 decibars at the latitude of Tocopilla (22°10' S.) for winter 1972.

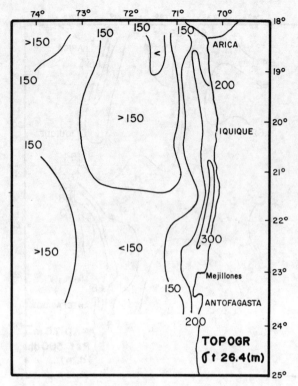

Fig. 28(a). Topography of sigma-*t* 26,4 (m) for winter 1972.

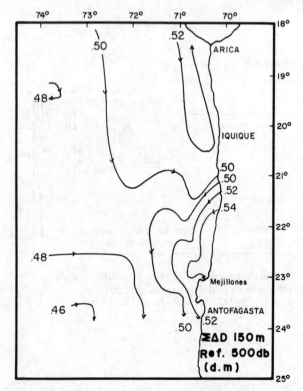

Fig. 28(b). Dynamic topography at 150 m (dynamic metres) with reference to 500 decibars for winter 1972.

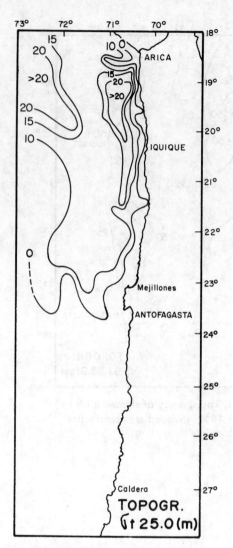

Fig. 29. Topography of sigma-*t* 25.0 (m) for spring 1972.

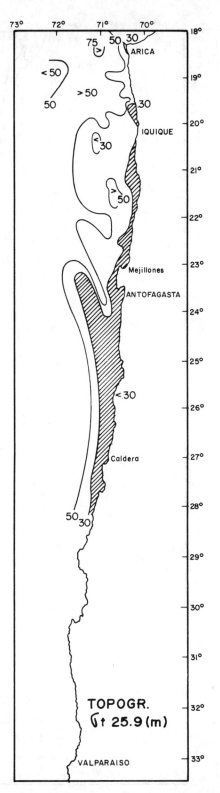

Fig. 30(a). Topography of sigma-*t* 25.9 (m) for spring 1972. (Shaded areas represent topographies less than 30 m.)

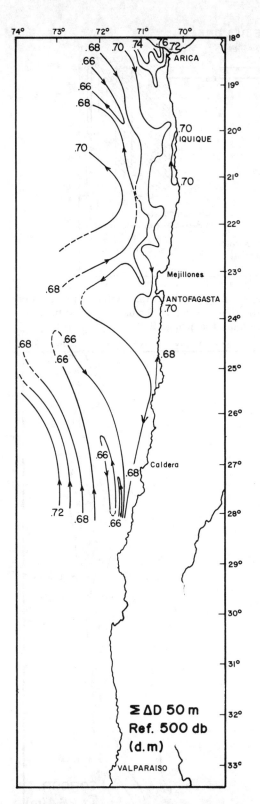

Fig. 30(b). Dynamic topography at 50 m (dynamic metres) with reference to 500 decibars for spring 1972.

MEJILLONES

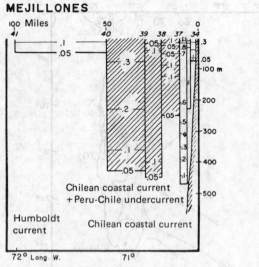

Fig. 31. Relative geostrophic velocity profile (knots) with reference to 500 decibars at the latitude of Mejillones for spring 1972.

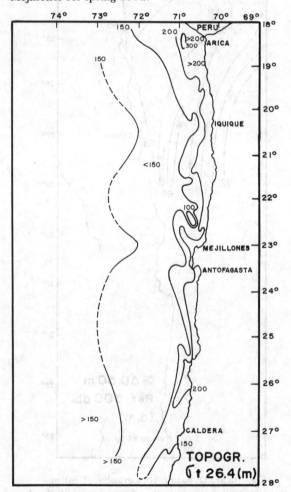

Fig. 32(a). Topography of sigma-*t* 26.4 (m) for spring 1972.

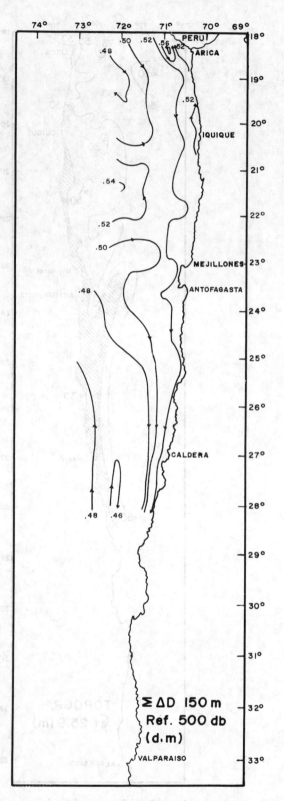

Fig. 32(b). Dynamic topography at 150 m (dynamic metres) with reference to 500 decibars for spring 1972.

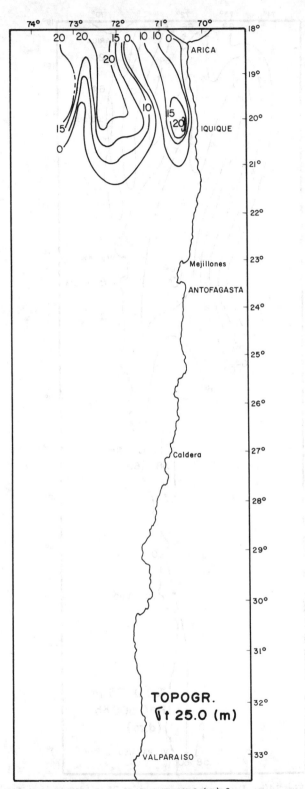

Fig. 33. Topography of sigma-*t* 25.0 (m) for autumn 1969.

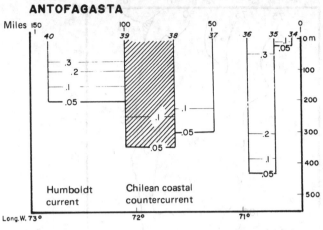

Fig. 34. Relative geostrophic velocity profile (knots) with reference to 500 decibars at the latitude of Antofagasta for autumn 1969.

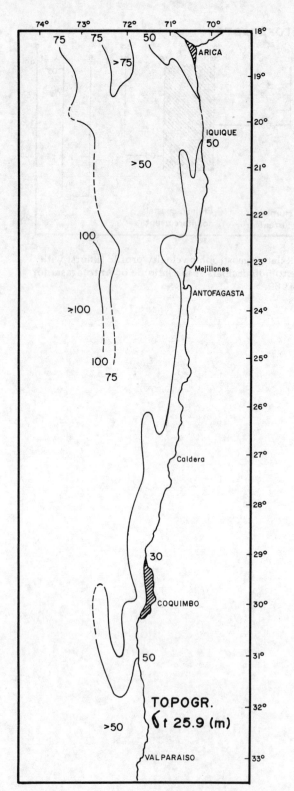

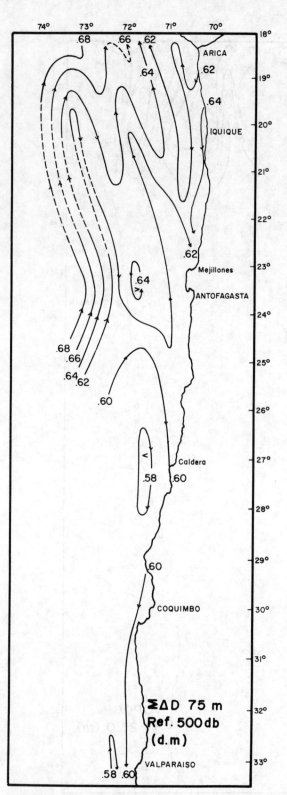

Fig. 34(a). Topography of sigma-*t* 25.9 (m) for autumn 1969. (Shaded areas represent topographies less than 30 m.)

Fig. 34(b). Dynamic topography at 75 m (dynamic metres) with reference to 500 decibars for autumn 1969.

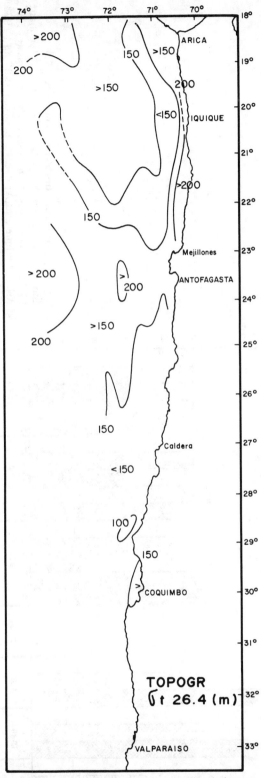

Fig. 36(a). Topography of sigma-*t* 26.4 (m) for
autumn 1969.

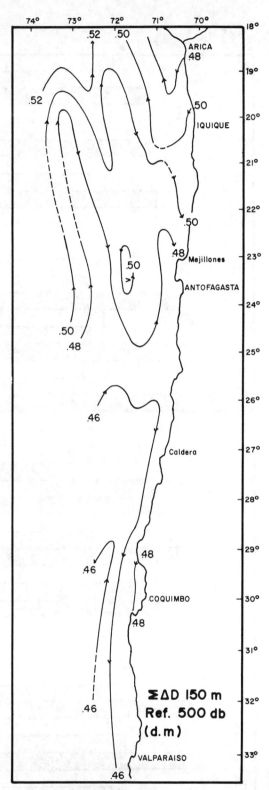

Fig. 36(b). Dynamic topography at 150 m
(dynamic metres) with reference to 500
decibars for autumn 1969.

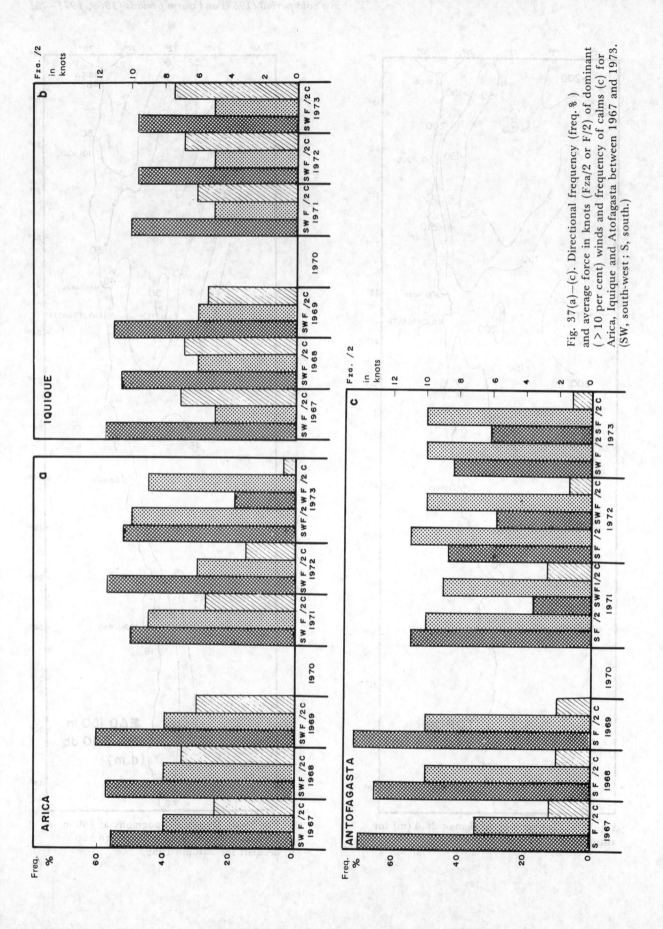

Fig. 37(a)–(c). Directional frequency (freq. %) and average force in knots (Fza/2 or F/2) of dominant (>10 per cent) winds and frequency of calms (c) for Arica, Iquique and Atofagasta between 1967 and 1973. (SW, south-west; S, south.)

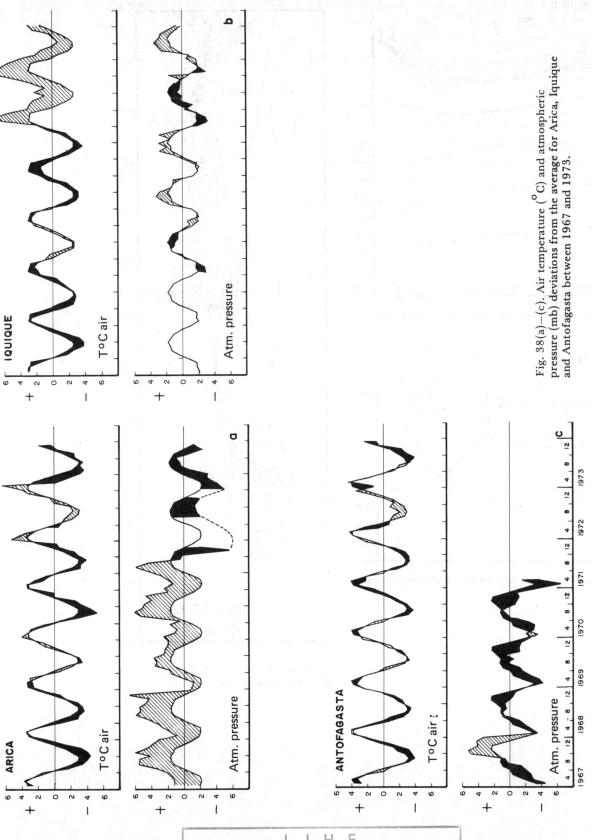

Fig. 38(a)—(c). Air temperature (°C) and atmospheric pressure (mb) deviations from the average for Arica, Iquique and Antofagasta between 1967 and 1973.

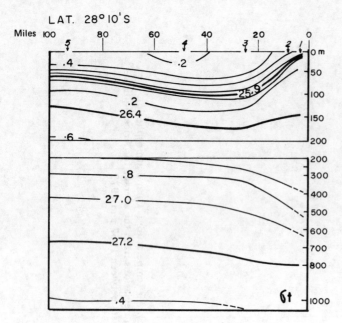

Fig. 39(a). Sigma-*t* profile at latitude 28°10′ S. for autumn 1969.

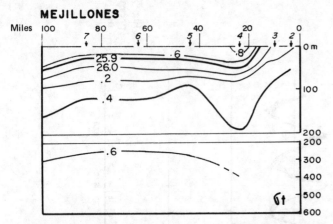

Fig. 39(b). Sigma-*t* profile at latitude of Mejillones for winter (late) 1971.

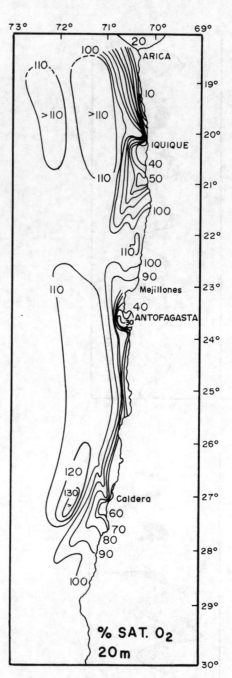

Fig. 39(c). Percentage O_2 saturation at 20 m for autumn 1967.

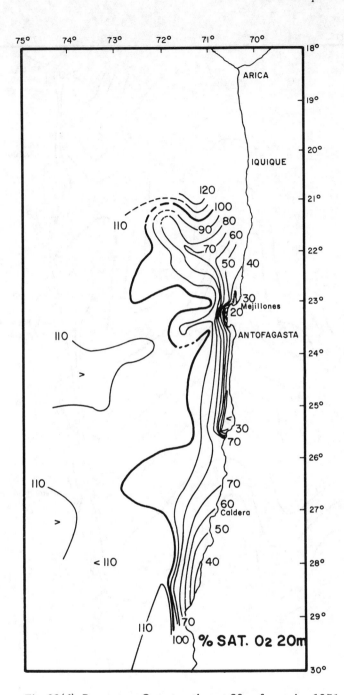

Fig. 39(d). Percentage O$_2$ saturation at 20 m for spring 1971.

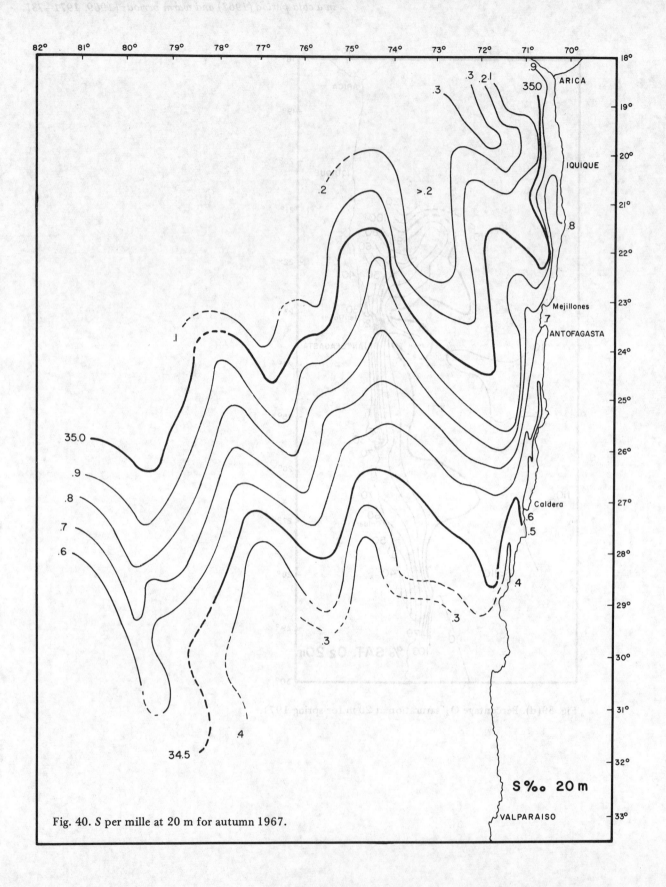

Fig. 40. *S* per mille at 20 m for autumn 1967.

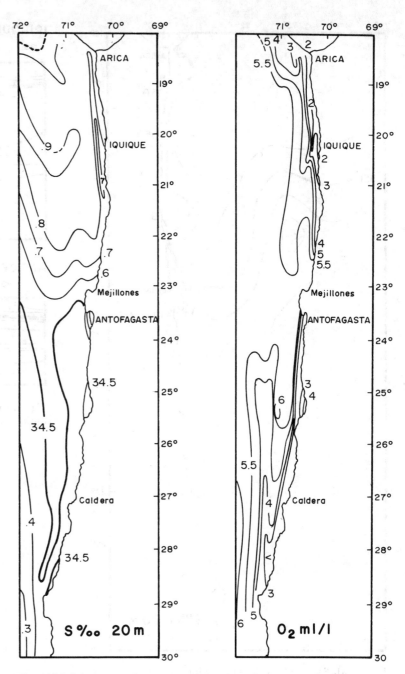

Fig. 41(a),(b). *S* per mille and O_2 ml/l at 20 m for winter 1967.

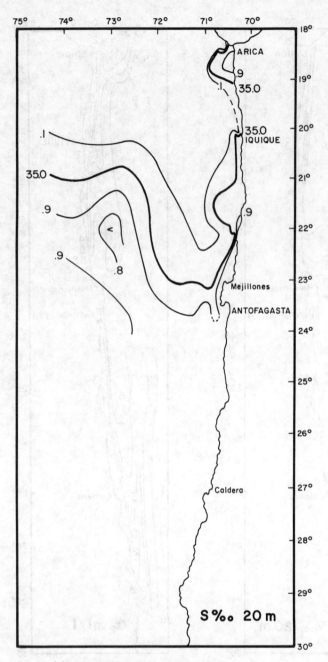

Fig. 42(a). *S* per mille at 20 m for winter 1972.

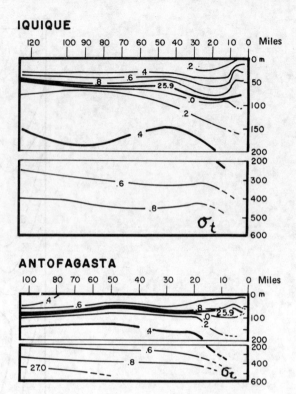

Fig. 42(b)-(c). Sigma-*t* profiles at latitudes of Iquique and Antofagasta for winter 1972.

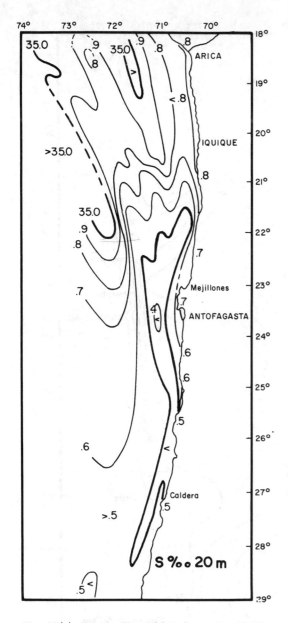

Fig. 43(a). *S* per mille at 20 m for spring 1967.

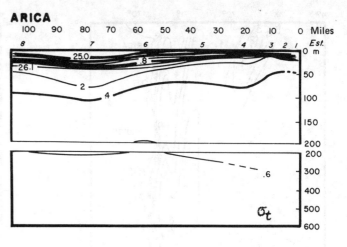

Fig. 43(b). Sigma-*t* profile at latitude of Arica for spring 1967.

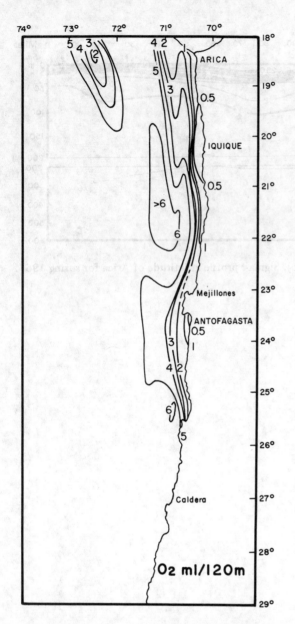

Fig. 43(c). O$_2$ ml/l at 20 m for spring 1967.

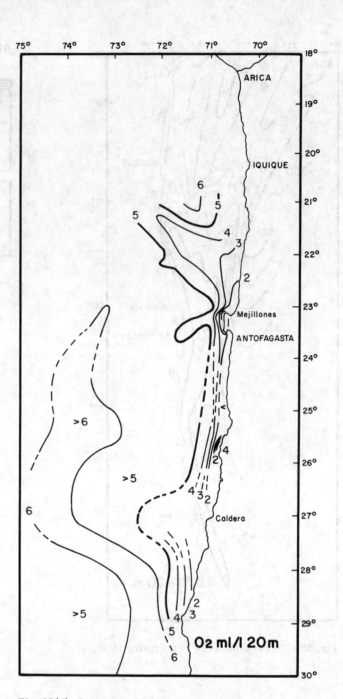

Fig. 43(d). O$_2$ ml/l at 20 m for spring 1971.

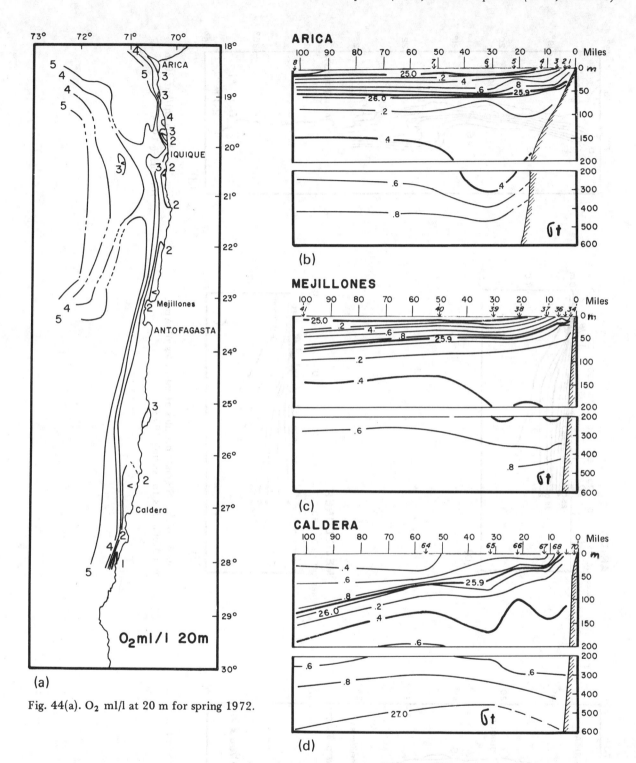

Fig. 44(a). O_2 ml/l at 20 m for spring 1972.

Fig. 44(b),(c),(d). Sigma-*t* profiles at latitudes of Arica, Mejillones and Caldera for spring 1972.

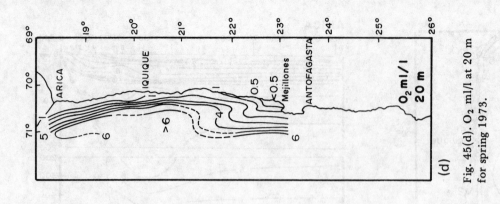

Fig. 45(d). O$_2$ ml/l at 20 m for spring 1973.

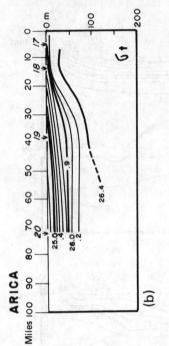

Fig. 45(b),(c). Sigma-*t* profiles at latitudes of Arica and Mejillones for spring 1973.

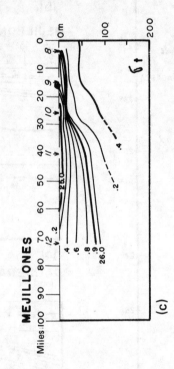

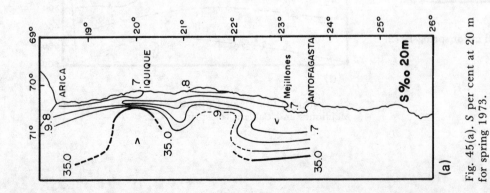

Fig. 45(a). S per cent at 20 m for spring 1973.

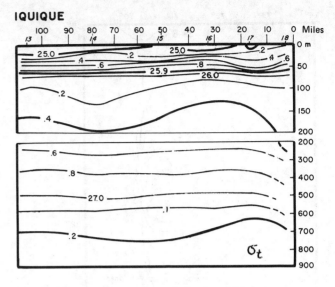

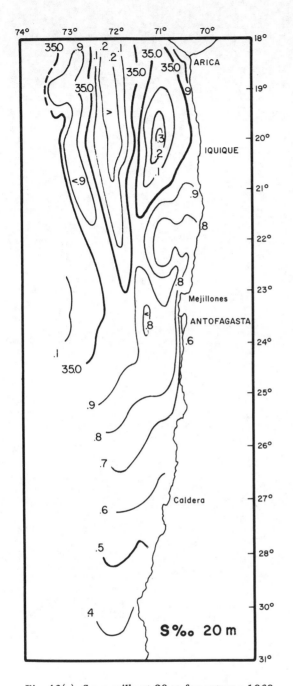

Fig. 46(b). Sigma-*t* profile at latitude of Iquique for autumn 1969.

Fig. 46(a). *S* per mille at 20 m for autumn 1969.

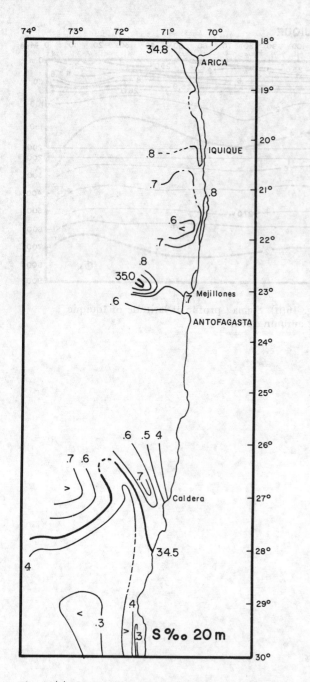

Fig. 46(c). *S* per mille at 20 m for autumn 1973.

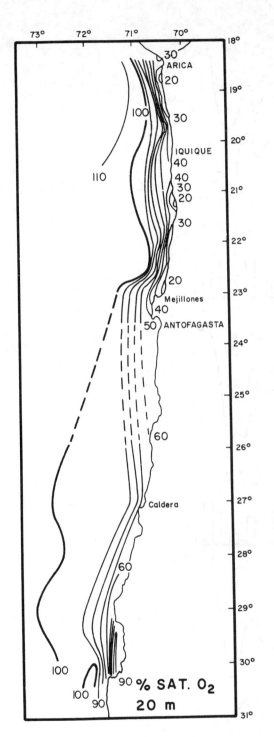

Fig. 47(a). Percentage O_2 saturation at 20 m for autumn 1973.

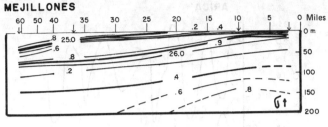

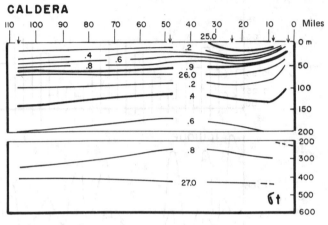

Fig. 47(b),(c). Sigma-t profiles at latitudes of Mejillones and Caldera for autumn 1973.

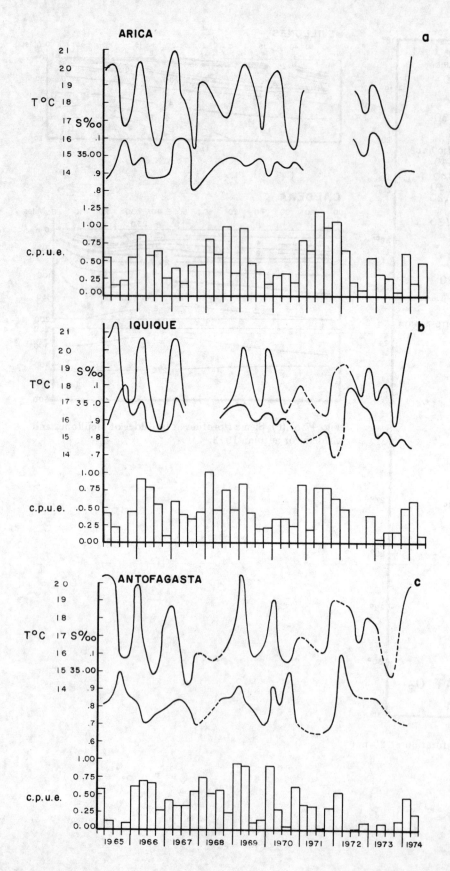

Fig. 48(a),(b),(c). Quaterly catch per unit of effort (c.p.u.e.) of anchovy versus quarterly averages of surface T° C and S per mille for the fishing areas of Arica, Iquique and Antofagasta (between 1965 and 1974).

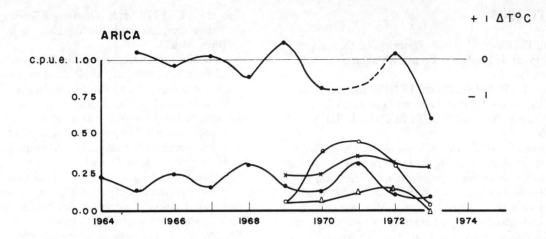

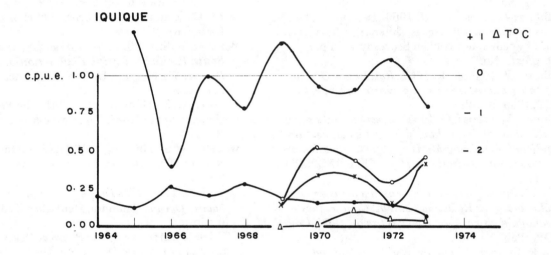

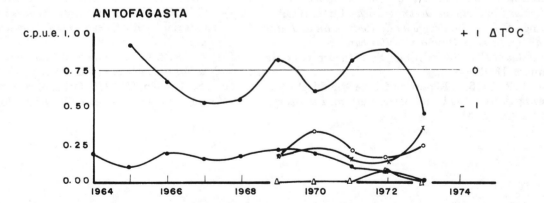

Fig. 49. Monthly average of the annual c.p.u.e. of anchovy (1964-73), and Spanish sardine, jack, and bonito (1969-73) versus the annual deviation of the surface temperature on nine-year average (1965—73) for the fishing areas of Arica, Iquique and Antofagasta.

- • anchovy
- × Spanish sardine
- ○ jack
- △ bonito

References

Alarcón, E.; Pineda J. 1969. Descripción Oceanográfica Estacional de las Aguas Frente a Valparaíso. *Bol. Cient.*, No. 11.

Bjerknes, J. 1961. Estudio del El Niño Basado en el Análisis de las Temperaturas de la Superficie del Océano de 1935–57. *Bol. IATTC* (La Jolla), Vol. V, No. 3.

Brandhorst, W. 1963. *Descripción de las Condiciones Oceanográficas en las Aguas Costeras entre Valparaíso y el Golfo de Arauco, con Especial Referencia al Contenido de Oxígeno y su Relación con la Pesca.* Chile, Lab. Oceanog. Biol. Pesq., Min. Agr.

——. 1971 Condiciones Oceanográficas Estivales Frente a la Costa de Chile. *Rev. Biol. Mar.* Valparaíso), Vol. 14, No. 3.

Brandhorst, W.; Inostroza, H. 1969. Descripción Gráfica de las Condiciones de Aguas Chilenas en Base a Datos de las Expediciones William Scoresby y Chiper. *Bol. Cient.*, No. 1.

Brandhorst, W.; Cañón, R. 1967. *Resultados Oceano-gráfico-pesqueros Aéreos en el Norte de Chile.* Chile, IFOP, (Pub. No. 29.)

Brandhorst, W.; Rojas, O. 1967. *Investigaciones sobre los Recursos de la Anchoveta y sus Relaciones con las Condiciones Oceanográficas en Agosto—Septiembre de 1963 y Marzo—Junio de 1964.* Chile, IFOP. (Pub. No. 31.)

——. 1968. *Investigaciones sobre los Recursos de la Anchoveta y sus Relaciones con las Condiciones Oceanográficas en Agosto a Octubre de 1964.* Chile, IFOP, (Pub. No. 36).

Cañón, R. In press. *Distribución y Abundancia de Anchoveta en la Zona Norte de Chile en Relación a Algunas Condiciones Oceanográficas.* Chile, IFOP.

Cummings, S. R. 1969. *Programa de Reducción de Datos Oceanográficos de Diseño Modular para un Computador IBM 360/50.* Chile, Sección Oceanografía Pesquera, IFOP.

Gunther E. R. 1936. A Report on Oceanographical Investigations in the Peru Coastal Current. *Discovery.* London (Rep. 13).

Inostroza H. 1972. *Atlas Oceanográfico de Chile.* Valparaíso, Instituto Hidrográfico de la Armada. (Pub. 3041).

——. 1972. Some Oceanographic Features of Northern Chilean Waters in July 1962. *International Symposium on Oceanography of the South Pacific.* Wellington, New Zealand National Commission for Unesco.

Robles, F. 1966. *Graphical Description of Oceanographic Conditions off Tarapacá Province, Based upon Data from* Marchile II *Expedition.* Valparaíso, Instituto Hidrográfico de la Armada.

——. 1968. *Descripción General de las Condiciones Oceanográficas en Aguas Chilenas. En Sinopsis sobre Algunos Aspectos de las Pesquerías Chilenas.* Valparaíso, Universidad Católica.

Sandoval, E. 1971. The Summer Distribution of Tuna in the Relation to the General Oceanographic Conditions off Chile and Peru. *Far Seas Fish. Res. Lab. Bull.* (Shimizu), No. 5.

Wooster, W.S. 1970. *Eastern Boundary Currents in the South Pacific. Scientific Exploration of the South Pacific.* Washington, D.C., National Academy of Sciences.

Wooster, W.S.; Gilmartin, M. 1961. The Peru-Chile Undercurrent. *Journal of Marine Research*, Vol. 19, No. 3.

Wooster, W.S.; Guillén, O. 1974. Characteristics of El Niño in 1972. *Journal of Marine Research*, Vol. 32, No. 3.

Wyrtki, K. 1964. *The Thermal Structure of the Eastern Pacific Ocean.* Hamburg, Deutsches Hydrographisches Institute.

——. 1965. *Summary of the Physical Oceanography of the Eastern Pacific Ocean.* San Diego, Calif., Institute of Marine Resources, University of California.

——. 1967. Circulation and Water Masses in the Eastern Equatorial Pacific Ocean. *Int. J. Oceanol. and Limnol.*, Vol. 1, No. 2.

Zuta, S. 1972. El Fenómeno El Niño. *Revista de Estudios del Pacífico* (Valparaíso), No. 5.

Zuta, S.; Guillén, O. 1970. Oceanografía de las Aguas Costeras del Perú. *Boletín IMARPE,* Vol. 2, No. 5.

Primary production of the coastal and oceanic waters of the northern and central zones of Chile (oceanographic cruise 'Marchile VIII', 1972)

Boris Ramirez R. [1]
Sergio Palma G.
Hector Barrientos C.

Introduction

In the past some cruises have been made along the northern and central Chilean littoral for the purpose of studying the production capacity of these waters (Expeditions Shoyo Maru, 1964; Anton Bruun, 1965–66; Marchile V, 1965, and Marchile VII, 1967). However, the resulting information has been presented only in the form of data reports which lack adequate interpretation from which to obtain an integrated picture of primary productivity and its relation to oceanographic phenomena.

For this reason, during the oceanographic cruise Marchile VIII, a collection and analysis of water was made in order to study the quantity of chlorophyll produced by phytoplankton and thus gain knowledge of the distribution and abundance of these organisms, both latitudinal and longitudinal, through the study zone.

In addition, these studies are designed to add to the knowledge of the phytoplanktonic potential of these waters; this is especially important for the maintenance of pelagic fisheries of herbivorous character, particularly the anchoveta, whose economic importance is centred in the northern zone of the country.

Materials and methods

The oceanographic operation Marchile VIII was carried out by the Chilean navy vessel AGS *Yelcho* between 10 August and 8 September 1972, and covered an area of the south-eastern Pacific extending between 18° and 33° S. and between the Chilean coast and 80° W.

A total of 112 samples was collected at 66 stations distributed over four sections perpendicular to the coast (section 1, 3, 4 and 5), each of a length of approximately 450 miles (Fig. 1). Surface samples were taken at all these points and samples were taken with Van Dohrn bottles at depths of 0, 10, 20 and 30 m at the four most coastal stations of each section.

Two litres of water were filtered through 0.45 μm millipore membranes and the cold ketone extract of pigments was obtained after forty-eight hours according to the methods of SCOR/Unesco (1966). The supernatant was measured in a Hitachi Perkin Elmer 124 spectrophotometer with a 1 cm light path. The concentration of chlorophyll a/m^3 was calculated from optical density values (SCOR/Unesco, 1966); the diversity of the specific pigment composition was obtained by the quotient D430/D665 (Margalef, 1960), and the planktonic biomass (grams dry weight of plankton/m^3), from the expression given by Margalef and Herrera (1961).

In the graphic representation of the concentration of chlorophyll a at the surface, the following ranges of productivity were indicated: 0.01–0.30 mg/m^3, areas of low productivity; 0.31–0.70 mg/m^3, areas of average productivity; > 0.71 mg/m^3, areas of high productivity.

SOME OCEANOGRAPHIC CHARACTERISTICS OF THE AREA

In the area under study it was found that the temperature and salinity values increased slowly from the south towards the north from 14° C to 17° C and from

1. Centro de Investigaciones del Mar, Universidad Católica de Valparaíso.

34.0 per mille to 35.1 per mille respectively. In this region Gunther (1936) distinguished two surface currents, the Peruvian coastal current and the Peruvian oceanic current, respectively the coastal and oceanic branches of the Humboldt current (Sievers and Silva, 1975). Wyrtki (1963) indicated that the two current are separated to the north of 25° S. by the southward-flowing Peruvian countercurrent.

On the basis of the surface dynamic topography relative to the 1,000 db/level (Fig. 18 of Sievers and Silva, 1975) it can be seen that the Peruvian counter-current would presumably have two branches, the first of which is more oceanic, situated west of 77° W., and would extend to 27° S.; this coincides with the location given by Wyrtki. The second would be more coastal and would penetrate south along 75° W., extending its effect as far as Valparaíso.

The coastal region of the northern zone (sections 1 and 3) would be influenced by upwelling phenomena caused by the action of the dominant winds of the region. Otherwise the zone off Huasco (section 4) showed characteristics of surface currents a little different from those of the other sections due to the presence of an eddy of anti-cyclonic character whose nucleus was located approximately 90 miles from the coast.

In the region south of the area off Valparaíso, the northerly flows in the coastal zone were influenced by upwelling phenomena and, in the oceanic zone (79° W.), probably by a southerly flow (see Fig. 18, Sievers and Silva, 1975).

SURFACE DISTRIBUTION OF PRIMARY PRODUCTION

Comparing the graphs of chlorophyll *a* and the surface dynamic topography relative to the 1,000 db level (Sievers and Silva, 1975), a close relation can be detected. Thus, in the sections in the more northern part of the region (sections 1 and 3), a wealth of phytoplankton was found in the coastal zones coincidentally with the upwelling phenomena. This section contained high concentrations of chlorophyll *a* compared with the other zones (Table 1). The ocean richness in the north is due to very young phytoplanktonic populations which correspond to the cocolithophorid group. It is possible to make this supposition on the basis of background information both of the low diversity index (< 1.0), and of the low values of biomass (< 1.04 mg/m³).

The coastal populations which grow old in the course of this displacement are moved to the north-east by the predominant winds. This coincides with the band of low productivity lying between 72° and 73° W. (Fig. 2). A zone of high productivity is located at about 75° W. It is coincident with the flow of the Peruvian countercurrent and associated with two zones of medium productivity. The latter zones are probably caused by the divergence between the southerly flows (oceanic and coastal branch of the Humboldt current) and the Peruvian countercurrent (Forsbergh and Joseph, 1963).

In section 4, the low productivity (with a mean of 0.12 mg/m³) was almost general with the exception of an area of medium productivity between 74° and 75° W.; this coincided with the southerly flow of the Peruvian coastal current (Fig. 2). The values of all the other sections was some four times greater than this value. In further support of this, it was found that the greater percentage of stations in this section yielded chlorophyll values which were in the range of low productivity (Table 1).

This difference in the measured phytoplankton of these sections raises some questions, considering that what had been expected for the coastal areas was the gradual increase in production to the north caused by local upwellings (Forsbergh and Joseph, 1963). However, in general it is seen that there is a greater photosynthetic potential in the coastal waters than the oceanic.

In the region south of the area (section 5), the greater chlorophyll values are centred some 12 miles from the coast and diminish gradually towards the ocean (Fig. 12). West of 73° W., a zone of medium productivity is found with width varying between 17 and 18 miles (Fig. 2). Finally, it can be seen that to the west of this section, there was located a broad zone of low productivity which was interrupted by two regions of average production. The region located at about 78° W. might have been due to the divergence between the northern flow of the oceanic branch of the Humboldt current and the southern flow detected in the neighbourhood of the Juan Fernández Archipelago.

In general, we can say:
The regions of high productivity (Fig. 2) were situated in the coastal zones between 18° and 25° S. and in an oceanic region located at about 75° W. off Arica.
The regions of average productivity (Fig. 2) are situated in the southern zone of the area under study and in the oceanic zones which extend along

all the area and which coincided with southward flow from the Peruvian countercurrent.

The regions of low productivity (Fig. 2) are generally situated off Huasco and in the regions coinciding with the northern flow of the oceanic and coastal branches of the Humboldt current.

VERTICAL DISTRIBUTION OF PRIMARY PRODUCTION

Analysis and discussion of data for the four most coastal stations in each section can be made on the basis of the relationship that exists between chlorophyll a, the diversity index and the total pigment biomass (Margalef, 1972), while taking into consideration the influence that some abiotic factors have on the coastal production systems.

In section 1 on the basis of the chlorophyll a isopleths, it can be seen that the maximum values were centred between 10 and 25 m depth (Fig. 3), associated with a low diversity almost uniform for the section—with the exception of station 4 where it was higher (Fig. 4). Moreover, the increase in chlorophyll from the coast (station 1) towards the ocean (station 4) was associated with an increase in their rate of cellular renewal, indicated by the low diversity index. This increase would be produced by the displacement of physiologically mature populations with diversity values greater than 3 caused by the Eckman effect. Finally, the pigment biomass is low, especially at station 4 (Fig. 5).

In section 3, a wedge of water of medium production capacity, centred at station 32, was detected. Zones of high productivity (> 20 mg/m^3) are located on both sides of this wedge, especially in the first 20 m (Fig. 6). The values of the diversity index remain low almost throughout the section (Fig. 7). The pigment biomass shows a distribution similar to that of production, there being a poor zone of wedge shape (< 20 mg/m^3) which coincides with the belt of low-production capacity water (Fig. 8). Section 4 situated off Huasco showed low concentrations of chlorophyll a which did not exceed 0.30 mg/m^3 (Fig. 9). The greatest values of the diversity index were centred within the first 10 metres at stations 35, 36 and 37, the last of which had a low pigment diversity (Fig. 10) low biomass values (< 30 mg/m^3) and this biomass was distributed in the first 10 m (Fig. 11).

In section 5, the chlorophyll a values increase outwards from the coast to the neighbourhood of station 64, at the same time showing a greater increase in value with dpeth. Beyond station 64 a reduction in production was seen (Fig. 12). The diversity index increased towards the stations furthermost from the coast (Fig. 13) and the pigment biomass shows two areas of high values (> 50 mg/m^3), the first located at 30 m depth at station 65, and the second on the surface at station 64 (Fig. 14).

In general, it can be said that section 4 was the only section which showed great variation within it, since it showed low productivity and pigment biomass countering the high diversity which indicated very mature phytoplankton populations.

Table 1. Surface distribution of chlorophyll a (mg/m^3), in number of stations per section, grouped in ranges of productivity.

Chlorophyll a range mg/m^3	Primary production	Number of stations per section in each category			
		1	3	4	5
0.01—0.30	Low	7	8	14	5
0.31—0.70	Medium	5	5	1	7
0.71	High	5	2	0	1

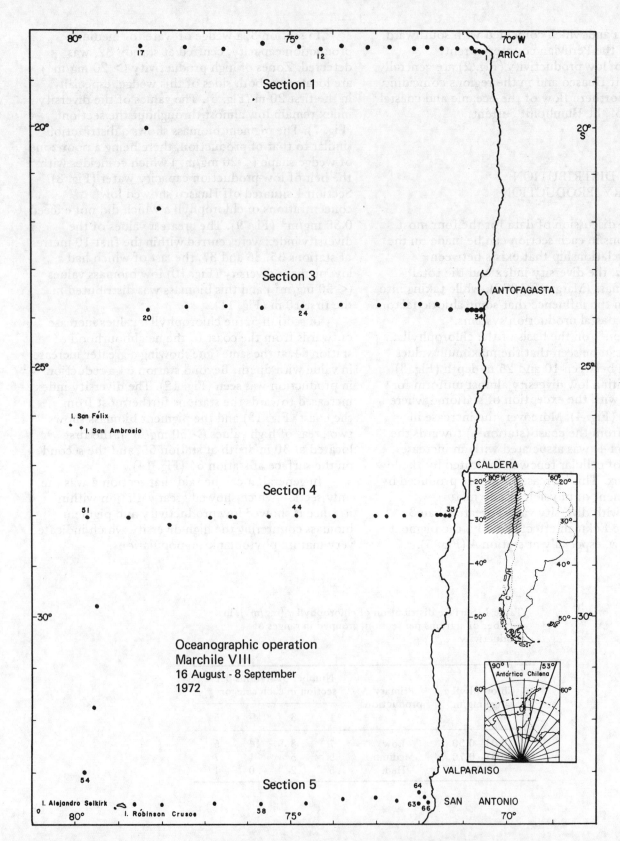

Fig. 1. Geographical location of stations (Marchile VIII, 16 August—8 September 1972).

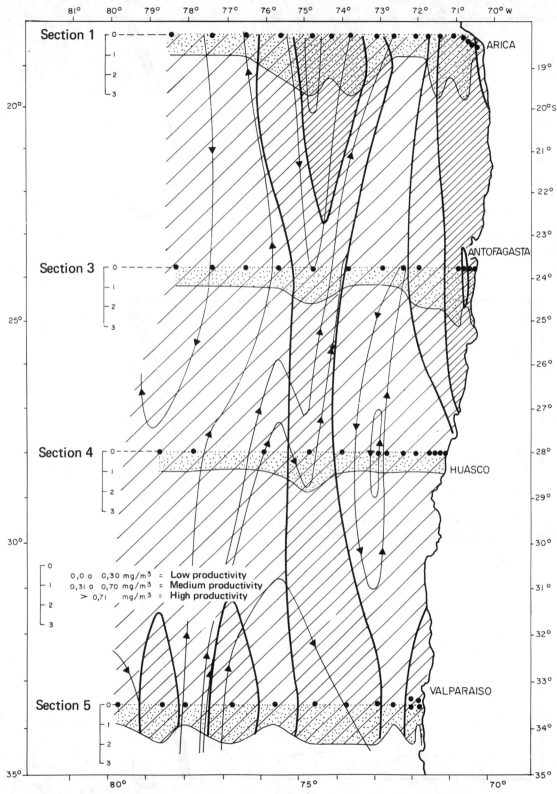

Fig. 2. Surface distribution of chlorophyll *a*   (mg/m^3). Values shown on the scale of : low (1), medium (2) and high (3) productivity of the area. The errors indicate the dynamic topography relative to the 1,000-decibar surface (adapted from Sievers and Silva, 1975).

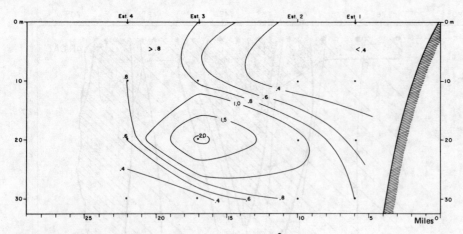

Fig. 3. Vertical distribution of chlorophyll *a* (mg/m^3) for the four stations of section 1 nearest the coast.

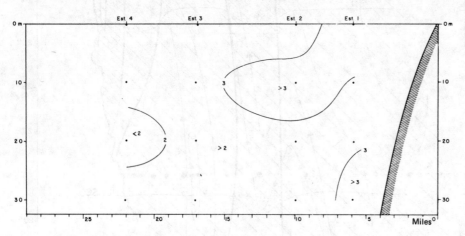

Fig. 4. Vertical distribution of the diversity index (D430/D665) for the four stations of section 1 nearest the coast.

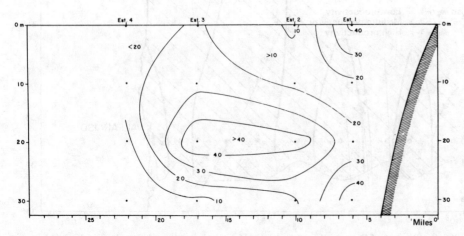

Fig. 5. Vertical distribution of plankton biomass (mg/m^3) for the four stations of section 1 nearest the coast.

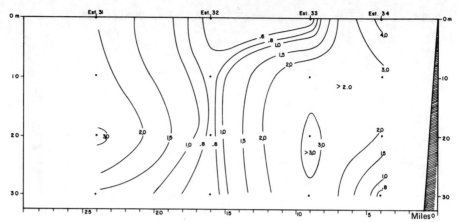

Fig. 6. Vertical distribution of chlorophyll *a* (mg/m³) for the
four stations of section 3 nearest the coast.

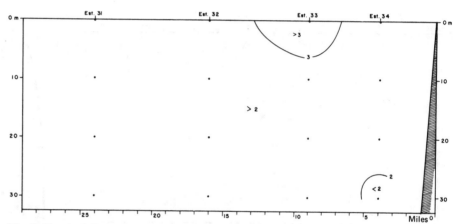

Fig. 7. Vertical distribution of the diversity index (D430/
D665) for the four stations of section 3 nearest the coast.

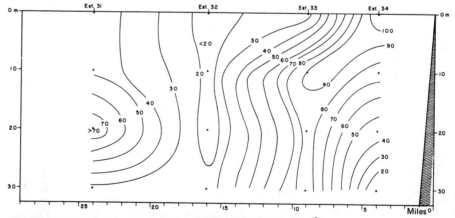

Fig. 8. Vertical distribution of the plankton biomass (mg/m³)
for the four stations of section 3 nearest the coast.

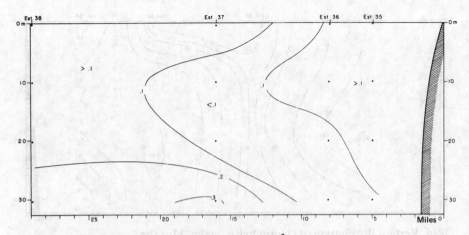

Fig. 9. Vertical distribution of chlorophyll *a* (mg/m³) for the four stations of section 4 nearest the coast.

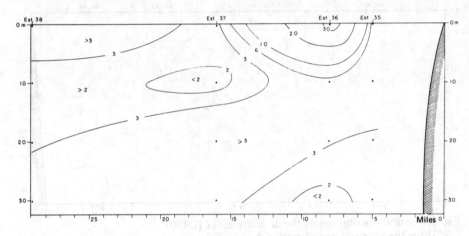

Fig. 10. Vertical distribution of the diversity index (D430/D665) for the four stations of section 4 nearest the coast.

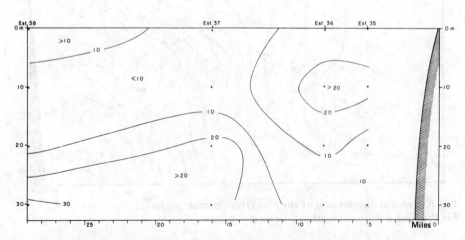

Fig. 11. Vertical distribution of the plankton biomass (mg/m³) for the four stations of section 4 nearest the coast.

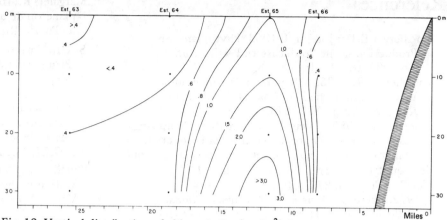

Fig. 12. Vertical distribution of chlorophyll *a* (mg/m³) for the four stations of section 5 nearest the coast.

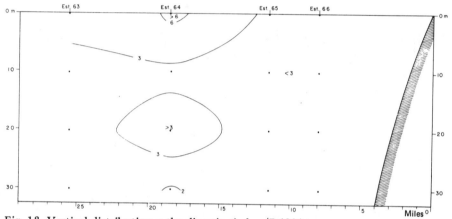

Fig. 13. Vertical distribution o the diversity index (D430/ D665) of the four stations of section 5 nearest the coast.

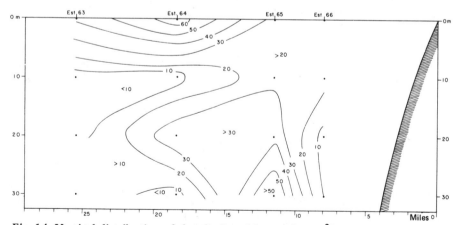

Fig. 14. Vertical distribution of the plankton biomass (mg/m³) for the four stations of section 5 nearest the coast.

References

Forsbergh, E.D.; Joseph, J. 1963. Phytoplankton Production in the Southeastern Pacific. *Nature,* Vol. 200, No. 2901, p. 87—8.

Gunther, E.R. 1936. A Report on Oceanographical Investigation in the Peru Coastal Current. *Discovery Rep.,* Vol. 13, p. 107—276.

Margalef, R. 1960. Valeur Indicatrice de la Composition des Pigments du Phytoplankton sur la Productivité, Composition Taxonomique et Propriétés Dynamiques des Populations. *Rapp. Comm. int. Mer. Médit.,* Vol. 15, No. 2, p. 277—81.

——, 1972. Ecología Marina. *El Ecosistema.* Fundación La Salle de Ciencias Naturales. (Cap. 12 : 447—53.)

Margalef, R.; Herrera, J. 1961. Hidrografía y Fitoplancton de un Area Marina de la Costa Meridional de Puerto Rico. *Inves. Pesq.,* Vol. 18, p. 33—96.

SCOR/Unesco. 1966. Determination of Photosynthetic Pigments in Sea-water. *Monogr. Oceanogr.,* Method I, 69 p.

Sievers, C., H. A. Silva, S., N. 1975. Masas de Agua y Circulación en el Océano Pacífico Sudoriental. Latitudes 18°—33° S. (Operación Oceanográfica Marchile VIII). *Cienc. y Tec. del Mar. Contrib. CONA,* No. 1 ; p. 7—67.

Wyrtki, K. 1963. The Horizontal and Vertical Field of Motion in the Peru Current. *Bull. Scripps Inst. Ocean.,* Vol. 8, No. 4, p. 313—46.

The Peru current system. 1: Physical aspects

Oscar Guillén G. [1]

Introduction

Zuta and Guillén (1970) have carefully described the oceanographic conditions of the Peruvian current, based upon data up to 1969. Mujica (1972) has reviewed the information on the Peruvian Sea. In some abnormal years, such as occured recently in 1957–58, 1965 and 1972–73, warm waters reached much further south than their normal position, causing catastrophic effects on the marine fauna, the guano-bird populations and on the climate along the coast. This situation is known as the 'El Niño' phenomenon, which is dealt with in detail in Zuta *et al.* (1974). However there are still no integrated studies specifically of the Peruvian current which could lead to better understanding of the coastal upwelling phenomena, 'El Niño' itself, the productivity of waters, etc.

Topography

The maritime region of Peru is situated between 3°23' and 18°21' S., with a littoral estimated as being approximately 2,900 km. The topography of the sea floor off the Peruvian coast is extremely irregular and presents characteristics described in the following section.

The coastline is also considerably irregular and influences the orientation of the Peruvian current. The variation of the form and width of the continental shelf is defined approximately by the 100-fathom isobath and the greatest width is between latitudes 7° and 10° S., reaching 65 miles from the coast approximately off Pimentel and Salaverry. To the south of 14° S., e.g. at San Juan, Pescadores and Mollenglo, it extends approximately five miles from the coast. The slope is moderate between latitudes 7° and 14° S., becoming more marked to the north and south of these latitudes.

Another feature is the Peru-Chile trench, which lies parallel to the coast and is interrupted by the Nazca Ridge. The axis of this ridge lies between 40 and 140 miles from the coast, coming closest to the coast at 6° S. (approximately 40 miles) and 15° S. (approximately 70 miles) and its greatest distance from the coast at 9° S. and 17° S. The greatest depths have been recorded to the south of latitude 17° S. (6,643 m at 18° S.). To the north of 17° S., the greatest depth recorded was 6,490 m, between latitudes 10° and 11° S. This trench has been studied by Zeigler *et al.* (1957) from the profiles made by the vessels *Horizon* (1952) and *Atlantis* (1955). Menzies and Chin (1966) recently studied the Nazca ridge which extends roughly perpendicularly to the coastline at Punta Doña María. The highest part of this ridge is at about 1,000 fathoms from the sea surface. West of the trench and north of the Nazea ridge is the South-east Pacific basin, with mean depths of about 2,400–2,600 fathoms.

Along the coast there are also canyons and eroded and irregular ground, conspicuously in two general areas. One is located between latitudes 14° and 18° S., the other to the north of latitude 6° S., extending to the Gulf of Guayaquil.

1. Instituto del Mar del Perú, Esq. Gamarra y Gral. Valle, Chucuito, Callao (Peru).

Physical properties

TEMPERATURE

Horizontal distribution of temperatures

The distribution and variation of temperature are tied to the oceanic currents and to variations of solar radiation. Wyrtki (1965) has published monthly mean sea-surface temperature maps which are very similar to those published by the Meteorological Office in the United Kindgom (1944, 1960) and those of the United States Navy Hydrographic Office (1944) which showed the presence of a warm tongue located to the west of upwelled waters off Peru from October to May. However, this tongue is not shown by Schott (1935) and although the atlas of the United States Navy Hydrographic Office (1944) shows it, it does so with lower temperatures.

Whether the warming of this tongue is a local effect, or is due to advection, or is the horizontal transfer of water masses in the horizontal ocean currents caused by the Peruvian countercurrent (Wyrtki, 1964a, b), has not yet been clarified; this has been discussed by Bjerknes (1961). Zuta and Urquizo (1972) indicated that the warm tongue oriented towards the south-east appeared in November to June, being most marked between January and April.

The area of lowest temperatures along the Peruvian littoral lies between 14° and 16° S. although there are cold areas between 4°−6° S. and 7°−9° S. The Equatorial front (Zuta and Urquizo, 1972) lies north of 5° S. in a strip 70 to 130 nautical miles wide, with a maximum gradient of 0.6° C/10 nautical miles in summer and of 0.7° C/10 nautical miles in winter.

The maps of Wyrtki (1964) also distinguished the cold area near San Juan and especially the warm tongue of summer and autumn which approached 30° S. in March, disappearing almost completely from July to September.

The maps of the sea surface temperatures (Zuta and Guillén, 1970; Zuta and Urquizo 1972) along the Peruvian coast showed an increase in temperature westward and northward, giving rise to zonal and latitudinal gradients to the south and north respectively of 6° S. During summer (Fig. 1(a)) and autumn (Fig. 1(b)), the distribution of isotherms less than 24° C was approximately parallel to the coast with a prominent warm tongue well off the coast. During winter (Fig. 1(c)) and spring (Fig. 1(d)), this parallelism of the isotherms was practically lost.

Zuta and Urquizo (1972) indicated the 22° C isotherm on the sea-surface chart as the outer boundary of strictly coastal waters in summer, that of 20° C in autumn and predominantly that of 17° C in winter; on the other hand, for spring they indicated 17° C (for October), 18° C (for November), and that of 19° C for December.

Vertical distribution of temperature

In general, temperature falls with depth. Only occasionally do small inversions appear. The coastal upwelling areas are characterized by the homogeneous distribution of temperature (Figs. 1(a),(b),(c),(d)). The mixing layer or 'napa' is in general approximately 50 m deep within 100 miles of the coast of Peru but this depth can be greater in winter; occasionally layers of 125 m have been observed 150 miles out (Zuta and Guillén, 1970).

Near the coast the thermocline generally lies closer to the surface than it does at greater distances. The thermocline may have up to 11 isotherms during the spring/summer period and 3 and 4 isotherms during winter. Close to the coast, at depths of approximately 100 m, it has been observed that isotherms often diverge, with a sinking of the 13°−15° C isotherms; this is associated with the flow of the subsurface Peruvian/Chilean Equatorial current.

Temperature variations

Temperature varies both with geographic position and season of the year. The monthly variations of surface temperature showed that warming occurred from October to February and cooling from April to August, March and September showed a balance between warming and cooling (Zuta and Urquizo, 1972).

Maximum temperatures were observed in February/March, with a mean range of 17°−27° C; minimum temperatures with a mean range of 21°−13° C occurred during August/September, with a mean annual variation along the coast of Peru of 5°−7° C (Zuta and Guillén, 1970).

In coastal areas (Fig. 2(b)) up to three regimes of variations in the annual cycle of temperature at the sea surface have been found (Zuta and Urquizo, 1972); the first is composed of two phases (one of continuous cooling, the other of continuous warming), the second is composed of three phases (the first phase of continuous cooling, followed by a second phase of seasonal cooling, and the third of continuous warming); and the third regime is also composed of three phases (the first phase of continuous cooling, followed by a second phase of short, alternate periods of warming or cooling and the third phase of continuous warming).

An example of temperature variation in the 0—100 m layer was shown by Zuta and Guillén (1970) for the areas of Callao and Punta Falsa, in which it was observed that warming occurred from September to January at Punta Falsa or until February at Callao. Below 50 m a further cooling occurred for two and three months respectively in the two areas. The annual amplitude at the sea surface was 5.26° C and 5.03° C for Punta Falsa and Callao respectively, diminishing with depth.

Wyrtki (1965) subjected the annual means of sea-surface temperature for the period 1947—60 to harmonic analysis to determine the amplitude and phase of the variation of annual and semi-annual temperatures. He found annual amplitudes greater than 3° C in the Peruvian current—which decreased as they approached the coast—whilst the semi-annual amplitudes were around 0.5° C.

THERMAL STRUCTURE

Wyrtki (1964) defined the thermocline as the layer in which the temperature gradient exceeded values of 0.3° C/10 m.

The thermal structure of the Eastern Pacific Ocean has been well described. Monthly maps of sea-surface temperatures, changes of sea-surface temperature, depths of the mixing layers and depths of the centres of the thermoclines have already been prepared. Also maps of annual mean variation of surface temperatures, occurrences of maximum and minimum temperatures, temperature gradients in the thermoclines, temperature differences in the thermoclines, characteristic parts of the summer thermocline and variation of the annual mean of the thermal structure for selected areas have all been described (Wyrtki, 1964).

Zuta and Guillén (1970) distinguished the following types of thermocline off the Peruvian coast :
The permanent surface thermocline was characterized by its relatively superficial position and by a strong temperature gradient which usually exceeded 1° C/10 m—also by its large temperature difference between upper and lower parts of the thermocline. The temperature fluctuations in the mixing layer were small and did not cause the formation of a summer thermocline but rather joined the permanent thermocline. It was found generally to the north of 4° S., above 75 m and below mixing layers thinner than 25 m.
The permanent subsurface thermocline, extended over a large part of the Peruvian coast with moderate gradient. A seasonal, surface thermocline developed above it.
The seasonal superficial thermocline developed during the warming period, principally in summer. It was characterized by a very intense gradient and, in some cases, extended to the surface.
The permanent deep thermocline was found to be separated from the permanent subsurface thermocline by the thermostatic layer. The deep subsurface thermocline resulted from the combination of the permanent deep thermocline and the permanent subsurface thermocline at depths from 150 to 700 m.

HEAT EXCHANGE

The distribution of the annual mean of measured radiation showed considerable dependence on latitude. The variations along the parallels reflected variations of cloud cover. The maximum measured radiation to the South Pacific occurred between the Equator and 10° S. The dense clouds which covered the Peruvian current regions contributed to the very low levels of measured radiation.

The distribution of the annual mean of the measured radiation (Wyrtki, 1965) varied between 80 and 130 cal. cm^{-2} day^{-1}. The irradiated radiation was low (< 100 cal. cm^{-2} day^{-1}) in high latitudes (due to dense cloud cover) and in Equatorial regions (due to high vapour pressure) whilst in subtropical regions it was comparatively high (> 100 cal. cm^{-2} day^{-1}).

The quantity of heat lost by evaporation (Wyrtki, 1965) was less than 100 cal. cm^{-2} day^{-1} and evaporation was less than 60 cm per year in high latitudes because of small differences of vapour pressure. High evaporation occurred (> 250 cal. cm^{-2} day^{-1} or 156 cm/year) in subtropical regions where the difference of vapour pressure was larger.

The distribution of the annual means of heat exchange (Wyrtki, 1965) reflected differences between sea-surface temperatures and air temperatures ; these reached negative values only in the upwelling regions off Peru. The distribution of annual mean, total heat exchange (Wyrtki, 1965) showed a heat gain in the upwelling areas off Peru as a result of low evaporation.

SALINITY

Sea surface salinity (Fig. 3).

The changes in salinity off the Peruvian coast are subject principally to the surface circulation process which results from advection of more or less saline waters, vertical mixing processes and evaporation and precipitation phenomena. The influence of the fresh water running into the ocean was insignificant off the Peruvian coast (Zuta and Guillén, 1970).

Maps of monthly distribution of salinity at the sea surface have been made by Bennett (1966), from which it can be seen that salinity always increased from 10° S. to about 20° S. and from the western coast of South America to approximately 125° W. reaching values of 36.5 per mille or more in the middle of the high-salinity cell of the South Pacific. As a consequence of the great extension of this cell, the monthly maps show a tongue of high salinity open to the west reaching values of 36.8 per mille in June and July. Near the latitude 4° S., the southern part of the salinity front was found to intersect with the coast at a salinity of approximately 34.5 per mille for the entire year. Also it has been found that salinities to the south of 16° S. never exceeded 35.0 per mille, in spite of the existence practically throughout the year of a tongue of high salinity of western origin which almost touched the coast near 18°–20° S.

Zuta and Guillén (1970) showed the zonal gradients to the south of 6° S., where salinity increased far from the coast as a result of the effect of surface subtropical waters. To the north of 6° S., the longitudinal gradients were more pronounced since the salinity fell to the north due to the Equatorial and tropical surface waters.

The vertical distribution of salinity

Salinity does not always diminish with depth but maxima and minima can occur at different levels, produced by flows towards the Equator or pole. In the surface layer which is relatively homogeneous, a surface maximum occurs above 100 m, which is associated with the incursion of surface subtropical waters towards the coast. To the north of 6° S. and farthest offshore from the region studied, another maximum is seen within the thermocline which goes deep towards the north to below 100 m depth acting as a penetration of subtropical waters towards Equatorial regions. Another subsurface maximum is observed along a great part of the Peruvian coast, caused by the presence of subsurface Equatorial waters between 75 and 300 m of depth; these were notable to the south of 10° S. (Wyrtki, 1967).

A minimum salinity was observed south of 12° S. —generally above 100 m—and caused by the flow of subantarctic waters towards the north. Another salinity minimum was observed between 700 and 1,000 m (especially south of 14° S.), generally with a salinity less than 34.6 per mille; this was associated with the northerly flow of intermediate and antarctic waters. The coastal upwellings caused the surface salinity to increase or diminish according to upwelled water, thus waters of less than 34.9 per mille generally appeared south of 14° S., and of greater than 35 per mille further to the north.

Seasonal variations in salinity

The seasonal variations of salinity (Fig. 3) are more marked above 50 m of depth and are much greater in the northern areas. Notable salinity changes were found in the surface layer off Punta Falsa from November to April (which were most marked between December and February), associated with the pronounced Equatorial front. The change off Callao did not show large seasonal variations. The annual amplitude at the surface was 0.2 and 0.9 per mille for Callao and Punta Falsa and diminished with increasing depth (Zuta and Guillén, 1970).

Chemical properties and productivity

DISSOLVED OXYGEN

Oxygen at the surface of the sea (Fig. 4)

Generally it can be said that in Peruvian coastal waters, dissolved oxygen increases with distance from the coast, with minimum values of 2 ml/l in the upwelling areas and maximum values up to about 7 ml/l in the areas of high photosynthesis. The distribution of dissolved oxygen within 100 miles of the coast during autumn and spring and within 15 miles during the summer and winter is very irregular.

Vertical distribution and oxygen

The vertical distribution of oxygen off the Peruvian coast is found in the following layers:

A surface layer with relatively uniform values generally greater than 5 ml/l,

A discontinuity layer—called the oxycline—in which the dissolved oxygen falls sharply generally from 5 to 1.0 ml/l. To the north of 6° S., the sinking of the isolines from 2 to 0.5 ml/l below 50 m (Zuta and Guillén, 1970) was associated with the extension of the Cromwell current,

A minimum layer, with values less than 0.5 ml/l between 50 and 800 m, which is closer to the surface near the coast and towards the south. The mean absolute minimum is found between 50 and 450 m depth with values greater than zero but less than 0.5 ml/l.

Below the minimum layer where dissolved oxygen content increases rapidly with depth.

Variations of oxygen levels

Off the coast, the range of dissolved oxygen is greater in summer and autumn than in winter and spring. Zuta and Guillén (1970) found a variation of 1.88 ml/l off Punta Falsa, between the July/August and December/February values in the surface layer; at Callao, however, the oxygen variation showed an annual amplitude of 2.29 ml/l at the surface (with a maximum of 5.88 ml/l in November and minimum of 3.59 ml/l in September); this diminished directly with depth.

NUTRIENTS

Phosphate

Mean phosphate at the surface of the sea (Fig. 5)
The high phosphate concentration off the coast of Peru is due in part to coastal upwelling associated with the trade winds.

    Off the Peruvian coast the mean ranges of phosphate concentration fell to between 0.2 and 3.20 μg—at/l reaching the highest values and their maximum concentrations (> 2.5 μg—at/l) in the upwelling coastal areas (Guillén and Izaguirre, 1973b). The lowest concentrations (< 1.0 μg-at/l) occurred in subtropical and Equatorial surface waters (Fig. 5).

Vertical distribution of phosphate
Off the coast of Peru, the vertical distribution of phosphate appears in four well-marked layers:
The superficial layer (0—50/100 m) in which the values were relatively uniform and low with concentrations generally around 1 μg—at/l.

The transition layer, in which the phosphate content increased sharply, with values generally from 1 to 2 μg-at/l.

The layer of maximum concentration, in which the phosphates attained their maximum concentration (with values of 2.5 to 3.5 μg—at/l, at depths between 500 and 1,200 m). The absolute maximum of phosphates occurred approximately 200 and 900 m deeper than the absolute minimum of oxygen (Zuta and Guillén, 1970),

The lowest layer, in which the phosphates diminished gradually with depth.

Variations of phosphate
Phosphate varies according to season of the year and to geographic position, the greatest concentrations being at the sea surface in the upwelling areas. In general, the maximum values occur in winter and the minimum in summer.

    Zuta and Guillén (1970) found that, off Punta Falsa and Callao, the greatest changes occurred above 50 m with an annual amplitude at the surface of the sea of 1.23 μg—at/l and 1.25 μg—at/l respectively. The amplitude off Punta Falsa was greater than 1 μg—at/l for the entire 100 m column whereas at Callao the amplitude diminished appreciably with depth.

Silicate

Mean silicate at the sea surface (Fig. 6)
Off the Peruvian coast, the mean ranges of silicate at the surface of the sea (Guillén *et al.*, 1974) reached between 0 and 24 μg—at/l with highest concentrations near the coast. The lowest concentrations (< 5 μg—at/l) occurred in surface subtropical and Equatorial waters.

Vertical distribution
The distribution of silicate with depth occurred also in four well-marked layers.
The surface layer (0—50/100 m), in which the concentration of silicate was low and relatively homogeneous with values less than 10 μg—at/l.

A smooth discontinuity layer, in which silicates increased sharply, with concentrations generally varying between 10 and 30 μg—at/l.

An intermediate layer, in which the changes were slight and with concentrations generally from 30 to 40 μg—at/l.

A deep layer, in which the content increased with the depth.

Variations

The concentration of silicate varies according to geographic position and season of the year (Guillén and Izaguirre, 1973*b*); the greatest concentrations were attained in winter and the lowest in summer.

Nitrate

Mean nitrate at the sea surface (Fig. 7)

The distribution of nitrate off the Peruvian coast at the sea surface occurred over a mean range of 0.5–21 µg–at/l, reaching highest values close to the coast. The greatest level of nitrate occurred in upwelling waters and the lowest in the surface subtropical and Equatorial waters.

Vertical distribution

The vertical distribution of nitrate is similar to that of phosphate and occurs in four layers:

The surface layer (0–50/100 m), which was relatively poor throughout, with concentrations generally less than 5 µg–at/l.

A transition layer, in which the nitrates increased sharply from concentrations of 5–35 µg–at/l.

The maximum layer (500–1,300 m), in which the nitrates reached mean values of 40 to 55 µg–at/l.

A deeper layer, in which the nutrients diminished gradually with depth.

Variations

The concentration of nitrate varied according to the season of the year and the geographic position (Guillén *et al.*, 1974), reaching maximum concentrations during the winter due to intensification of the upwelling processes; it was at its lowest in summer due to its utilization in the photosynthetic process.

Nitrites

Mean nitrite at the sea surface

The distribution of mean values of nitrite off the Peruvian coast was very irregular, ranging between 0.1 and 1.6 µg–at/l, with highest concentrations near the coast and falling off further out. The lowest values (< 0.25 µg–at/l), were found in surface subtropical and Equatorial waters.

Vertical distribution

The vertical distribution of nitrite appeared in three marked layers:

In the surface layer (from 0–50/100 m) the values were generally low.

In the intermediate layer the concentrations were variable and usually showed one or two maxima. The first nitrite maximum appeared with a mean range of 0.1–3.5 µg–at/l, and the second with the mean range of 0.1–5.5 µg–at/l. The origin of two or more maxima appeared to be related to the interaction of two opposite flows across a large cyclonic eddy which apparently had as its centre 12°30′ S. and 80°30′ W., with the flow of subsurface Equatorial waters and the subantarctic waters on the coastal side (Zuta and Guillén, 1970).

In the deepest nitrite layer the values generally fell to near zero.

Variations

The nitrite values vary at the surface as a function of time and space, reaching highest values close to the coast with maximum concentrations during winter and minimum values close to zero during summer.

Relation between nutrients

Guillén and Izaguirre de Rondan (1973*b*) suggested that the relations between apparent oxygen utilization (AOU) and nutrients were associated with circulation processes and mixing of the waters. They found three well-developed layers in relation with AOU and the nutrients: AOU:N:Si:P was 286:16:16:1. They also found a linear correlation between nitrate and phosphate in the relationship 15:6:1 (layer: 260–80 cl/*t*) and 16:1 for the relationship of Si:P for the layer of 260–180 cl/*t*.

Guillén (1973) found a relationship for P:N:Si of 1:10.9:7.4 for the euphotic zone which suggested that the silicates might be one of the most important limits of the photosynthetic system. This would agree with what had been previously found by Guillén and Izaguirre de Rondan (1973*b*) and Dugdale (1972), since the dominant phytoplankton populations off the Peruvian coast are diatoms (Guillén *et al.*, 1971, 1973; Blasco, 1971; Calienes, 1973).

Zuta and Guillén (1970) examined the distribution of the differing relationships of N/Si, N/P and Si/P according to depth and described four distinct layers:

In the surface layer the relationships showed light variations of silicate with other nutrients due to photosynthetic effects.

In the discontinuity layer the relationships varied according to the vertical gradients of nitrate, silicate and phosphate.

In the subsurface layer between 100 and 150 m depth the changes in the ratios of Si/P and N/Si were gradual, whereas the N/P ratio changes were more rapid owing to a tendency to homogeneity of nitrate, silicate and phosphate, and furthermore because of the greater homogeneity of phosphate. Between 100 and 300 m, the great influence of subsurface Equatorial waters was seen, as was evident in the relationship of N/Si, Si/P and AOU.

In the deep layer below 500 m the relationships of Si/P and N/Si generally showed opposite trends because of the steeper increase of silicate with respect to nitrate and phosphate.

PRODUCTIVITY

The biological abundance of the surface waters of the Peruvian current is due principally to the upwelling process which develops above 100 m depth. Another important factor is the turbulent upward transport of nutrients (Posner, 1957; Wyrtki, 1965).

Posner (1957) calculated the productivity of the Peruvian current, assuming a total area of 1.44×10^{12} m^2 and a total area of upwelling of 2.14×10^{10} m^2. Guillén (1964) studied the distribution of phosphate off Callao as a measure of primary production (Guillén and Izaguirre de Rondan, 1968). Various studies of the productivity of waters off Peru have been made by: Guillén, 1973; Guillén et al., 1969, 1971, 1973; Zuta and Guillén, 1970; and Guillén and Rojas de Mendiola, 1974. In abnormal years, for example during the 'El Niño' phenomena of 1965 and 1972 (Guillén, 1971, 1974), the productivity under the influence of tropical and surface Equatorial waters was extremely low.

Chlorophyll a

Mean distribution at the surface (Fig. 8)
Off the Peruvian coast, the annual mean of surface chlorophyll *a* is 1.47 µg/l, within a range of 0.18–5.27 µg/l (Guillén *et al.*, 1973a). High values were found near the coast, with concentrations greater than 2.0 µg/l and the highest concentrations were found off Pucusana (> 5.0 µg/l), Chimbote, Punta Doña María and Ilo (> 4.0 µg/l); these areas coincide with those of the best anchovy fishing. The lowest values (1.0 µg/l) were found in surface subtropical and Equatorial waters (Guillén and Izaguirre, 1973a).

Vertical distribution
The vertical distribution of chlorophyll was studied by Zuta and Guillén (1970) and Guillén and Izaguirre (1973a, b). Guillén *et al.* (1974) deduced that its distribution was not homogeneous in surface layers and was usually characterized by regional maxima. Generally a maxium was located close to the bottom of the euphotic zone in the region of the thermocline. The origin of this maximum has been discussed by Riley *et al.* (1949). Steele and Yentsch (1960), Lorenzen (1967) and Hobson and Lorenzen (1972).

The distribution of chlorophyll *a* off Peru is low and homogeneous well off the coast, whereas close to the coast it is irregular and generally shows more than one maximum. Maximum values of chlorophyll *a* were found in the 0–20 m layer.

Guillén *et al.* (1973a) found in the 60-mile band along the coast, a mean for the euphotic zone, the 0–25, 0–50 and 0–100 layers of 63, 64, 93 and 123 mg/m^2, respectively. Zuta and Guillén (1970) found a maximum value of 212 mg/m^2 of chlorophyll *a* for the 0–100 m layer.

Variation
The concentration of chlorophyll *a* varied according to latitude and season of the year. During the winter when stability diminished, the distribution of chlorophyll *a* was highly uniform with depth (Guillén *et al.*, 1973a).

Primary production

Mean primary production at the surface (Fig. 9)
Off the Peruvian coast, primary production values of from 0 to 500 mg C/m^3/day were found. The highest mean concentrations were close to the coast, off Salaverry (> 200 mg C/m^3/day), and off San Juan (> 400 mg C/M^3/day).

However, 100 miles further out, values of no more than 50 mg C/m^3/day are observed and, in the surface Equatorial and subtropical waters still lower values of (10 mg C/m^3/day) have been found.

Vertical distribution
The total production (Fig. 10). Off the Peruvian coast, the mean values of total production were between 0.1 and 4.0 g C/m^2/day, showing the richness of the zone within 100 miles from the coast;

exceptional values were found within 50-mile limits as a result of upwelling. The greatest concentrations were found off Salaverry ($>$ 1.5 g C/m²/day) and off San Juan ($>$ 3.5 g C/m²/day). Highest production values were found at the latter (8.88 g C/m²/day) on the Unanue 6705 cruise and 11.4 g C/m²/day, obtained in the Anton Brunn expedition, cruise 15. In strictly coastal waters, values of 0.5 g C/m²/day were found and values less than 0.2 g C/m²/day were common for surface Equatorial and subtropical waters.

The mean distribution of the productivity indexes (Guillén, 1973) showed greatest concentrations along and near the coast, the maximum values being in the upwelling areas off Talara, Paita. ($>$ 140 mg C/mg Cla/day), Huacho—Callao ($>$ 120 mg C/mg Cla/day) and Pisco—San Juan ($>$ 80 mg C/mg Cla/day). These were associated with high nutrient concentrations. The lowest values of the productivity index ($<$ 20 mg C/mg Cla/day) corresponded to surface subtropical waters which were characterized by low production and low nutrient contents. Guillén also found a mean productivity index of 29.0 mg C/mg Cla/day for the euphotic zone and, considering all the data concerning different light intensities in the euphotic zone, established a mean of 42 mg C/mg Cla/day. Relating the productivity index to radiation showed no correlation which implied that in surface subtropical waters the nutrients are more important than radiation.

Variations

The distribution of productivity showed geographical and seasonal variations (Zuta and Guillén, 1970; Guillén, 1973; Guillén *et al.*, 1974). Guillén (1973) showed the variations of productivity in relation to the different water masses off the Peruvian coast. Zuta and Guillén (1970) reported the variation of mean total production along the entire coast for a coastal band of 30 to 60 miles in width in which four maxima were seen around 5°, 8°, 11° and 15° S., with mean values of 2.2 and 1.3 g C/m²/day at 8° and 15° S., respectively (for the 30-mile band). The mean total production for the entire coast was 1.2 g C/m²/day, equivalent to a production of 438 g C/m²/year (Guillén *et al.*, 1974).

Values given for selected upwelling areas were averaged in the tables published by Cushing (1969): California, 0.22 g C/m³/day; Peru, 0.67 g C/m³/day; Canarias, 0.39 g C/m³/day; Bengala, 0.88 g C/m³/day; north/west Australia, 0.28 g C/m³/day.

It is thought that the primary production values given for the Peruvian coast by Guillén and Izaguirre de Rondan (1968), Cushing (1969), Zuta and Guillén (1970) and Guillén *et al.* (1974) may be lower than the true value, largely owing to the scarcity of data.

Water masses

Wyrtki (1967) made a detailed study of the water masses of the eastern Pacific Ocean. The water masses which penetrated the area off the Pacific coast of Peru did so by horizontal flow towards the pole and Equator. This movement was followed by mixing.

SURFACE WATER MASSES

The following masses and types of water are distinguishable at the sea surface off Peru (Wyrtki, 1967; Zuta and Guillén, 1970):
Surface subtropical waters characterized by high temperature and low salinity, normally appeared north of 4° S. with salinity less than 33.8 per mille.
Surface, Equatorial waters normally appeared north of 6° S., reaching their greatest intensities during spring and summer with salinities less than 34.8 per mille. The variation of these waters was apparently caused by displacements of the Equatorial front.
Surface subtropical waters of high salinity also had variable temperature ranges and appeared to have salinities greater than 35.1 per mille.
Cold coastal waters were characterized by salinities of 34.8—35.1 per mille. The limits between these water masses were subject to seasonal fluctuations. In most cases, these were limiting zones rather than fronts.
For vertical maps of temperature, salinity and nutrients see Figures 11—15. Also see Figures 16—19.

SUBSURFACE WATER MASSES

According to Zuta and Guillén (1970), the two water masses were found in the subsurface.

The subsurface Equatorial waters between 50 and 300 m had temperatures of 13°—15° C and salinities of 34.9—35.1 per mille. As they advanced southwards they diminished in density, temperature and salinity. These waters were characterized by being relatively saline and having a relatively high oxygen content; this was the result of the fact that they came from the southern branch of the divisions of the Cromwell current.

The deep Equatorial waters between 150–700 m were characterized by temperatures of 7°–13° C and salinities of 34.6–34.9 per mille.

Taking into account the common characteristics of these waters, Wyrtki (1967) identified the layer. with minimum dissolved oxygen and temperatures of 5° to 15° C (found off Peru) as a single water mass. Called the subsurface Equatorial waters, this mass had almost the same characteristics of temperature and salinity as indicated by Sverdrup *et al.* (1946) for the 'Equatorial Pacific water mass' (temperature 5° to 15° C and salinities 34.55-35.00 per mille). The temperate waters of the subantarctic off Peru (0–100 m) had temperatures of 13°–15° C and salinities of 34.6–34.8 per mille. They were characterized by a salinity minimum above the salinity maximum of the subsurface Equatorial waters. The intermediate antarctic waters had temperature of 7°–4° C and salinities of 34.45–34.60 per mille (below 600 to 700 m in depth down to about 1000 m).

Circulation

The flow which moves northwards as part of the anticyclonic circulation of the South Pacific along the coast off Peru is called the Peruvian current. It should be referred to as the Peruvian 'system of currents', since it consists of several more or less independent branches which interact in a complex way. Schott (1931) interpreted these currents on the basis of observations of surface currents, temperature and salinity. The results of research in the waters along the South American coast by the vessel *William Scoresby* in 1931 was described by Gunther (1936), who distinguished a subsurface coastal current which carries high salinity waters southwards from the Peruvian coastal current and the Peruvian oceanic current further from the coast. Moreover, he maintained that upwelling was a process of little depth which carried waters from a mean depth of 130 m to the surface, and was irregular in time and space both as a structure and appearance. Sverdrup *et al.* (1946) supplemented Gunther's investigations with evidence that the northerly transport by the Peruvian current was 10–15 × 10¹² cm³/sec., and that the water of the subsurface coastal current was probably of Equatorial origin. Yoshida and Tsuchiya (1957) theoretically established a connection

between upwelling and coastal poleward flows. Wooster and Reid (1963) likewise dealt with a subsurface coastal current off California, Peru and Chile.

A detailed study of circulation and the eastern Pacific Ocean has been made by Wyrtki (1965a, 1966 and 1967) particularly of the Peruvian current, by Wyrtki (1963), Stevenson *et al.* (1970) and Zuta and Guillén (1970).

SURFACE CURRENTS

Along the Peruvian coast, the Peruvian coastal current and the Peruvian oceanic current (further from the coast) flow to the north-east as parts of the anticyclonic circulation of the South Pacific Ocean. These two currents are generally separated by a weak and irregular flow to the south, the Peruvian countercurrent. The latter is subsurface (though it occasionally reaches the surface, Wyrtki, 1963). Stevenson *et al.* (1970) found that the Peruvian coastal current could be followed from Arica up to 5° S. at normal speeds of 4–15 cm/sec., sometimes reaching speeds of 40–80 cm/sec. Wyrtki (1965a) found the mean speed to be 0.2–0.3 knots along the coast. It attained speeds of 0.5–0.7 knots when it reached the coast off Punta Aguja and flowed westwards to form subsequently part of the sub-Equatorial current. The flow of the Peruvian coastal current was more intense during the period from April to September and its transport was generally confined to the top 200 m of water (Stevenson *et al.*, 1970).

To the east of 82° W., the Peruvian oceanic current, as it is called by Gunther (1936), flowed northwards (Wyrtki, 1963). It reached depths of 700 m, then turned westward and moved into the region south of 10° S. The Peruvian oceanic current was more intense than the Peruvian coastal current; this was explained in a theoretical treatise by Stommel (1958).

Wyrtki (1963) calculated the transport of the Peruvian current as 6 × 10⁶ m³/sec. and that of the Peruvian oceanic current as 8 × 10⁶ m³/sec., i.e. a total of 14 × 10⁶ m³/sec.

The countercurrent was absent from the sea surface from July to October, showing its greatest intensity from November to February. The Peruvian coastal current and the Peruvian oceanic current formed a single uniform northward flow from July to October, which thereafter joined the sub-Equatorial current. The contribution of the Peruvian current to the sub-Equatorial current is 14×10^6 m³/sec. When the countercurrent develops, the waters of the coastal current pass through the countercurrent to the oceanic current.

SUBSURFACE CURRENTS

The subsurface Peruvian/Chilean current (Wooster and Gilmartin, 1961) flowed southwards at speeds of 4–10 cm/sec. off Peru, except off Punta Falsa where speeds of 20 cm/sec. were registered.

The transport of geostrophic flow diminished southwards, from 21×10^6 m³/sec at 5° S. to about 3×10^6 m³/sec. at 15° S. At 15° S. it is characterized by relative high salinity and temperature and low dissolved oxygen content. South of Chile it is also evident by its phosphate and silicate maxima.

Wyrtki (1963) found a new subsurface current, the Peruvian countercurrent, which was distinct and more intense than the Peruvian/Chilean subsurface countercurrent. The countercurrent was seen clearly in vertical sections published by Wooster and Gilmartin (1961). The profiles showed that the countercurrent was separated from the subsurface current in all sections south of Punta Aguja and that, in its turn, it was more intense than the subsurface current. The countercurrent (Wyrtki, 1966) was stronger near 100 m depth and reached approximately 500 m, transporting about 10×10^{12} cm³/sec. at 5° S. Afterwards it diminished rapidly to 6×10^{12} cm³/sec. at 15° S., and 2×10^{12} cm³/sec. at 22° S. Cochrane and Zuta (1968) and White (1969) did not find such differences, they rather established that the subsurface countercurrent originated at the union of the Cromwell current extension and the south Equatorial countercurrent. Zuta and Guillén (1970) named this current the Peruvian subsurface current. A part of the 'extension of the Cromwell current' moves south close to the coast. This contributes principally to upwelling north of 9° S.

The south Equatorial countercurrent flows from west to east at about 9° S. between depths of 100 and 500 m. This countercurrent was discussed by Reid (1959, 1961) and Wooster (1961*b*) and later by Wyrtki (1963). According to Reid it flowed from 8° to 10° S. at the surface of the sea (at speeds of 8–15 cm/sec.), transporting 10×10^6 m³/sec. Wooster (1961) and Wyrtki (1963) indicated that the entry of the Equatorial countercurrent from the south of the eastern tropical Pacific occurred along the meridian 95° W., between 5° and 8° S.

The Chilean current (Wooster, 1968) flows to the north and north-east between depths of 50 and 150 m near the Peruvian coast.

Upwellings

The coastal upwelling is a vertical movement which renews the surface waters with subsurface waters rich in nutrients and low in dissolved oxygen content. Along the coast, upwelling is limited principally to depths less than 100 m, whereas further from the coast the ascending movements may come from greater depths. The area in which ascent takes place within the discontinuity layer extends out to 700 km from the coast. The mean spead of such ascending movements is 20×10^{-5} cm/sec., equal to 5 m per month.

Hidaka (1954), Yoshida (1955, 1958 and 1967), Yoshida and Tsuchiya (1957), Yoshida and Mao (1957), and Smith (1968) have all dealt with upwelling processes and their effects on the distribution of properties, climate and biological wealth. With respect to upwellings along the Peruvian coast, Schweigger (1958) indicated six different areas in contrast with the four areas described by Schott (1931) and Gunther (1936).

The total contribution of upwelling to the area off Peru is approximately of 3×10^{12} m³/sec. The greater part of these waters are supplied by subsurface movement from the north and north-west with a mean ascending movement (Wyrtki, 1963) of from 1 to 2×10^{-4} cm/sec. at depths of about 100 m. A mean upwelling speed of 1.67 m/day was calculated by Posner (1957), whereas those reported by Schott (1931), Wyrtki (1963), and Zuta and Guillén (1970) were 0.5 m/day, 0.6 m/day, 5 m/month and 10–7 m/month respectively.

If the limit of coastal upwelling were measured at the point where the isotherms began the descending loop at the base of upwelling layer, it could have been said that the coastal upwelling extended 80–220 miles (145–400 km) from the coast, however, the limit of coastal upwelling was generally at 140–160 miles (250–290 km) from the coast (Stevenson *et al.*, 1970). The upwelling speed along the Peruvian coast was estimated at approximately 1.9×10^{-5} cm/sec. by Posner (1957), and $5 - 30 \times 10^{-5}$ cm/sec. by Wyrtki (1963).

A comparative study of all the eastern limitrophic currents of the oceans and their zones of upwelling has been made by Wooster and Reid (1963). The total divergence of wind drift along the Peruvian coast between 5° and 24° S. has been estimated at 4.6×10^{12} m³/sec. (Wyrtki, 1966), which is partially compensated for by the horizontal convergent flow and by upwelling.

The intensity of coastal upwellings varied according to geographical position and season; thus Zuta and Guillén (1970) found the following variations: spring, 7°, 12°, 15° S.; summer, 9°, 12°, 15° S.; autumn, 5°, 7°, 10°, 15° S.; winter, 5°, 7°, 9°, 12°, 14°, 16° S.

The upwelling waters along the Peruvian coast were principally from three sources: (a) waters of the Cromwell current extension which were upwelled principally between 4 and 6° S. and contributed in part to upwelling north of 9° S.; (b) waters coming from the Peruvian/Chilean subsurface countercurrent which upwelled principally to the north 12° S., and which during summer and autumn could possibly influence upwelling further south; and (c) temperate subantarctic waters, which came from the south across the Chilean flow, upwelled principally to the south of 14° S. (see Zuta and Guillén, 1970).

The typical and almost permanent upwelling along the coast appeared between 14° and 15° S. whereas areas between 4 and 6° S., 7 and 8° S. and 11 and 12° S. were regions of secondary importance.

Zuta and Guillén (1970) calculated 25,250 square miles as the mean upwelling area. This area was located at 850 miles from the coast line and had a width of approximately 30 miles. The seasonal variations of this area are as follows: summer, 12,000; autumn, 25,000; winter, 36,000 and spring, 28,000 square miles respectively.

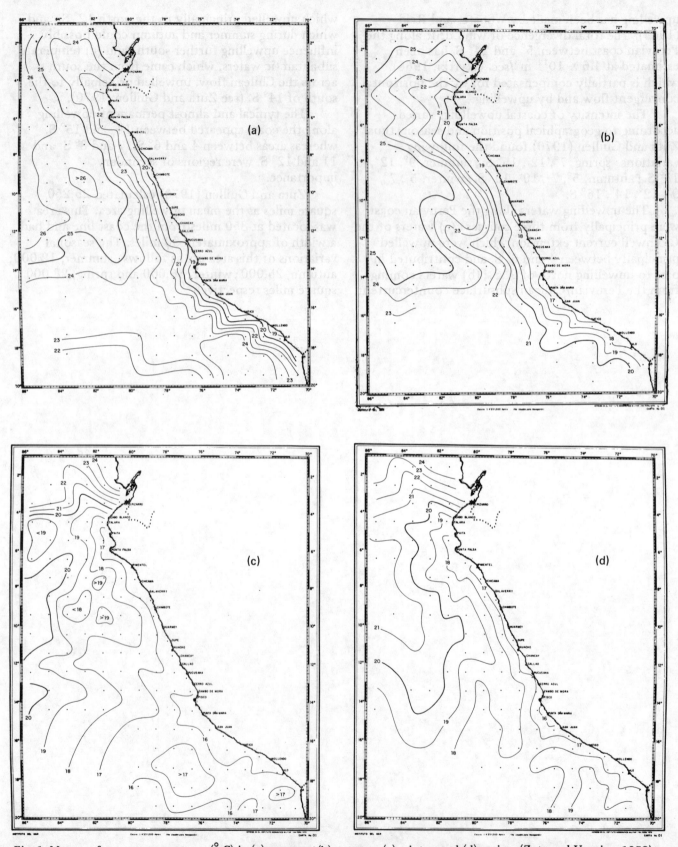

Fig. 1. Mean surface sea temperatures (°C) in (a) summer, (b) autumn, (c) winter, and (d) spring. (Zuta and Urquizo, 1972).

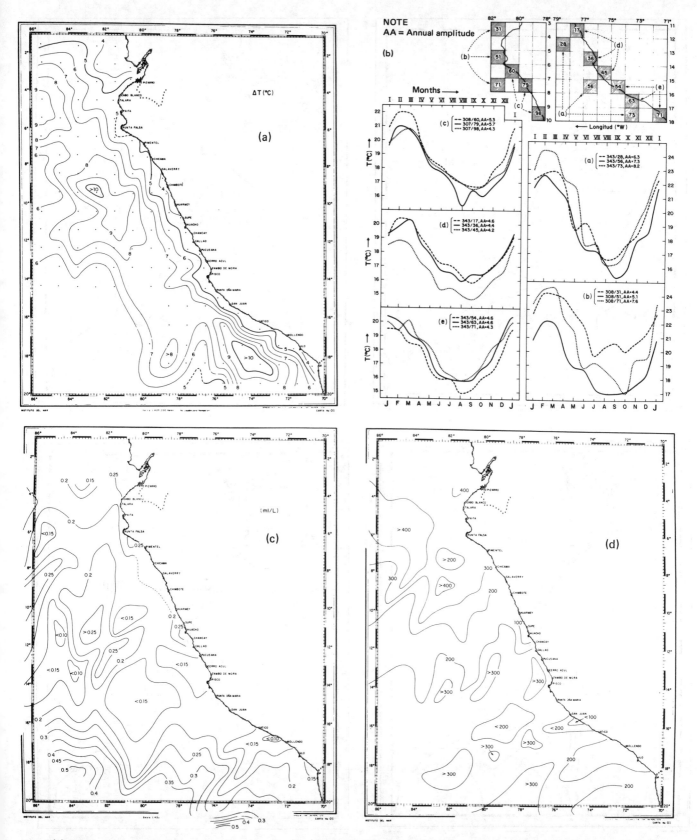

Fig. 2(a). Mean annual variation sea surface temperature (Zuta.and Urquizo, 1972); (b) Mean Monthly variation sea surface temperature (Zuta and Urquizo, 1972); (c) Minimum mean oxygen saturation; (d) Topographical mean of oxygen saturation (Zuta and Guillén, 1970).

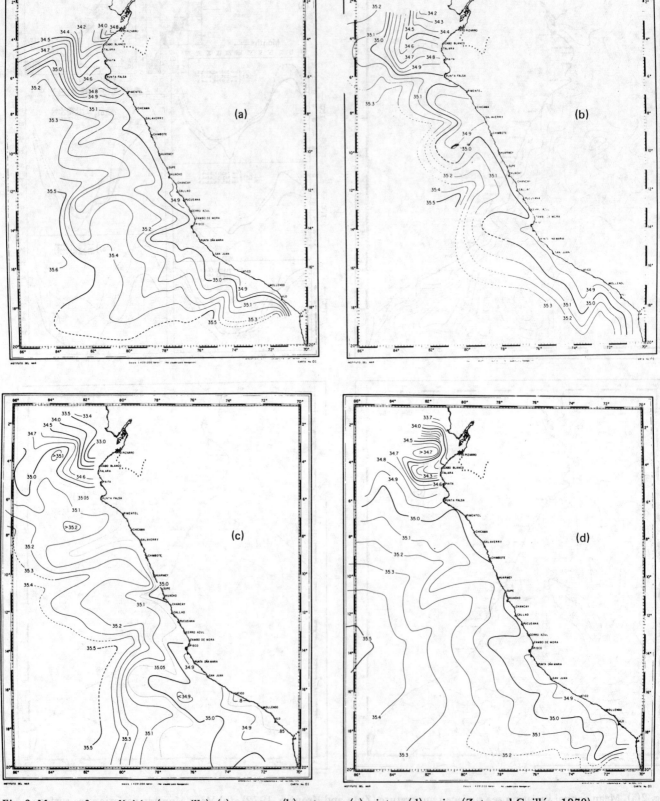

Fig. 3. Mean surface salinities (per mille). (a) summer; (b) autumn; (c) winter; (d) spring (Zuta and Guillén, 1970).

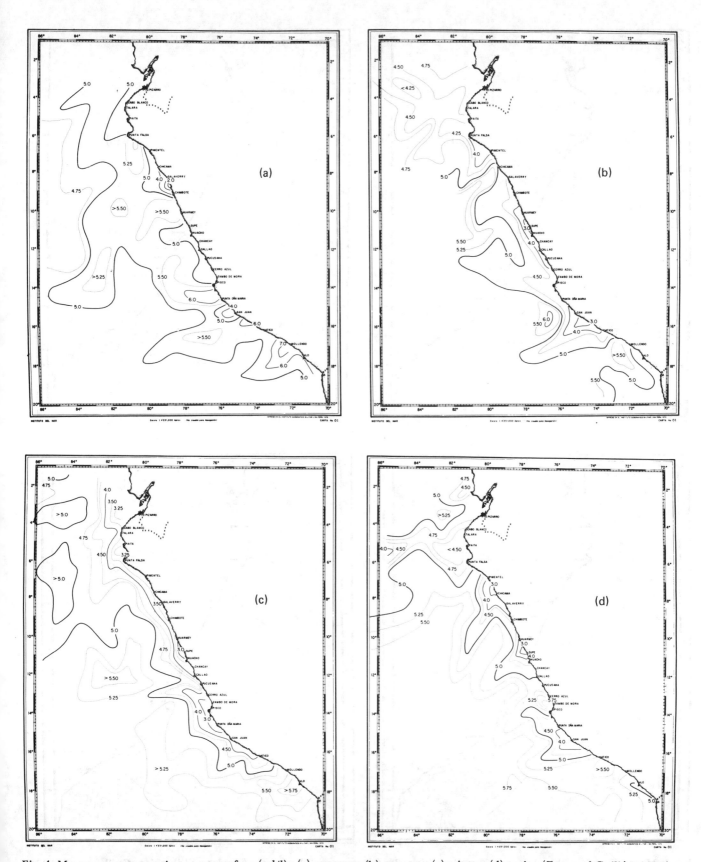

Fig. 4. Mean oxygen saturation at sea surface (ml/l): (a) summer; (b) autumn; (c) winter; (d) spring (Zuta and Guillén, 1970).

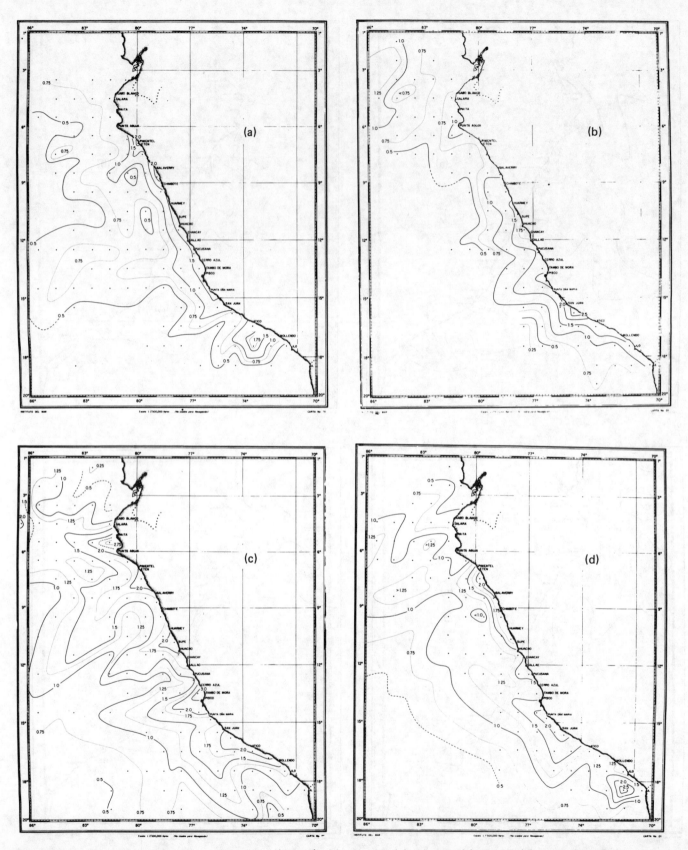

Fig. 5. Mean sea surface phosphate concentrations (μg-at/l): (a) summer; (b) autumn; (c) winter; (d) spring (Guillén *et al.*, 1974).

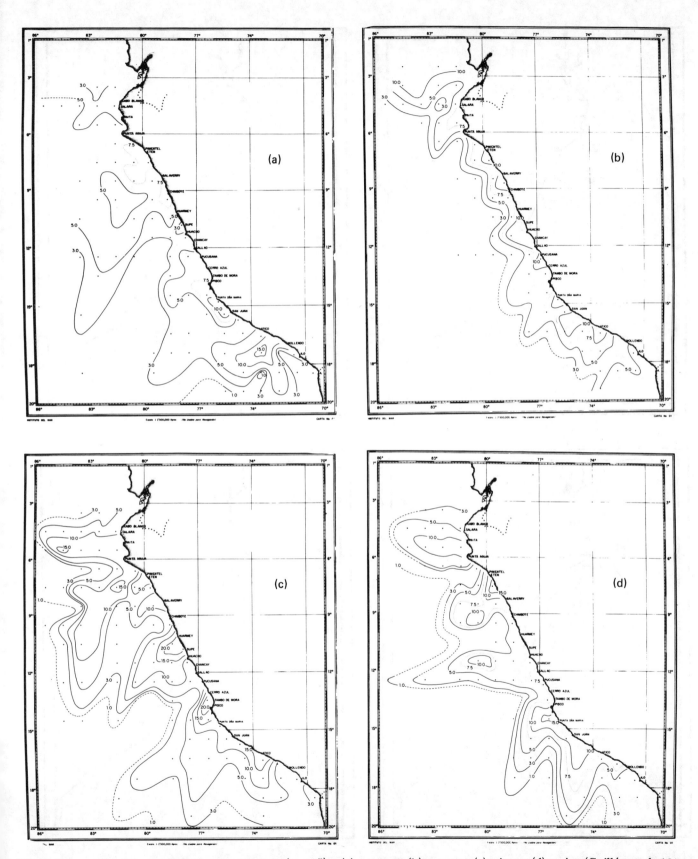

Fig. 6. Mean sea surface for silicate concentrations (μg-at/l): (a) summer; (b) autumn; (c) winter; (d) spring (Guillén *et al.*, 1974.

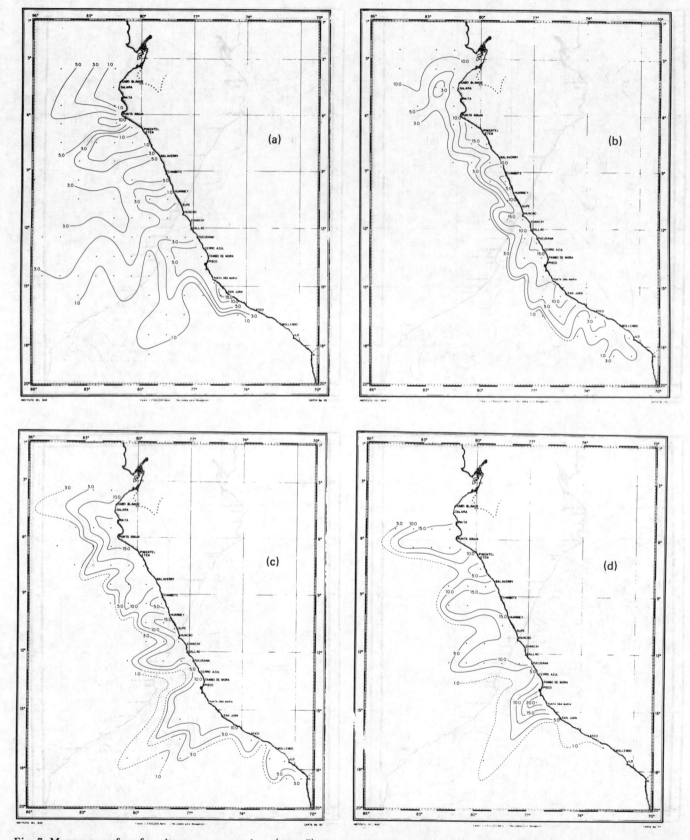

Fig. 7. Mean sea surface for nitrate concentrations (μg-at/l): (a) summer; (b) autumn; (c) winter; (d) spring (Guillén, *et al.*, 1974).

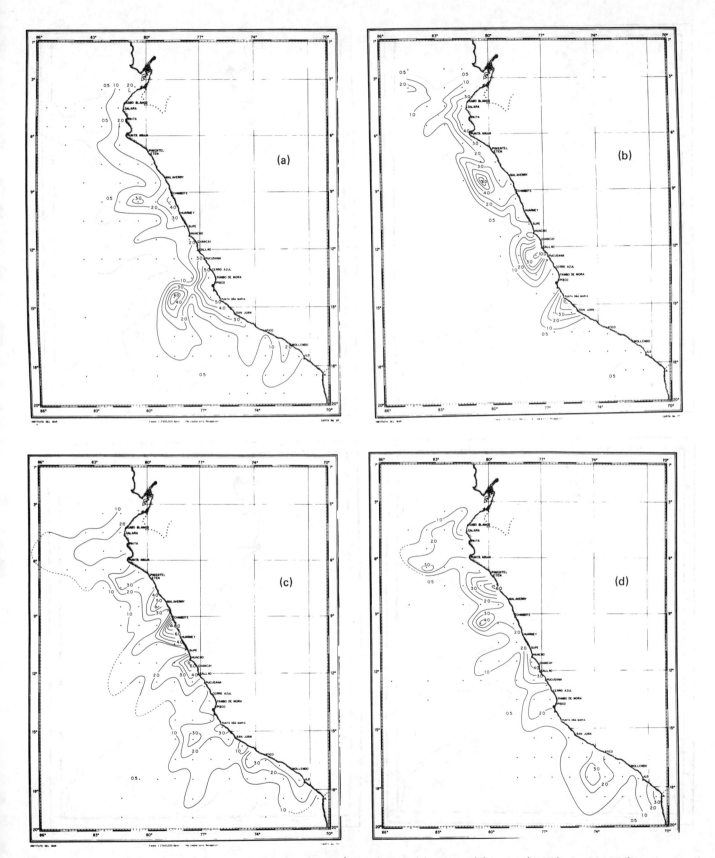

Fig. 8. Mean sea surface for chlorophyll *a* (μg/l) (a) summer;|(b) autumn; (c) winter; (d) spring (Guillén *et al.*, 1974).

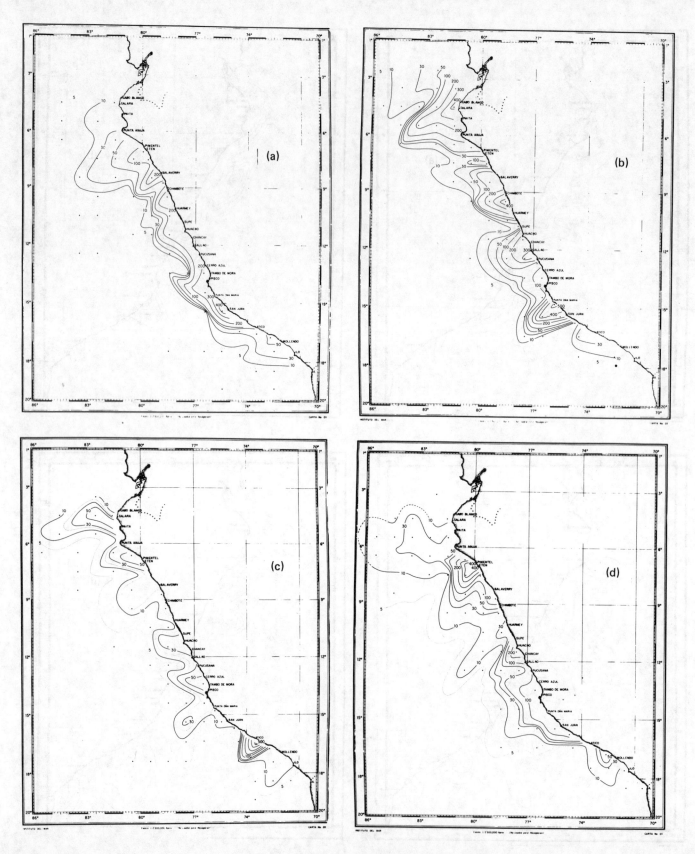

Fig. 9. Mean sea surface for primary production (mg C/m³/day): (a) summer; (b) autumn; (c) winter; (d) spring (Guillén *et al.*, 1974).

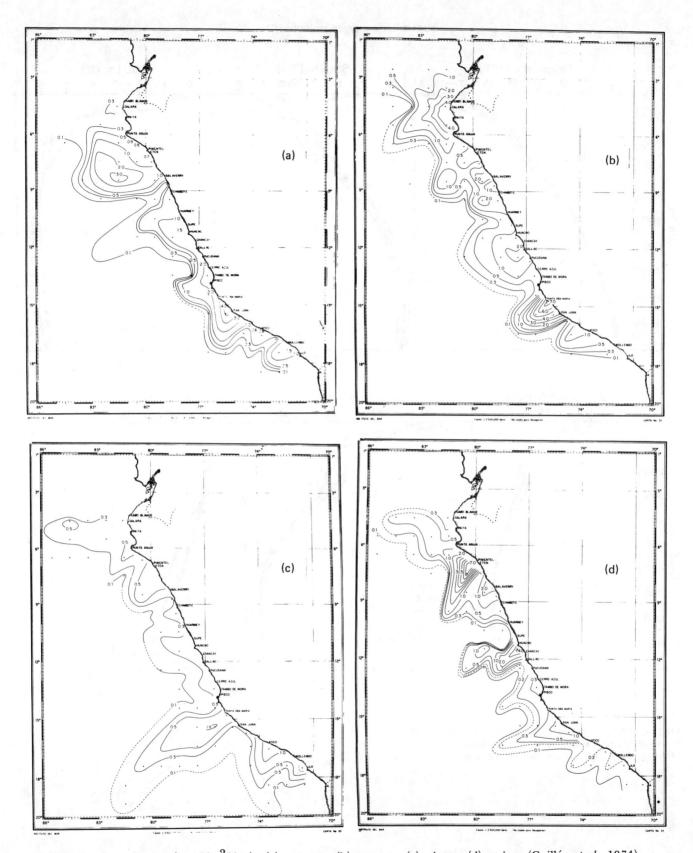

Fig. 10. Total production (mg C/m^2/day) : (a) summer ; (b) autumn ; (c) winter ; (d) spring ; (Guillén *et al.*, 1974).

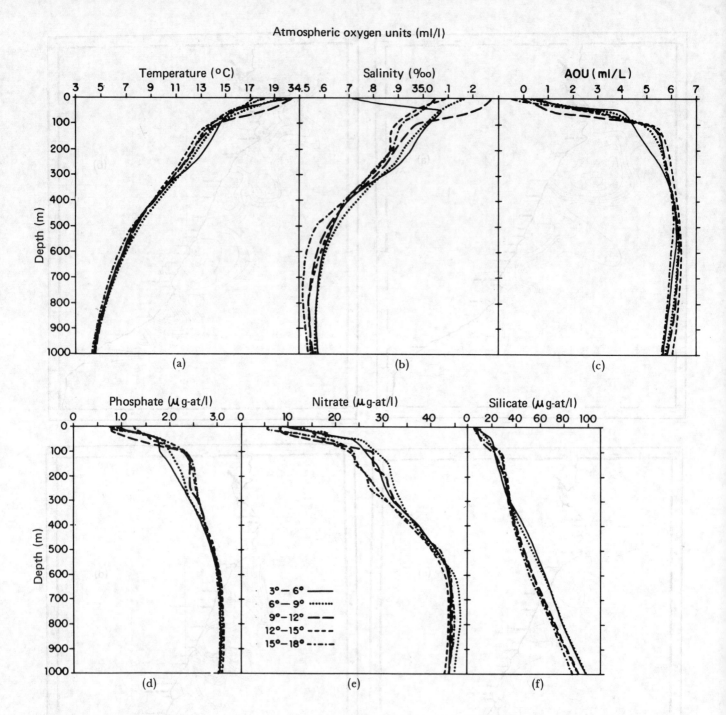

Fig. 11. Vertical sea distribution of : (a) temperature ;
(b) salinity ; (c) atmospheric oxygen units ;
(d) phosphate ; (e) nitrate and (f) silicate.

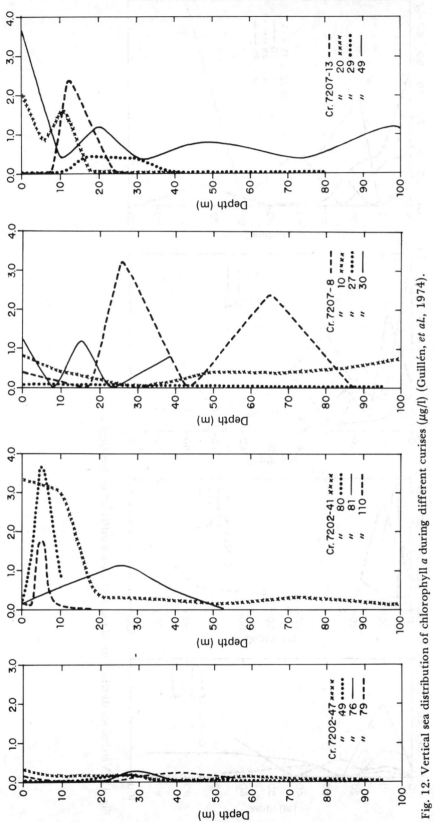

Fig. 12. Vertical sea distribution of chlorophyll *a* during different curises (µg/l) (Guillén, *et al.*, 1974).

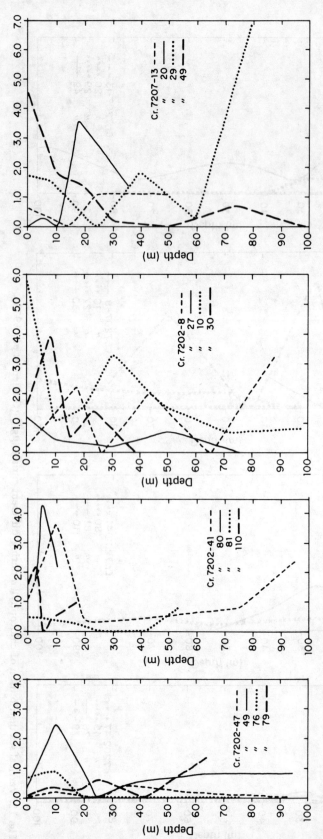

Fig. 13. Vertical sea distribution of pigment during different cruises (μg/l).

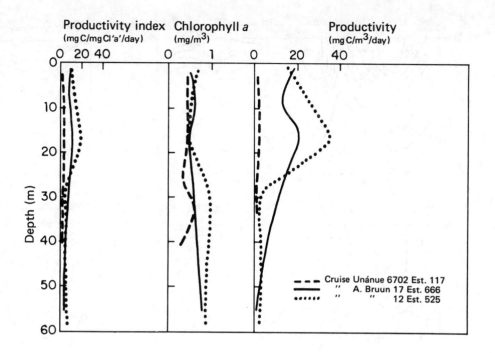

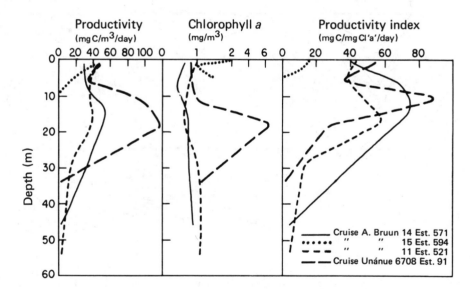

Fig. 14. Vertical sea distribution of total productivity, chlorophyll *a* and productivity index for two different periods (Guillén, 1973).

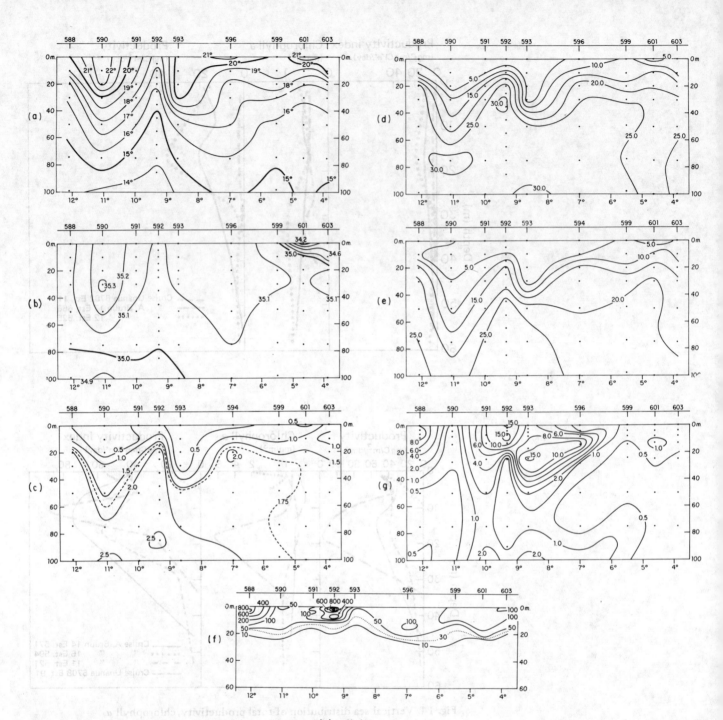

Fig. 15. Parallel zone to coast. Data of (a) temperature; (b) salinity
(c) phosphate; (d) nitrate; (e) silicate; (f) primary production
and (g) chlorophyll *a*.

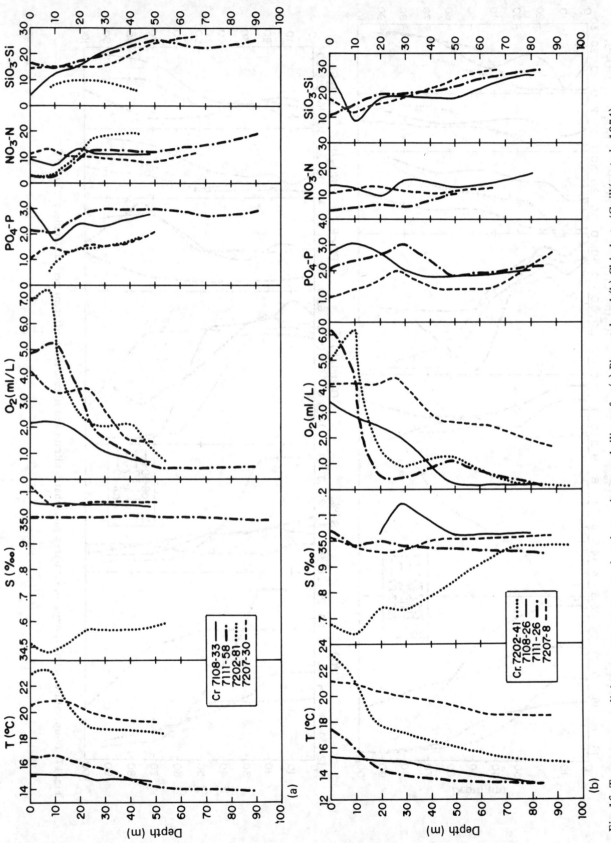

Fig. 16. Temperature, salinity, oxygen saturates, phosphate, nitrate and silicate for (a) Pimentel and (b) Chimbote (Guillén *et al.*, 1974).

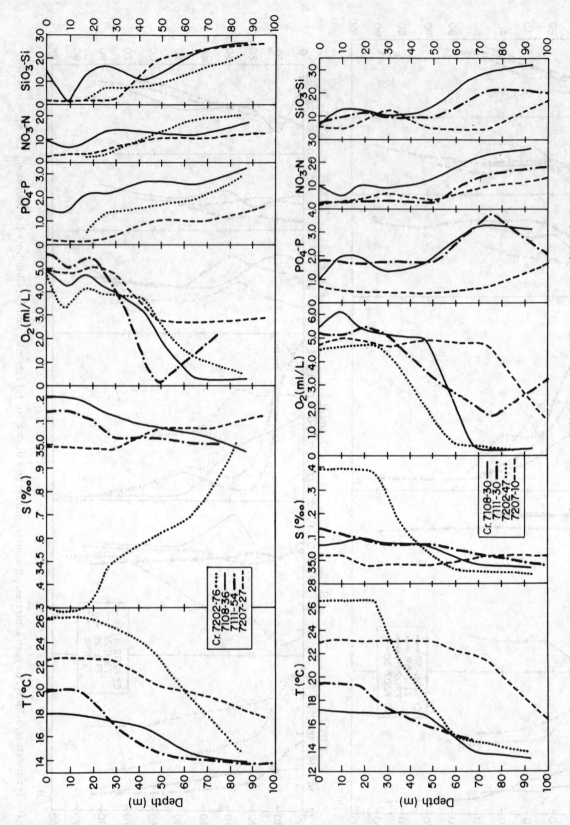

Fig. 17. Temperature, salinity, oxygen, saturates, phosphate, nitrate and silicate for a different period (Guillén, *et al.*, 1974).

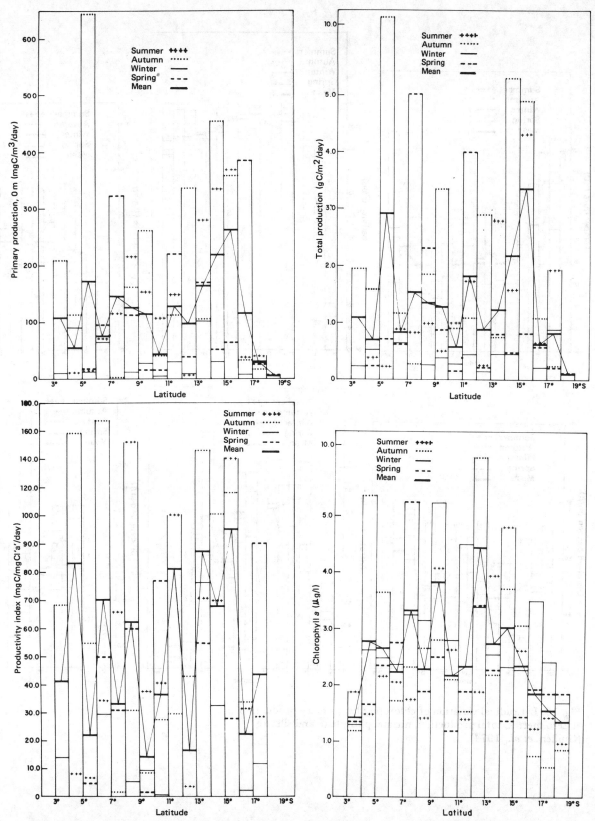

Fig. 18. Latitudinal variation of temperature, salinity, oxygen structure, phosphate, nitrate and silicate for the various seasons against productivity of chlorophyll *a*. (Guillén and Izaguirre, 1974).

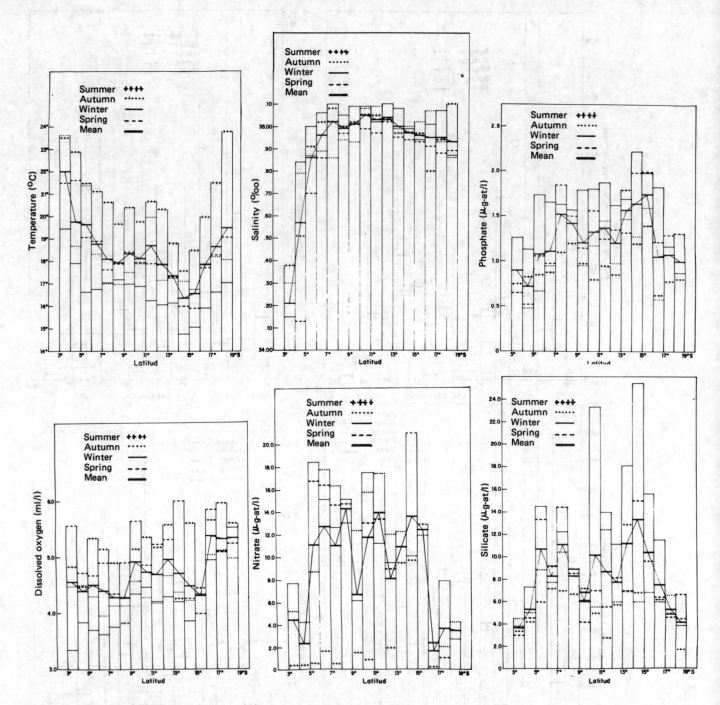

Fig. 19. Latitudinal variation of chlorophyll *a*, primary production at zero metres, total production, nitrate, phosphate and silicate. (Guillén, *et al.*, 1974).

References

Bennett, E. B. 1966. Monthly Charts of Surface Salinity in the Eastern Tropical Pacific Ocean. *Inter-Amer. Trop. Tuna Comm. Bull.*, Vol. 11 No. 1, p. 1–44.

Bjerknes, J. 1961. 'El Niño' Study Based on Analysis of Ocean Surface Temperatures 1935–1957. *Inter-Amer. Trop. Tuna Comm. Bull.*, Vol. 5, No. 3, p. 217–304.

Blasco, D. 1971. Composición y Distribución del Fitoplancton en la Región del Afloramiento de las Costas Peruanas. *Inv. Pesq.*, Vol. 35, No. 1, . p. 61–112.

Calienes, R. 1973. Diversidad y Asociación de Fitoplancton en el Callao. Arequipa, Univ. Nac. San Augustin. (Thesis.)

Cochrane, J. D.; Zuta, S. 1968. *Equatorial Currents East of the Galápagos Islands in February–March, 1967.* Texas A. and M. University, Department of Oceanography.

Cushing, D. H. 1969. *Upwelling and Fish Production.* 40 p. (FAO Fish. Tech. Pap., 84).

Dugdale, R. C. 1972. *Chemical Oceanography and Primary Productivity in Upwelling Regions.* University of Washington.

Guillén, O. 1964. Distribución del Contenido de Fosfatos en la Región de la Corriente Peruana, *Inf. Inst. de Inv. de los Rec. Mar.*, Vol. 28, p. 1–15.

——. 1971. The 'El Niño' Phenomenon in 1965 and its Relations with the Productivity in Coastal Peruvian Waters. In: J. Costlow (ed.), *Fertility of the Sea,* Vol. 1, p. 187–96. New York, N.Y., Gordon & Breach.

——. 1973. Carbon Chlorophyll Relationships in Peruvian Coastal Waters. *Oceanography of the South Pacific 1972,* Wellington: New Zealand National Commission for Unesco.

——. 1974. The 'El Niño' Phenomenon in 1972 and its Relations with the Productivity in Coastal Peruvian Waters. Paper presented at Twentieth Eastern Pacific Oceanic Conference, 2–4 Ocotbur 1974.

Guillén, O.; Izaguirre de Rondan, R. 1968. Producción Primaria de las Aguas Coteras del Perú en el Año 1964. *Inst. Mar Perú, Bol.*, Vol. 1, No. 7, p. 349–76.

——. 1973a. Distribution of Chlorophyll a in the Peru Coastal Current. *Oceanography of the South Pacific 1972,* Wellington, New Zealand National Commission for Unesco.

——. 1973b. Nutrients in the Peru Coastal Current. *Oceanography of the South Pacific 1972,* Wellington, New Zealand National Commission for Unesco.

Guillén, O.; Izaguirre de Rondan, R.; Calienes, R. 1969. Contribucción al Estudio del Ambiente de la Anchoveta (*Engraulis ringens* J.). *Bol. Mar. Perú,* Vol. 2, No. 2, p. 49–76.

Guillén, O.; Izaguirre de Rondan, R.; Rojas de Mendiola. 1971. Primary Productivity and Phytoplankton in the Coastal Peruvian Waters. *Fertility of the Sea,* Vol. 1, p. 157–85. New York, N.Y., Gordon & Breach.

——. 1973. Primary Productivity and Phytoplankton in the Coastal Peruvian Waters. *Oceanography of the South Pacific 1972.* Wellington, New Zealand National Commission for Unesco.

——. 1974. Productividad Biológica de las Aguas Costeras del Perú. *Inst. Mar Perú. Bol.*

Gunther, E. R. 1936. A Report on Oceanographical Investigations in the Peru Coastal Current. *Discovery Rep.*, Vol. 13, p. 107–276.

Hobson, L. A.; Lorenzen, J. 1972. Relationships of Chlorophyll Maxima to Density Structure in the Atlantic Ocean and Gulf of Mexico. *Deep-sea Res.,* Vol. 19, p. 297–306.

Hidaka, K. 1954. A Contribution to the Theory of Upwelling and Coastal Currents. *Trans. Amer. Geophy. Un.,* Vol. 35, p. 431–44.

Lorenzen, J. 1967. Vertical Distribution of Chlorophyll and Phaeo-pigments: Baja California. *Deep-sea Res.,* Vol. 14, p. 735–45.

Mujica, R. 1972. El Mar Peruano. *Historia Marítima del Perú.* Vol. 1.

Posner, G. S. 1957. The Peru Current. *Bull. Bingham Oceanogr. Coll.,* Vol. 16, No. 2, p. 106–55.

Reid, J. L. Jr. 1959. Evidence of a South Equatorial Countercurrent in the Pacific Ocean. *Nature* (London), Vol. 184, p. 209–10.

——. 1961. On the Geostrophic Flow at the Surface of the Pacific Ocean with Respect to the 1000-decibar Surface. *Tellus,* Vol. 13, No. 4, p. 489–502.

Riley, G. A.; Stommel; Bumpus, D. F. 1949. Quantitative Ecology of the Plankton of the Western North Atlantic. *Bull. Bingham Oceanogr. Coll.,* Vol. 12, p. 1–169.

Schott, G. 1931. Der Peru Strom und seine Nordlichen Nachbargebiete in Normaler Ausbildung. *Ann. Hydro. Mar. Meteorol.,* Vol. 59, p. 161–9, 200–13, 240–52.

——. 1935. *Geographie des Indischen und Stillen Ozeans.* Hamburg.

Schweigger, E. H. 1958. Upwelling along the Coast of Peru. *J. Oceanogr. Soc. Japan,* Vol. 14, No. 3, p. 87–91.

Smith, R. L. 1968. Upwelling. *Oceanogr. Mar. Biol. Ann. Rov.,* Vol. 6, p. 11–46.

Steele, J. H.; Yentsch, C. S. 1960. The Vertical Distribution of Chlorophyll. *J. Mar. Biol. Assoc. U.K.,* Vol. 39, p. 217–26.

Stevenson, M. R.; Guillén, O.; Santoro de Icasa, J. 1970. *Marine Atlas of the Pacific Coastal Waters of South America.* University of California Press, 23 p.

Stommel, H. 1958. A Survey of Ocean Current Theory. *Deep-sea Res.,* Vol. 4, p. 149–84.

Sverdrup, H. U.; Johnson, M. W.; Flemming, R. H. 1946 *The Ocean, Their Physics, Chemistry and General Biology.* New York, N.Y., Prentice-Hall, 1087 p.

U.S. Navy Hydrographic Office. 1944. *World Atlas of Sea Surface Temperatures.* Washington, D.C. (H. O. Publ. 225).

White, W. B. 1969. The Equatorial Undercurrent, the South Equatorial Undercurrent and their Extension in the South Pacific East of the Galapagos Islands, During February—March 1967. *Tech. Rep. ONR Contract No. 2119(04).* Texas A and M. University, (69—4—1), 44 p.

Wooster, W. S. 1961. Further Evidence of a Pacific South Equatorial Countercurrent. *Deep-sea Res.,* Vol. 8, No. 3/4, p. 294—7.

——. 1968. Eastern Boundary Currents in the South Pacific. Paper presented at SCOR Symposium on Scientific Exploration of the South Pacific, June 18—20.

Wooster, W. S.; Gilmartin, M. 1961. The Peru—Chile Undercurrent. *J. Marine Res.,* Vol. 19, p. 97—122.

Wooster, W. S.; Reid, J. L. 1963. Eastern Boundary Currents. In: M. N. Hill (ed.) *The Sea,* Vol. 2, p. 253-80. New York and London, Interscience.

Wyrtki, K. 1963. The Horizontal and Vertical Field of Motion in the Peru Current. *Bull. Scripps Inst. Oceanogr.,* Vol. 8, p. 313—46.

——. 1964. Total Integrated Mass Transports and Actual Circulation in the Eastern South Pacific Ocean. *Studies on Oceanography,* p. 47—52. Tokyo.

——. 1964. The Thermal Structure of the Eastern Pacific Ocean. *Deutsche Hydrog. Zeits., Erganzungsheft,* p. 1—84.

——. 1965a. Surface Currents of the Eastern Equatorial Pacific Ocean. *Inter-Amer. Trop. Tuna Comm. Bull.,* Vol. 9, No. 5, p. 270—304.

——. 1965b. The Annual and Semiannual Variation of Sea Surface Temperature in the North Pacific Ocean. *Limnol. Oceanogr.,* Vol. 10, p. 307-13.

——. 1964. Oceanography of the Eastern Equatorial Pacific Ocean. *Ocenaogr. Mar. Biol. Ann. Rev.,* Vol. 4, p. 33—68.

——. 1967. Circulation and Water Masses in the Eastern Equatorial Pacific Ocean. *Int. J. Oceanol. and Limnol.,* Vol. 1, No. 2, p. 117—47.

Yoshida, K. 1955. Coastal Upwelling Off the California Coast. *Res. Oceanogr. Wks. Japan,* Vol. 2, 13 p.

——. 1958. *Coastal Upwelling Off the California Coast, and Its Effects on Productivity of the Waters.* Tokyo, Geophysical Institute, Tokyo University.

——. 1967. Circulation in the Eastern Tropical Oceans with Special References to Upwelling and Undercurrents. *Japanese Journal of Geophysics,* Vol. IV, No. 2, 75 p.

Yoshida, K.; Mao, H. L. 1957. A Theory of Upwelling of Large Horizontal Extent. *J. Mar. Res.,* Vol. 16, p. 40—54.

Yoshida, K.; Tsushiya, M. 1957. Northward Flow in Lower Layers as an Indicator of Coastal Upwelling. *Rec. Oceanogr. Wks. Japan,* Vol. 4, p. 14—22.

Zeigler, J. M.; Athearn, W. D.; Smali, H. 1957. Profiles across the Peru—Trench. *Deep-sea Res.,* Vol. 4, p. 238—49.

Zuta, S. 1972. El Fenómeno 'El Niño'. *Revistas Estudios del Pacífico* (Valparaíso), No. 5, p. 27—42.

Zuta, S.; Enfield, D.; Valdivia, J.; Lagos, P.; Blandi, C. 1974. Aspectos Físicos del Fenomeno el Nino 1972—73. IOC El Niño Workshop, December, Guayaquil. Ecuador.

Zuta, S.; Guillén, O. 1970. Oceanografía de las Aguas Costeras del Perú. *Bol. Inst. Mar. Perú,* Vol. 2, No. 5, p. 157-324.

Zuta, S.; Urquizo, W. 1972. Temperatura Promedio de la Superficie del mar Frente a la Costa Peruana. Período 1928—1969. *Bol. Inst. Mar. Perú—Callao,* Vol. 2, No. 8.

The Peru current system. 2: Biological aspects

Haydee Santander[1]

Introduction

The Peruvian current is a complex biotic community which, though famous for great abundance of anchovy therein, has still been insufficiently studied. Much is known of the anchovy and of several other elements, but the knowledge of the community as a whole is extremely poor; and still poorer is the knowledge of the total ecosystem with respect to the interrelationships between biotic and abiotic elements.

Although Peruvian research on elements in this community has, from the beginning, been organized to take in parallel environmental and biological observations, the accumulated results still do not permit the kind of analysis that is required. Therefore this document seeks to provide a sketch of the existing knowledge of the living community as a base for the planning of further research on it.

Biological pattern of the Peruvian current

One of the greatest upwelling areas of the oceans is located off the Peruvian coast. The upwelled waters, on entering the Peruvian current, fertilize it and thus encourage photosynthesis. Therefore, in a treatment of the biological aspects of this current, it is impossible to neglect the effect of upwelling and its variations.

The current is not an isolated phenomenon but is part of oceanic circulation which, through vertical movements, brings water from subsurface strata to the surface, which is subsequently carried away by horizontal flows (Wyrtki, 1963). The current exercises a marked influence along the Peruvian coast. The permanent winds move surface water away from the coast throughout the year but at times cause very intense upwellings which may last for more than a week (Zuta and Guillén 1970). The effects of upwelling in the principal regions affect the biological abundance particularly at shallow depths (less than 100 m). The greater intensities of upwelling are related to cool periods, hence the abundance zones tend to occur during the winter.

Both typical and permanent upwelling occurs between 14° and 16° S. but significant upwellings also occur during a large part of the year between the latitudes 4°−6°, 7°−8° and 11°−12° S. Although upwelling usually occurs throughout the year, it is commonly less intense in summer, from December to February. During these months warm waters advance south-west along the coast of Peru normally as far as 5° S. In some past years the warm waters have extended further south still, raising the surface temperatures as high as 7° C (Wooster and Gilmartin, 1961; Wyrtki, 1966).

It is interesting to note that in winter, when upwelling is at its greatest intensity, the enrichment of phytoplankton or zooplankton help nourish the great numbers of fish whose larvae use the biological material that will be produced prior to their spawning. Subsequently, at the end of winter or beginning of spring, the maximum spawning activity of abundant fish species such as the anchoveta, hake, sardine, etc., occurs. Guillén *et al.* (1971),

1. Instituto del Mar del Perú, Esq. Gamarra y Gral. Valle, Chucuito, Callao (Peru).

investigating the productive areas of the Peruvian coastal waters between 4° and 22° S. throughout each season of the year 1964, found that the greatest quantities of phytoplankton occurred along and around the the coast. The greatest concentration lay south of 6° S. which was favoured by the supply of nutrients from the upwelling process, the maximum occurring in summer and the minimum in winter (Fig. 1).

Calienes (1973), who studied the population structure in the Callao zone by means of variations in the diversity of phytoplankton during 1961—62, also found that the seasonal maxima occur in spring and summer and minima in autumn and winter, greater population levels being at the surface (0—10 m) and decreasing from 30 to 50 m. The most frequent species in this study were: *Rhizosolenia delicatula* and *Thalassiosira subtilis*; *Skeletonema costatum* was also found but limited principally to the coast.

The areas of greatest concentration of phytoplankton coincided with the zones of highest productive capacity during summer in the areas of Pimentel, Salaverry, Supe and Callao. The lowest concentrations of phytoplankton occurred in areas north of 6° S. and at a considerable distance from the coast (Fig. 2) (Guillén *et al.*, 1971). Nevertheless, at times (March—April 1966) incongruencies have been found between highly fertile areas of high concentration of nutrients with low phytoplankton standing stock and one of the reasons principally proposed was that the rate of nutrient utilization of the plant cells exceeded the rate of growth (Stickland *et al.*, 1969). In turn, Calienes (1964), studied the development of the phytoplankton off Callao. In one season he observed that the phytoplankton influenced the phosphate cycle, obtaining reduced values of maximum photosynthetic activity in summer and autumn and higher values when the phytoplankton diminished during the winter.

In addition, silicate, whose greatest concentrations occur in winter and the lowest in summer and are increased by the intensity of coastal upwelling (Zuta and Guillén, 1970), appears to be reduced by the direct actions of the phytplankton population who by absorption reduce it to a summer minimum.

Guillén *et al.* (1971) found that the concentration of phytoplankton generally decreased during autumn from the summer levels. In winter, the phytoplankton concentrations were the lowest of the year for the area south of 6° S., with the exception of Chimbote and Salaverry, where winter coincides with the

highest production of these organisms. To the north of 6° S., significant plankton concentrations were detected, except in the area of Cabo Blanco which is, in fact, the area of greatest overall annual productivity.

In spring, the concentrations generally increase from winter values due to the improvements in light intensity and upwelling (with consequent transport of necessary nutrients to the surface), especially off Pimentel, Huarmey and Callao. The three planktonic species throughout the years to the north of Callao are *Eucampia zoodiacus*, *Skeletonema costatum* and *Rhizosolenia delicatula*.

In addition to the seasonal variations which determine normal fluctuations in phytoplankton production, other factors exist which affect in certain areas, making them more or less productive.

According to Blackburn (1966), the production of phytoplankton in the eastern tropical Pacific appeared to be limited more by nutrients than by light, but the identity of the limiting nutrient or nutrients is still in doubt. The distribution of inorganic phosphate (the only compound closely studied) agrees closely with that of zooplankton concentrations. Observations from 1961 to 1965, show that the phosphate maximum occurs in the Pimentel—Chimbote and the Callao—Pisco areas at different times of the year; during the spring for the former region and summer for the latter (Guillén and Mendiola, 1974).

One of the elements which determines fluctuations in the phytoplankton population is the herbivorous zooplankton (Strickland *et al.*, 1969; Ryther *et al.*, 1970). Beers *et al.* (1971) also discussed zooplankton as the limiting factor in phytoplankton abundance in their study of an area close to Supe (10°45′ S.), calculating that the zooplankton consumed 25 per cent of phytoplankton produced. One of the most important upwelling areas in terms of secondary production is that of the Peruvian Current where production is about 4×10^6 tonnes per year (Cushing, 1969).

Blackburn (1966), who investigated the chlorophyll and primary production of zooplankton at the surface of the eastern Pacific, showed that the maximum values (0.70 mg/m^2) for chlorophyll *a* in the area off the Peruvian coast occurred in the July—December period. The observations of zooplankton off the Peruvian coast, made by taking Henson net samples from the surface to 50 m gives us a general table of volumetric estimates of zooplankton. From 1964 to 1969, these values indicated that the greatest volumes were distributed principally in the southern area between 15° and 17° S. The seasonal maximum occurred in spring and the minimum in autumn for the southern and central areas and in winter for the northern area (Fig. 3). Highest values recorded reach over 25 mg C/m³/day.

Santander (1974), studying the area from 6° to 9°20′ S. in the period 1971−72, found the lowest value of zooplankton (mean number of zooplankton per m³) was in the winter of 1971. He also noted that the maximum occurred in summer. However, an analysis of the copepod group (a dominant group of the zooplankton) showed that the greatest harvest was produced in spring, which indicated that an increase in other zooplankton groups (doliolids, pteropodos, apendicularias and siphonophores) must have contributed to the summer maximum.

This type of information is valuable in an overall appreciation of the regular, seasonal and regional variations. However, we know comparatively little about the species composition of zooplankton and of the factors that control the zooplankton concentrations.

The copepods, which are holoplanktonic organisms, are numerically dominant over the entire Peruvian littoral (Santander, 1967; Vasquez, 1967; Alvarado, 1972). Although the euphausiids are incorrectly collected in the Hensen net, there is evidence of a great abundance existing at levels lower than that sampled by this apparatus; e.g. collection of a large number of larval stages in surface layers and their enormous volumes obtained during the expedition of Krill III (July, 1974). The species *Euphausia mucronata* which is endemic to the Peruvian current (Brinton, 1962), appears to be an important element of the biotic environment of this current.

A global panorama of the ichthyologic wealth is given by the ichthyoplankton. Einarsson *et al.* (1966), analysing the composition of the ichthyoplankton of the northern and central areas of the Peruvian littoral where the fishing activity is principally centred, found that the number of eggs and larvae of other fishes, with respect to the anchovy, reached 25 per cent during the main spawning periods of these fish (excluding anchovy), whereas in winter and spring (maximum period for anchovy) it could fall to as low as 4 per cent.

The increase which the highly productive areas of the Peruvian current stimulates in the spawning of many species is unquestioned. The anchovy is the best example of localization of spawning in areas with bio-oceanographic characteristics favourable

to the process and the success of subsequent larval stages. According to Zuta and Santander (1974), the conditions most appropriate for anchovy spawning appear to be mixed waters with temperatures of 14.5−17.5° C and salinities from 31.1−34.9 per mille. Physical aspects such as the configuration of the coastal line with the salients at 6° and 14° S. and the greater width of the continental shelf to the north of 14° S., favour the location of the principal spawning area which lies between 6° and 12° S.

The duration of the spawning period from July to March with maximum intensification in September (Santander and de Castillo, 1973; de Vildoso and de Haor, 1969; Miñano, 1968) is closely related to the period of greatest planktonic production, i.e. spring and summer (Calienes, 1973; Santander, 1974; Guillén and de Mendiola, 1974). The alteration of a favourable condition, such as in the case of 'El Niño' in 1972, causes decreased spawning activity. Before the marked reduction in upwelling and consequent fall of production, the traditional spawning zone (northern and central) is changed, moving to the south. It moves considerably closer to the coast (particularly in the central area). It is evident that the localization of maximum spawning of Peruvian fish (Einarsson *et al.*, 1966) is closely tied to the mode of phytoplankton and zooplankton production since they constitute the food for the early fish stages. Thus fishes such as bonito (*Sarda s. chilensis*), sardine (*Sardinops sagax sagax*), jurel (*Trachurus symmetricus murphyi*), caballa (*Scomber japonicus peruanus*), cojinoba (*Seriorella violacza*), etc., have spawning periods principally in the spring and summer.

An explanation has already been given as to how the biotic community of the Peruvian current supports an abundant phytoplankton vegetation, or first trophic level, which, in turn, supports the life of the great zooplankton population. The two make up the basic diet of the fish population, of which the anchovy is a significant part.

One of the most important aspects of the anchovy is that its feeding is based upon plankton —principally phytoplankton (Rojas de Mendiola *et al.*, 1969)—which, in consequence, yields greater production by shortening the food chain. Linked to the great productivity of the area in which it is distributed, it constitutes the largest single species of fish caught in the area.

The interactions which take place between the species that inhabit the same system as the anchovy have a common point of contact in the trophic relations between them. Thus, in the ecological system of the Peruvian current, the anchovy plays a fundamental role as the basic food of many fish, birds, mammals and even invertebrates. The interspecific relations between the components of the ecosystem of the Peruvian current are little known. The basis for study of trophic levels is the knowledge of the feeding regimes of the marine organisms. Until now, the work in this field in most cases has yielded only quantitative data on organisms found in the stomachs of fish. The disadvantage of this type of research is that the identifiable organisms only make up a part of the food ingested. In Figure 4 is the existing knowledge on the components of the ecosystem of the Peruvian current related to the anchovy.

Other species, such as the sardine and the machete, occupy the same trophic level as the anchovy, perferring phytoplankton organisms, although zooplankton also are found in their stomach contents (Rojas de Mendiola, 1966). In this manner, they are both competitors of the anchovy and also its predators since they ingest anchovy eggs in the filtered zooplankton mass (particularly for the sardine—anchovy up to 4 cm, have been observed in sardine stomachs—IMARPE, 1973*b*). These two species are constituents of the neritic fauna characteristic of the Peruvian current.

The sardine is distributed off Peru in two areas, one in the north-central part of Peru and the other between southern Peru and northern Chile. Until 1972, its catch on the Peruvian littoral was very irregular. From data up to 1971, it is known that the greatest volume landed came from the zone between Paita and Chimbote and the second greatest volume from the southern area in front of Ilo (Mejia *et al.,* 1970). From the presence of eggs and larvae in the plankton, the spawning is known to occur from August to February in the north and central area (Santander and de Castillo, 1974). Taking 80,000 tons as an estimate of the stock, IMARPE (Mejia *et al.,* 1974) calculated a sardine-fishing potential of 30,000 tons annually.

Since 1972, when the last strong 'El Niño' phenomenon appeared, the sardine has become remarkably abundant. Enlarging its catch and spawning areas by September 1972, the species covered the entire coast where previously it has occupied only the northern and central areas (Santander and de Castillo, 1974). Indeed, in 1973, 150,000 to 170,000 tons were caught (IMARPE, 1974*a*) which, as shown by the localization of a mode

at about 17.5 cm, was a result of the successful spawning in the previous year.

The machete is a neritic species distributed along almost all the Peruvian coast and part of Chile, and according to Schweigger (1964), occurs principally in the zone between Punta Aguja and Isla San Gallán (13°55′–76°30′S.). Economically useful, the areas of greatest landing stretch from Chimbote to Pisco, particularly from January to October. According to the latest available statistics (Mejia *et al.,* 1974), it was the second largest species in 1972 with respect to quantity caught for human consumption.

The bonito lives like the anchovy, in the Peruvian current, and ranges up to the edge of the current where there is the confluence with oceanic water. Its habitat extends along the Peruvian and Chilean coast from 5° to 36° S., with greatest abundance from Chimbote to Iquique. It prefers depths between 4 and 30 fathoms, temperatures of 15° to 23° C and salinities of 34.5 to 35.1 per mille (IMARPE, 1970*b*). It shows marked seasonal fluctuation in catches, reaching its highest in spring and summer when the Peruvian current is narrow. Frequently, the increases are associated with the presence of anchovy, its principal diet (de Vildoso, 1963). Its distribution with 15 to 20 miles on the coast may well be related to the approach of the anchovy. It is during this period too that spawning occurs.

The feeding of the bonito, although based principally on anchovy, consists also of the genus *Munida* and occasionally of other organisms, such as *Euphausids,* sardine, pejerrey, jurel, camotillo, etc. It is considered to be a species of the greatest importance for human consumption (both fresh and canned) and, according to IMARPE statistics, it was the species most heavily fished for direct human consumption in 1972. The mean quantity of annual catch until 1972 was about 60,000 tons (IMARPE, 1970*b*) with a peak, in 1961, of 110,000 tons.

The bonito population suffered a marked decline between 1962 and 1971, as shown by changes in average length and weight, and in catch per unit effort (IMARPE, 1974*b*). It is calculated that the catch level of this species fell to a present (1974) potential of about 40,000 tons.

Species such as the jurel, caballa and cojinoba are of undoubted importance in the ecological community of the Peruvian current. Their relationships with anchovy nutrition (since it is the principal food of the three species) seems to confirm that they share the same habitat. These three species are distributed along the entire Peruvian coast (Miñano and Castillo, 1971; IMARPE 1973a). Part of the jurel's distribution to the north of 7° and the highest caballa concentrations between 4° and 9° S. did not exactly coincide with the distribution of the anchovy. Thus it appears that distribution is affected in some way by the extension of the southern branch of the Cromwell current (Zuta and Santander, 1974).

The principal spawning areas for jurel (between San Juan and Ilo, within 120 miles of the coast at the end of winter (Santander and de Castillo, 1971), are associated with the borders of the upwelling areas, with temperatures of 15°–16° C and salinities of 34.9–35.0 per mille at the surface in the area of maximum spawning. A fishing potential of 30,000 tons from a stock of 90,000 tons has been estimated (Mejia *et al.*, 1974).

The spawning area of the caballa extends northwards from 15°30′ S., with the highest concentrations off Eten (7°10′ S.), the principal spawning period being the summer (Santander and de Castillo, 1972; Miñano and de Castillo, 1971). The stock of these species is estimated in 40,000 tons and the possible annual catch estimated by IMARPE was 10,000 tons (Mejia, *et al.*, 1974). Like the jurel and bonito, they play a substantial role in the Peruvian economy. Records and analyses of other species of fish by IMARPE will soon produce an evaluation of the fish resources of the ecological community of the Peruvian current.

Within the ecological system of the Peruvian current, the guano birds play a very important role, occupying the third trophic level and constituting the greatest natural predators of the anchovy. The populations of guano birds are made up of three major species, the cormorant, *Phalacrocoax bougainvilli,* the gannet, *Sula variegata,* and the pelican, *Pelecannus occidentalis thagus.* The cormorant represents 83 per cent, the gannet 15 per cent and the pelican 2 per cent of this majority group of guano birds. Their distribution extends from 6° to 12° S. during spring and summer and from 1° N to 38° S. in autumn and winter (Jordán and Fuentes, 1966).

The censuses of 1961 and 1963 provide data from which it was estimated that 1.8 to 2.8 million tons of anchovy were consumed annually by a population of 12×10^6 to 18×10^6 birds (Jordán, 1967). This direct dependency of the birds on their food is decisive in the fluctuation of the birds: when the anchovy are affected by environmental changes it often becomes less accessible. In 1974, according to the last census carried out for 1973–74 productive

cycle (Tovar, 1974), the guano-bird population was estimated at 2.5 million.

The effect of the Peruvian current on its wildlife is an unquestionable but not isolated phenomenon. Other factors are involved, such as the coastal projection of the southern branch of the Cromwell current which becomes more important north of 9° S. Due to its high content of oxygen, it appears to influence the distribution of some species. That seems to be the case for the jurel, the caballa, the cojinoba all of whose greatest concentrations are under the combined influences of these waters.

The hydrological fronts formed from currents and the water masses, upwelling, etc., favour the formation of an environment conducive to the development of some organisms. The anchovy is associated with the cold edges of these fronts (Zuta and Santander, 1974). Physical aspects such as the configuration of the coastal line, the extent of shelf, the degree of water movement also contribute to the improvement of the environment. In the transition zones, where there is contact between the tropical waters of the gulf and the cold waters of the Peruvian current, the best catches of demersal species are taken (Del Solar, 1968). Among these, the hake, *Merluccius gayi,* whose greatest density occurs over the edge of the continental shelf—between the islands Lobos de Afuera and Huarmey—is the most abundant species of the Peruvian coast.

Even the minimum oxygen layer, which is limiting for a large number of organisms, could favour others should they be so adapted; this appears to be the case for *Euphausia mucronata.*

Variations in some components of the biotic community of the Peruvian current

Even when studies began in the early part of this century, they were directed mainly at a very few species. Our current knowledge of the trophic relations between most species of the ecological community of the Peruvian current makes it impossible to comment on fluctuations. Only in the cases of the anchovy and guano birds has the work been sufficient to give us some knowledge of the direct relations between their respective communities. Mortalities suffered by the guano birds have been noted since 1616.

Since 1909, the bird fluctuations have been evaluated by the indirect method with respect to guano production (Vogt, 1942). By means of these records, it is possible to estimate the falls in number produced by the mortalities of the years 1917, 1939—41 and 1957—58 (Fig. 5). The years considered as abnormal are indicated on the upper line of this figure and some of these do not seem to have decreased the population (Jordán and Fuentes, 1966). But the marked decreases in the years 1939—41 and 1957—58 are noteworthy. The latter fall occurred just after the population had attained its maximum value in 1955.

The records obtained by direct method, based on graphical census, have given better information and show considerable agreement with the indirect method. Thus, since 1954, the fluctuations have been analysed by this method (Fig. 6) (Jordán, 1967). In this and the previous figure, it can be appreciated that the bird population increased considerably up to 1955, principally due to protection of the nesting zones. In 1955—57, the population suffered a marked decrease from about 28 million to about 6 million birds by 1957, but afterwards and until 1962 the population recovered until it reached 18.1 million, remaining at this level until the beginning of 1965.

During 1966 and 1967, lowest values were detected as a result of 'El Niño' which caused a fall to about 5 million birds. Then until 1971, the population remained at about this same level. As a consequence of the 1972—73 'El Niño', the population was about 2 million at the end of 1973 and in 1974 was 2.51 million (Tovar, 1974).

The food of the guano birds consists of about 90 per cent anchovy and a geographic distribution showed their greatest concentrations to lie between 8° and 14° S. (Jordán, 1967) coinciding with the principal anchovy areas. When oceanographic changes occur, the pattern of horizontal and vertical distribution of the anchovy changes, making it less accessible to the birds. This was evident when the catches per unit of effort in 1972 during 'El Niño' were less than one-tenth of the minimum encountered during 1961—72 (IMARPE, 1972). The anchovy schools move closer to the coast and prefer different areas of distribution; the consequence is mass mortality of birds due to lack of food. Typical cases occurred during the years 1957—58, 1963, 1965 and 1972.

Although not all the elements necessary to determine the influential factors of the fluctuations of bird population are available, it is reasonable to conclude that since the anchovy is the primary food of all these species, any factor which causes appreciable diminution of the anchovy, be it oceanographic, biological or man himself, will cause drastic effects on the birds. It is apparent that anchovy fishing over a limit of 16 million tons per year limits the guano-bird population (IMARPE, 1970*a*).

A further indication of the repercussions which low anchovy availability have on the bird life is the change in the proportions of the three most abundant species—the cormorant, which constituted 82 per cent of this group in 1963 (Jordán and Fuentes, 1964), fell to 41 per cent, less than that reached by the gannet (45 per cent, Tovar, 1974). This effect was probably due to the higher percentage occupied by anchovy in the diet of the cormorant (96 per cent) in comparison with 80 per cent for the gannet, which evidently can count on other fish species for its food.

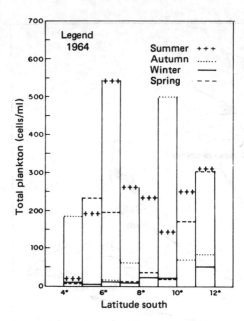

Fig. 1. Variation with latitude
of total plankton concentration
(cells/ml) in the first 10 m of water
during the four seasons of 1964.

Fig. 2. Total plankton distribution in the summer
of 1964 in the topmost 10 m of water (cells/10^5 l).

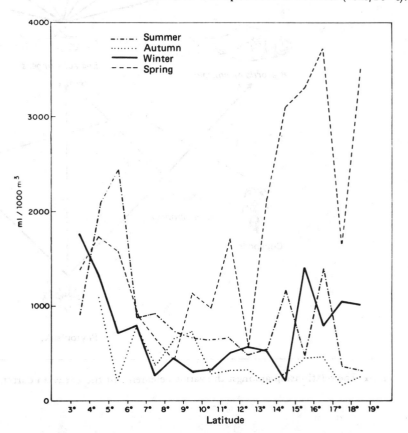

Fig. 3. Variation with latitude of mean zooplankton volume
(ml/1,000 m^3) in each of the four seasons from 1964 to
1969.

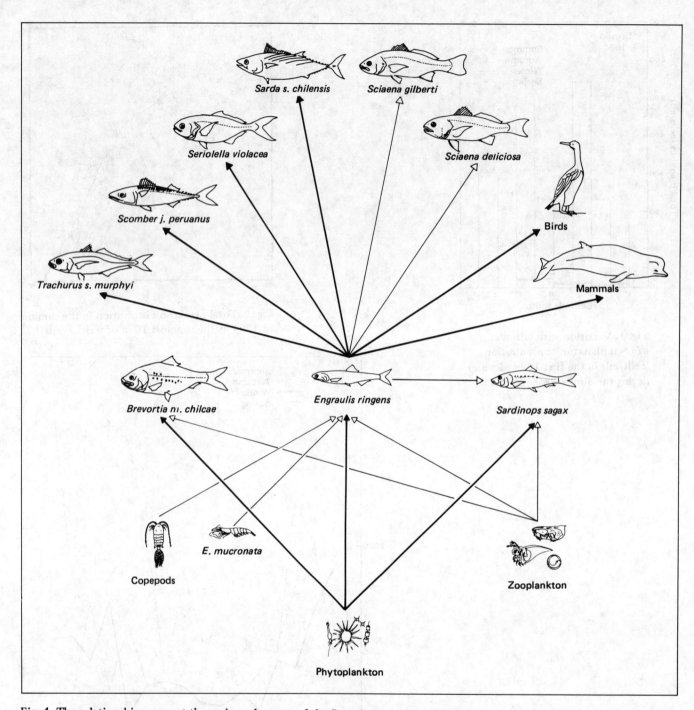

Fig. 4. The relationship amongst the various elements of the Peruvian current ecosystem.

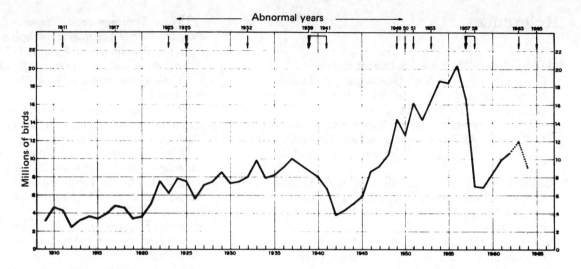

Fig. 5. Fluctuation of average annual numbers of guano birds
based on guano production.

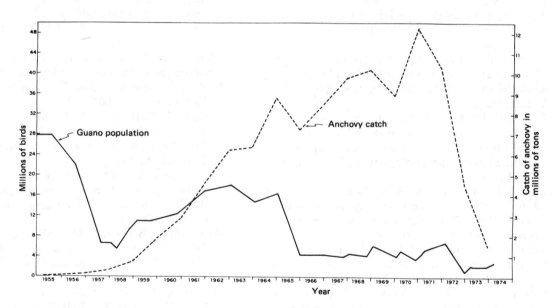

Fig. 6. Number of guano birds and catch of anchovy over the
years 1955 to 1974.

References

Alvarado, A. 1972. Variación Cuantitativa de Copepodos, Eufausidos y Quetognatos de la Zona Norte Peruana (07°01' y 08°56' Lat. Sur), Summer—Winter, 1967. Trujillo. (Thesis.)

Beers, J. R.; Stevenson, M. R.; Eppley, R. W.; Brooks, E. R. 1971. Plankton Populations and Upwelling off the Coast of Peru, June 1969. *Fish. Bull.*, Vol. 69, No. 4.

Blackburn, M. 1966. Relationships between Standing Crops at Three Successive Trophic Levels in the Eastern Tropical Pacific. *Pac. Sci.* Vol. 20. No. 1, p. 36—59.

Brinton, E. 1962. The Distribution of Pacific Euphasuiids. *Bull. Scrips Inst. Oc. Univ. Calif.*, Vol. 8, No. 2, p. 51—270.

Calienes, R. 1964. Fluctuaciones del Fitoplancton en Relación con los Fosfatos, Temperatura y Desove de la Anchoveta en el Area de Callao, 1961—1962. Arequipa, Peru. (Thesis.)

——. 1973. Diversidad y Asociación del Fitoplancton en Callao, 1961—62. Arequipa, Peru. (Thesis.)

Cushing, D. H., 1969. *Upwelling and Fish Production.* 40 p. (FAO Fish. Tech. Pap., 84).

de Vildoso, A. C., 1963. Especies del Género Sarda en el Pacifico Oriental. *FAO Fish. Rep., (6),* Vol. 3, p. 1542—56.

de Vildoso; de Haro, B. 1969. La Madurez Sexual de la Anchoveta (*Engraulis ringens* J.), en los Períodos Reproductivos, 1961/1968. *Inst. Mar. Perú. Bol.*, Vol. II, No. 3.

Del Solar, E. 1968. *La Merluza* Merluccius gayi *(Guichenot), como Indicador de la Riqueza Biótica de la Plataforma Continental del Norte del Perú.* (Published under the auspices of the Soc. Nac. de Pesq. Perú.)

Einarsson, H.; de Mendiola, B. R.; Santander, H. 1966. El Desove de los Peces en Aguas Peruanas Durante 1961/1964. *Memoria 1º Seminario Lat. Amer. Oc. Pac. Orien. Lima, Perú.*

Guillén, O.; de Mendiola, B. R.; de Rondán, R. Y. 1971. Primary Productivity and Phytoplancton in the Coastal Peruvian Waters. In: J. Costlow (ed.), *Fertility of the Sea,* New York, Gordon & Breach.

——. 1974. Productividad de la Corriente Peruana. *Anales del Primer Seminario Nacional de Sistemas Ecológicos.*

IMARPE, 1970a. Informe del Cuadro de Expertos sobre Dinámica de la Población de Anchoveta Peruana. *Bol.*, Vol. II, No. 6.

——. 1970b. *Información General sobre la Pesca de Consumo.* (Serie de Inf. Esp. No. IM-61).

——. 1972. *Operación Eureka XXIII, 3—6 Agosto, 1972.* (Serie de Inf. Esp. No. IM—112).

——. 1973a. *Resumen de los Trabajos Cientifico-Pesqueros de la Segunda Expedición del Bec Professor Mesyatsev en Aguas del Océano Pacífico, Adyacente a la Costa Peruana.* (Inf. Esp. No. IM-145).

——. 1973b. *Operación Eureka XXVIII.* Inf. Esp. No. IM—146).

——. 1974a. Informe de la Cuarta Sesión del Panel de Expertos de la Evaluación del Stock de Anchoveta Peruana. *Bol. Inst. Mar, Perú* (Callo), Vol. 2, No. 10.

——. 1974b. *Informe sobre el Bonito.* (Inf. IMARPE Dpto de Peces de Consumo. No. 6.)

Jordán, R. 1967. The Predation of Guano Birds on the Peruvian Anchovy (*Engraulis ringens J.*). *Calcofi Report,* Vol. XI.

Jordán, R.; Fuentes, H. 1964. *Resultados de los Censos Gráficos de Aves Guaneras Efectuadas Durante el Ciclo Reproductivo, 1962—1963.* p. 1—15. (Inf. Invest. Recurs. Mar. Callao, No. 22).

——. 1966. Estudio Preliminar sobre las Fluctuaciones de las Poblaciones de Aves Guaneras. *Memoria 1º Seminario Lat. Amer. Oc. Pac. Orien. Lima, Perú.*

Mejia, J.; Samamé, M.; Pastor, A. 1970. *Información Básica de los Principales Peces de Consumo.* (Serie Inf. Esp. No. IM—62.)

Mejia, J.; Samamé, M.; Esquerre, M. 1974. *Informe sobre Stocks Disponibles para la Pesca de Consumo en la Costa Peruana.* (Inf. IMARPE, Dpto de Peces de Consumo, No. 5.)

Miñano, J. 1968. Estudio de la Fecundidad y Ciclo Sexual de la Anchoveta (*Engraulis ringens* J.), en la Zona de Chimbote. *Bol. Inst. Mar, Perú* (Callao), Vol. 1, No. 9, p. 505—52.

Miñano, J.; Castillo, J. 1971. *Primeros Resultados de la Investigación Biológico-Pesquera de la Caballa,* Scomber japonicus peruanus, *J. y H.* (Série de Inf. Esp. No. IM-84).

de Mendiola, B. 1966. Notas sobre la Alimentación de la Sardina y el Machete, en la Aguas Cosimeras del Perú. *Memoria 1º Seminario Lat. Amer. Oc. Pac. Orien. Lima, Perú.*

de Mendiola, B.; Ochoa, M.; Calienes, R.; Gómez, O. 1969. *Contenido Estomacal de Anchoveta en 4 Aréas de la Costa Peruana.* (Inst. 27, Inst. Mar Perú, Callao.)

Ryther, J. H.; Merzel, D. W.; Hulburt, E. M.; Lorenzen, C. J.; Crowin, N. W. 1970. *Production and Utilization of Organic Matter in the Peru Coastal Current.* (Contribution No. 2402, Woods Hole Ocean. Instn.)

Santander, H. 1967. Los Euphausidos en la Zona Callao—Chimbote y la Composición General del Zooplancton. Lima. (Thesis.)

——. 1974. *Cosecha Estable del Zooplancton.* Inst. Mar., Perú (Série de Inf. Esp. No. IM-148.)

Santander, H.; de Castillos, O. S. 1971. *Desarrollo y*

Distribución de Huevos y Larvas de Jurel, Trachurus symmetrius murphyi *(NICHOLS) en la Costa Peruana.* (Inst. Mar., Perú, Inf. No. 35.)

——. 1972. *Distribución de Huevos y Larvas de 'Caballa' Scomber japonicus peruanus, en la Costa Peruana.* (Série de Inf. Esp. No. IM-103.)

——. 1973. *Estudios sobre las Primeras Etapas de Vida de la Anchoveta.* (Inst. Mar., Perú, Inf. No. 41.)

——. 1974. Variaciones en la Intensidad del Desove de la Sardina *Sardinops Sagax* (J) en la Costa Peruana en los Años 1966—1973. In: *Anales del IV Congreso Nacional de Biologia, Perú.*

Schweigger, E. 1964. *El Litoral Peruano,* 2nd ed. Lima.

Strickland, J. D. H.; Eppley, R. W.; de Mendiola, B. R. 1969. Poblaciones de Fitoplancton, Nutrientes y Fotosíntesis en Aguas Costeras Peruanas. *Bol. Inst. Mar, Perú,* Vol. 2. No. 1, p. 4—12.

Tovar, H. 1974. *Censos Gráficos de Aves Guaneras para los Ciclos Reproductivos de 1969/70 a 1973/74.* (Inf. Int. s/n.)

Vásquez, F. 1967. Ensayo sobre la Relación de los Factores Abióticos con la Distribución. Trujillo. (Thesis.)

Vogt, W., 1942. Informe sobre las Aves Guaneras. *Bol. Cia. Admora. Guano.,* Vol. 18, No. 3, p. 1—132.

Wooster, W. S.; Gilmartin, M. 1961. The Peru—Chile Undercurrent. *J. Mar. Res.,* Vol. 19, No. 3; p. 97—122.

Wyrtki, K., 1963. The Horizontal and Vertical Field of Motion in the Peru Current. *Bull. Scripps Inst. Oceanogr.,* Vol. 8, No. 4, p. 313.

——. 1966. Oceanography of the Eastern Equatorial Pacific Ocean. *Oceanogr. Mar. Biol. Ann. Rev.,* Vol. 4, p. 33—68.

Zuta, S.; Guillén, O. 1970. Oceanografía de las Aguas Costeras del Perú. *Bol. Inst. Mar Perú* (Callao), Vol. 2, No. 5.

Zuta, S.; Santander, H. 1974. El Ambiente Oceánico y su Relación con los Organismos Marinos. *Anales del Primer Seminario Nacional de Sistemas Ecológicos.*

The oceanography of the region north of the Equatorial front: biological aspects

Roberto Jimenez Santistevan[1]

Introduction

The following review is not a complete treatment of the biological aspects of the eastern tropical Pacific, but rather an effort to collate the information on the area north of the Equatorial front. Very few references were available for this approach and the biological data on the trans-Equatorial flows during 'El Niño' occurrences were still scarcer.

Basic information on planktonic and benthic flora and fauna communities in Ecuadorian waters is rare and with this in view, the Instituto Oceanográfico de la Armada del Ecuador created a marine-biology division, in December 1972, to organize oceanographic research.

From the cruises carried out since, data are now available for the better understanding of the marine environment around the coast of Ecuador.

Review of the biological aspects of the region: Panama Bight

Nichols and Murphy (1944) first designated the waters between the Gulf of Panama and Punta Santa Elena, Ecuador, the 'Panama Bight'; the region was defined more precisely by Wooster (1959) 'as the part of the Eastern Tropical Pacific Ocean that lies between the Isthmus of Panama (about 9° N.) on the north and Punta Santa Elena (about latitude 2° S.) on the south and that extends westward from the coasts of Panama, Colombia and Ecuador to about longitude 81° W.'

The oceanographic programme conducted by the Inter-American Tropical Tuna Commission in 1965–66 was entitled the Augmented Colombian 'El Niño' Tuna Oceanography (ACENTO) Programme. It was a continuation and expansion of the surveys conducted jointly by the Republic of Colombia and the commission during 1963–65 as part of the so-called 'El Niño Project' designed to study the coastal waters of western South America from Panama to northern Chile.

During the ACENTO cruises, nutrients, chlorophyll *a*, carbon fixation and zooplankton volumes were studied.

Nitrate is the most important of the principal micro-nutrients in the surface waters of the north-eastern tropical Pacific, as due to its low concentrations it is the limiting factor in the growth of phytoplankton. Minimum nitrate values in the Panama Bight were usually found between 10 m and 20 m rather than at the surface—where the values tended to be higher due to enrichment of nutrients at the surface from rainfall and *in situ* production. Indications that nitrates may severely limit production in wide areas of the euphotic zone of the Panama Bight during most of the year was shown by Forsbergh (1969).

The distribution of nitrate concentrations at the surface was generally less than 1.0 g-at/l, though during ACENTO 4, a high value of 3.0 g-at/l was found at 6°07′ N., 79°25′ W. Other values at this station increased with depth as opposed to the usual distribution with a minimum at 10 m or 20 m. During nearly all the ACENTO cruises, phosphate

1. Instituto Oceanográfico de la Armada del Ecuador, División de Biología Marina, Guayaquil (Ecuador).

concentrations at the surface were very low, mostly less than 0.2 g-at/l. However during ACENTO 4 a tongue of water with a phosphate concentration greater than 0.2 g-at/l at the surface extended southwards from the Gulf of Panama. This coincided with similar coldwater and high-salinity tongues, indicating that upwelling in the gulf and in the centre of the bight was resulting in some enrichment of surface waters.

Forsbergh reported on the distribution of chlorophyll *a* at the surface. Concentrations were low (0.20 mg/m^3) at the salinity maximum in the centre of the bight but were higher (0.40 mg/m^3) to the east and west. This distribution was interpreted by Forsbergh as suggesting newly upwelled water low in phytoplankton and high in micro-nutrients near the centre of the thermal dome in the cyclonic circulation cell, which had originated below the euphotic zone. This water then moved outwards from the centre of upwelling and by the time the rapidly growing phytoplankton had reached its peak, it was located some distance from the centre.

The remarkably high chlorophyll *a* values (up to 3.30 mg/m^3) found south-east of Punta Mala were attributed, in part, to rapid growth in the nutrient-rich water upwelled in the gulf. The micro-nutrients in this presumably once rich surface water apparently had been severely depleted by the phytoplankton.

Only during ACENTO 4 were subsurface measurements made of chlorophyll *a* and phaeo-pigments. The values of chlorophyll *a* at the surface were as low as those in the rest of the water column (19 mg/m̃^{2}) at adjacent stations; it was very high (36–41 mg/m^2) at and just south of the western part of the mouth of the Gulf of Panama. Phaeo-pigments in the water column were relatively high ($\geqslant$ 25 mg/m^2) south of the Península de Azuero, reaching a maximum of 45 mg/m^2 (at station 4). Lorenzen (1967) concluded that 'the quantity of phaeo-pigment in the water column is related to the quantity of herbivorous zooplankton'.

Forsbergh, during ACENTO 4 (February–March), reported high rates of production (> 40 mg C/m^3/day) offshore. The maximum offshore rate was 63 mg C/m^3/day at 5°00′ N., 79°38′ W., 19 nautical miles west of the centre of upwelling as indicated by maximum surface salinity and 35 miles north of this position a rate of 42 mg C/m^3/day was found; both positions are close to that of the secondary surface chlorophyll *a* maximum with a transparency of 8 m as measured by a Secchi disc—the minimum registered in the Panama Bight during ACENTO cruises.

During ACENTO 1, zooplankton volumes were high ($\geqslant$ 200 ml/10^3 m^3) both in the eastern part of the Panama Bight and at station 3. This distribution may perhaps be related to that of surface chlorophyll *a*, where high values (> 0.40 mg/m^3) were found upstream from the centres of zooplankton abundance.

During ACENTO 2, high zooplankton values were found only in the Gulf of Panama. The low values ($\geqslant$ 200 ml/10^3 m^3) outside the gulf, reflected the low chlorophyll values throughout the area. During ACENTO 3 zooplankton values, with one exception, were low throughout the bight reflecting the uniformly low chlorophyll *a* values.

During ACENTO 4, zooplankton values were low in the south-east portion of the bight and high in the north-west, roughly following the distribution of surface chlorophyll *a*. The maximum of 1,000 ml/10^3 m^3 occurred north of Malpelo Island, about 180 nautical miles south-west of the chlorophyll *a* maximum and about 100 nautical miles south-south-west of the phaeo-pigment maximum for the water column.

This downstream displacement of the zooplankton maximum relative to the phaeo-pigment maximum is perhaps explained by the fact that zooplankton volumes are comprised of several trophic levels whereas phaeo-pigments simply indicate herbivore concentration.

Forsbergh (1963), in seeking relationships between measurements of the standing crops of phytoplankton and zooplankton in the Gulf of Panama, found some significant correlation which showed a strong tendency for positive slopes to occur during the upwelling seasons and for negative slopes to occur during the rainy season (Table 1).

Forsbergh pointed out that, except for the period from September 1958 to January 1959, where no apparent relationship exists, the signs of the slopes are consistent for each season.

Smayda (1963) studied the phytoplankton conditions of the Gulf of Panama during July and November 1957 and March 1958. Unusually warm conditions occurred during the March survey, attribuable to considerably weaker upwelling winds than would normally occur at the time. This contributed to the considerably lower standing crop and a retardation in succession of three to five weeks relative to that observed during 1955–57.

Smayda also pointed out, during the March survey, a well-defined inverse relationship existed between mean temperature and mean diatom abundance in the upper 10 metres, and between transparency and mean diatom abundance. A direct relationship occurring between surface salinity and mean diatom abundance primarily reflects the nutrient concentrations associated with a given upwelling intensity rather than describing casual relationships.

Smayda (1963), through a comparison of the average March standing crop at the permanent station with those during the 1958 survey, revealed a considerably lower diatom density during the latter period (Table 2).

The much lower standing crop during March 1958 undoubtedly reflects the unusually high temperatures prevalent during the survey; the delayed phytoplankton succession might be explained by the observation that upwelling winds were 'considerably weaker' than usual during March 1958, following an unusually warm February. These meteorological conditions would also explain the 3°–5° C higher temperatures noted in the upper 25 metres during the March 1958 survey compared with previous years. In this year was reported one of the most disastrous 'El Niño' phenomena in the eastern Pacific.

Smayda in a later paper (1966) suggested that the mean monthly abundance of phytoplankton, expressed as cell numbers and biomass, during the rainy season, was significantly and directly related to the three-day northerly winds at Balboa.

These results suggest that general phytoplankton growth during the rainy season, as well as during the upwelling season, primarily depends on the occurrence of northerly winds, whereas short-term phytoplankton fluctuations may not.

Wooster (1959) described the climatology of the Isthmus of Panama, and pointed out the influence of the north-east trade winds on the upwelling formation in the Gulf of Panama from January to April (but occasionally including December and May when the Doldrums are displaced to the south). The north-east trade winds usually weaken and disappear in late April or May when the wind system moves northward. The Gulf of Panama then becomes increasingly influenced by the Doldrums and the rainbearing south-west winds of the onshore south-east trade-wind systems within the Doldrums is called the (Smayda 1966). The actual convergence of these trade-wind systems within the Doldrums is called the 'intertropical convergence', and is accompanied by heavy rains. The Tradewind–Calm Belt (Doldrums) System lies at its farthest southward position during the northern winter (February) and migrates to its most northerly position during the northern summer (August).

The dry northerly offshore winds associated with the north-east trade winds displace the water mass in the upper 40–78 m offshore, lowering the sea-level and causing an upwelling of colder, more saline and nutrient-rich water to the surface during January through to April. The rain-bearing, southerly onshore winds associated with south-east trade winds and intertropical convergence within the Doldrums prevail during the remainder of the year. The sea level rises, the water mass becomes warmer, more dilute and nutrient-impoverished, and flushing and admixture with more fertile waters are hindered. A slight resurgence of northerly winds during July and/or August may induce mixing or even cause a slight upwelling.

Smayda (1966) indicated that upwellings appeared to be limited to the Gulf of Panama. The seasonal decline in sea-surface temperature characteristic of upwelling does not occur in the Panama Bight where the mean monthly temperature ranges from 26.1°–27.8° C (Scjaefer *et al.*, 1958).

Review of the biological aspects of the region: Ecuadorian waters

PHYTOPLANKTON, PRIMARY PRODUCTION AND PHOTOSYNTHETIC PIGMENTS

The EASTROPAC Atlas (1974) reported nutrient data from cruises run in oceanic waters of Ecuador during October–November 1967. Distributions of nutrient concentrations at 10 m and 100 m deep were shown. Nitrate concentrations at 10 m were high (0.6–0.8 µg-at/l) to the south, off the coast of Ecuador and to the west of the Galápagos Islands. The same distribution pattern was reported for nitrite, phosphate and silicate at the same depths. Lower values were reported north of these areas. A nutrient maximum was shown at 100 m.

A cruise conducted by INOCAR in coastal waters off Ecuador in October 1973, revealed high nitrate concentrations, ranging from 5 to 20 µg-at/l from the surface to 50 m deep in the Gulf of Guayaquil. Less than 0.5 µg-at/l was reported between Punta Pedernales and Salinas from the suface to 10 m deep. Increasing values of nitrate below 20 m were recorded along the coast of Ecuador. High values of phosphate of up to 0.5 µg-at/l were reported along the coast with a maximum deeper than 50 m in the Gulf of Guayaquil.

Marshall (1972) had studied the phytoplankton composition in four stations between Ecuador and Galápagos during the Stanford Oceanographic Expedition No. 19 aboard the r/v *Te Vega* in August 1968. Generally, the diatoms were found at all the depths sampled down to 300 m, though several diatom species were found restricted to depths above or below 100 m. Low counts were common in surface samples. Concentrations were most abundant in depths up to 100 m, and then the numbers fell sharply. The oxygen values at the four stations (averaged) were 4.87, 2.56, 1.45, 0.27 ml/l respectively for the surface and approximate depths of 100, 200, and 300 m.

Desrosieres (1959), sampling along the Equator from east to west, noted a decrease in phosphate and nitrate content accompanied by a temperature rise and a decline in the standing crop. High nutrient values were reported in the Peru current and waters east and west of the Galápagos Islands by Forsbergh and Joseph (1964). Holmes *et al.* (1957) further reviewed the primary production of the tropical eastern Pacific and showed that chlorophyll data and zooplankton volumes support the presence of high productivity off north-west South America and west of the Galápagos Islands.

The phytoplankton described by Marshall represented a mixture of oceanic and neritic species from both tropical, subtropical and Equatorial water masses. The Peru current system, dominated by *Chaetoceros* and *Rhizosolenia* species, moves into this Equatorial region marked by changing temperature and salinity values. The presence of large numbers of coccolithophores, *Emiliana huxleyi* (*Coccolithus huxleyi*), *Gephyrocapsa oceanica* and *Coccolithus pelagicus* indicated the important role of this group in the standing crop of the tropical Pacific (Hasle, 1960; Marshall, 1972).

Hasle (1959) studied the phytoplankton conditions in the south Equatorial current west of the Galápagos Islands, and found high phytoplankton concentrations restricted to the uppermost 50 to 100 m of water. Maximum levels of diatoms were found nearer the surface where dinoflagellates were less evident, while the coccolithophorids showed different patterns in their vertical distribution. A phytoplankton maximum of 70,000 cell/l at a depth of 50 m was reported by Hasle (1959).

Owen and Zeitschel (1970), using data from a series of year-long cruises in the eastern tropical Pacific, gave evidence of a significant seasonal cycle of plant production in tropical oceanic regions

(Fig. 1). Average values of the seasonal cycle were found to range from 127–318 mg C/m²/day. Annual production was 75 g C/m²/year. They suggested that probable reasons for the seasonal cycle were time variation of thermocline pattern and variations of nutrient supply from local source areas such as the Costa Rica Dome, Gulf of Tehuantepec, Peru current extension and Equatorial undercurrent domain.

Barber and Ryther (1969), during cruise 15 of the r/v *Anton Bruun,* collected material from five stations between 2° S. and 2° N. at 92° W. in water upwelling out of the subsurface Cromwell current at the current at the Equator in the eastern Pacific. The upwelled water was found to be high in inorganic nutrients, relatively low in dissolved organic carbon and supported less phytoplankton growth than more northerly or southerly waters. One degree north or south of the Equator, dissolved organic carbon concentrations were higher and phytoplankton growth was increased. Barber and Ryther suggested that natural organic chelators, released by organisms as the water ages at the surface, might be partly responsible for the increased phytoplankton growth north and south of the Equator.

Cross-sectional profiles of oxygen concentrations, temperature and dissolved organic carbon from stations straddling the Equator show vertical homogeneity in the immediate vicinity of the current and, in contrast, steep, vertical gradients just north and south of the current. Knauss (1966) suggested that in this way the water in the current is continuously being replaced with water converging at the Equator and moving eastward, finally upwelling and downwelling out of the current. At the surface, the recently upwelled water would spread out to the north and south, flowing slowly away from the Equator. This pattern of flow would bring to the surface water that is rich in inorganic nutrients but relatively low in ability to support phytoplankton growth (Barber and Ryther, 1969).

During the second oceanographic cruise of R.V. *Orion* in May 1973, surface-water temperatures were related to the Peru current in the south, and to the Panama Bight System in the north (Fig. 2). The Equatorial front was limited by the isotherms 20°–25° C. The highest values of chlorophyll were found in the Gulf of Guayaquil. Chlorophyll maxima ranged from 0.6 to 2 mg/m³. The warm tropical waters in the north contained less than 0.2 mg/m³ chlorophyll. Primary production (by Carbon-14 assimilation) ranged from 10 to 20 mg C/m³/day in these areas and showed the highest values in the

Gulf of Guayaquil and its western areas—with values of 20–50 mg C/m^3/day. (Later investigations in coastal waters of Ecuador yielded the same distribution pattern for primary production and chlorophyll standing crop as those in oceanic waters. The high values were located in the south and in the Gulf of Guayaquil where chlorophyll ranged from 0.5 to 1.0 mg/m^3. The subsurface chlorophyll maximum was recorded between 10 and 20 m in depth (Figs. 3–6). The highest plankton value found in coastal areas was 332,600 cells/l.

The analysis of phytoplankton composition of this area have shown the predominance of diatoms, followed by coccolithophorids (in the order of 100,000 cell/l in the 10 to 20 m zone (Figs. 7–10)). The euphotic zone was limited to 20 m. Dinoflagellate and ciliate communities were less marked in these areas.

Hobson *et al.* (1973) pointed out that microflagellates were an important part of the phytoplankton crop at all times both in open ocean and coastal waters, even when upwelling was occurring and diatoms abundant.

North of these areas, near the Esmeraldas and Manabí coasts, the warm, tropical water (24°–25° C) contained chlorophyll at less than 0.2 mg/m^3. When the standing crop of phytoplankton was estimated, the number of ciliates reached more than 3,000 cell/l. (Primary production in coastal waters of Ecuador ranged from 140 to 430 mg C/m^2). An average photosynthetic rate of 4.3 mg C/mg Chl a/m^3 was obtained in the same areas. This value is very high if compared with the values given by Strickland *et al.* (1969) for the upwelling waters off the Peruvian coast. A predominance of detritus and particulate organic matter over the phytoplankton was evident in all the coastal waters of Ecuador.

BIOLOGICAL INDICATORS

Planktonic organisms have been used by some authors as indicators of water movement. Indicator organisms are often so sensitive to changes of physico-chemical properties that they can be used to identify water masses where traditional oceanographic techniques fail. Bradshaw (1959) and others have used chaetognaths, euphausiids and pteropods, respectively, to recognize large faunal regions that appear to be closely related to the surface oceanographic water masses in the Pacific.

Sund and Renner (1959), during the 'Eastropic' expedition of 1955, found that chaetognaths could serve as biological indicators to distinguish different oceanic environments in eastern tropical Pacific waters. *Sagitta bedoti* may indicate water movements in the region of the boundary between the Peru and south Equatorial currents and the warmer Equatorial waters to the north. *S. pulchra* may also be an indicator of the cold–warm water boundary in the Equator, especially near the South American coasts. Finally, *S. regularis* and *Krohnita pacifica,* which appear to inhabit warm waters, are widely distributed in moderate numbers throughout much of the tropical region. They are absent from the colder waters of both the California and the Peru currents. Therefore, they hold definite promise as indicators of the boundaries separating the Equatorial waters from those of different character to the north and south.

In the same way, Brinton (1962), during the 'Shellback' expedition, sampled a normal southern autumn within the Peru current in 1952. The 'Downwind' expedition in January 1958 surveyed as far as 12° S.; this was a southern summer during which 'El Niño' was exceptionally severe and destructive, and the plankton from these cruises indicated that zoogeographical changes accompanied temperature changes. For example, the widespread warm-water species *Stylocheiro carinatum* was abundant in coastal waters during the warm January 1958 period, but it was absent in the main part of the current—cooler than 18° C—in July 1952. High densities of the eastern Equatorial species *Euphasia distinguenda* and *E. lamelligera* extended farther south into the Peru current during 'El Niño' than during the survey carried out in the southern winter. Similarly, *E. tenera* was numerous off Callao in January 1958, but not in July 1952.

A widely accepted concept of 'El Niño' holds that warming of the region by the current takes place as a consequence of a southward shift of the tropical rain belt, bringing about a disruption of upwelling and a southerly deflection along the coast of the water from the Equatorial countercurrent. These changes are initiated in December but the peak period of warming is during February and March.

The difference in the euphausiid distribution suggests that, in January 1958, the water off Peru was generally warm but was not dominated by strong currents. During the 'Downwind' expedition, the current was nearly static from the standpoint of water movement. Temperatures off Callao were 5°–8° C higher than at the time of the 'Shellback' survey. The species composition of the euphausiid fauna of the region was constant for the two survey periods, though the dominating Equatorial species were observed to be numerous farther south (e.g., *E. lamelligera*) and nearer the shore (e.g., *Stylocheiron carinatum*) during the 'Downwind' expedition than during the 'Shellback' expedition the latter was carried out when upwelling prevailed (Brinton, 1962).

Gonzales (n.d.) reported the occurence and the relative abundance of the tropical equatorial species, *Euphausia diomedae, E. tenera, E. lamelligera* and *Stylocheiron carinatum* in Ecuadorian waters during 'El Niño' of 1972.

The high density of *Euphausia lamelligera*, which made up 52.4 per cent of the total fauna in 1972, suggested the same distribution pattern as reported by Brinton (1962) of 'El Niño' of 1958 in the eastern Pacific. The indicator value potential of this species for these abnormal conditions is considerable.

Nyctiphanes simplex is a transition species from the Peru current. Although normally restricted to the area south of the coasts of Ecuador, it was found in healthy condition in the northern warmer waters influenced by 'El Niño'.

Planktonic foraminifera have been used by some authors as indicators of water movements. Bradshaw (1959) found that these organisms could be grouped into four faunae in the Pacific: a cold water fauna, a transition fauna and two warm water faunae. The regions they inhabited appeared to be differentiated by temperature and salinity characteristics.

He also suggested that there were indications of the presence of a transition fauna in the Peru current, and pointed out that the warm-water faunae included the Equatorial region and the North and South Pacific. The 20° C isotherm associated with this boundary also presumably marks the southern extent of these (warm) faunae in the South Pacific.

Miró and Luzuriaga (1974) studied the occurrence and distribution of the planktonic foraminifera in Ecuadorian waters waters in relation to the oceanic Equatorial front as well as to the species found in the sediments in two different years, in August 1971 and December 1972. The warm (25° C) surface waters were present at 1° N. while the temperature was less than 19° C in the Gulf of Guayaquil in August 1971. On the contrary, warm (25° C) waters were present at 4° S., and still warmer waters (up to 27° C) were reported north of Ecuador in December 1972. The abundance and predominance of warm-water faunae were reported in the oceanic waters off Ecuador in December 1972 while the

cold-water faunae were abundant in the previous year.

Cruz (n.d.) in a detailed analysis of the conditions of planktonic foraminifera during 'El Niño' of 1972, concluded:

The warm-water faunae of *Globoquadrina dutertrei, Globigerinoides ruber, G. sacculifer* and *Globorotalia menardii* made up 80 per cent of the total foraminifera fauna in Ecuadorian waters (Figs. 11–14).

There were some indications that the presence of *Globigerinoides ruber* and *G. sacculifer* were good *indicators* of the warm oceanic water poor in phytoplankton during 'El Niño' of 1972.

The cold-water species *Globigerinita glutinata* was almost absent in Ecuadorian waters in 1972, while it was abundant in 1971;

The presence of the cold-water species, *Globigerina bulloides, G. quinqueloba* and *Globigerinita bradyi*, suggest the mixture of two kinds of water masses south of Ecuador in 1972, and the adaptation of this species to these abnormal conditions.

RED TIDES

Red waters, caused by ciliates, have been reported in the Pacific from Point Barrow, Alaska (Holm-Hansen *et al.*, 1970) to Valparaíso, Chile. Avaria (1970) reported the phenomenon during a period (March 1968) when water temperature was rather high and preceded by a long period of windless isolation.

The occurrence of extensive red water patches in the oceanic waters in the vicinity of the Gulf of Guayaquil (81°05′ W.–2°44′ S.) was recorded (Jimenez, 1974). The organism causing this water discoloration was a ciliate protozoa with chlorophyll,, *Cyclotrichium meunieri* Powers, a positively phototropic organism. The movement of warm oceanic water from the north and west towards the Peru current system favours the occurrence of red tide patches and culminates with the concentration of these micro-organisms that colours the water with a deep rusty red. No toxic disturbance of the local fauna was observed.

The red pigment of the ciliate was water-soluble, and highly labile. The residual green pigment was acetone-soluble and its absorption spectrum was similar to that of the photosynthetic pigments of marine plankton algae. Values of 93.71 mg Chl/m^3 and 3,700 mg C/m^3/day were recorded in this water discoloration.

It was concluded that the ciliate contains either symbiotic algae or chlorophasts but, in both cases, functions as a plant. Normal hydrographic conditions were reported for this period of the year.

Ryther (1966) and Barber (1967) described the occurrence of a red water patch (100 square miles) between Punta Aguja and Cabo Blanco in April 1966. The causative organism was identified as the ciliate *Cyclotrichium meunieri*. The red water occurred in a region of turbulence at the boundary of two opposing currents. The warmer offshore water had a temperature of 21.64° C and a salinity of 35.132 per mille. The colder inshore water had a temperature of 19.6° C and a salinity of 35.078 per mille. It should be observed that the warm intrusions have high salinities, distinguishing these warm waters from the warm, low-salinity tropical surface water that occupies the area north of the Peru current boundary. Wyrtki (1966) showed the position of the boundary which be called the 'Equatorial front', which separates the tropical surface water and the Peru current system. According to Schott (1931), Posner (1957) and others, it is the Peru current region during 'El Niño' whereas the *Aquaje* (red tide)-producing warm water fronts reported by Barber were intrusions of high-salinity oceanic waters.

These intrusions could have spun off from the Peru countercurrent, but this is by no means clear. The water making up the countercurrent could come from the south Equatorial countercurrent (Forsbergh and Joseph, 1964) or from the surfacing of the Cromwell current east of the Galápagos Islands (Bjerknes 1961, 1966).

Whatever the origin of the warm water meeting the Peru coastal current in the area where the red water blooms were observed, considerable mixing occurred therein (Barber, 1967).

At a later date, Barber *et al.* (1969) reported two areas (02° 33' S, 82° 31' W. and 02° 35' S., 82° 01' W.) of red water in February 1968 during cruise 17 of the R.V. *Te Vega*. These locations were 90 and 60 miles respectively off Ecuador, and 160 miles north of the site of the 1966 red water occurrence described by Ryther. Each area was approximately one mile wide and stretched to both horizons. The causative organism was identified as *Cyclotrichium meunieri*. The authors suggested the presence of a cryptomonad symbiont in these ciliates.

Whatever the intensity of red tide, it is clearly distinct from the mass mortalities associated with the disastrous 'El Niño' invasions of warm water. The difference between 'El Niño' and the red-tide-producing warm countercurrent is well stated in the following quote from Brongersma and Sanders (referred to by Barber, 1967):

Schweigger . . . states that two different phenomena are involved. One is the development of a strictly coastal countercurrent, called 'El Niño' by Peruvian fishermen, originating in the Gulf of Guayaquil and flowing southwards in the northern winter along the most northern part of the Peruvian littoral. The other phenomenon (erroneously called 'El Niño' by oceanographers outside Peru) is the movement of warm oceanic water from the north and west towards northern Peru and sometimes far southward along the coast.

Although this statement seems to be correct, the information available is not adequate to deduce any conclusion. It is interesting to note the past occurrences of 'El Niño' and the appearances of red tides caused by the ciliate *Cyclotrichium meunieri* Powers (Table 3).

Although the literature is scanty, a bibliographic review of red tide in the tropical Pacific suggests that the hydrographic conditions near the Gulf of Guayaquil favours the occurrence of these water discolorations.

The relationship between the 'El Niño' phenomenon, the surface circulation and the phytoplankton production in coastal waters of Peru and Ecuador has been noted by several authors.

Guillén (1971), during 'El Niño' of 1965 reported very low concentration of phytoplankton and very low productivity associated with the flow of the surface Equatorial waters with temperatures and salinities between 24°−27° C, and 34.8−33.8 per mille respectively, along the Peruvian coast.

The higher values during the 'El Niño' phenomenon were still lower than the average value found in the same areas during normal years, and general coastal upwelling was reduced.

Jiménez (n.d.) noted local disturbances in the phytoplankton communities in the Gulf of Guayaquil, especially with reference to the 1972 'El Niño' phenomenon. When the highest surface water temperatures (25°−26° C) were registered in November 1972 to February 1973, a phytoplankton community dominated by coccolithophorids, dinoflagellates, and ciliates was abundant.

An increase of diatoms was observed when the surface temperature decreased to 22°−23° in the

Gulf of Guayaquil in March 1973, and a normal population dominated by diatoms was recovered.

Wooster and Guillén (1974) studied the 'El Niño' phenomenon of 1972 and reported the intensity of warming by November and December 1972 in the northern regions of the Peruvian coasts. Not until March 1973, did coastal temperatures of Peru return to normal.

Summary and conclusions

The relatively well studied Panama Bight presents seasonal variations for some oceanographic properties in response to meteorological changes caused by the southward movement of the Intertropical Convergence Zone.

Strong southerly and south-westerly surface currents occur, caused by the northerly winds funnelled through the mountains. These wind-induced circulations result in enrichment of the surface layers by mixing processes which permit a high rate of primary production, specially when upwellings in the Gulf of Panama occur.

The distribution values of micronutrients for the Panama Bight were smaller than the values reported for the Equatorial Front between continental Ecuador and the Galápagos Islands.

An extremely high-standing crop (expressed as chlorophyll *a* cell/l) and primary production were observed in the Gulf of Guayaquil and to the south and west of the Ecuadorian coast. These values were higher than the values reported for the Panama Bight.

Smayda (1963) reported, for the Panama Bight during March 1958, that upwelling winds were 'considerable weaker' following an unusually warm February and that water temperatures 3°-5° C higher than in the previous years were measured in the upper 25 metres. A much lower standing crop and a retardation in phytoplankton succession were also observed. These abnormal conditions occurred during the 1958 'El Niño' phenomenon.

Low concentrations of phytoplankton were also reported for the Peruvian waters during 'El Niño' of 1965 (Guillén, 1971) and for Ecuadorian waters during 'El Niño' of 1972.

There are indications that some planktonic organisms can be used as indicators of water masses, especially during the abnormal conditions that prevail during the 'El Niño' phenomenon. During 'El Niño' of 1972 in Ecuadorian waters, euphausiids and foraminifera proved to be most useful indicators of water movements.

Acknowledgement

Special thanks must go to the Ecuadorian Navy and, in particular, to Capitán de Corbeta UN Raúl Toledo, Director of the Instituto Oceanográfico, and Teniente de Fragata UN Pedro Cabezas, Head of Department of Marine Sciences, for supporting the preparation of this article. The writer also thanks the officers and crew of Ecuadorian R.V. *Orion* in which all the cruises were run. Dr Humberto Aguier provided the nutrient data, and Ing. Hector Ayon read the English manuscript.

Table 1

Period	Approximate season	Sign of slope
January—March 1957	Upwelling	+
March—November 1957	Rainy	—
November 1957—March 1958	Upwelling	+
March—September 1958	Rainy	—
September 1958—January 1959	End of rainy	?
January—April 1959	Upwelling	+
April—May 1959	Beginning of rainy	—

Table 2

Micro-organisms	1955—57 (cells/l)	1958 (cells/l)
Diatoms	907,645	449,096
Dinoflagellates	3,415	1,903
Gymnodiniaceae	2,864	2,535
Coccolithophores	9,628	5,000
Monads	21,156	14,430

Table 3. Red tide

Intensity Niño year	Location/year	Organism	Reference
Major, 1957—58	Valparaíso, Chile 1957	Ciliate?	
	Arica, Chile 1958	Ciliate?	Avaria (1970)
Major, 1965	Northern Peru April, 1966	*C. meunieri*	Ryther (1966)
Minor 1969	Point Barrow, Alaska, United States September, 1968	Ciliate sp.	Holm-Hansen *et. al* (1970)
	Gulf of Guayaqui, Ecuador February, 1968	*C. meunieri*	Barber *et al.* (1969)
	Valparaíso, Chile March, 1968	*C. meunieri*	Avaria (1970)
Major, 1972—73	Gulf of Guayaquil, Ecuador May, 1973	*C. meunieri*	Jiménez (1974)

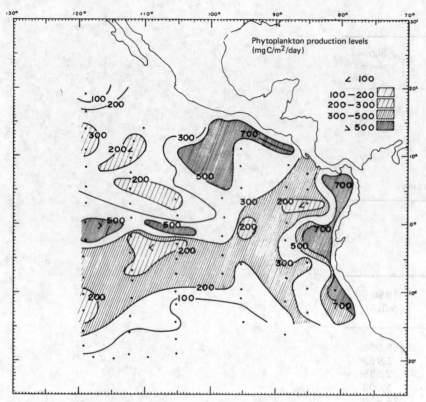

Fig. 1. Phytoplankton production in the Eastern Tropical
Pacific. (Owen and Zeitzschell, 1970).

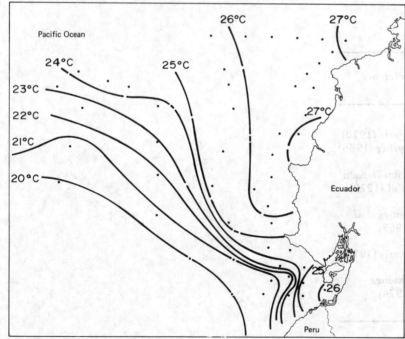

Fig. 2. Geographic distribution of sea-surface temperature,
R.V. *Orion* cruise 13–30 May 1973.

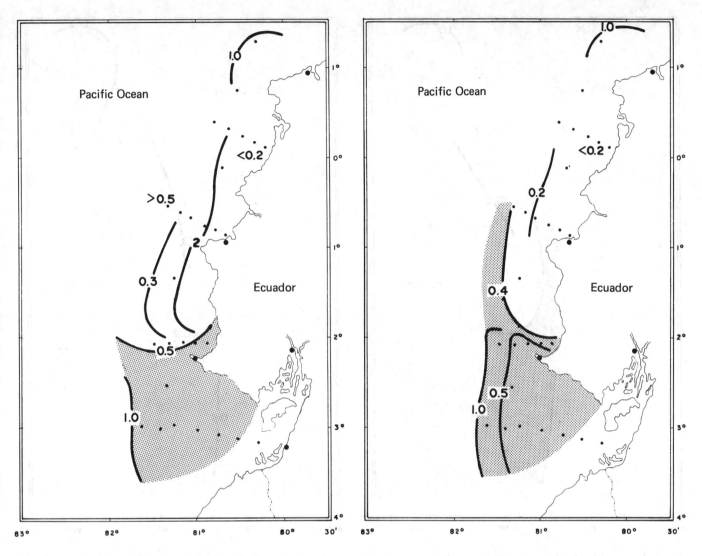

Fig. 3. Geographic distributions of chlorophyll *a* at the surface (mg/m³) R.V. *Orion* cruise 25—29 October 1973.

Fig. 4. Geographic distributions of chlorophyll *a* at 20 m deep, R.V. *Orion* cruise 25—29 October 1973.

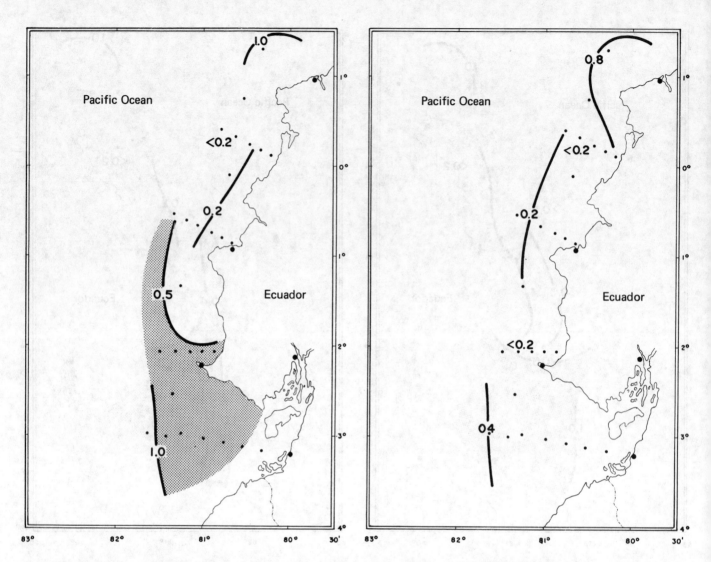

Fig. 5. Geographic distributions of chlorophyll *a* at 10 m deep, R.V. *Orion* cruise 25—29 October 1973.

Fig. 6. Geographic distributions of chlorophyll *a* at 30 m deep, R.V. *Orion* cruise 25—29 October 1973.

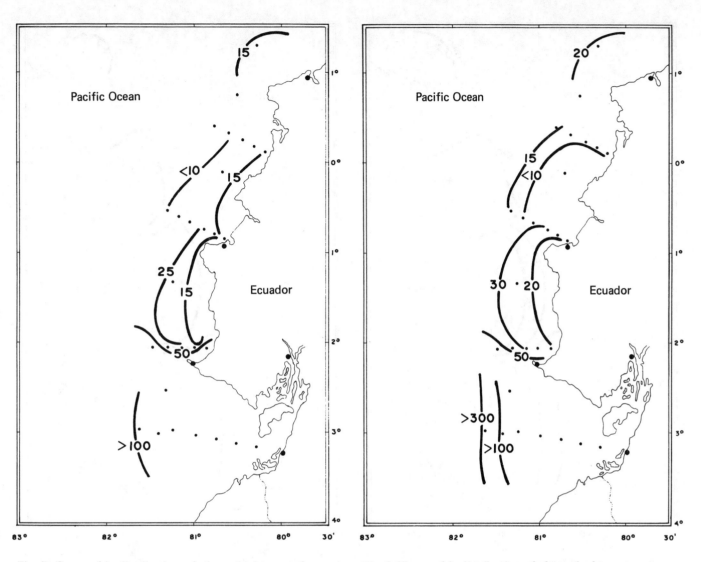

Fig. 7. Geographic distribution of phytoplankton at the surface (cell/ml), R.V. *Orion* cruise 25–29 October 1973.

Fig. 8. Geographic distribution of phytoplankton at 10 m deep, R.V. *Orion* cruise 25–29 October 1973.

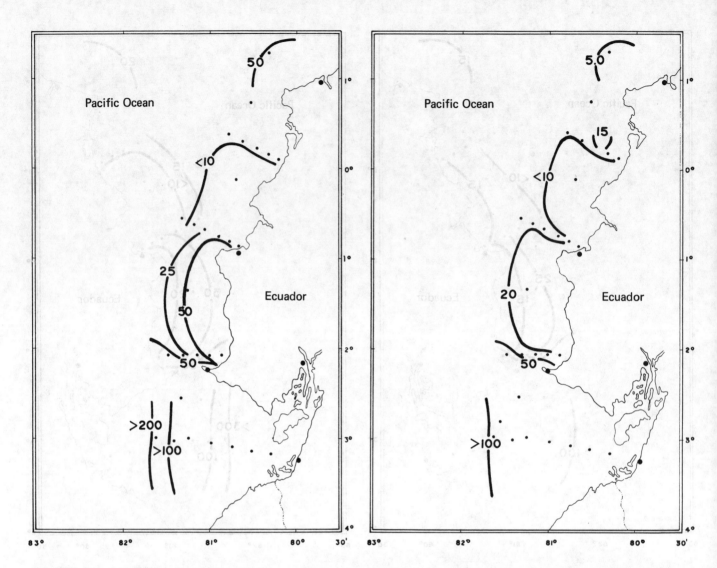

Fig. 9. Geographic distribution of phytoplankton at 20 m deep, R.V. *Orion* cruise 25–29 October 1973.

Fig. 10. Geographic distribution of phytoplankton at 30 m deep, R.V. *Orion* cruise 25–29 October 1973.

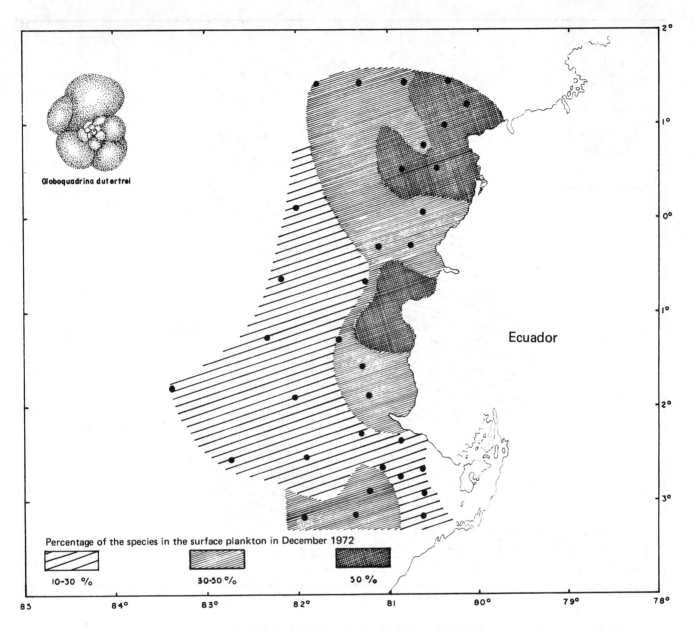

Fig. 11. Geographic distribution of planktonic foraminifera *(Globoquadrina dutertrei).*

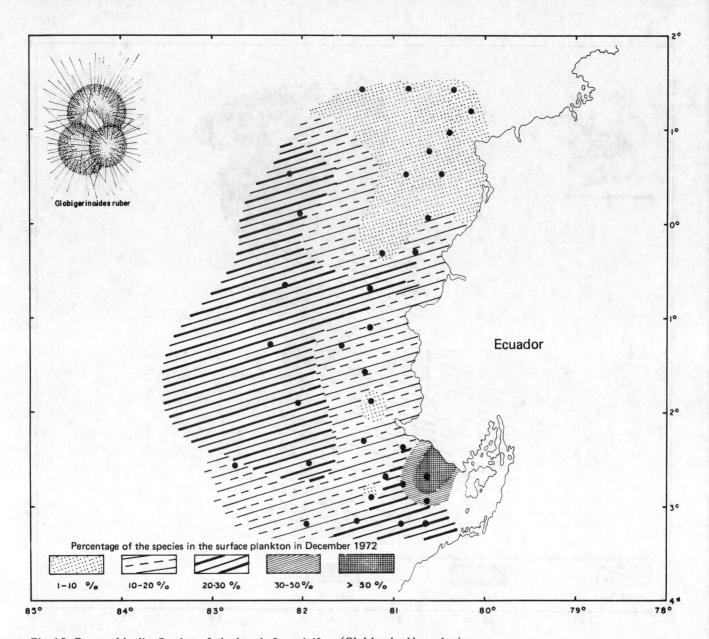

Fig. 12. Geographic distribution of planktonic foraminifera *(Globigerinoides ruber)*.

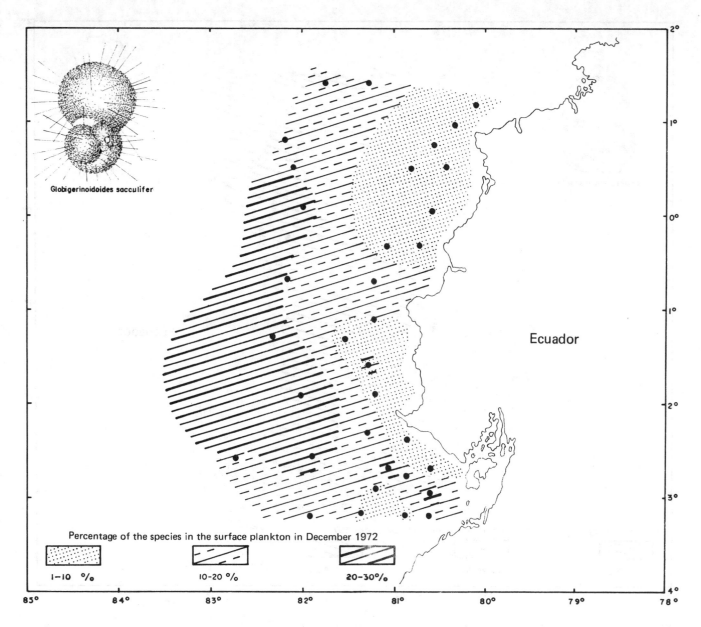

Fig. 13. Geographic distribution of planktonic foraminifera *(Globigerinoides sacculifer).*

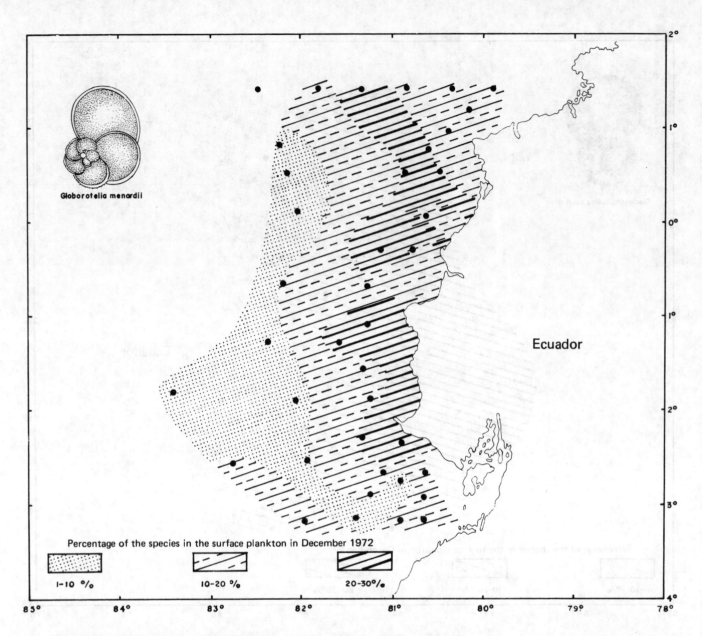

Fig. 14. Geographic distribution of planktonic foraminifera *(Globorotalia menardii).*

References

Avaria, S. 1970. Observación de un Fenómeno de Marea Roja en la Bahía Valparaíso. *Rev. Biol. Mar.* (Valparaíso), Vol. 14, No. 1, p. 1–15.

Barber, R. 1967. The Distribution of Dissolved Organic Carbon in the Peru Current System of the Pacific Ocean. Stanford University. (Ph.D. Dissertation.)

Barber, R. T.; Ryther, J. H. 1969. Organic Chelators: Factors Affecting Primary Production in the Cromwell Current Upwelling. *J. exp. mar. Biol. Ecol.,* Vol. 3, p. 191–9.

Barber, R.; White, A.; Siegelman, H. W. 1969. Evidence for a Cryptomonad Symbiont in the Ciliate, *Cyclotrichium meunieri, J. Phycol.,* Vol. 5, No. 1, p. 86–8.

Bennett, E. B., 1963. An Oceanographic Atlas of the Eastern Tropical Pacific Ocean, Based on Data from Eastropic Expedition. October–December 1955. *Inter-Amer. Trop. Tuna Comm.,* Vol. 8, No. 2, p. 33–65.

——. 1965. Currents Observed in Panama Bay During September–October 1958. *Inter-Amer. Trop. Tuna. Comm.,* Vol. 10, No. 7, p. 399–457.

Bjerknes, J. 1961. 'El Niño' Study Based on Analysis of Ocean Surface Temperatures 1935–57. *Inter-Amer. Trop. Tuna Comm. Bull.,* Vol. 5, No. 3, p. 219–307. (P/0-02-00033).

——. 1966. Survey of 'El Niño' 1957–58 in its Relation to the Tropical Pacific Meteorology. *Inter-Amer. Trop, Comm. Bull.,* Vol. 12, No. 2; p. 1–62 (MET-01-00010.)

Boltovskoy, E.; Gualancañay, E. 1974. Foraminiferos Bentónicos Actuales de Ecuador. 1: Provincia de Esmeraldas. *Bol. Inst. Ocean. de la Armada.*

Bradshaw, J. 1959. Ecology of Living Planktonic Foraminifera in the North and Equatorial Pacific Ocean. *Contr. Cushman Found. for Foram. Research* Vol. 10, No. 2, p. 25–64.

Brinton, E. 1962. The Distribution of Pacific Euphausiids. *Bull. Scripps Inst. Oceanogr.,* Vol. 8, No. 2, p. 51–270.

Cromwell, T.; Bennett, E. 1959. Surface Drift Charts for the Eastern Tropical Pacific Ocean. *Inter-Amer. Trop. Tuna. Comm.,* Vol. 3, No. 5, p. 217–35.

Cruz, M. L. de. n.d. Distribución de los Foraminíferos Plantónicos Vivos del Mar Ecuatoriano. (Mimeo.)

Desrosières, R. 1969. Surface Macrophytoplankton of the Pacific Ocean Along the Equator. *Limnol & Oceanogr.,* Vol. 14, p. 626–32.

EASTROPAC Atlas. 1974. Biological and Nutrient Chemistry Data. In: C. M. Love (ed.). (United States Department of Commerce, Vol. 8, Circ. 330.

Forsbergh, E. 1963. Some Relationships of Meteorological, Hydrographic and Biological Variables in the Gulf of Panama. *Inter-Amer. Trop. Tuna Comm.,* Vol. 7, No. 1, p. 1–109.

Forsbergh, E.; Joseph, J. 1964. Biological Production in the Eastern Pacific Ocean. *Inter. Amer. Trop. Tuna Comm.,* Vol. 8, No. 9, p. 477–527.

Forsbergh, E. D. 1969. On the Climatology, Oceanography and Fisheries of the Panama Bight. *Inter-Amer. Trop. Tuna Comm.,* Vol. 14, No. 2, p. 49–365.

Gonzalez, M. de. n.d. Estudio Preliminar de los Eufásidos de las Aguas Superficiales del Ecuador. (Mimeo).

Guillén, O. 1971. The 'El Niño' Phenomenon in 1965 and its Relation to the Productivity in Coastal Peruvian Waters in Fertility of the Sea. In: J. D. Costlow, (ed.).

Hasle, G. R. 1959. A Quantitative Study of Phytoplankton from the Equatorial Pacific. *Deep-sea Res.,* Vol. 6, p. 38–59.

——. 1960. Phytoplankton and Ciliate Species from the Tropical Pacific. *Norske, Vidensk, Akad., Hvalrad. Skr.,* Vol. 2, p. 5–50.

Hobson, L. A.; Menzel, D. W.; Barber, R.; 1973. Primary Productivity and Sizes of Pools or Organic Carbon in the Mixed Layer of the Ocean. *Mar. Biol.,* Vol. 19, No. 4, p. 298–306.

Holmes, R. W.; Schaefer, M. G.; Shimada, B. M. 1957. Primary Production, Chlorophyll and Zooplankton Volumes in the Tropical Eastern Pacific Ocean. *Bull. Inter.-Amer. Trop. Tuna Comm.,* Vol. 2, p. 129–69.

Holm-Hansen, O. F.; Taylor, J. R.; Bardate, R. J. 1970. A Ciliate Red-Tide at Barrow, Alaska. *Mar. Bio.,* Vol. 7, No. 1, p. 36–46.

Jimenez, R. 1974. Marea Roja, Debida a un Ciliado en el Golfo de Guayaquil. *Bol. Inst. Ocean. de la Armada.* (CM-Bio-2).

Jimenez, R. (n.d.) Diatomeas y Silicoflagelados del Fitoplancton del Golfo de Guayaquil. (Mimeo).

Jimenez, R.; Tesantes, F. (n.d.) Palncton, Producción Primaria y Pigmentos en Aguas Costeras Ecuatorianas. (Mimeo.)

Knauss, J. A. 1957. An Observation of an Oceanic Front. *Tellus,* Vol. 9, p. 234–6.

——. 1966. Further Measurements and Observations of the Cromwell Current. *Journ. Mar. Res.,* Vol. 24, No. 2, p. 205–40. (P/O-02-00121.)

Marshall, H. G. 1972. Phytoplankton Composition in the Southeastern Pacific Between Ecuador and the Galápagos Islands. *Proc. Biol. Soc. Wash.,* Vol. 85, No. 1, p. 1–38.

Miró, M. de; Jimenez, R.; Gualancañay, E.; Luzuriaga, M. 1974. Producción Primaria y Pigmentos Fotosintéticos del Fitoplancton Marino del Ecuador. *Bol. Inst. Ocean. de la Armada* (CM-Bio-1).

Miró, M. de ; Gualancañay, E. 1974. Foraminíferos Bentónicos de la Plataforma Continental de la Provincia de Esmeraldas, Ecuador. *Bol. Inst. Ocean. de la Armada.* (CM-Bio-4.)

Miró, M. de ; Luzuriaga, M. 1974. Foraminíferos Planctónicos Vivos en Aguas Ecuatorianas. *Bol. Inst. Ocean. de la Armada.* (CM-Bio-3).

Owen, R. W. ; Zeitschel, B. 1970. Phytoplankton Production Seasonal Change in the Oceanic Eastern Tropical Pacific. *Mar. Biol.,* Vol. 7, No. 1, p. 32—6.

Posner, G. S. 1957. The Peru Current. *Bull. Bingham Oceanogr. Coll.,* Vol. 16, No. 2, p. 106—51. (P/O-04-00034).

Ryther, J. H. 1966. *Cruise Report Research Vessel 'Anton Bruun'. Cruise 15.* Mar. Lab. Texas, A. & M University (Special Rep. No. 5).

Schaefer, M. ; Bishop, Y. M. M. ; Howard, G. V. 1958. Some aspects of Upwelling in the Gulf of Panama. *Inter-Amer. Trop. Tuna Comm.,* Vol. 3, No. 2, p. 79—131.

Schott, G. 1931. Der Peru—Strom und seine nordlichen Nachbargebiete in normaler Ausbildung. *Ann. Hydrog. Mar. Meteorol.,* Vol. 59, p. 161—9, 200—13, 240—52. (P/0-02-00258.)

Smayda, T. 1963. A Quantitative Analysis of the Phytoplankton of the Gulf of Panama: I. *Inter-Amer. Trop. Tuna Comm.,* Vol. 7, No. 3, p. 193—253.

——. 1965. A Quantitative Analysis of the Phytoplankton of the Gulf of Panama: II. *Inter-Amer. Trop. Tuna Comm.,* Vol. 9, No. 7, p. 467—529.

——. 1966. A Quantitative Analysis of the Phytoplankton of the Gulf of Panama: III. *Inter-Amer. Trop. Tuna Comm.,* Vol. 2, No. 5, p. 355—612.

Sund, P. N. ; Renner, J. 1959. The Chaetognatha of the Eastropic Expedition, with Notes as to their Possible Values as Indicators of Hydrographic Conditions. *Inter-Amer. Trop. Tuna Comm.,* Vol. 3, No. 9, p. 395—436.

Stevenson, M. R. ; Santoro, J. 1968. Resultados Preliminares e Informe de Datos del Crucero-2 de EASTROPAC. *Inter-Amer. Trop. Tuna Comm.* (S/R.)

Stevenson, M. R. ; Taft, B. 1971. New Evidence of the Equatorial Undercurrent East of the Galápagos Islands. *Mar. Research,* Vol. 29, No. 2, p. 103—15.

Strickland, J. D. H. ; Eppley, R. W. ; Mendiola, B. R. 1969. Poblaciones de Fitoplancton Nutrientes y Fotosíntesis en Aguas Costeras Peruanas. *Bol. Inst. Mar. Perú,* Vol. 2, No. 1, p. 4—45.

Wooster, S. W. ; Guillén, O. 1974. Características de 'El Niño' en 1972. *Bol. Inst. Mar del Peru,* Vol. 3, No. 2. p. 44—71.

Wyrtki, K. 1965. Surface Currents of the Eastern Tropical Pacific Ocean. *Inter-Amer. Trop. Tuna Comm.,* Vol. 9, No. 5, p. 271—303.

Biology of the anchoveta. 1: Summary of the present knowledge

Romulo Jordán S.[1]

Identity

NOMENCLATURE

Valid name: *Engraulis ringens*. taxonomy: Vertebrata, craneata, Gnathostomata, Pisces, Teleostomi, Actinopterygie, Clupeiformes, Engraulidae; Engraulis. Subspecies: no subspecies has been described, but the existence has been postulated of three subpopulations more or less distinguishable on the basis of meristic characters, degrees of mixing by marked fish, differences in reproductive rhythm and other characteristics.

Accepted common name and vernacular names

The scientific literature regularly uses the name of 'anchovy' for *Engraulis ringens,* although the name anchovy appears in the literature due to its resemblance to *E. mordax* found off the coast of California.

The following vernacular names are used: Peru—Anchovy (adult individuals), Anchoveta negra, Peladilla (juvenile individuals); Chile—Anchoveta (Arica), Chicora (Iquique), Sardina bocona (Valparaíso), Sardina (Talcahuano and San Vicente), Anchoa.

Morphology

The description of coloration is usually according to preserved specimens and is usually confused in the literature; therefore, it should be clarified. The dorsal aspect presents a clear brilliant green pigmentation of all tones, becoming dark and blueish in adult individuals. It contrasts with the side and belly which are of brilliant silver colours. The pectoral, dorsal and ventral fins are of clear tones and the caudal fin is dark, almost black.

The principal proportions and meristic characteristics are the following: head 3.0 to 3.7; height 4.4 to 5.3 in adult specimens, between 5.5 to 6.5 in individuals less than 90 mm; D. 15 to 18; A. 19 to 24; P. 15 to 18; scale about 43 to 47, V. 46—49, B. 38 to 48 + 35 to 43. Detailed descriptions can be found in Hildebrand (1943; 1946) and Jordán and Vildoso (1965).

The male and female cannot be distinguished externally (Clark, 1954) and comparison of length frequence with sex of fishes collected at Chimbote, Callao, and Pisco showed no differences. The analysis of numbers of vertebrae (Jordan, 1963), gill rakers (Tsukayama, 1966) or anal or dorsal radii permitted no means of distinction between male and female (see Fig. 1).

Distribution

The records of the species which appear in the literature are listed in Table 1; from these we can deduce only a latitudinal distribution. Commercial fishery for the species shows that longitudinally the greatest concentrations are caught within 40 to 50 miles of the Peruvian coast or within an even lesser distance from that of Chile. The exploratory and experimental fishing carried out by IMARPE through the Eureka operations has shown the existence of anchovy up to 80 to 100 miles from the coast.

1. Romulo Jordán S. Instituto del Mar del Perú, Esq. Gamarra y Gral. Valle s/n, Chucuito, Callao (Peru).

Vestnes and Saetersdal (1964) and Vestnes *et al.* (1965) had previously indicated that anchovy was not found further than 20 miles from the shore.

A better way of establishing an accurate dimensional distribution of the adult anchovy is to study the occurrence of anchovy eggs in plankton. This is almost certain evidence of spawning individuals near by since the hatching time of the eggs is scarcely 50 hours (Santander and Castillo, 1973) and the speed of the drift current off the Peruvian coast is relatively slow—some 0.5–0.7 m/sec. (Wyrtki, 1965). Figure 2 shows that the greater concentrations predominate near the coast but the maximum limits of distribution extend up to 210 miles approximately. Even if objection is raised to distribution based on eggs, the presence of the species at even greater distances of the coast has been proved by the distribution of larvae of the species (see below).

In summary, the *E. ringens* is distributed horizontally from Zorritos, Peru (04° 30′ S.) to Valdivia, Chile (39° 47′ S.), with areas of great abundance off the Peruvian central and northern zones. Longitudinally, they are found up to approximately 230 miles from the coast, but harbour from north to south. The area of greatest abundance is up to 40 miles from the Peruvian coast and 20 miles from the Chilean coast.

Vertical distribution, was noted first by Clark (1954) using the 'floating trawl' and echo-sounding method. He failed to collect anchovy at depths greater than 50 m, and the majority of the schools were located at depths less than 25 m. However, recent work by IMARPE showed that the depths at which the anchovy occur can be greater. Jordan *et al.* (1971) condensed these observations, showing that during the day schools could be encountered at up to 100 m and only by night less than 50 m. In general, about 70 per cent of the anchovy schools were detected between 10 and 30 m. The presence of shoals of the different levels appeared to be independent of the sea-floor depth:

The mean depth of schools during winter is
double that during summer—probably because in
winter the mixing layer is much deeper, with
consequently greater dispersion of the food supply.

At the depths at which the schools swim, the
extreme temperatures of 13.5 to 23° C rarely
occur.

The school prefer a temperature range of 14.5 to
21° C.

During summer, the schools appear to be able to
tolerate a temperature range of up to 4.6° C in

the main body of the school and up to 10° C at the extremes.

Bionomics and life history

REPRODUCTION (MATURITY, GONADS AND FECUNDITY)

The sexes are separate in the anchovy and show a marked gonochorism. No cases of hemaphroditism have been described.

It has been possible to establish a general pattern, for the entire area of distribution, of two maturation waves each year, one of which has its maximum between September and October, and the other between January and February. March, April and May are months principally of sexual inactivity at the start of a new cycle, in such a way that sexual activity occurs almost throughout the year in this species. The development during the second maturation wave is very rapid, which could be explained by the higher sea temperatures during spring and summer (Einarson *et al.*, 1966; Simpson *et al.*, 1969). Individuals begin gonad development at about 11 cm and only a few reach full maturity at 12 cm (approximately one year old); about 50 per cent of those at 14 cm, and practically all those at 15 cm reach the spawning stage.

Completely mature female gonads have been observed occasionally and apparently their presence is only momentary. The enlarged turgid ovary has a globular appearance and is orange-coloured. It is full of microscopic ovules which are oval in shape and have translucid cytoplasm with large vitelline granules. The latter give them a typical reticulated appearance, central nucleus and swollen membrane. The ovules are 1,000 to 1,370 μm in size (Jordán 1959). The distribution of maturing ovules shows bimodality, suggesting that two spawnings might be produced in one season.

Miñano (1968), studying fecundity, established a relationship between fecundity and length:

$$F = 277.68 + 2.96 \, L$$

with $r = 0.94$.

The mean number of ovules in the more mature fish varies from 9,000 for 12 cm individuals to 21,000 for 17 cm fish. The relationship of fecundity to weight is expressed by the equation:

$$F = 47.20 + 4.45\,P$$

with $r = 0.91$.

SPAWNING

Systematic studies carried out by the Peruvian Sea Institute and the Chilean Institute for Fisheries Development over more than 10 years have provided considerable information. Some investigations have been summarized by Jordán and Vildoso (1965) for Peru.

The anchovy spawns all along the Peruvian coast beginning in the vicinity of Talara (5° 40′ S.). The centre of distribution lies off Peru from a point south of Punta Aguja to Cerro Azul (see Fig. 2) with a density of greater than $1,000/m^2$. In the spawning foci the number of eggs is sometimes greather than $40,000/m^2$. Further south from Cerro Azul, spawning takes place in progressively more limited areas.

The principal spawning period off the Peruvian coast, as shown by egg and larvae collections and maturity studies (see Fig. 3), lasts 6 to 8 months, from August to February or March, although spawning occurs sporadically throughout the year. The peak falls generally between August and October and in consequence the principal recruitment period is January to March. A secondary peak occuring in summer (January–February) results in a secondary recruitment in winter (see below).

The occurrence and limits of the spawning season show certain changes by zones according to ecological conditions and perhaps to as yet unknown physiological conditions. Thus, in the northern and central Peruvian littoral zones two peaks occur: one at the end of winter and the other in summer whereas, in the southern zone, a single winter spawning season occurs somewhat before that in the other regions.

Recently, following the 'El Niño' phenomenon of 1972–73, spawning occurred off the Peruvian coast almost constantly.

The spawning season off the Chilean littoral in some years appears to differ slightly from that of Peru. Off Valparaíso, Fischer (1958) found the greater quantity of eggs in May, June and July, then diminished in the succeeding months and because scarce or absent between November and January.

Material presented by Simpson and Carreno (1967) for Arica and Iquique showed high levels of spawning anchovy from June to October and again from January to February, with sporadic spawning throughout the year. This resembles the Peruvian situation, especially that of the Ilo area—where spawning takes place somewhat in advance of that in the central and northen areas of Peru. In Talcahuano maximum spawning takes place from April to September and July to August, with sporadic spawning throughout the year. In the southernmost area of distribution (Valdivia), samples taken in June and September and in March indicate spawning.

Eggs

The eggs are pelagic, ovoid, translucent, with visible nuclei and smooth and somewhat swollen membranes. The vitellum is granular in appearance, divided into numerous clearly visible alveoli and is of amber colour in preserved specimens; and possesses no oil globule.

The measurements quoted by different authors are:

	Barreda (1950)	Fischer (1958) n = 75	Einarrson et al. (1963) n = 2,121
Major axis (mm)	1.25–1.50	1.22–1.49	1.19–1.60 $\bar{x} = 1.42$
Minor axis (mm)	0.65–0.80	0.54–0.68	0.57–0.86 $\bar{x} = 0.71$

Fischer obtained hatching of the eggs *in vitro* at temperatures of 10.5 to 12.5° C. Santander and Castillo (1973), following the developmental sequence, calculated that hatching occurs at the natural medium temperatures 14.9–16.9° C. after 50 hours. The eggs are distributed through a column of at least 70 m and in cases of great density, about 77 per cent at less than 30 m, falling off towards both extremes. Spawning takes place chiefly between 22.00 h and 02.20 h.

PRE-ADULT PHASE

Embryonic Phase

The embryonic developmental sequence takes place in three phases as described by Einarsson and Mendiola (1963) and by Santander and Castillo (1973):

Phase 1 : from beginning of fertilization to closure of the blastopore. At the end of this phase the embryo appears with 6 to 8 miomeres, and the optic vesicles have formed although they are not clearly distinguishable.

Phase 2 : from closure of the blastopore to separation of the caudal extremity of the embryo from the vitelline sac. The optical vesicles become clearly visible and the number of miomeres rises to 13—15.

Phase 3 : from separation of the tail from the vitelline sac to hatching.

The chronological sequence of the described phases is shown in Figure 4. A comparison of the development rhythm at different depths from 0 to 70 m showed no significant differences, although the temperature range was as much as 5° C. (from 13.5° to 18.5° C.) ; Santander *et al.* (1973) also found that the eggs during phase 1 are the most susceptible to the mechanical action of the sampling causing death in high proportions but falling to zero in the prehatching period. Natural mortality fluctuated from 0 to 30 per cent per sample, the lowest values being at the depth of 30 m.

Larval phase

The sequence of larval development was described by Fischer (1958) and Einarsson *et al.* (1963) and is as follows :

1—5 hours : 2.9—3.1 mm, 34—36 preanal miomeres. The tail is 24.4 per cent and the vitelline sac about 60 per cent of total length. Pectoral fins not yet formed. Hood and body pigmented. On the sixth day it changes into a prelarva at temperatures of 11—13° C.

24 hours : melanophores appear on each side of the digestive tube.

Sixth day (prelarva) : notable increase in length up to 3.8—4.1 mm in 24 hours. The tail is now 27.6—28.2 per cent of body length, the vitelline sac much diminished ; a small, rounded pectoral fin develops.

Seventh day : 5.4 mm, thirthy-three pre-anal of this length. Disproportionately big head and five branchials visible. The vitelluna absorbed or only residual.

Seventh day : 5.4 mm, thirty-three pre-anal miomeres. Tail 30 per cent of total length. Body has considerably increased in height and breadth. The digestive tube is clearly distinguishable.

The horizontal distribution of larvae is shown in Figure 5 and the degrees of dispersion from the centres of spawning can be seen by comparison with Figure 2.

The maximum depth reached by larvae is unknown but apparently the number diminishes markedly below 70 m. The changes in the proportion of larvae at different levels of a column of water allows deduction of processes of phototrophic migration. During the night they are found chiefly in mid-water between 20 and 40 m, and during the day at or near the surface. These migrations are partial since both by night and by day larvae can be found at different depths.

Adolescent phase

According to Einarsson and Rojas de Mendiola (1963), juvenile forms are characterized by a definite head conformation and proportions, and by a change in pigmentation pattern from larva to adult. They are greater than 32 mm in size. In a juvenile of 46 mm, the head is one-quarter of the total length, and four to five rows of pigmentation already are in evidence. The presence of juveniles in plankton samples is rare, as is their appearance in commercial fishing nets (normally due to entanglement in the mesh). The information on distribution and behaviour of the first stages of this phase is sparse. The catch records of juveniles in the literature can be summarized as shown in Table 2.

Adult phase

Longevity

The year class structure of the catches allows identification of groups up to 3 years old. Recent information derived from individuals marked in July 1970 has shown that anchovy released at sizes between the extremes of 9 and 17 cm (mostly between 14—15 cm) have been recovered up to May 1974, indicating a lifespan greater than 4 years. The sequence of recoveries from September 1970 until May 1974 was as shown in Table 3.

Competitors

Rojas de Mendiola (1966) gave the preliminary information shown in Table 4 on the diet of the sardine (*Sardinops sagax*) and machete (*Brevoortia maculata*) species, which, like the anchovy, feed preferentially on phytoplankton.

Sardine and machete populations are much smaller than that of the anchovy (principally on the Peruvian coast) so that the competition effect is reduced.

Predators

Various records and verifications of anchovy in the stomachs of fishes, birds and mammals have been given by Lavalle (1917), Del Solar (1942), De Buen (1958), Schweigger (1964) and others. Table 5 summarizes what is presently known of the anchovy's predators.

The three species that produce guano, i.e. *P. bougainvillii, S. variegata* and *P. occidentalis thagus,* are held to be the chief predators of anchovy, which is certain so long as those populations were maintained at high levels. The maximum guano-bird population was 28 million (1955) and the minimum 1.8 million (1973). The most abundant species over the last seventy years has been *P. bougainvillii* at 82 per cent of the total, followed by *S. variegata* at 15 per cent and *P. occidentalis thagus,* 2 per cent.

Among the various values given as estimates of the ingestion by *P. bougainvillii,* the most reasonable is considered to be 430.9 fish per day, of which some 96 per cent is anchovy. The variation in bird populations from 28 million in 1955 to 1.8 million in 1973 would suggest that predation varied from 4×10^6 tons to 0.3×10^6 tons, respectively. Another important predator of the anchovy is the bonito, *Sarda chilensis,* an abundant pelagic fish of Peru and Chile. Its predation has been estimated at a minimum of 10^6 tons per year (Boerema *et al.,* 1967). For seals, between 100,000 and 500,000 tons per year has been estimated. Other predators of importance are squid, cuttlefish, blackruff, and others for which no estimates exist. The sardine, chaetognaths and other planktonic organisms are also involved as predators of eggs and larvae. It has been calculated that the total annual predation of anchovy fluctuated from 11×10^6 tons in 1965 to 6.4×10^6 tons in 1970 (Panel of Experts, 1970).

NUTRITION AND GROWTH

Feeding

The anchovy has special adaptations to filter and assimilate planktonic organisms, particularly phytoplankton, e.g. a disproportionately large mouth, a large number of densely disposed gill rakers, and a long intestine which may measure up to twice the total length of the body.

According to aquaria studies, the anchovy feeds on microscopic particles by prolonged filtration, swimming at a more or less constant speed and only capturing larger particles, e.g. *Artemia salina,* with specific movements; Pastor and Málaga (1966) stated that feeding can continue in aquaria for 15 to 20 minutes and the anchovy can ingest 2 to 39 grams of food per day.

Food

The studies made by Rojas de Mendiola (1966) showed that the anchovy of the north and centre of Peru fed mainly on phytoplankton (about 98 per cent), whereas, in the south, predominately on zooplankton. According to De Buen (1958), its food off the Chilean coast consisted principally of zooplankton.

The dominant species of food in the Chimbote area (based on collections between 1955 and 1958) were *Skeletonema costatum, Shoroderella delicatula, Thalassiosira subtilis* and various species of the genera *Chaetoceros* and *Coscinodiscus.*

The most outstanding characteristics of feeding are described in a study made in the summer of 1968 in four different areas of the Peruvian coast (Rojas de Mendiola *et al.,* 1969). Their results can be summarized as shown in Table 6.

Rojas de Mendiola (1969) noted a dietary difference according to age. Larvae and juveniles, principally the latter, showed a predominance of zooplanktonic organisms especially copepods (*Centropages brachiatus, Calanus australis* and *Oncaea*) and euphausiids (*Euphausia mucronata* and *Nyctiphanes simples*). The author also mentioned that the significant change in phytoplankton diet took place in adults larger than 12 cm.

Bio-oceanographic changes such as the 1972 'El Niño', caused an area-dependent change in the nominal diet composition. As a result, anchovy in the northern and central zones of Peru fed on zooplankton, almost exclusively euphausiids (Eureka XXIII) and in the south on phytoplankton (Eureka XXIV).

Growth rate

Saetersdal and Valdivia (1964), examining the displacement of modal sizes of length frequencies off the Peruvian coast, decided that fish of 9 cm total length were in their first 6 months of life, and after a year were of about 12 cm; at the age of 18 months, fish were 13–14 cm in length. They noted that modal groups higher than 15 cm were rarely

found although individual fishes could measure up to
17.5 cm. Off the coast of Chile, Simpson *et al.* (1969)
gave lengths of 9.5 and 15.5 for fish of 6, 12 and
18 months, respectively.

The parameters of the growth equation have
been calculated independently for fish caught off the
Peruvian and Chilean coasts, with the values shown
in Table 7.

Saetersdal and Valdivia (1964) noted that the
median growth increment of fish from 9 to 12 cm
was more than 0.5 cm, with maximum noted at 1 cm
per month in summer (October to May), and less
than the mean during winter (June to September).
Simpson *et al.* (1967) reached a similar result for
Chile establishing that the mean increment reached
its maximum from November to January and
diminished in winter. The rate is probably related
to changes in the rates of production and to the
environment.

The maximum lengths (*L max*) given by
Simpson *et al.* (1967) for fish caught off the coast
of Chile were: Arica, 18.5 cm; Iquique, 18.5;
Antofagasta—Mejillones, 18.5; Coquimbo, 18.0;
Talcahuano, 21.0; and Valdivia, 19.5, are much
higher than those given for the Peruvian coast.

Recent information for the Peruvian coast
(1973—74) indicated an evident shift of *L max.* up
to 20.5 cm since it has been found in different
regions (with modes between 17 and 18 cm, see
below). This situation might be the result of a
changing growth rate. The growth pattern calculated
for an anchovy generation off the Peruvian coast is
given in Table 8 (Table 4 from the Panel of Experts,
1970). This table can be compared also with that
given by Schaeffer (1967, Table 10, p. 241).

BEHAVIOUR

Migrations and local movements

The results of two marking experiments, with
liberation at different points on the Peruvian coast,
gave information on displacements and mixing.

The marking of 170,051 anchovy, carried out
in July 1970 at thirty-four different localities, chiefly
of fish from 12 to 16 cm, yielded 4,196 recoveries in
four months. The monthly distribution of the marked
fish is shown in Figure 7. The principal results are
summarized as follows:
The marked anchovy moved equally to the north and
    south independent of the geographic area in which

they were liberated, with the sole exception of a
group released in the north (8° 30′ S.) whose
southward movement was more marked.
During the four months following the marking
    (September—December 1970) about 80 per cent of
    the liberated fish remained within the same zone
    (about 90 miles).
A proportion of the fish moved considerably,
    reaching up to 480 miles from the marking place in
    only two months. This record comes from fish
    recovered in September and October off Callao
    (12° S.) coming from Ilo (18° S.). Various fish
    marked off Pisco (13° S.) and Huacho (11° S.)
    were recaptured in November 30 miles to the north
    and 360 miles to the south respectively.
Some of the fish marked in the southern area moved
    to northern Chile. Fish from Atico (16° S.),
    Mallendo (17° S.) and Ilo (18° S.) were recovered
    at different Chilean localities as far as Antofagasta
    (22° S.).
In spite of the wide movements noted, definite
    migratory movements did not show themselves.
    The general tendency was of a latitudinal
    dispersion in both directions from the marking
    locality, with a more southerly movement by
    fishes in northern zones. These movements are
    probably of trophic type and related with
    oceanographic changes which occur principally
    in the northern zone of the Peruvian coast during
    spring and summer.
The fish of the southern zone (Atico—Tacna)
    intermingled actively in their own area but in a
    much smaller proportion with those of the centre
    and north, suggesting somewhat independent
    population subunits.
Anchovy marked by the Chileans and liberated from
different areas of the north coast of the country since
1971 have been recovered in southern Peru. All the
above information relates to adult fish. The juvenile
fish are found principally very close to the coast and
if this distribution is compared with that of the larvae
it implies that each year there is a movement of the
fish towards the coast, according to the rate of
growth.

Schooling

Villanueva *et al.* (1969), Jordán *et al.* (1971) and
other reports from the Instituto del Mar indicated
that the anchovy schools appeared to be at their
greatest density during the day, causing traces known
as 'feather' on the echogram; by night they were

dispersed with light traces of the 'layer' type. There were also indications of discrete vertical displacements towards the surface at night.

There is little information with regard to the conformation of the schools and their structure; it is known that males and females school together indifferently, though with certain segregation by size. However, with some frequency it is possible to encounter mixed schools with wide ranges of sizes. Saetersdal and Valdivia (1964) showed that the size composition from a single catch could comprise fish between 8 to 15 cm and two modal groups— an almost equal result to that obtained with samples from two to five catches.

Each school can be formed of some hundreds (and, at times, thousands) of tons. There are records of boats which could bring in between 200 and 300 tons in a single catch; the degree of independence of each school and the length of time for which it can exist as a unit are unknown, but it is known from fishing operations that a group of schools can remain in the same area for several weeks. A marking of 18,000 individuals off Cerro Azul (13° S.) demonstrated that some individuals remained in the marking area for at least four weeks.

The density of the school is variable; during marking operations, schools have been observed with fish maintaining themselves at distances of 5 to 10 cm from one another.

Schweigger (1964) gave indications with respect to the movements of schools estimating a speed of 8 to 9 knots when attacked by predators. Vestnes and Saetersdal (1964) observed that the fish moved at a speed of 5 knots during fishing operations.

Population

SEX RATIO

The sex ratio in multiple samples taken in different months showed a relation about 1 : 1 though with a consistent bias in favour of the female, as can be seen in Table 9.

In material both from the Peruvian and Chilean coasts, sexual segregation varies with size in a consistent manner. The ratio was moderately in favour of females in the small fish of up to approximately 12 cm. There was an equal sex ratio among sizes of 12 to 15 cm, but a quite noticeable preponderance of females in the old fish. The disproportion in the smaller sizes could indicate a

difference of genetic origin in favour of females thus reflecting a real difference of abundance between the sexes. The disproportion of sexes in those of larger sizes might be caused by differences of behaviour between males and females expressed as a greater vulnerability of the males or the effect of a lower mortality rate of females.

AGE AND LENGTH COMPOSITION

The anchovy population is regularly formed by three-year classes which correspond to six cohorts arising from the double annual spawning.

In general at the beginning of the year, the number of small fish from 8 to 10 cm begins to increase until it reaches its maximum between February and March, constituting the year-class born in winter of the previous year. Fish of the old classes are present throughout the year being predominant between June and October with modes between 13 and 15 cm. A decline in the proportion of large fish was detected in the years before 1972 (Fig. 10).

In May 1974, after the last 'El Niño' phenomenon of 1972–73, the age and size structure of the population was calculated as follows: (a) fish smaller than 9 cm, from the spawning of November 1973 and February 1974, approximately 5 months old; (b) fish up to 13 cm, from the 1973 winter spawning, older than 11 months; (c) fish 14–14.5 cm, from the spawning of summer 1972–73, approximately 18 months old; (d) fish greater than 15 cm, from spawnings of winter 1972 and earlier, aged 2 to 3 years (modes at 17–17.5 cm); and (e) fish greater than 17.5 cm, probably up to 4 years of age.

At that time, May 1974, the most important modal groups were those of 14–18 cm.

The most salient characteristic during 1974 was that up until and during November the Peruvian catches were composed of a strong year-class with modes from 18 cm up to 20.5 cm, and lengths which had never been recorded before 1972, except in the area of Talcahuano, Chile.

ABUNDANCE AND DENSITY

The fluctuations in abundance and density of the anchovy stock are measured by means of a monitoring system which utilizes echosounders and echosonar equipment on fishing vessels.

The echo-acoustic recordings are classified as: 0, nil; 1, very dispersed; 2, dispersed; 3, dense; 4, very dense. The area totals, obtained by summing the various categories observed, gives primarily a distribution of the different densities of concentration and of relative abundance.

The results indicate that during 1972 and 1973 the area of distribution diminished to one-third of the mean of previous years both in latitudinal sense and in the extension seawards. The outer limits of category 2 in nautical miles were as follows: 1968, 50–70; 1970, 50–60; 1971, 50–70; 1972, 0–10; 1973, 20–30.

So as to be able to estimate absolute abundance by the technique of echo-integration and to convert the density traces to quantitative estimates, calibration experiments with live anchovy had been previously carried out. The resulting conversion factor was 18.3 tons/nm^2 for each mm of reading per mile. The first application of this method was made in February 1973 aboard the IMARPE research vessel, with an estimate of the biomass at 4 million tons from the north of the Peruvian coast down to Atico. This value has ± 18,000 tons as confidence limits.

The validity of the application of the calibration values to the synoptic results of echo traces in the Eureka operations has yet to be verified.

The cohort analysis through the virtual population method developed by Burd and Valdivia leads to estimates of mean monthly abundance taking the instantaneous natural mortality coefficient at $M = 0.09$ per month and the instantaneous fishing mortality coefficient as $F = 0.10$. A modification of this method with varying values of M was proposed by Clark taking into account the changes which had taken place in the populations of the principal predators.

The stock estimates thus calculated varied between values somewhat more than 17×10^6 tons for the years 1963, 1964, 1965 and 1970 and of 10×10^6 tons for 1972.

An estimate of biomass for the period 1972–73 was attempted on the basis of egg production, arriving at values between 2.5 and 3 million tons. By applying the De Lury method an independent estimate of 2.1 million tons in March 1973 was obtained (Panel of Experts, 1970).

Another type of independent estimate was made by using calculations from the value of the coefficient of fishing mortality and data of catch and effort; the mean stock was estimated to be between 6.5

and 7.5×10^6 tons during the March to May 1974 fishery with values of between 8 and 10.5 at the beginning of March and between 5.3 and 6.2×10^6 tons at the end of May.

Finally, the method of yield by year-class was employed by Tsukayama, leading to an estimate for March 1973 of approximately 1.5×10^6 tons of adult fish remaining from the 1971 recruitment, fish which still appeared to constitute an important part of the 1974 fishery.

NATALITY

It is known that, in general, the number of ovules produced per female is approximately 20,000. The number of planktonic eggs collected at sea diminished significantly after 1967 (Fig. 8). The number for 1974 was similar to that for 1971. The spawning produced a very low recruitment probably owing to an extraordinarily high mortality rate among the embryos and larvae.

The total number of eggs in the sea during the 1972 spawning season in the area between 6° and 14° S. was 5.1×10^{14}; this value was obtained by assuming that the number of eggs per square metre was 55 in August; 108 in September, and 43 in October; that the total area was 16.5×10^{10} m^2; and that the eggs developed in some fifty hours (approximately two days).

The result of reproduction depends on a series of interrelated and complex factors, e.g. age structures of the population, density of the spawning stock and the mesological conditions which affect behaviour, the variability of the fertilized eggs and mortality of the larval stages.

RECRUITMENT

In a fish with short life such as the anchovy, which is subject to high levels of exploitation, renewal of the population by the annual recruitment of new generations is vital for the future of the fishery. The fundamental concept relating the magnitude of recruitment with the adult spawning stock has been dealt with in accordance with a specific model. The adjusted curve suggested that recruitment increases in direct relation with the adult stock up to a critical level, after which it decreases even though the density of the adults increases. When the adult stock is less than the critical point recruitment can fall sharply, a rule which seems to have been confirmed by what occurred in 1972–73; however, a compensatory factor seems to operate with an increase in fecundity (greater number of spawnings per season) at low population levels. The spawnings during 1972 and particularly 1973 were almost continuous throughout the year, although the resulting recruitment continued to be low.

The general pattern of recruitment begins in November/December and reaches its highest values in February/March. This is a consequence of the spawnings of winter and spring (with fish of 8 cm and more), and of secondary recruitment in winter coming from the summer spawnings (see Fig. 9).

Estimates of the magnitude of annual recruitment, calculated as number of fish per unit of effort in different years are presented in Table 10. The recruitment of 1972 was the lowest since records began, at approximately one-seventh of the mean; that of 1973 was one-quarter, and that of 1974 was expected to be similar to that of 1965.

MORTALITY

Since the fish are not totally accessible to fishing until they have reached a length of about 14 cm, i.e. over one year old, it is not possible to measure total mortality by the classical method of apparent abundance of modal groups as they pass through the fishery. Boerema *et al.* (1967) calculated an exploitation rate, E of 0.67, which would indicate a fishing mortality rate approximately twice the natural mortality rate. Schaefer (1967), applying a computer simulation model of the fishery and, on the basis of catch rates in the first and second years of the fishery, obtained values of total mortality, $Z = 2.0$, $F = 1.0$, and $M = 1.0$, as the most reasonable. Similar values were obtained by Burd.

Gulland (1968) recognized that it was not easy to separate mortality due to fishing from that of other causes, and that it might be more convenient to express it in terms of the exploitation rate, $E = F/(F + M)$. E can be estimated directly on the basis of the decline in numbers taken per unit effort (see Fig. 9); arriving finally at the approximate value of $E = 0.5$. The values calculated for different year-classes between 1961 and 1966 were the following: 1961, 0.37; 1962, 0.43; 1963, 0.48; 1964, 0.44; 1965, 0.52; 1966, 0.33.

Gulland finally reached the conclusion that the exploitation rate could be broken down to probable

values of $F = 0.7$ to 1.0 and $M = 1.0$ to 1.3 with $Z = 2$. Table 23 of the report of the Panel of Experts (1970) gave the last calculations of annual mortality for recruits and adults between 1962 and 1972. The values of Z averaged approximately 1.3 for the recruits and 2.4 for adults.

POPULATION DYNAMICS

The general production model was applied in the case of the anchovy. This model has the Verhulst–Pearls sigmoid curve as its base and was applied to the fishery by Murphy (1967), Schaefer (1967) and Gulland (1968). Its advantages are that it requires limited information on catch and effort and an adequate historical series. The resulting parabolas were calculated according to three variants of the model: logistic, exponential, and hyperbolic, including in the calculations the catches and efforts made by man and birds (principal predators of the anchovy) so as to obtain values of maximum sustainable yield (MSY). The statistical series which was analysed covered the period from 1960 to 1971 (Fig. 11). The advantages and disadvantages of these models are well known but for the anchovy, although they gave valid standards for administration even while the annual fluctuations of recruitment were small—varying only by a factor of 2 or 2.5—their application was ineffective after the sharp changes in the rate of recruitment and the fall in total biomass caused by the 'El Niño' phenomenon of 1972–73.

The analytical model put forward by Beverton and Holt (1957) has been only partially applied to the anchovy and, given its complex characteristics, at the present time it is the system of monitoring which makes it possible to follow changes in the characteristics of the stock and in the effects of fishing.

It must be noted that it is desirable to develop integral models which take into account not only the characteristics of a single-species population, but also its relation with ecological factors and with other populations of the community, i.e. the Peruvian current ecosystem of which the anchovy is a fundamental pillar.

THE POPULATIONS IN THE COMMUNITY AND ECOSYSTEM

The physical, dynamic and productivity characteristics of the Peruvian current ecosystem have been described by numerous authors and agreement exists that this constitutes one of the areas of highest productivity and great energy transfer; however the operation of the system still must be more deeply studied.

The productivity maps of Reid (1962) with respect to productive richness, the high values for carbon conversion by Guillen *et al.* (1970) with up to 330 c/m^2/year, and that of Posner (1957) with 8×10^5 metric tons of phosphate/year, are some of the values which characterize the richness of this zone.

The anchovy is probably one of the most important consumers of phytoplankton in the marine system. The vertical circulation of upwelled water—rich in nutrients—towards the euphotic zone permits the growth of phytoplankton populations which assimilate the phosphate, nitrate and silicate. It has been suggested that there could exist a daily rhythm of this process, falling off during the night. The number of cells in the high productivity areas shows low diversity in the seas around the upwelling focus. The spatial succession consists of a nucleus of small diatoms followed by cells of greater size and greater concentrations, appearing after the dinoflagellates.

The mechanisms of nitrate assimilation by phytoplankton and the analysis of the activity of enzymes which reduce nitrate are important aspects. Concerning anchovy excretion, Whitledge and Packard (1971) detected appreciable quantities of nitrogen in the form of ammonia, creatine and urea, suggesting that about one-third of the ammonia came from the fish and the rest from other organisms; in this sense the fish could constitute the most important single source of regeneration of nutrients in the Peruvian current system.

Strickland *et al.* (1969) suggested that a correlation between the incidence of anchovy and the brown waters where phytoplankton predominate should be sought. It has been suggested that the anchovy was associated with cold edges of water currents.

Dugdale and MacIsaac (1971) discussed the development of a prediction model for estimation of primary production on the basis of measurements of nitrogen in parallel with the traditional carbon method. Margaleff (1967), proposed the simulation of the flow of nitrogen as well as the employment of matrices to study the physiology of the ecosystem in terms of structure, stability, energy flow per unit of mass and diversity. He suggested that a knowledge of the relationship of the environment to the anchovy (studied through analytical models with which it would be possible to analyse the interaction between populations occupying different trophic levels) could lead to a more efficient use of marine resources since it functions as regulator of the most advanced trophic levels.

Exploitation

At the beginning of the 1950s, the small anchovy industry emerged vigorously with only 126 small boats of 2,400 tons gross register, and 16 processing plants in 1954, to reach (in only 10 years) 1,700 boats of about 140,000 TGR and 150 plants. The first wooden boats, of 60 tons and almost without mechanical equipment for fishing and recovery of the nets, have given way to boats of 300 to 350 tons equipped with modern systems of echo-sounding, radar, automatic pulleys, pumps, and nylon nets of more than 300 m in length. The annual increase in boats and plants was 68 per cent between 1962 and 1963 and has been without significant reduction since.

The creation of jobs (which reached approximately some 100,000 persons directly or indirectly related to the industry) as well as the boost to the economy of the country were the greatest benefits obtained. In spite of this, the imprudent overinvestment in fleet and plants—with capacities far above the biological possibilities of the resource—made the industry highly vulnerable; nevertheless, the legal structure of the country made this grave problem insoluble. The years 1963 and 1965, when the availability of anchovy fell owing to small oceanographic changes, led to the bankruptcy of various enterprises.

In 1970, the capacity of the processing plants was some 8,000 tons/hour. By working 20 hours per day, 300 days per year, more than 48×10^6 tons could be processed annually; although the existing fleet was theoretically capable of fishing such quantities, in reality estimates of maximum sustainable yield of the anchovy stock were only of about 10×10^6 tons annually, approximately one-fifth that of the theoretical level. The rate at which the Peruvian fleet has been catching anchovy can be seen in Table 11.

The 1972–73 'El Niño' had a drastic effect on the industry and created various social problems without ready solutions due to the persistence of low stock availability along the entire coast. In early 1973, the government reorganized the fishing industry, making it a State enterprise known as 'Pesca Perú'. It then became possible to reduce the excesses of fleet and plants by more than 50 per cent. The achievement of adequate reduction with more rational exploitation had been made possible.

Regulations and administration

The research on anchovy, which began practically simultaneously with development of the fishery, has given bases on which to establish administrative policies and the necessary conservation measures.

Since 1964, when research drew attention to the excessive fishing and the dangers that could follow, regulatory measures were imposed with a closed season in winter and a limitation on the catch of small fish.

In the following years, the scientific assessments recommended a series of measures insisting on a limitation of effort and protection of small fish during periods of high recruitment.

Up to 1973 the limitation of effort could be effected only indirectly, by the following means:

(a) closed seasons of two months in winter; (b) limitation of the fishing to five days per week (and sometimes to four); and (c) a catch quota for each season after which fishing was stopped.

The protection of the peladilla, or small fish, was accomplished by: (a) the closure of the fishery during one month (and sometimes two) in summer; and (b) the prohibition of fishing when the young fish (less than 12 cm) reached or exceeded 50 per cent of the catch.

Since 1972 the measures have been even more drastic, with prolonged closures, limitation of the fleet and plants and protection of small fish. The future projection of research, vital for more adequate monitoring of the stock, is set out by Dr Kesteven in the following article.

Table 1. Records of distribution of *E. ringens,* listed in chronological order

Country	Area	Geographic co-oordinates	References
Chile	Iquique	20°14' S.; 70°10' W.	Jenyns, 1842
Peru	Chimbote	9°05' S.; 78°31' W.	
Peru	Lobos de Tierra	6°26' S.; 80°53' W.	Evermann and Radcliffe, 1917
Peru	Eten	6°56' S.; 79°51' W.	
Peru	Ilo	17°38' S.; 71°22' W.	Nichols and Murphy, 1922
Peru	Pescadores	16°24' S.; 73°17' W.	
Peru	Callao	12°00' Q.; 77°07' W.	Jordán and Seale, 1926
Peru	Peruvian coast	13°30' S. 78°20' W.	Coker, 1918
Peru	Peruvian and Chilean coast	23°55' S.; 70°08' W.	Hildebrand, 1946
Chile	Talcahuano	36°40' S. 73°30' W.	Mann, 1954
Peru	Cabo Blanco (extreme north)	4°15' S. 81°14' W.	Fiedler *et al.,* 1943
Chile	Iquique	20°14' S.; 70°10' W.	De Buen, 1955
Peru	Pta Aguja (extreme north)	6° S.; 81°05' W.	Schweigger, 1964
Chile	Valdivia paral. 40 (extreme south)		De Buen, 1958
Chile	Valdivia	39°47' S.; 74°40' W.	Brandhort, 1963; Simpson *et al.,* 1967
Peru	Zorritos	04°30' S.; 81°18' W.	Chirichigno, 1965. n.d. [1]
Chile	Valdivia	39°50' S.; 74°40' W.	Simpson *et al.,* 1967[2]

1. Identification made on the basis of specimens collected at 30 fathoms depth. Gives meristic counts, proportions and comparison with similar species.
2. Gives information about commercial fishing in the zone 1964–66.

Table 2.

Area	Date	Sizes[1]	No. of samples	Catch method	Reference
Chimbote	26 October	21–57	500	Floating trawl	Clark (1954)
Callao Ilo	4 December 1953				
Mollendo Ilo	26 March 4 April 1954	28–46	100	Floating trawl	Clark (1954)
Ilo	1954	27–52	100	One stomach of barrilete (*K. pelamis*)	Clark (1954)
Huacho	October 1955	30–43		Many stomachs of guanay (*P. bougainvilii*)	Jordán (1959)
Huacho	October 1956	20–50			

1. Sizes expressed in standard lengths.

Table 3. Recoveries[1]

Month	Year				
	1970	1971	1972	1973	1974
January	–	29	–	1	4
February	–	15	4	–	–
March	–	154	1	22	5
April	–	29	–	5	3
May	–	17	1	2	1
June	–	6	–	14	–
July	–	5	–	–	–
August	–	87	–	–	–
September	1,742	–	–	–	–
October	1,793	41	–	–	–
November	587	15	–	–	–
December	326	24	–	–	–

1. Expressed as numbers caught per calendar month.

Table 4. Percentage of diet : sardine and machete.

	Sardine	Machete
Diatoms	62.92	69.53
Dinoflagellates	28.48	20.29
Copepods	5.68	6.47
Others	2.92	3.71

Table 5.

Animal	Common name	Place
Fishes		
Sarda chilenis	Bonito	Peru/Chile
Katsuwonus pelamis	Barrilete	Peru/Chile
Thunnus macropterus	Yellow fin tuna	Peru/Chile
Thunnus germo	Albacora	Peru/Chile
Thyrsistes atún	Sierra	Chile
Trachurus murphi	Jurel	Peru
Neptomenus crassus	Cojinoba	Peru/Chile
Squatina armata	Angelote	Peru
Paralichthys adspersus	Lenguado	Peru
Sciena gilberti	Corvina	Peru
Sciaena deliciosa	Lorna	Peru
Sea birds		
Phalacrocorax bougainvillii	Guanay	Peru/Chile
Sula variegata	Piquero	Peru/Chile
Pelecannus occidentalis thagus	Alcatraz	Peru/Chile
Larosterna inca	Zarcillo	Peru/Chile
Spheniscus humboldti	Pájaro niño	Peru/Chile
Puffinus griseus	Pardela	Peru/Chile
Sula nebouxi	Camanay	Peru
Larus pipixcan	Gaviota	Peru/Chile
Mammals		
Otaria flavescens	Lobos marines	Peru/Chile
Delphinus delphis	Delfín	Peru/Chile

Table 6.

	Chimbote (9°S.)	Supe (11°S.)	Callao (12°S.)	Tambo de Mora (14°S.)
Time	7:00–10:30	6:00-11:30	7:30-11:30	8:30-18:00
Fish length (mm)	137–170	105-137	85-165	85-160
Stomach content (cc)	$\bar{x} = 151$ 0.31	$\bar{x} = 116$ 0.16	$\bar{x} = 109$ 0.14	$\bar{x} = 123$ 0.21
Predominant type of food	phyto-plankton *T. subtilis*	phyto-plantkon *T. subtilis*	zoo-plankton *Copepods*	zoo-plankton *Copepods*
Predominant organisms	*Actinocyclus* sp.	*Chaetoceros* sp.	*T. subtilis* *T. bacillaris*	*T. bacillaris* *T. subtilis*

Table 7.

	L_{oo}	K	t_0	Unit of time	Im/L_t	Method	Reference
Peru	15	1.7	—	Year	0.8	Von Bertalanffy	Saetersdal and Valdivia (1964)
Peru	16.8	1.26	0.60	Month	—	Gompertz	
Peru	16.0	0.17	0.68	Month	—	Von Bertalanffy	
Chile	16.9	1.6	0.02	Year	0.6—0.8	Von Bertalanffy	Simpson *et al.* (1967)

Table 8. Estimated growth pattern of anchoveta.

Age (months)	Mean length (cm)	Mean weight (g)	Natural logarithm of weight	Period	Instantaneous rate of growth (G)
5	6.3[1]	1.3[1]	0.262	5—6	0.654
6	7.7[1]	2.5[1]	0.916	6—7	0.365
7	8.5[1]	3.6[1]	1.281	7—8	0.267
8	9.2	4.7	1.548	8—9	0.260
9	9.8	6.1	1.808	9—10	0.138
10	10.3	7.0	1.946	10—11	0.194
11	10.9	8.5	2.140	11—12	0.023
12	11.1	8.7	2.163	12—13	0.149
13	11.6	10.1	2.312	13—14	0.156
14	12.2	11.8	2.468	14—15	0.112
15	12.5	13.2	2.580	15—16	0.135
16	13.0	15.1	2.715	16—17	0.112
17	13.3	16.9	2.827	17—18	0.012
18	13.5	17.1	2.839	18—19	0.046
19	13.7	17.9	2.885	19—20	0.075
20	14.0	19.3	2.960	20—21	0.094
21	14.3	21.2	3.054	21—22	0.037
22	14.6	22.0	3.091	22—23	0.091
23	14.8	24.1	3.182	23—24	0.008
24	15.0	24.3	3.190	24—25	0.013
25	15.1	24.6	3.203		—

1. Extrapolated values.

Table 9.

Place	Percentage of females	X^2	Reference
Huacho, Peru	60.1	122.6	Jordán (1959)
Chimbote and Callao	52.9	—	Einarsson *et al.* (1966)
Chimbote, Peru	52.8	71.9	Miñano (1968)
Arica, Chile	54.0	24.8	Simpson *et al.* (1967)
Iquique, Chile	55.1	41.54	Simpson *et al.* (1967).

Table 10. Estimate of recruitment in hundreds of fish per GRT-trip based on the length compositions by regions

Year	Northern region	Central region	Northern and central
1961	264.57	400.10	332.34
1962	254.25	220.36	237.30
1963	198.88	167.44	183.16
1964	496.89	310.94	403.92
1965	195.20	189.91	192.56
1966	452.69	425.81	439.25
1967	189.22	577.45	383.34
1968	124.56	550.95	337.76
1969	273.17	480.23	376.70
1970	545.82	560.22	553.02
1971	564.46	513.81	539.14
1972	68.24	36.06	52.15
1973	150.00[1]	170.00[1]	160.00[1]

1.   Up to March 1973.

Table 11. Statistical history of the anchovy fishery in Peru

	Fishing days	Voyages	Catch (tons)
1959	294	—	1,908,698
1960	279	73,235	2,943,602
1961	298	94,352	4,579,709
1962	294	123,730	6,274,625
1963	269	130,875	6,423,237
1964	297	160,512	8,863,367
1965	265	131,293	7,233,479
1966	190	134,947	8,529,821
1967	170	132,599	9,824,624
1968	167	147,877	10,262,661
1969	162	153,534	8,960,460
1970	180	148,216	12,276,977
1971	89	91,030	10,281,784
1972	89	55,206	4,448,511
1973	103	24,907	2,035,425
1974[1]	—	—	3,692,212

1.   January to 26 November.

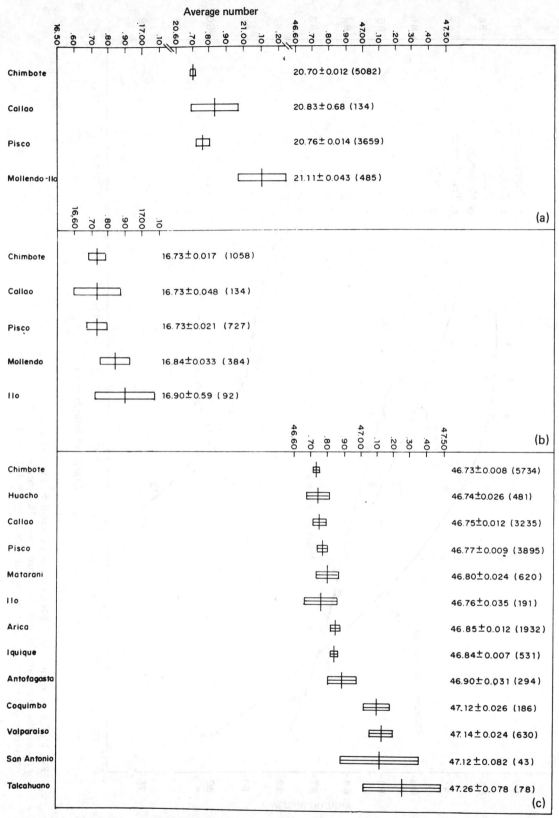

Fig. 1. Variation in (a) anal and (b) dorsal fin rays and
number of vertebrae of the anchovy.

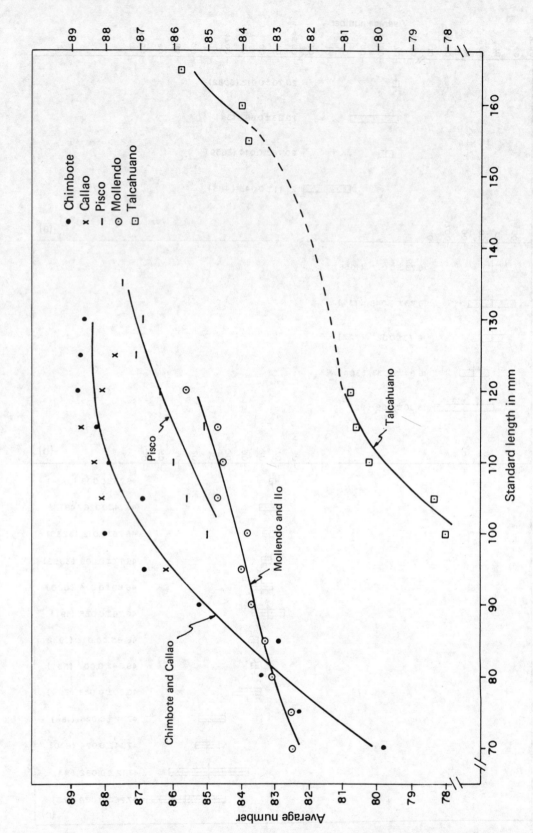

Fig. 1(d). Size of anchovy related to average number of branchial rays on the first branchial arch. Standard length (L_s) can be converted to total length (L_t) by the formula $L_t = 2.5 + 1.154 \, L_s$

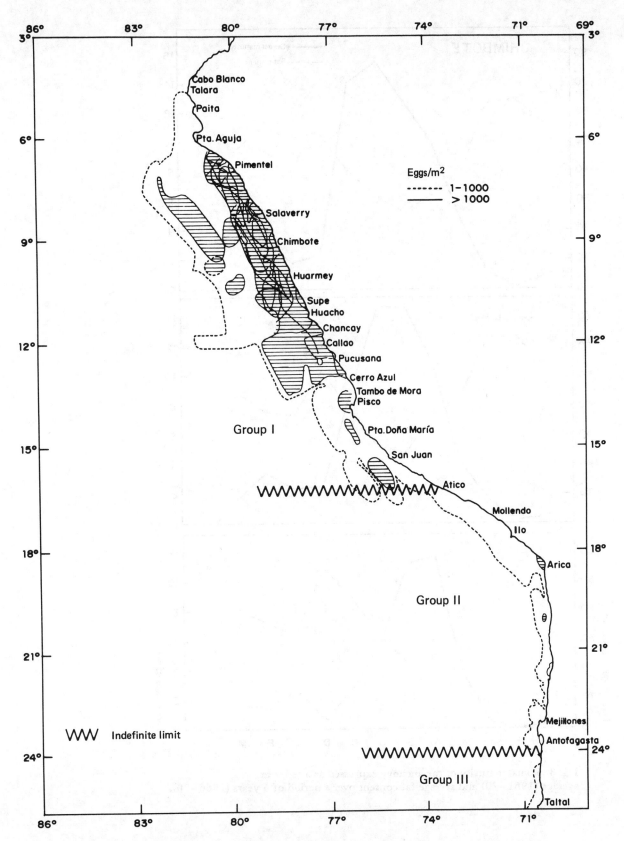

Fig. 2. Distribution of the anchovy (*E. ringens*) determined by spawning areas.

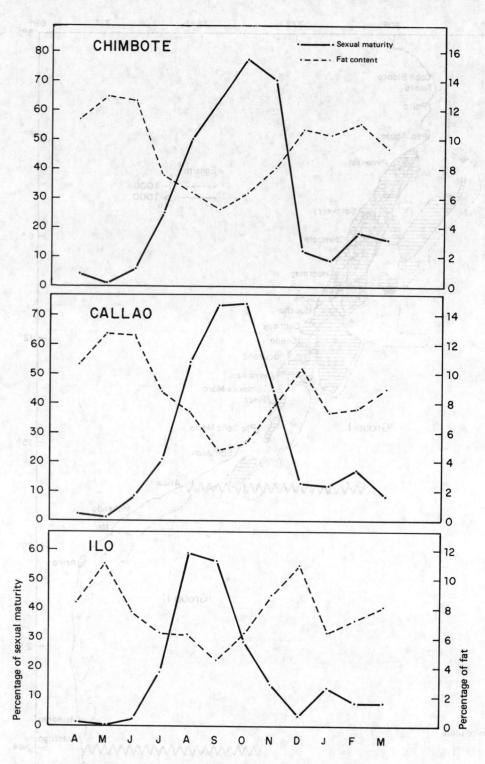

Fig. 3. Sexual maturity of the anchovy expressed as a ten-year
average (1961—70) and average fat content over a period of 5 years (1966—70).

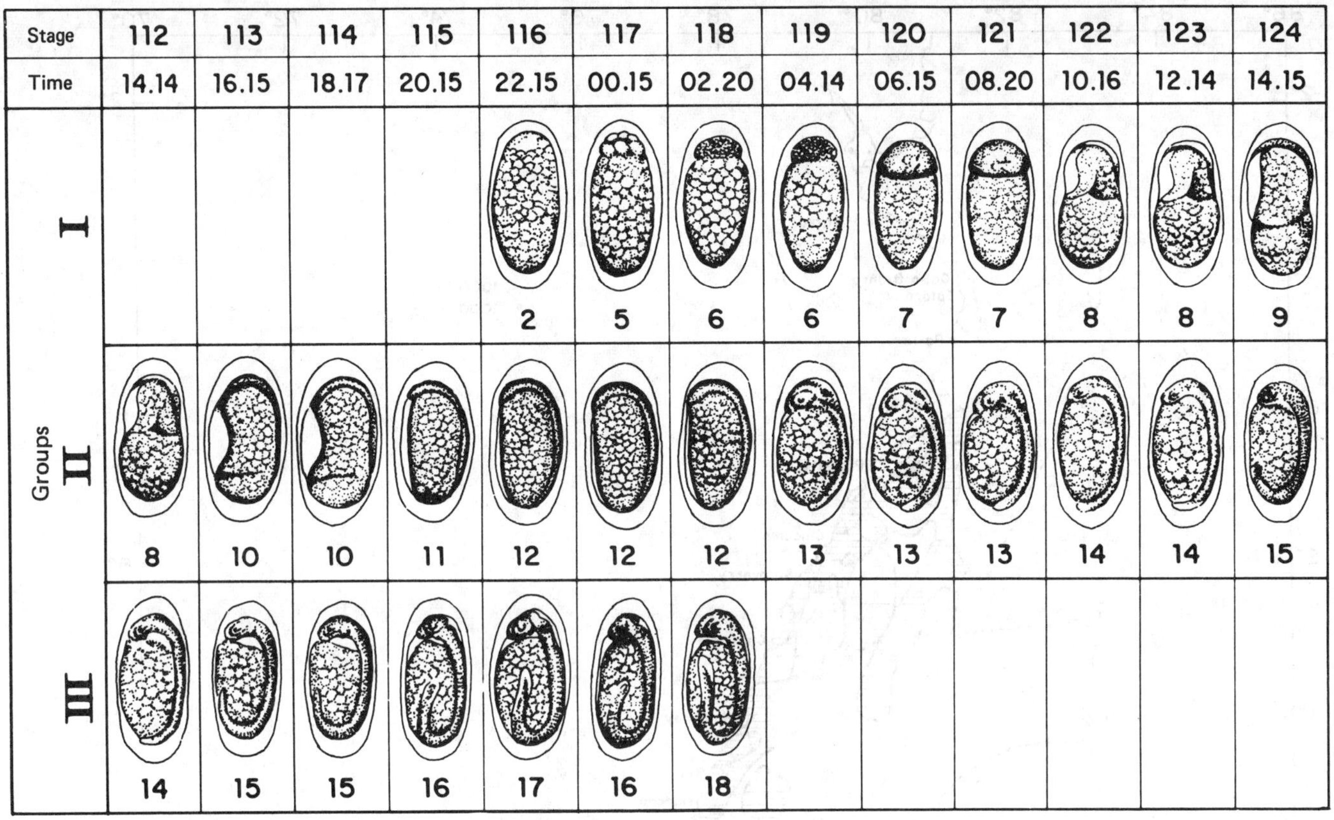
Stage
112 113 114 115 116 117 118 119 120 121 122 123 124
Time
14.14 16.15 18.17 20.15 22.15 00.15 02.20 04.14 06.15 08.20 10.16 12.14 14.15
Groups
I
2 5 6 6 7 7 8 8 9
II
8 10 10 11 12 12 12 13 13 13 14 14 15
III
14 15 15 16 17 16 18

Fig. 4. Embryonic development sequence of the young anchovy at 30 m depth (from Santander and Castillo, 1973).

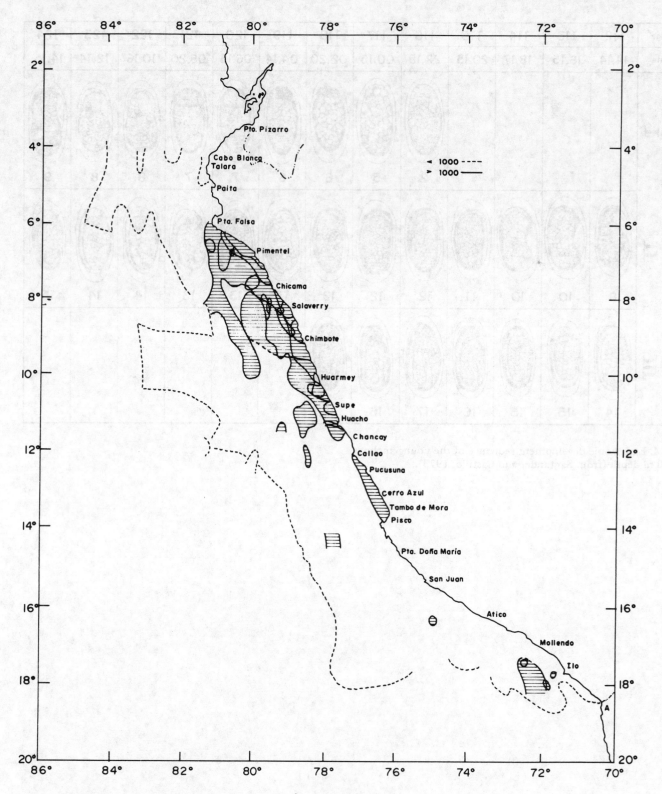

Fig. 5. Anchovy larva distribution (numbers per m^2) over the
period 1964—73.

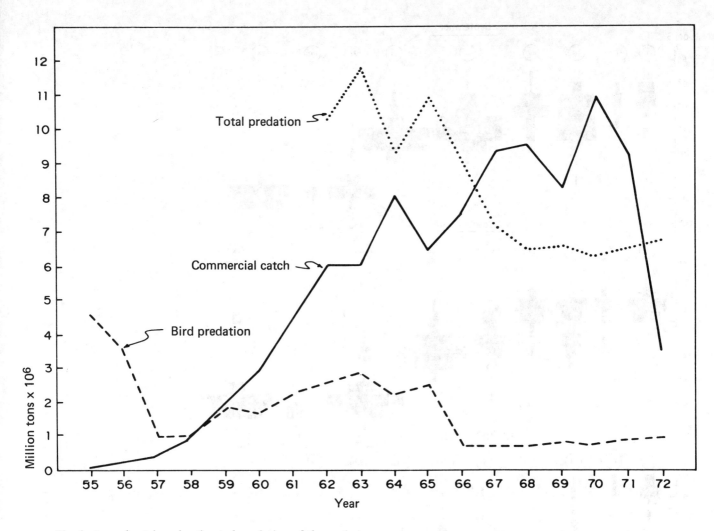

Fig. 6. Annual catch and estimated predation of the anchovy
by birds, fish and other predators.

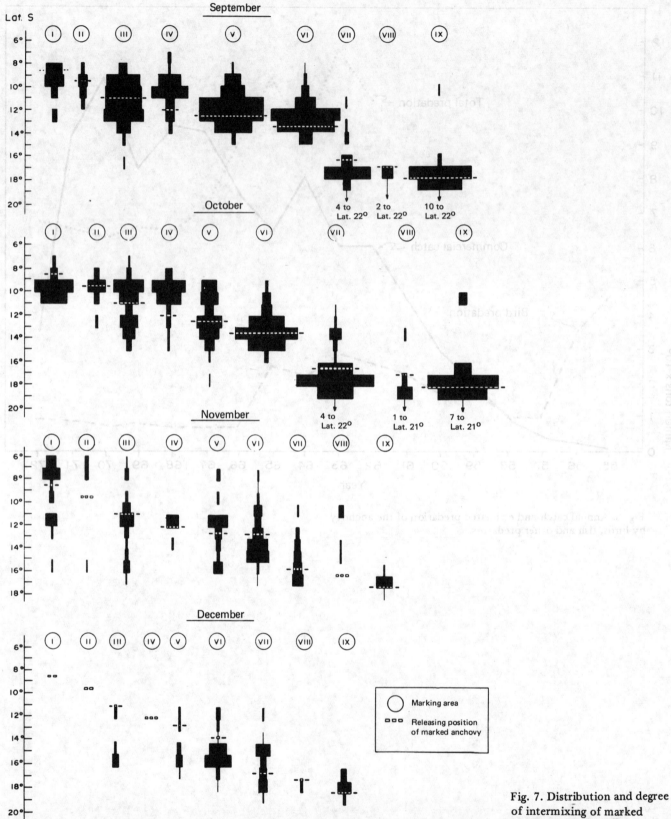

Fig. 7. Distribution and degree of intermixing of marked anchovy in July 1970.

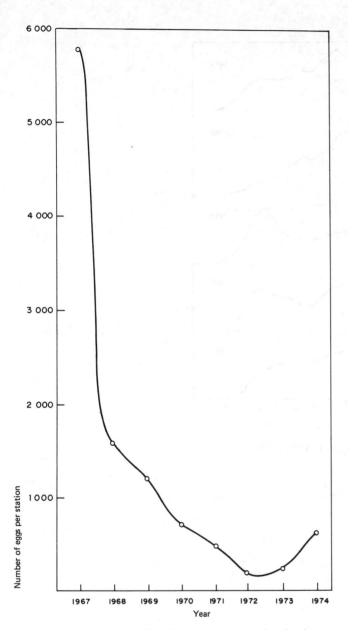

Fig. 8. Average number of anchovy eggs per station in the area 6°–14° S. during the period August to September in the years 1967–74.

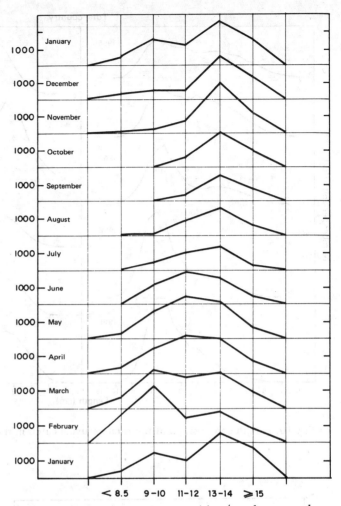

Fig. 9. Mean monthly catch composition (numbers at each length) of the anchovy (calculated by catch per unit of effort (from Gulland, 1968)).

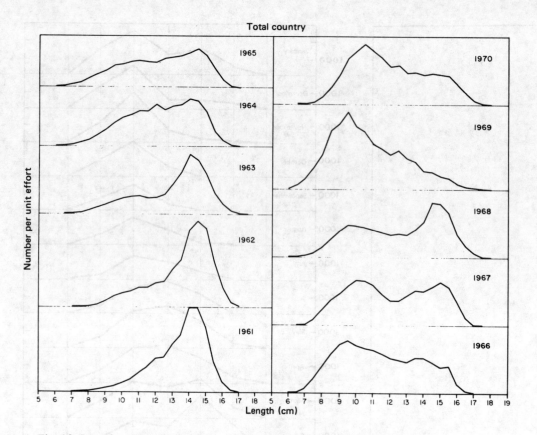

Fig. 10. Length composition of the total Peruvian catch in the years 1961—70.

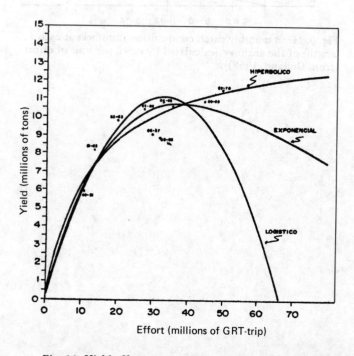

Fig. 11. Yield-effort curves with efficiency correction.

References

Barreda, M. 1950. Informe sobre las Investigaciones Efectuadas en Relación al Desove de la Anchoveta. *Bol. Cía. Adm. Guano,* Vol. 26, No. 5, p. 55–63.

——. 1953. Un método Cientifico para Estudiar la Edad y Crecimiento de los Peces. *Bol. Cient. Cia. Adm. Guano,* Vol. 1, No. 1, p. 51–62.

——. 1957. El Plancton en la Bahía de Pisco. *Bol. Cía. Adm. Guano,* Vol. 33, No. 9, p. 7–22, 33; No. 10, p. 7–22, 33; No. 11, p. 11–18.

Beverton, R. J. H.; Holt, S. J. 1957. On the Dynamics of Exploited Fish Populations. *Fish. Invest., Serv. II. U.K.,* Vol. 9, No. 533.

Bjerknes, J. 1961. 'El Niño' Study Based on Analysis on Ocean Surface Temperature 1935–57. *Inter-Amer. Trop. Tuna Comm. Bull.,* Vol. 5, No. 3, p. 217–72 (English); 273–304 (Spanish).

Boerema, L. K.; Saetersdal, G.; Tsukayama, I., Valdivia J.; Alegre, B. 1967. Informe sobre los Efectos de la Pesca en el Recurso Peruano de Anchoveta. *Bol. Inst. Mar, Perú–Callao,* Vol. 1, No. 4.

Brandhorst, W.; Méndez, M.; Rojas, O. 1966. *Observaciones Oceanográficos-Biológicas sobre los Recursos de la Anchoveta* (Engraulis ringens, *Jenyns) en la Zona Norte de Chile.* Part. I. 43 p. (Serie Pub. Inst. Fom. Pesq. (Santiago), N. 22, p. 43.)

Branchorst, W.; Rojas, O. 1967a. *Distribución Geográfica de la Pesca de la Anchoveta en el Norte de Chile y su Composición del Tamaño, de Marzo de 1961 a Julio de 1963.* 69 p. (Serie Pub. Inst. From. Pesq. (Santiago), No. 24).

——. 1967. *Investigaciones sobre los Recursos de la Anchoveta* (Engraulis ringens *J.) y sus Relaciones con las Condiciones Oceanográficas en Agosto–Setiembre de 1963 y Marzo–Junio de 1964.* 38 p. (Serie Pub. Inst. Fom. Pesq., (Santiago), No. 31.)

Brandhorst, W.; Simpson, J. G.; Rojas, O.; Pineda, J.; Mendéz, M. 1967. *Observaciones Oceanográfico-Biológicas sobre los Recursos de la Anchoveta* (Engraulis ringens, *Jenyns) en la Zona Norte de Chile.* Part. II. (serie Pub. Inst. Fom. Pesq. (Santiago), No. 23.)

Chirichigno, N. Ampliación de la Distribución de la Anchoveta Peruana (*Engraulis ringens,* Jenyns, (1843). (Inf. Interno IMARPE. Dpto Biología. No. 50 (unpublished).)

Chirinos de V., A.; Alegre de Haro, B. 1969. La Madurez Sexual de la Anchoveta (*Engraulis ringens* J.) en los Periodos Reproductivos 1961/1968. *Bol. Inst. Mar, Perú–Callao,* Vol. II, No. 3.

Chirinos de V., A.; Chumán, E. 1966. Variaciones en el Crecimiento de la Anchoveta Peruana Estuiada por Medio de la Medida de sus Otolitos, *1er Sem. Lat. Amer. Oc. Pac. Prien., Lima.*

——. 1968. *Validez de la Lectura de Otolitos para Determinar la Edad de la Anchoveta* (Engraulis ringens). (Inf. Inst. Mar, Perú–Callao, No. 22.)

Chuman de Flores, E. 1969. *Variación Estacional de la Naturaleza del Borde de los Otolitos de Anchoveta en las Zonas de Chimbote e Ilo.* Instituto del Mar del Perú. (IMP-52).

Clark, F., 1954. Biología de la Anchoveta. *Bol. Cient. Cía. Adm. Guano,* Vol. 1, No. 2, p. 98–132. (Translated by Enrique Avila.)

Coker, R. E. 1918, Ocean Temperatures off the Coast of Peru. *Geogr. Rev.,* No. 5, p. 127–35. (P/0-02-00257.)

De Buen, F. 1955. El Estudio de la Edad y el Crecimiento de Peces, Viviendo en Medios Oceánicos Diferentes, y Especialmente en la Anchoveta ó Chicora (*Engraulis ringens). Bol. Cient. Cia. Adm. Guano,* No. 2, p. 41–7.

——. 1958. Peces de la Superfamilia Clupeoidae en Aguas de Chile. *Rev. Biol. Mar. Publ. por la Est. de Biologia Marina de la Univ. de Chile,* Vol. 8, No. 1, 2, 3, p. 83–110.

Del Solar, E. 1942. Ensayo sobre la Ecología de la Anchoveta. *Bol. Cía. Adm. Guano,* Vol. 18, No. 1, p. 1–23.

Dugdale, R. C.; MacIsaac, J. J. 1971. A Computational Model for the Uptake of Nitrate in the Peru Upwelling Region. *Inv. Pesq.,* Vol. 35, No. 1, p. 299–308.

Einarsson, H.; Flores, L. A.; Miñano, J. 1966. El Ciclo de Madurez de la Anchoveta Peruana (*E. ringens* J.) *1er Sem. Lat. Amer. Oc. Pac. Orien. Lima.*

Einarsson, H.; Rojas de Mendiola, B. 1963. Descripción de Huevos y Larvas de Anchoveta Peruana (*Engraulis ringens). Bol. Inst. Invest. Recurs. Mar. Callao,* Vol. 1, No. 1, p. 1–23.

——. 1967. An attempt to Estimate Annual Spawning Intensity of the Anchovy (*E. ringens* J.) by Means of Regional Egg and Larval Surveys during 1961–1964. *CALCOFI Conference.*

Einarsson, H.; Rojas de Mendiola, B.; Santander, H. 1966. El Desove de los Peces en Aguas Peruanas durante 1961–1964. *1er Sem. Lat. Amer. Oc. Pac. Orien. Lima.*

Evermann, B.W.; Radcliffe, L. 1917. The Fishes of the West Coast of Peru and Titicaca Basin. *U.S. Nat. Mus. Bull.,* No. 95, p. 1–166. (B/0-04-00019, 00020.)

Fiedler, R. H.; Jarvis, N. D.; Lobell, M. J. 1943. La Pesca y las Industrias Pesqueras en el Perú. *Comp. Admin. Guano, Lima.* 371 p.

Fischer, W. 1958. Huevos, Crias y Primeras Prelarvas de la Anchoveta (*Engraulis ringens,* Jenyns). *Rev. Biol. Mar. Valparaíso,* Vol. 8, No. 3, p. 113–23.

Guillén, O. 1964. *(a) Distribución del Contenido de Fosfatos en la Región de la Corriente del Perú,* p. 1–12. Inf. Inst. Invest. Recurs. Mar., Callao, No. 28.

Guillén, O.; Calienes, R.; de Rondán, R. I. 1969. Contribución al Estudio del Ambiente de la Anchoveta. *Bol. Inst. Mar, Perú–Callao,* Vol. II, No. 2.

Guillén, O. ; de Mendiola, B. R. ; de Rondán, R.I., 1971. Primary Productivity and Phytoplankton in the Coastal Peruvian Waters. *Fertility of the Sea,* Vol. I. Sao Paulo.

Gulland, J. A. 1968. Informe sobre la Dinámica de la Población de Anchoveta Peruana. *Bol. Inst. Mar, Perú—Callao,* Vol. I, No. 6.

Gunther, E. R., 1936. A Report of Geographical Investigations in the Peru Coastal Current. *Discovery Report,* No. 13, p. 107—276.

Hildebrand, S. 1943. A Review of the American Anchovies (Family *Engraulidae*). *Bull. Bingham Oceanographic Coll.,* Vol. 8, No. 2.

—. 1946. A Descriptive Catalog of the Shore Fishes of Peru. *Smithsn Inst. U.S. Nat. Mus. Bull.* No. 189. 530 p.

IMARPE. 1965. *Las Pesquerías de la Anchoveta.* (Inf. Inst. Mar, Perú—Callao, No. 1.)

—. 1967. *Informe Complementario sobre la Pesquería de la Anchoveta.* (Inf. Inst. Mar. Perú—Callao, No. 15.)

—, 1968. *El Estado del Stock de Anchoveta y Recomendaciones para el Año Pesquero 1968/69.* Instituto del Mar del Perú (IMP-30).

—, 1968. *Encuasta sobre las Embarcaciones Anchoveteras Realizada en Junio de 1967.* (Inf. Inst. Mar, Perú—Callao, No. 23.)

—, 1968. *Informe Complementario sobre las Regulaciones de la Pesquería de la Anchoveta en la Temporada 1968/69.* Instituto del Mar del Perú. (IMP-33).

—, 1968. Informe del Cuadro de Expertos sobre Dinámica de la Población de Anchoveta Peruana. *Bol. Inst. Mar., Perú—Callao,* Vol. II, No. 6.

—, 1968. *La Pesquería de la Anchoveta durante la Temporada de Pesca 67/68.* Instituto del Mar del Perú (IMP-28.)

—, 1968. *Las Pesquerías de la Anchoveta Recomendaciones para la Temporada 1967/68.* (Inf. Inst. Mar, Perú—Callao, No. 20.)

—, 1968. *Tonelaje Máximo de Captura de Anchoveta para la Temporada 1967/68.* Instituto del Mar del Perú (IMP-27.)

—. 1969. *Meidas Reguladoras de la Pesquería de la Anchoveta en la Costa Peruana para la Temporada 1960/70.* Instituto del Mar del Perú. (IMP-51.)

—. 1970. *Tonelaje Máximo de Captura de Anchoveta. en la Temporada 1969/70.* Instituto del Mar del Perú. (IMP-59).

—, 1972. *Exploración de Peladilla y Distribución de Cardúmenes de Anchoveta.* Instituto del Mar del Perú (IMP-98.)

—, 1972. Informe sobre la Segunda Reunión del Panel de Expertos en Dinámica de Población de la Anchoveta Peruana. *Bol. Inst. Mar, Perú—Callao,* Vol. II, No. 7.

—, 1972. *La Anchoveta en Relación con el Fenómeno de 'El Niño' 1972.* Instituto del Mar del Perú.

—. 1972. *La Pesca en el Sur y la Situación del Stock de Anchoveta.* Instituto del Mar del Perú. (IMP-119.)

—. 1972. *'Operación Anchoveta I'.* Instituto del Mar de Perú. (IMP-100.)

—. 1972. *'Operación Eureka XX', 28—29 Abril de 1972.* Instituto del Mar del Perú (IMP-105.)

—. 1972. *'Operación Eureka XXI', 17—18 Junio de 1972.* Instituto del Mar del Perú. (IMP-110.)

—. 1972. *'Operación Eureka XXII' 18—19 Julio de 1972.* Instituto del Mar del Perú. (IMP-111.)

—. 1972. *'Operación Eureka XXIII', 3-6 Agosto de 1972.* Instituto del Mar del Perú. (IMP-112.)

—. 1972. *'Operación Eureka XXIV', 5—8 Septiembre de 1972.* Instituto del Mar del Perú. (IMP-116.)

—. 1972. *'Operación Eureka XXV', 20—23 Octubre de 1972.* Instituto del Mar del Perú. (IMP-117.)

—. 1972. *'Regulación de la Pesquería de Anchoveta para el Año Calendario 1972'.* Instituto del Mar del Perú. (IMP-97.)

—. 1972. *Resultados de la Pesca Exploratoria Realizada del 4 al 7 de Diciembre 1972 (Paita—Punta Lamas).* Instituto del Mar del Perú (IMP—121).

—. 1973. *Informe sobre la Primera Semana de Pesca de Anchoveta Realizada del 5 al 9 de Marzo de 1973.* Instituto del Mar del Perú. (IMP-124.)

—. 1973. *'Operación Eureka XXVI', 20—23 de Enero 1973.* Instituto del Mar del Perú. (IMP-122.)

—. 1973. *'Operación Eureka XXVII', 23—26 Septiembre de 1973.* Instituto del Mar del Perú. (IMP-141.)

—. 1973. *'Operación Eureka XXVIII' (12—13 Nov. 1973) y la Pesca de Comprobación (14—17 Nov. 1973). Diagnóstico del Estado del Stock de Anchoveta en Noviembre de 1973.* Instituto del Mar del Perú. (IMP-146.)

—. 1973. *Situáciòn del Stock de Anchoveta a Principios de 1973.* Instituto del Mar del Perú. (IMP-125.)

—. 1974. *Informe sobre el Estado del 'Recurso Anchoveta' a Fines de Setiembre y las Perspectĩvas para la Pesquería en la Temporada Octubre—Diciembre 1974.* Instituto del Mar del Perú. (IMP-165.)

—. 1974. *'Operación Eureka XXIX'. 28—30 de Mayo 1974.* Instituto del Mar del Perú. (IMP-158.)

Jordan, D. S.; Seale, A. 1926. Review of the *Engraulidae* with Descriptions of New and Rare Species. *Bull. Mus. Comp. Zool.* Vol. 67, No. 11, p. 355—418.

Jordan, R. 1959. Observaciones sobre la Biología de la Anchoveta (*Engraulis ringens,* J.) de la Zona Pesquera de Huacho. *Bol. Cía. Adm. Guano,* Vol. 35, No. 11, p. 1—22.

—. 1963. Un Análisis del Número de Vértebras de la Anchoveta Peruana (*Engraulis ringens* J.). *Bol. Inst. Invest. Recurs. Mar. Callao,* Vol. 1, No. 2, p. 27—43.

—. 1967. The Predation of Guano Birds on the Peruvian Anchovy. (*E. ringens,* J.). *CALCOFI Conference.*

Jordan, R.; de Vildoso, A. 1965. *La Anchoveta, Conocimiento Actual sobre la Biología Ecologia y Pesqueria* (Inf. Inst. Mar, Perú–Callao, No. 6.)

Jordan, R.; Málaga, A. 1972. *Resultado de la Primera Marcación Experimental de Anchoveta* (Engraulis ringens, *J.*) *en el Mar.* (Inf. Inst. Mar, Perú–Callao, No. 39.)

Jordan, R.; Málaga, A., Pastor, A. 1971. *Los Estudios de Factibilidad de Marcaciones de Anchoveta.* Instituto del Mar del Perú (IMP-92.)

Landa, A. Datos sobre la Migración, Madurez, Variaciones Meristicos y Determinación de Edad de la Anchoveta Peruana en Chimbote. 1951–53. (Unpublished.)

Lavalle, J. A. de, 1917. Informe Preliminar sobre la Causa de la Mortalidad Anormal de las Aves Ocurrida en el Mes de Marzo del Presente Año. *8va. Memoria de la Cía. Adm. Guano.*

Málaga, A. 1974. *Las Marcaciones de Anchoveta en el Mar durante Febrero y Agosto 1973.* Instituto del Mar del Perú (IMP-155.)

Mann, F. G. 1954. Vida de los Peces en Aguas Chilenas. *Inst. Invest. Vetern., Santiago de Chile.* 342 p.

Margaleff, R. 1967. Some Concepts Relative to the Organization of Plankton. *Oceanogr. Mar. Biol. Ann. Rev.*, No. 5, p. 257–89.

Miñano, J. 1958. Algunas Apreciaciones Relacionadas con la Anchoveta Peruana (*Engraulis ringens*) y su Fecundidad. *Bol. Cía. Adm. Guano,* Vol. 34, No. 2, p. 9–16; No. 3, p. 11–24.

——. 1963. Estudio de la Fecundidad y Ciclo Sexual de la Anchoveta. *Bol. Inst. Mar, Perú–Callao, Ser. C,* No. 9.

Murphy, G. 1967. *Análisis Preliminar de la Dinámica de Población de la Anchoveta Peruana.* Instituto del Mar del Perú. (IMP-15.)

Nichols, J. T.; Murphy, R. C. 1922. On a Collection of Marine Fishes from Peru. *Amer. Mus. Nat. Hist. Bull.* No. 46, p. 501–16. (B/0-04-00073.)

Panel of Experts. 1970. *Informe sobre los Efectos de Diferentes Medidas Regulatorias de la Pesquería de la Anchoveta Peruana.* (Inf. Inst. Mar, Perú–Callao, No. 34.)

Pastor, A.; Málaga, A. 1966. Experimentos Preliminares con Anchovetas Adultas y Larvas (*Engraulis ringens*) en Acuario. *1er Sem. Lat. Amer. Oc. Pac. Orien. Lima.*

Posner, G. S. 1957. The Peru Current. *Bull. Bingham Oceanogr. Coll.,* Vol. 16, No. 2, p. 106–51. (P/0-04-00034.)

Reid, J. L., Jr. 1962. On Circulation, Phosphate-Phosphorus Content, and Zooplankton Volumes in the Upper Part of the Pacific Ocean. *Limnol. and Oceanogr.,* Vol. 7, No. 3, p. 287–306. (B/0-02-00008.)

Rojas Escajadillo, B. 1953. Estudios Preliminares del Contenido Estomacal de las Anchovetas. *Bol. Cient. Cía. Adm. Guano,* Vol. 1, No. 1, p. 33–43.

Rojas de Mendiola, B. 1958. Breve Estudio sobre la Variación Cualitativa Anual del Plancton Superficial de la Bahía de Chimbote. *Bol. Cía. Adm. Guano,* Vol. 24, No. 12, p. 7–17.

——. 1964. *Abundancia de los Huevos de Anchoveta* (Engraulis ringens) *con Relación a la Temperatura del Mar en la Región de Chimbote.* 24 p. (Inf. Inst. Invest. Recurs. Mar., Callao, No. 25.)

——. 1966. Cosecha Estable en Relación con el Desove y la Alimentación de la Anchoveta. (*Engraulis ringens*) en las Costas del Peru. *1er Sem. Lat. Amer. Oc. Pac., Lima.*

——. 1971. *Some Observations on the Feeding of the Peruvian Anchoveta* Engraulis ringens *J. in Two Regions of the Peruvian Coast.*

Rojas de Mendiola, B.; Ochog, N. 1971. *Observaciones sobre el Alimento de la Anchoveta* (Engraulis ringens) *durante el Crucero 6908-09.* Instituto del Mar del Perú (IMP-82).

Rojas de Mendiola, B.; Ochoa, N.; Calienes, R.; Gomez, O.; 1969. *Contenido Estomacal de Anchoveta en Cuatro Areas de la Costa Peruana.* (Inf. Inst. Mar., Perú–Callao, No. 27.)

Saetersdal, G.; Tsukayama, I.; Alegre, B. 1965. *Fluctuaciones en la Abundancia Aparente del Stock de Anchoveta en 1959–1962.* (Inf. Inst. Mar., Perú–Callao, No. 2.)

Saetersdal, G.; Valdivia, J. E. 1964. Un Estudio del Crecimiento, Tamaño y Reclutamiento de la Anchoveta (*Engraulis ringens*). *Bol. Inst. INvest. Recurs. Mar., Callao,* Vol. 1, No. 4, p. 35–136.

Saetersdal, G.; Valdivia, J. E.; Tsukayama, I.; Alegre, B. 1967. Preliminary Result of Studies on the Present Status of the Peruvian Stock of Anchovy (Engraulis ringens, J.). *CALCOFI Conference.*

Santander, H.; Sandova, de Castillo, O. *El Desove de la Anchoveta* (Engraulis ringens, J.) *en los Periodos Reproductivos de 1961 a 1968.* Instituto del Mar del Perú. (IMP-40.)

——. 1973a. *Estudio sobre las Primeras Etapas de Vida de la Anchoveta.* (Inf. Inst. Mar, Perú–Callao,

——. 1973b. Estudios sobre las Primeras Etapas de Vida de la Anchoveta. *Ser. Inf. Inst. Mar. Perú,* Vol. 1, No. 5.

Schaefer, Milner D. 1967. Dinámica de la Pesquería de la Anchoveta (*Engraulis ringens*) en el Perú. *Bol. Inst. Mar, Perú–Callao.* Vol. 1, No. 5.

——. 1969. *Informe Provisional sobre Investigaciones de Ecología y Dinámica de Población de la Anchoveta* (Engraulis ringens) *en el Perú.* Instituto del Mar del Perú (IMP-47.)

——. 1970. *Investigaciones Adicionales de la Dinámica*

de las Pesquerias de la Anchoveta (Engraulis ringens) en el Perú. (Inf. Inst. Mar, Perú—Callao, No. 31.)

Schott, G. 1931. Der Perú Strom and Seine nordlichen Nachbangebiete in normaler und anomaler. *Ausbildung Ann. Hydrogr.*, No. 59, p. 161—9, 200—13, 140—52.

Schweigger, E. 1964. *El Litoral Peruano.* Second edition, under the auspices of the Universidad Nacional Federico Villarreal. Lima, 414 p.

Simpson, J. G.; Buzeta, R.; Gil, E. 1969. *Relación Longitud-Peso de la Anchoveta,* Engraulis ringens, *durante 1966.* 26 p. (Serie Pub. Inst. Fom. Pesq. (Santiago), No. 44.

Simpson, J. G.; Carreño, M. 1967. *Distribución Geográfica Mensual y Trimestral y Composición Mensual de Frecuancia de Longitud por Zona de la Anchoveta Desembarcada en Arica, Iquique, Tocopolla, Antofagasta, Coquimbo y Talcahuano de Enero a Junio de 1966.* 117 p. (Serie Pub. Inst. Fom. Pesq. (Santiago), No. 27.

Strickland, J. H. D.; Eppley, R. W.; Rojas de Mendiola, B. 1969. Poblaciones de Fitoplancton, Nutrientes y Fotosintesis en Aguas Costeras Peruanas. *Bol. Inst. Mar. Perú,* Vol. 2, p. 4—45.

Tsukayama, I. 1966. El Número de Branquispinas como Carácter Diferencial de Subpoblaciones de Anchoveta (*Engraulis ringens,* J.) en las Costas del Perú. *1er Sem. Lat. Amer. Oc. Pac. Orien.,* Lima.

——. 1969. Una Nueva Medida de la Pesca por Unidad de Esfurerzo en la Pesquería de Anchoveta (*Engraulis ringens,* J.) en el Perú. *Bol. Inst. Mar, Perú—Callao,* Vol. II, No. 4.

Valdez, V.; Castillo, J.; Villanueva, R. 1964. *Operación Quizás II.* (Inf. Inst. Mar del Perú, Comunicado, No. 6.)

Vasquez, A. I. 1969. *Resumen General de la Pesquería de Anchoveta durante el Año 1968.* Instituto del Mar del Perú. (IMP-35.)

——. 1970. *Resumen General de la Pesquería de Anchoveta durante el Año.1969.* Instituto del Mar del Perú. (IMP-57.)

Vasquez, A. I.; Hidalgo, R. 1971. *Resumen General de la Pesquería de Anchoveta durante el Año 1970.* Instituto del Mar del Perú. (IMP-76.)

Vasquez, A. I.; Hidalgo, R.; Pérez, E. 1971. *Resumen*

General de la Pesquería de Anchoveta durante la Temporada 1970—71. Instituto del Mar del Perú. (IMP-87.)

——. 1972. *Resumen General de la Pesquería de Anchoveta durante el Año 1974.* Instituto del Mar del Perú (IMP-101.)

——. 1973. *Resumen de la Pesquería de Anchoveta y Otras Especies, para Reducción Enero—Julio 1973.* Instituto del Mar del Peru. (IMP-143.)

——. 1973. *Resumen General de la Pesquería de Anchoveta durante 1972.* Instituto del Mar del Perú. (IMP-127.)

Vestnes, G.; Saetersdal, G. 1964. *Informe sobre la Prospección de Anchoveta en el Norte de Chile, entre Marzo y Junio de 1964, Realizada en el B/M Stella Maris.* (Serie Pub. Inst. Fom. Pesq. (Santiago) No. 3.)

——. 1965. *Informe sobre la Prospección de Anchoveta en el Norte de Chile entre Agosto y Octubre 1964 Realizada con el B/I Carlos Darwin,* 19 p. (Serie Pub. Inst. Fom. Pesq. (Santiago), No. 5.)

Vestnes, G.; Stroem, A.; Saetersdal, G.; Villegas, L. 1965. *Informe sobre Investigaciones Exploratorias en la Zona de Talcahuano—Valdivia y Puerto Montt, Junio—Julio 1965, Realizadas con el B/I Carlos Darwin.* 27 p. (Serie Pub. Inst. Fom. Pesq. (Santiago), No. 10.)

Vestnes, G.; Stroem, A.; Villegas, L. 1965. *Informe sobre Investigaciones Exploratorias entre Talcahuani y Bahia de San Pedro. Diciembre 1965, Realizadas con el B/I Carlos Darwin.* 33 p. (Serie Pub. Inst. Fom. Pesq. (Santiago), No. 6.)

Villanueva, A. R.; Jordán, R.; Burd, A. 1969. *Informe sobre el Estudio de Comportamiento de Cardúmenes de Anchoveta.* Instituto del Mar del Perú. (IMP-45.)

Whitledge, T.; Packard, T. T. 1971. Nutrient Excretion by Anchovies and Zooplankton in Pacific Upwelling Regions. *Inv. Pesq.,* Vol. 35, No. 1, p. 242—50.

Wyrtki, 1965. Surface Currents of the Eastern Tropical Pacific Ocean. *Inter. Am. Trop. Tuna Comm., Bull.,* Vol. 9, No. 5.

Zuta, S.; Guillén, O. 1970. On the Oceanography of the Peru Coastal Waters. *Inst. Mar. Peru. Bol.,* No. 5. (P/0-02-00131, 00132.)

Biology of the anchoveta. 2: Projected Peruvian research

G. L. Kesteven [1]

Introduction

Research on the Peruvian anchovy, *Engraulis ringens*, in progress for many years, has resulted in a number of principal conclusions[2] which constitute the basis for an intensive monitoring procedure. The depth of the statistical record of commercial fishing on which the system operates, the intensity of its sampling of commercial catches, the array of other information which is compiled and analysed, and the immediacy of its results are all important features of the procedure.

The procedure is undoubtedly unique with respect to the magnitude of the resource upon which it is directed and probably unique with respect to the relationship it has to the control of exploitation. Admirable as the system is, however, its prognoses fall short of the degree of accuracy required for managerial decisions, and it is seriously deficient in its predictive power.

A measure of the inadequacy of its predictive capability is to be found in the forecasting of the contemplatable catch, i.e. the catch that can be taken from the stock available in a given interval of time (say, a particular month, or quarter). This is a function not solely of the size of the stock at the beginning of that interval, or even of that stock size plus the properties of growth and reproduction of that stock, but also a function of the environmental conditions during the exploitative interval. These will determine recruitment into that stock and the growth of its individuals, as well as of the conditions that, in subsequent periods, will determine the survival and growth of the residue of the stock and of its new generations. But these functions are still unknown, and hence the current forecasts, which carry large assumptions of persistence of system characteristics, cannot meet the demands even if environmental behaviour could be predicted. Hence, accompanying the programmes that study the Peruvian Current and associated systems —from which will come prediction of events such as 'El Niño'—research must be carried out into these other functions.

It may be supposed *a priori* that more accurate prognoses might be of much value to management, but this would not justify the assumption that every kind of measurement (of stock or environment) would be valuable; much less can it be assumed that limits need not be set to the intensity and frequency of measurement. Therefore, the plans for research aimed at improving the monitoring system must be controlled by an evaluation of the contribution of existing elements and of each new element of the system.

The existing system is briefly described here so that the significance of the proposed new lines of research may be appreciated in context; the new ideas are then described and a brief account is given of the principles to be observed in the design of the new research, the introduction of the results to the system, and the monitoring of the operation of the monitoring system itself.

1. UNDP/FAO/Per/008/72 Project, Callao, Peru.
2. See previous article.

The existing monitoring system

The structure given to a monitoring system (MonS) must be decided with reference to: (a) the size, structure and dynamic of the object-system (ObS); (b) the ObS characteristics whose behaviour is to be predicted; and (c) the anticipation-time required in the predictions.

The monitoring system is dominated by what is known of item (a), and is essentially a set of procedures for obtaining information, on ObS characteristics, to be operated on in a set of component models whose results then flow to a principal model. The MonS, then, is as good as its models, but inclusion of cybernetic links in the MonS means that its operation can contribute to refinement of the information of item (a), and hence of the models and, indeed, that is precisely the situation of IMARPE at present with its anchovy MonS.

Items (b) and (c) imply two levels of decision: that of the user, and that of the MonS operators; the latter need predictions of the behaviour of characteristics underlying those characteristics of which the user requires prediction.

THE AIMS OF THE MONITORING SYSTEM (Mons)

The reason for maintaining a monitoring system is to be in possession of reliable information on the state of the stock and thus to be able to specify the quantity and composition of catch that can be taken (in accordance with established criteria) in the course of some limited interval of time; also to specify a suitable regime for fishing operations. The specification of catch would be made on the basis of the condition of the stock at the time and the condition in which the stock might be at distinct intervals of time in the future. This implies, in each case, for the stocks as well as for the environment: (a) the taking of observations and measurements of various characteristics at the time under consideration, for the purpose of immediate diagnosis, and (b) the processing of these data through models so as to predict the conditions that might be expected.

Thus the operational objectives are:
To organize and maintain a system for collection of data with respect to: (a) the catch taken and the fishing effort expended together with other information concerning these operations so as to relate them strictly with the fishing grounds; (b) the composition of the catch with respect to species, length, weight, age, maturity and fat content of the individuals; (c) the distribution and abundance of the non-fishable, aionomorphic populations of eggs, larvae and pre-recruits; and (d) the environmental conditions.
To process these data rapidly by the operation of appropriate models.

THE OBJECT-SYSTEM (ObS)

The object-system is the resource of anchovy, *Engraulis ringens,* in its habitat, together with the industrial elements involved in exploitation of the resource.

Structurally, the following classes of components of the system can be identified: (a) the aionomorphic populations of anchovy; in addition, although only one species of anchovy is recognized in Peruvian waters, the possibility exists that the species population is composed of a number of autonomous populations; (b) the water masses in which the anchovy population lives; (c) the populations of other species, both plants and animals, which hold biotic relations with the anchovy; (d) the operating units of the fishery which are principally the purseseine boats but which include elements for servicing, managing and controlling the purse-seine boats; (e) the shore-plants to which the purse-seiners deliver their catches; and (f) the effects of public and private sectors which determine exploitation of the resource.

The central component is, of course, the anchovy with respect to the magnitude of the resource, its distribution, accessibility and vulnerability to fishing, as well as the variations that take place in each of these aspects.

The components of groups (b) and (c) are of first order in that they exercise direct influence on the anchovy population and normally these components operate so as to maintain the anchovy population at equilibrium; however, from time to time these components change to such an extent that they cause a perturbation of the anchovy population; therefore it is necessary to have a description of the normal condition and to establish a system through which to detect the imminence of environmental change which would cause such a perturbation.

At the same time the operations of the components of group (d) cause important changes in the anchovy population, not only with respect to its magnitude and its population processes, but also to its behaviour and other properties. For this reason the measurement of fishing activity (fishing effort) and of its results, either as catch or mortality rate, is an indispensable element of the data.

The components of groups (e) and (f) are of second order, exercising a determinant influence on the operation of the components of group (d). Best estimates of each of the attributes of the resource species are being assembled in a species synopsis, which then will serve as a companion manual.

SOURCES OF INFORMATION

The MonS currently operates with information and data drawn from the following sources:

1. The industry, from which it obtains: (a) daily fishing-log sheets, from each boat; (b) daily reports of landings, of each boat; (c) daily reports of fleet operations; and (d) a detailed inventory of the fleet, all of which furnish data on catch and effort.
2. Its own catch-sampling system, from which it obtains data on composition of the catch as to length, weight, age (?), sex and reproductive conditions of individual fish; the sampling also determines the species composition of the catch and provides material for measurement of fat content.
3. Multi-shop survey operations (Eureka and Cateo), which furnish plankton samples, temperature measurements, and acoustic survey evidence on distribution and density, and catches from special fishing which are sampled as in 2.
4. Survey operations by the research vessel SNP-1, which provide acoustic measurement of distribution and density, and oceanographic observations.
5. Marking operations, which furnish information on movement of the anchovy and data on mortality.
6. Other operations at sea, which furnish oceanographic and ecologic information.
7. Census of the guano birds.

LINES OF ARGUMENT

There are five principal lines of argument, each resulting in a calculation of biomass, and the five values converging on an operation in which the calculations of biomass are compared; these comparisons are made in pairs so as to explain the differences between the values obtained by one line from contemporaneous values obtained by another method in terms of the characteristics of the other; hence:

$$B = f(_B X_1 ; _B X_2 \cdots _B X_n)A$$

in which A and B stand for results obtained by methods 'A' and 'B' respectively, and the terms $_B X_n$ signify values of separate characteristics of method 'B'. We then erect the reverse hypothesis:

$$A = f(_A X_1 ; _A X_2 \cdots _A X_n)B.$$

In this way the five results permit twenty comparisons. The result of this operation in the first place is to establish criteria for identification of the most acceptable value of biomass estimate; in the second place, the result is of cybernetic effect in assessing the methods with indication of defects which may exist in them.

The principal lines are:

First, the calculation of biomass by applying a proportion factor to the value of catch per unit of effort.

This operation is carried out with values for each separate statistical square or zone, the proportion factor is calculated by analysis of a time series which until now has been effected with relatively simple data but which in the near future will be calculated for each statistical square or zone separately, taking into consideration data with respect to environmental conditions.

A multifactorial analysis of data with respect to distribution of anchovy, catch per unit of effort, history of the fishery and environmental variables should make it possible to obtain values, of this proportion, each of which would be characteristic of particular conditions; perhaps also it will be possible to make this calculation of biomass with proportion factors more precisely identified with the existing conditions for each series of fishing operations. It may also be supposed that these results will reflect the accessibility and vulnerability of the stock.

Second, the yield to be expected from a stock can be calculated from an equation such as that of Beverton and Holt, given the existence of data with respect to growth characteristics of the species and the rate of mortality to which the stock is subject; and from that equation, following Gulland's equation, it is possible to calculate the biomass of fishable stock, from values of recruitment, infinite weight, the constants of the von Bertalanffy equation, and values of natural fishing mortality.

In addition, if real-time values of recruitment can be obtained and similarly the contants of the von Bertalanffy equation can be adjusted to represent the response to actual environmental conditions, it should be possible to make a much more precise calculation of biomass.

Third, biomass of fishable stock also can be calculated by a simple operation dividing the figures of quantity of catch by the value of fishing mortality In the case where the total catch from a cohort can be registered separately up to the end of its life, the calculation is simple: $B = C/F$; but in the case where calculation must be made of part of the life of a cohort, or with respect to part of the area of its distribution, it is necessary to make the calculation with the equation $D = C_{ij}/F_{ij}(1 - e^{-zt})$ with values separately calculated for the coefficient, F.

Fourth, collection of eggs and larvae by an efficient sampling system permits the calculation of the number of eggs and larvae in the sea during the sampling period; the calculation must take due account of dispersion of eggs and larvae by current, and of changes in the size of each population (of eggs and of larvae) which result, on the one hand, from spawning during the sampling time, and on the other hand from mortality occurring among the eggs and larvae during this time.

Given the calculation of the number of eggs in the sea and a regression of fecundity on length or weight it is possible to calculate the number of females spawning in the sampling period; however the measure of fecundity must be in respect to the number of eggs which a female can realease at each distinct spawning act; it is possible that a fecundity regression derived from histological study with respect to the number of ovules present in an ovary may represent a number of eggs which will be released in a series of spawning acts each taking place on a different day. This signifies that a distinction must be made between fecundity as the number of eggs which a female may release in a biotic year, fecundity as the number of eggs released in the spawning cycle, and fecundity as the number of eggs released in a single spawning act.

Furthermore, the number of females spawning at a particular time can be only a proportion of the number of females present in the area during the spawning time, since we know that the mature individuals do not all spawn simultaneously on the same day; therefore, we need an estimate of the proportion of females truly spawning in the sampling period. Given such information on true spawning proportions we can then calculate the number of mature females in the area in the fishable stock.

Given the population sex ratio we can calculate the number of individuals in the mature population and with a value for mean weight of the individuals in the fishable stock at the time of sampling, we can calculate the total weight of the fishable stock.

Finally, with acoustic equipment, we can make distinct measurement of biomass in the sea, but these measurements are of samples of the stock, therefore they must be adjusted according to statistical logic so as to yield an estimate of total biomass.

OPERATIONAL PROCEDURES

Assuming that the models incorporated in the MonS are valid, success in operating it depends, initially, entirely on the regularity and reliability of the procedures for collection of raw data records and the materials whose measurement and analysis yield raw data. Much attention has therefore been paid to the logistic problems of this phase, yet much more has still to be done.

Some of the steps being taken are as follows: (a) although the proportion of the fleet that turns in acceptable log-forms is high compared with most other fisheries (and, of course, there are many fisheries that give no such information), efforts are being made to increase it; (b) the sampling of catches to determine species and size composition is highly intensive, being taken at times from more than 30 per cent of the landings; the efficiency of the sampling design will be reviewed; (c) the sampling to determine sexual maturity will be reorganized so as to combine it with the length sampling; and (d) the marine operations, especially acoustic surveys, could be made more regular.

Development of ADP services for the compilation and analysis of these data has been advanced recently and will be continued so as to automate this work to a degree compatible with the time requirements of the system.

The organization of these procedures is represented in an arrow diagram which shows, in addition to the linear sequences of reduction of data, the transfer of data and, more importantly, of constants, from one line to another.

Output

The MonS is designed to give the following intermediate outputs:

State indexes: (a) distribution—a measure of the area occupied by the fishable stock and of the degree of its concentration; (b) composition—number of cohorts in the catch and mean size of each reproductive condition; (c) catch per unit effort; (d) condition and mean fat content; and (e) recruitment.

Biomass estimates: (a) from acoustic surveys; (b) from egg and larvae surveys; (c) from population properties through the Beverton—Holt model; (d) from catch-per-unit-of-effort data and estimates of fishing mortality coefficient; and (e) from catch-per-unit-of-effort data, oceanographic data significative of accessibility and vulnerability, and a time-series-derived factor of proportionality.

Obviously the state indices are simpler, preliminary measures of what is presented in the biomass estimates. The latter, in turn, are operated on in the final procedure where comparisons between the estimates lead to selection of a most acceptable estimate which is then related, so far as may be possible, to socio-economic objectives and to oceanographic forecasts in the formulation of a proposal for the fishing regime stated as total catch for an interval of time and as rate of capture.

The fact that these items are listed here is not to be taken to mean that a fully acceptable result is obtained consistently with respect to each of them; indeed, reservations, of one kind or another, must be made with regard to all of them. But then, neither are the reservations to be taken to mean that none of those items is reliable; on the contrary, they all have some diagnostic value. Moreover, steps have been planned both for measurement of the reliability of each of these results, and for improvement of the system of which they are the product; it is the purpose of this chapter to outline those steps.

Further development

The IMARPE strategy with respect to its anchovy monitoring system postulates three courses of action for improvement, to be taken concurrently with operation of the existing system.

The first course consists in stream-lining and rationalizing the existing procedures; this refers chiefly to the establishment of an automatic data-processing system, to accelerating the procedures for collection of the original data records, and to quality control of data; some of this has been discussed in the preceding section.

The second consists of an overhaul of all sampling plans and development of instrumentation which, given funds, would include the adoption of various automatic data-logging systems, for example, for the data from routine catch sampling and those from acoustic and oceanographic surveys.

The third is the conduct of research to elucidate particular features of the object system and hence to lead to improvement of the models. The present chapter deals mainly with this final course.

The line of research can conveniently be discussed with respect to three principal topics: accessibility and vulnerability; population properties, and environmental effects.

ACCESSIBILITY AND VULNERABILITY

It is well known that the anchovy can pass out of the 'reach' of the purse-seine net, either by swimming deep, or by being non-schooled; nevertheless, no measure of this condition is yet available, nor can an environmental element of biotic characteristic of the anchovy be identified as an indicator of it. It is possible that the whole of the fishable stock of a particular area alternates on each day between vulnerability and invulnerability, or that some proportion remains invulnerable all day, or even for an extended period; there is no evidence by which to determine which is the case.

Similarly, little can be said about the accessible proportion of the stock. By accessibility we mean here the condition of being within the reach of the bolicheros, in the sense of where they can or do go and in the sense of the range and sensitivity of the fish-searching equipment (chiefly acoustic). Even accessibility dependent on where the boats do go, as distinct from where they could go, is of importance in the result of the operations of a particular day, and hence of longer intervals of time.

Both these characteristics relate to the distribution and aggregative characteristics of the stock which, presumably, have their basis in the behavioural rhythms of the species and which, further, are to be assumed to be labile to particular environmental elements. The proposed research will be, in the first place, essentially descriptive and associative; that is, it will aim to give an account of the patterns of distribution of the anchovy in association with patterns of values of each of a number of environmental variables, and of the anchovy schooling behaviour, again in association with environmental variables. The results of such work would possibly be sufficient for the determination of measures of accessibility and vulnerability in real time but might not give a basis for prediction of these characteristics; however, it is not obvious that a prediction of the value of these characteristics would be important in management decisions. While it is clear that the resolution of these problems will be of importance to the estimates of biomass based on catch-per-unit-of-effort data (which include that which operates with the Beverton-Holt model), it is also the case that the relevance of accessibility and vulnerability indices is chiefly to real-time measurement of biomass. Nevertheless, if it should be thought that prediction of the characteristics would be useful, the research would proceed to an analysis of the behavioural rhythms of the anchovy, relating these to physiological rhythms and environmental variables.

POPULATION PROPERTIES

A central place in the anchovy MonS is given to assessment of biomass, and forecast of yield, from measures of population properties to be fed into the Beverton-Holt model. The values that now could be fed into the model are constant, estimated statistically in the past.

Although this procedure can give reasonable results, there exists evidence suggesting that mortality and growth are variable, and of course it is known that recruitment is highly variable. Research is therefore planned to ascertain the variability of the properties, to assess the possibility of measuring the changes in real time and perhaps of predicting them; also to evaluate the improvement in the models that might be obtained by introducing the indicated practices to the MonS.

Growth

The study of anchovy growth is difficult because of the difficulty of age-determination; moreover, practical considerations make it impossible to obtain some direct measure of growth through mark-and-recapture methods (the marks are detected and recovered in processing plants after reduction of the fish to meal and it is impossible to recover the individual fish before processing). Growth is studied

at present through the analysis of length frequency tables, with identification of cohorts. The line of progress would seem to be through more reliable identification and specification of the cohorts, with respect to the time of their spawning, the size range of each at any time, and their separation from other cohorts.

At the same time, it will be necessary to investigate the effect of variations in food supply and the variable effect of environmental factor on metabolic efficiency. One line of inquiry which suggests itself is a study of 'condition' related to these environmental variables.

Reproduction

Although, it is apparently futile as yet to seek a correlation between the amount of spawn shed in any interval of time and the number of individuals which develop therefrom and subsequently recruit to the fishable stocks, the measurement of reproduction must continue to have its place in the MonS and the data must be made more reliable than they are at present. Mention has already been made of the crosscheck of, on the one hand, the estimate of eggs in the sea (from egg surveys) and the estimate thus derived of the number of spawning females with, on the other hand, the estimate of the number of spawning females (from observation of reproductive condition of individuals in the catch) and the estimate thus derived of the number of eggs likely to have been produced. The reciprocal effect of this check will be obvious, and this might in itself be sufficient justification for continuance of the reproduction line of the MonS; but that line can be further justified (a) because an index of population reproductive state might well prove to be an indicator of environmental effects within the population, or of response of the population to environmental syndromes, and (b) there seems to be no reason for despairing of the possibility of being able to relate spawning to recruitment through a chain of relations between the successive aionomorphic populations, among themselves and with environmental variables, the maintenance and improvement of research on reproduction is advisable in anticipation of and as a contribution to achievement of that result.

Knowledge of reproductive behaviour and physiology of the anchovy is still somewhat scanty. The number of spawnings by each female during each year is thought to be two, but it is not known whether in fact this is so. It might be only one, or become three or more under certain environmental conditions. It is also not known whether each batch of mature eggs is released in a single act or in a series of acts, say, night after night. Thus, the effective fecundity number, by which to calculate spawning stock of a particular short interval of time from an estimate of eggs in the sea, is uncertain. In addition, the degree of lability of the fecundity/size relation, if labile it is, is unknown, although there seems to be evidence that the relation might vary with growth history and directly in response to environmental factors.

Research should therefore be carried out on reproductive physiology and behaviour; this will include the use of histological techniques, probably of aquarium studies, extensive planktonological investigations, associated ecology, and possibly an effort to make direct observation of natural spawning.

ENVIRONMENTAL EFFECTS

Each of the above lines of research includes an examination of ecological relations, but only in a general, theoretical sense. We may, for example, suppose that the metabolism of the anchovy is influenced by temperature and that, therefore, its growth at particular levels of food supply might vary as a function of prevailing temperatures. But this effect might be non-significant for all temperatures encountered by the anchovy and the critical relation might be simply the direct relation of density of anchovy to density of food supply.

The problem can be illustrated by reference to the 'El Niño' problem. The common assumption that the effect of this phenomenon on the anchovy stocks is that the stocks decline as a consequence of 'El Niño', and that, therefore, the correct strategy to adopt when an 'El Niño' arrives (or, better still, when one is predicted) must be to catch less anchovy. However, the following questions must be considered:
Is is true that a real change in anchovy abundance takes place before, during and/or after each 'El Nimo'?
Is it possible that some of the sequels of 'El Niño' (notably the mass mortalities of birds) result from a change in accessibility and vulnerability of the anchovy?
In the case that a change in anchovy abundance is associated with an 'El Niño' what is its nature?

Is it: (a) a heavier natural mortality of adult stock; (b) a result of reduced spawning (lowered fecundity or delayed spawning); (c) an unusually heavy mortality of eggs, larvae, post-larvae, juveniles; or (d) a combination of these?
If any or all of these are the case, from what do they result, and when and where do they occur?
In particular, to what degree are the effects a result of (a) variation in quantity and composition of food supply to the anchovy and/or (b) variation in anchovy living space?
If, instead, the change is in accessibility and vulnerability, what are its causes?
Moreover some of the effects must involve other biotic elements, notably food supply and predators.
In summary, the situation is that: (a) the nature of the change is not truly known; (b) the relations of anchovy to its habitat elements, through which the effects are produced, are not yet well identified; and (c) the relations cannot yet be expressed in equations and hence significance cannot yet be measured for any of them.

In this situation, the IMARPE strategy with regard to environmental effects comprises the following elements: (a) continuation and development of its current oceanographic programmes, especially with a view to development of an environmental frame; (b) participation in phenomenological research, more particularly that which may lead to prediction of the behaviour of the Peruvian current, including its 'El Niño' events; and (c) mounting of microclimatic studies, with simulation of the studied situations in aquaria and, later, by computer methods.

Methodological principles

The general strategy of this work may be represented by the frame below.

ANCHOVY STOCK

Characteristics	*Synoptic activities*
Adults:	
Real-time abundance	Analysis of catch and effort statistics
Survival	Analysis of catch
Growth	Eureka surveys
Maturation. fecundity	
Recruitment (timing, etc.)	As above
Pre-recruits, abundance distribution	Young fish survey

Larvae to pre-recruits

Egg production: potential realized

Stock/environment

Time-series correlations
Aquarium simulation
Micro-climate studies
Physiological analysis
Environmental programme

Juvenile stages survey
Sampling adult stock

Egg and larvae survey

For the particular lines of research referred to in the previous section opportunities offered by the above synoptic activities will be fully exploited and use will be made of materials drawn from them. Each line will of course require its own activities. In principle each particular line will be pursued according to the familiar paradigm: (a) measurement of associations, as far as existing data may permit (this phase may show a need for refinement of particular data series),

(b) experimental analysis (for example, in aquaria) of the anchovy side of each significant relationship; and (c) development of an environmental frame to lead to a more exact measure of association.

All this work will be controlled by reference to the monitoring system itself in the sense that initiating questions come from operation of the MonS, and the value of the results will be tested by a measure of the increase in reliability of the MonS to which they lead; in each case cost will be measured.

The critical cost-evaluation of new elements will be made within a general practice in application of linear-programming and similar methods. A conclusion as to appropriate fishing regimes will be reached by linear-programming evaluation of courses of action within constraints specified, on the one hand, from socio-economic considerations and, on the other, from resource considerations. Also, the inputs from the MonS will themselves be subject to similar evaluation.